BUSINESS STRATEGY

BUSINESS STRATEGY

An Introduction

Third edition

David Campbell

David Edgar

George Stonehouse

First published 2011 by
RED GLOBE PRESS

Red Globe Press in the UK is an imprint of Springer Nature Limited,
registered in England, company number 785998, of 4 Crinan Street,
London, N1 9XW.

Red Globe Press® is a registered trademark in the United States,
the United Kingdom, Europe and other countries.

ISBN 978–0–230–21858–1   ISBN 978–0–230–34439–6 (eBook)

This book is printed on paper suitable for recycling and made from fully
managed and sustained forest sources. Logging, pulping and manufacturing
processes are expected to conform to the environmental regulations
of the country of origin.

A catalogue record for this book is available from the British Library.

A catalog record for this book is available from the Library of Congress.

CONTENTS in brief

CONTENTS

LIST of figures

LIST of tables

ABOUT the authors

David Campbell has taught strategy since 1992 and is Senior Lecturer at Newcastle University Business School. He is the author of over 30 books, articles and monographs, and is on the editorial boards of several international journals in accounting and ethics. His research interests are in accountability, corporate governance, voluntary reporting and ethics.

David Edgar is Professor of Strategy and Business Transformation at Caledonian Business School. His main areas of research and teaching are in the field of strategic management, specifically dynamic capabilities, business uncertainty and complexity, and innovation. He has a wide range of academic experience from programme development to international collaboration.

David's consultancy experience is in the area of strategy process and review, using soft systems methodology, organizational analysis, innovation dynamics, business process analysis and design, scenario planning and strategic planning frameworks. He has worked with a wide range of private and public sector organizations, including Scottish Power, NTL, Telewest, the NHS, Scottish and Southern Electric and IBM.

George Stonehouse is Dean of the Business School at Edinburgh Napier University, having previously been Associate Dean and Professor of International Strategic Management at Newcastle Business School. He has wide international experience in both business and academia.

His research and consultancy interests lie in the areas of creativity, knowledge, organizational learning, strategic management and global business. He has published three books and numerous articles in leading academic journals in these areas. He has been engaged in research, consultancy and training with a number of leading international organizations, including Black & Decker, Hanson plc, Nike, Severstal JSC (Russia) and Yutong Corporation (China).

FOREWORD to the third edition and acknowledgements

This is the third edition of *Business Strategy: An Introduction*. From the introduction of the first edition in 1999, its primary purpose has been to provide a comprehensive but accessible guide to the main themes in strategy and to this end, the writing style was intentionally uncomplicated and it used cases and vignettes to convey and illustrate the main points of theory. The second edition in 2002 included a much richer suite of cases and expanded content to retain its currency with contemporary scholarship. The core features have been retained in the third edition: it is comprehensive, accessible and up to date.

Professor George Stonehouse and myself have been joined for this third edition by Professor David Edgar. It has been his energy and unremitting scholarship that has driven this third edition and it is his contribution that is the source of this edition's distinctiveness from the first two. As an outstanding scholar of international repute, Professor Edgar has updated and reframed much of the content of the text, while introducing new ideas, such as the 'Guru guides', which we are certain will be of value and interest to many people studying strategy for the first time.

As the coordinating author on all three editions, it has been my privilege to oversee an excellent and enthusiastic team of influential scholars who have contributed to the text in various ways including chapters, cases and in-chapter illustrations. These people include Kevin Grant and Margaret McCann at Caledonian Business School, Richard Pettinger at UCL and Arun Sukumar at Sheffield Hallam Business School.

The publisher subjected the manuscript to an extensive peer review process, and we are grateful to the anonymous reviewers who made valuable suggestions for improving the content and style of this book. In addition, we are also grateful to the copyright holders who permitted us to reprint tables and figures and to the various 'gurus' for allowing us to print their photographs.

This third edition is published by Palgrave Macmillan. We are grateful to Butterworth-Heinemann (later Elsevier) for their support of the first two editions. We are happy that Palgrave Macmillan are publishing this third edition and are grateful to its excellent editorial team. They have worked patiently with us to bring this text together including finding contributors for case content and other vignettes. We are particularly grateful to Martin Drewe who commissioned this third edition and was a continual source of support and encouragement throughout the preparation process.

David Campbell
Newcastle University
March 2011

PREFACE to the third edition

Business Strategy: An Introduction has been written specifically to fulfil the needs of students completing a final year degree and/or Masters course in business strategy (also entitled corporate strategy, strategic management, strategic management and leadership, and so on). This book analyses strategic decision-making within business, helping the student to develop a critical understanding of the strategic processes of business management and the interconnections between the numerous functional domains within businesses.

New for this edition

The book retains the clear, straightforward and accessible writing style from previous editions, but new to this edition are:

- additional figures and tables to help students make sense of often complex theories and processes
- the 'Guru guide' feature, giving an easy-to-digest snapshot of interesting biographical details and the central theories of key thinkers in the field
- a new 'Vocab checklist for ESL students', which links to free access to the Macmillan English Dictionary online, designed specifically for non-native speakers of English
- deeper coverage of the schools of strategy, with a dedicated chapter on perspectives on strategy
- broader coverage of contemporary themes in business strategy in the new Part 6
- global coverage, including new international case studies, a new chapter on emerging markets, a chapter on the international and global context and a global flavour throughout the analysis
- a brand new, attractive and clearly laid out page design, full of interesting features
- a companion website packed with additional learning materials, such as audio case studies and PowerPoint presentations
- free access to Strategic Planning Software. Find out more below.

While retaining core content from previous editions, the new edition contains several new chapters:

- Chapter 2: Perspectives on strategy
- Chapter 5: Knowledge, talent, culture and innovation
- Chapter 7: Information systems and technology
- Chapter 8: Strengths, weaknesses and strategic competence
- Chapter 12: Opportunities, threats and strategic position

- Chapter 17: Change management and leadership
- Chapter 18: The web, new technology and new organizational forms
- Chapter 21: Emerging markets and industry superpowers.

The book has been restructured and has a new Part 6, Contemporary Issues in Business Strategy, which consists of two new chapters and a much expanded chapter on social responsibility and business ethics, as well as a fuller consideration of contemporary quality management.

Content

Our approach to explaining business strategy is covered in detail below. We use a helpful 'Strategy process' diagram to help the student make sense of how strategy works (see Figure 0.1). Rather than thinking of strategy in strictly linear terms, we offer different 'stages', which present a structure for approaching the subject, while also demonstrating the fluidity in movement between each stage in real-life business strategy. We cover the four main areas of strategy – internal analysis, external analysis, the business strategy, and strategic implementation and management – and examine the issues and concepts that comprise the core of third year courses in the subject. However, unlike traditional strategy textbooks, the coverage of our new edition is much broader and deeper, global in focus and makes the subject accessible and engaging.

Business Strategy: An Introduction is divided into six parts. These parts are, of course, interconnected, but we believe that the division provides a convenient teaching device to guide the reader through the learning material. A brief outline of each part is given below:

- **Part 1** provides an introduction to the strategic process by defining what we mean by strategy and strategic management, profiling the evolution of the study of business strategy and establishing the different perspectives on (or schools of) strategic management.
- **Part 2** explores the internal environment of organizations and provides a range of tools and techniques to allow an internal analysis and to understand what constitutes the strengths, weaknesses and core competences of an organization.
- **Part 3** examines the organization's external environment through two layers of analysis – the macro- (or general) environment and the micro- (or competitive/ specific) environment. This highlights the opportunities and threats facing the organization and allows a complete SWOT analysis to be undertaken.
- **Part 4** relates to the formulation of the business strategy and involves using the information from the analysis in Parts 2 and 3 to make informed judgements and decisions as to potential strategic direction, methods and futures.
- **Part 5** examines the issues, tools and techniques associated with implementing a chosen strategy and managing the process to improve the chances of realizing an intended strategic goal.
- **Part 6** introduces a range of current and emerging issues in business strategy. In this section new technology, quality management, social responsibility, and emerging markets and industry superpowers are considered.

Our approach in this book is to recognize that business strategy is a complex art and often multiple stages are conducted in parallel, but that to understand and study strategy, we need a degree of order. So we adopt a structured approach to explaining business strategy but would ask the reader to remember that, in real life, things are not that simple.

Business strategy is never a once-and-for-all event – it goes on and on. There is a need to continually review strategic objectives because the environment is always changing. Depending on the stance your company adopts, the purpose of strategy is either to make a business 'fit' into its environment or to use the resources of the business to 'change the rules of the game' or reshape the environment. By achieving this, the probability that the organization will survive and prosper are enhanced.

Figure 0.1 shows the 'stages' involved in business strategy and also sets up the structure we adopt for our book.

Figure 0.1 **The strategy process**

We have structured our book to explore each of these areas. As you progress through Part 1, you will see that there are different views of strategy and different perspectives as to how business strategy is developed and implemented. In the past, emphasis often used to be placed on understanding the external side of a business, that is, markets, environmental changes, outputs and economy (Part 3). Now, however, organizations are emphasizing the softer side of the business, that is, innovation, competences, creativity, talent, resources and processes. These elements are mainly found and understood when undertaking the internal analysis (Part 2). So our book is structured to explore the internal analysis before the external and thus determine strengths, weaknesses and core competences before understanding how and where they can be used and how they can be influenced. We have, however, also ensured that each part can be used independently and interchangeably, so if you prefer, you can start your analysis with Part 3 and then do Part 2. Use what is most 'fit for purpose'.

TOUR of the book

Business Strategy: An Introduction includes a number of features that complement, supplement and reinforce the main text. In particular, they have been designed to promote critical thinking and to provide plentiful examples of real-life business strategy in a diverse range of countries and companies, prompting students to reflect on ideas, competing perspectives and implications of business strategy. These features will help students to relate to the ideas, tools and techniques in a way that is useful for future career development and deepens an understanding of how strategy works in practice.

The following pages act as a 'tour' through the book, highlighting the pedagogical features that will be useful to student and lecturer alike.

TOUR OF THE BOOK

Introduction and chapter overview

The introduction sets the scene while the chapter overview outlines the content of the chapter, so students know what to expect.

Learning objectives

Learning objectives set out what the student should have learned by the end of the chapter. Each is linked to a central topic or issue in business strategy, so students can see how each is relevant and how they fit together.

Introduction and chapter overview

Strategic thinking and strategic management are the most important activities undertaken by any organization. How effectively and skilfully these activities are carried out will determine the eventual long-term success or failure of the business. In this chapter, we introduce the basic concepts of business strategy by defining what we mean by strategy, examining the key elements of strategy and profiling the different schools of strategic thought. We close the chapter with a presentation of our strategy process framework and thus set the foundations for the chapters that follow.

Learning objectives

After studying this chapter, you should be able to:

- define what is meant by the word 'strategy'
- explain Mintzberg's '5 Ps' framework
- distinguish between deliberate (prescriptive) and emergent strategy
- describe the different elements associated with business strategy
- explain the different schools of strategy and their implications

GURU GUIDE

Coimbatore K. Prahalad was born in Coimbatore, India in 1941. He graduated from Loyola College, Chennai, with a BSc in physics before being recruited as an industrial engineer with Union Carbide in 1960. He graduated from Harvard with a DBA in 1975 before returning to India to teach management. He continued as a visiting research fellow at Harvard while in India. Prahalad was appointed to the position of the Paul and Ruth McCracken Distinguished University Professor of Corporate Strategy at the Stephen M. Ross School of Business at the University of Michigan. He has been honoured for his contributions with a Lifetime Achievement Award from the Ross School of Business. He received honorary doctorates from the University of London (Economics), Stevens Institute of Technology (Engineering) and University of Abertay, Dundee (Business). He was a member of the UN Blue Ribbon Commission on Private Sector and Development. He died in 2010.

Guru guides

The Guru guides provide fascinating snippets of information on key thinkers in the field, including their notable achievements and key theories.

Key concepts

Key concepts are highlighted throughout each chapter and contain explanations of key ideas, useful for revision.

KEY CONCEPT

A **paradigm** is a worldview – a way of looking at the world. It is expressed in the assumptions people make and their deep-rooted beliefs. The paradigm of an organization or a national culture is important because it determines how it will behave in a given circumstance. Given a certain moral dilemma or similar choice, we might expect the paradigms of, for example, an orthodox Jew and an atheist to lead them to arrive at different conclusions. The things that cause one culture to adopt one paradigm and another culture to espouse a different one are set out in the cultural web.

The **product life cycle** is the complete 'life' of a product or service from its inception and growth, through shake-out and maturity, to its eventual decline and death.

The product life cycle concept is based on the analogy with living things, in that they all have a finite life. All products would be expected to have a finite life whether it be long or short. The life cycle can operate at an individual product level, a product type or a product class level, where arguably a market life cycle would be a more appropriate title. At the individual product level, the product life cycle is a useful tool in product planning, so that a balance of products is kept in various stages of the life cycle.

Key terms

Key terms appear throughout each chapter and are glossed in the margin.

Case studies and questions

Each chapter contains an interesting case study on companies as diverse as Mattel, Swatch, Virgin and Ryanair to help students apply key concepts in strategy to the real world of business. These are accompanied by a set of questions to encourage analytical thinking and help students fulfil the learning objectives.

CASE STUDY CoffeeShops UK Ltd

CoffeeShops UK Ltd (CSUK) is a nationwide chain of cafés and restaurants. It has 200 outlets, of which 120 are coffee shops and bars, 40 are ice cream parlours, and 40 are franchise outlets at railway stations across the country.

Eleanor Young and Julia Richards founded CSUK 10 years ago. As an alternative to Starbucks, CSUK immediately took off. People liked the fact that it was a domestic UK company and that Eleanor and Julia were 'new entrepreneurs'. They opened their first coffee shop in Northampton, which gained them an immediate presence and recognition, not least because

Value chain activity	Areas of competence associated with differentiation strategies	Areas of competence asso cost/price-based strategie
Primary activities		
Inbound logistics	Control of quality of materials	Strict control of the cost o Tendency to buy larger vol standard inputs
Operations	Control of quality of output, raising standards	Lowering production costs achieving high-volume pr
Marketing and sales	Sales (and customer relations) on the basis of quality technology,	Achieving high-volume sa advertising and promotio

Figures and tables

The book makes full use of figures and tables, some classic and others new, to elucidate more complex theory.

Vocab checklist for ESL students

This is a list of some more difficult terms in business strategy, and more complicated items of vocabulary for non-native speakers of English to learn and check. On the book's companion website you will find definitions of all these terms and online access to the Macmillan English Dictionary.

VOCAB CHECKLIST FOR ESL STUDENTS

Analogue	Drawbacks	Pioneer
Brewers	Elite	Repute
Commonalities	Genteel	'Shake-out'
Constituent	Homogeneous	'Shop around'
Consumables	Impasse	Statistician
Dealership	Intrinsic	Strata
Discretionary income (see	Mailshots	Subcontract
'discretionary' and 'income')	Outsourcing	Telephony
Disincentive	Pedagogical	

Definitions for these terms can be found in the 'Vocab Zone' of the companion website, which provi access to the Macmillan English Dictionary online at www.macmillanihe.com/companion/business/

Review questions

Review questions are designed to test understanding and the ability to recall appropriate answers. Answers can be obtained by rereading the chapter.

REVIEW QUESTIONS

1. Explain the difference between an industry and a market.
2. Explain what is meant by market segmentation and profile the different ways in which can be segmented.
3. Explain what comprises Porter's five forces framework.
4. Define what is meant by strategic groups.

Discussion topics

Discussion topics consist of suggestions to encourage further thought and spark seminar debate.

DISCUSSION TOPIC

For business strategy to be effective, the strategy implementation process must occur at time as the strategy formulation process. Discuss.

Hot topics

These are research project ideas for students that suggest topics for investigation for an assignment or perhaps coursework.

HOT TOPICS – Research project areas to investigate

For your research project, why not investigate ...
- ... how organizations maintain control over resources during strategy implementation.
- ... what role culture plays in the implementation process.
- ... what the critical success factors are for ensuring the intended strategy is realized.

Recommended reading

These sections identify key texts for further research and include books and journal articles.

Recommended reading

Fuller, A.W. and Thursby, M.C (2008) 'Technology commercialization: cooperative versus competitive strategies', *Advances in the Study of Entrepreneurship, Innovation & Economic Growth*, 18: 227–50.

O'Reilly, T. (2007) 'What is Web 2.0: design patterns and business models for the next generation of software', *Communications and Strategies*, **65**(1): 17–38.

Shuen, A. (2008) *Web 2.0: A Strategy Guide: Thinking and Strategies behind Successf Implementations*, Cambridge: O'Reilly Be

Weitz, B.A. (2001) Electronic retailing: marke and entrepreneurial opportunities, in G.D *Entrepreneurship and Economic Growth Economy*, vol. 12, Elsevier Science.

For test questions, extra case studies, audio case stud and more to help you understand the topics covered i companion website at www.macmillanihe.com/comp

At the end of each chapter is a reminder for students to visit our companion website at www.macmillanihe. com/companion/business/campbell where they will find lots of extra material to help consolidate what they have learned and practise their critical thinking skills.

Business Strategy
an introduction
third edition

david campbell,
david edgar &
george stonehouse

| home | order title |

Welcome to the preview website for
Business Strategy: an introduction, 3rd edition
by David Campbell, David Edgar and George Stonehouse

What strategy did Mattel pursue to bring about the sale of one Barbie every seven seconds? How did Swatch overcome their barriers to change and compete with cheap digital watches? What difficulties has Virgin surmounted to secure its sources of competitive advantage?

Business Strategy: an introduction is a straightforward and plain-speaking textbook for those approaching strategy for the first time. Global in approach, it includes a full complement of international case studies and examples from companies as diverse as Ryanair, Mattel, Northern Rock and the National Bank of Poland to help students apply theory to real-world business scenarios. Business Strategy:

- contains chapters on contemporary themes such as **CSR** and **business ethics, emerging markets,** and **new technologies**
- includes a new **'Vocab checklist for ESL students'** feature to help international students get to grips with higher level vocabulary and key terms in strategy, as well as clear and simple language. This feature links to free online access to the Macmillan English Dictionary
- has full coverage of the **different schools of strategy** in a dedicated 'Perspectives on strategy' chapter and new 'Guru Guides' containing notable achievements and explanations of central theories of key strategists
- contains a wealth of helpful student features such as **review questions, suggestions for research project areas** to investigate, **on-page glossary, key concept boxes**, discussion points and **learning objectives**

About the book
What makes this book so special?
Guided tour of the book
Contents page
Sample chapter
About the authors

About the companion website
Website outline
Guided tour of the website

Order title/ Request inspection copy

Palgrave.com home

Palgrave.com help

Adobe Reader help

Companion website

The website for this book contains lots of additional material to help students get to grips with business strategy. Key features for students include:

- a selection of audio case studies
- online access to the Macmillan English Dictionary as part of the Vocab checklist for ESL students feature
- a searchable online glossary
- additional new case studies
- classic case studies from previous editions of the textbook
- self-test questions for each chapter
- useful weblinks
- links to interesting videos
- journal links relevant to each chapter

Those for lecturers include:

- PowerPoint presentations for each chapter
- a testbank of multiple-choice questions and essay questions
- a lecturer manual containing:
  - tutor's notes on teaching the case studies
  - answers to case study questions
  - additional new case studies

Strategic Planning Software (SPS)

Business Strategy: An Introduction includes free access to the exciting and innovative Strategic Planning Software. What is Strategic Planning Software?

- A step-by-step framework to help students **research and analyse a real company's** strategic position and to formulate strategies to overcome **real business problems.** It solves the most important problem faced by lecturers: **how to bring the world of business into the classroom.**
- It bridges the gap between theory and rigorous strategic planning and development and is used not only by students but by **practising strategy consultants.**
- It is ideal for lecturers to construct a **project or piece of coursework** around to assess students' understanding of their business strategy module. SPS generates reports that can be submitted for grading.
- **It is flexible:** lecturers can either set a research project on a real company or students can use SPS to analyse an existing case study, complete with facts and figures, on the book's companion website.
- It can span the length of a module, with students **completing sections week on week in tandem with the topics covered in class**, or be used as an end of course assessment.
- Students can work in **groups** or **individually.**

This interactive, engaging and intuitive software has been developed by strategy lecturers who are also **experienced strategy consultants**. It has been used by thousands of students and with real companies. SPS is divided into three main phases:

1. Strategic Position Analysis, including SWOT, External and Internal Analysis
2. Formulation of Strategy, including Business Portfolio Decision, Competitive Strategy and Development Strategy
3. Conclusions and Recommendations, where students bring together all their analyses and set out plans for the way forward, acting out their **future roles as managers and decision-makers**.

How can *Business Strategy: An Introduction* and Strategic Planning Software be used together?

This is a helpful chapter to refer to when completing both 1.1.2 Strategic Group Analysis and 1.1.4 Porter's Five Forces within the External Analysis section in Phase 1 of the **Strategic Planning Software** (www.planning-strategy.com). For more information on Porter's five forces, see also Chapter 13, particularly the section on competitive positioning.

- Links at the end of each chapter demonstrate which section of the software that chapter will help the student to complete
- References in each 'Theory' section of the software link that particular section to a relevant chapter or pages of the textbook
- The software's glossary is linked to *Business Strategy: An Introduction*'s online searchable glossary for quick definition of key terms in each section
- All major topics in business strategy are covered by the textbook and the software, and students can work through the software in the order dictated by their module structure.

Type in your purchase code and get going!

CASE STUDY GRID

Case study grid

The case study grid provides a list of specific, custom-written case studies that demonstrate concepts and issues to allow you to apply and evaluate models, frameworks and business strategy theories to different business contexts. Each chapter has an associated case that deals specifically with one or more areas of business strategy. These areas are indicated by a cross. Each case also allows for broader discussion around concepts and issues in the field, so your tutor may use the case to set up or stimulate a more wide-ranging debate to show you how the theory of business strategy relates to the real world. All bar two case studies were written by Richard Pettinger, while those in Chapters 7 and 18 were written by Dr Arun Sukumar.

Case study	Industry and market	Objectives and stakeholders	Internal analysis and SWOT	Generic strategy and value chain	External analysis: SPENT	External analysis: five forces, etc.
Chapter 1 ACN Inc.	x				x	
Chapter 2 Virgin	x	x		x		
Chapter 3 Gate Security Systems Ltd			x			
Chapter 4 Northern Rock			x	x		
Chapter 5 Barley Engineering			x	x		
Chapter 6 Hamilton Cars and World Motor Corp. Inc.		x	x			
Chapter 7 NHS Scotland		x	x		x	
Chapter 8 Bucks Burger Bars Inc.			x			
Chapter 9 City and Country Communications	x				x	
Chapter 10 National Bank of Poland	x				x	x
Chapter 11 Empire Supermarkets	x				x	x
Chapter 12 Celands Bank			x			
Chapter 13 Mattel				x		
Chapter 14 CoffeeShops UK Ltd						x
Chapter 15 British Airways						x
Chapter 16 Ryanair	x	x				x
Chapter 17 SMH						
Chapter 18 Facebook	x				x	
Chapter 19 Foreshore Engineering Ltd						
Chapter 20 Sunrise Farms Ltd						
Chapter 21 Swann Wind Farms Ltd	x	x			x	

Ethics	Financial analysis	Core competences, innovation and talent	Implementation	Ansoff and growth	Levels of strategy	International
					x	
				x	x	
		x				
		x				
		x				
	x	x				
						x
						x
					x	
				x	x	
			x	x		x
			x			
		x	x			
			x			
x			x			
x			x	x		x

PUBLISHER'S acknowledgements

The authors and publisher are grateful to the following 'gurus' or the institutions who allowed us to write about their achievements and theories and provided us with a photograph: Coimbatore Prahalad (courtesy of the Ross School of Business at the University of Michigan); John Kay; Geert Hofstede; Bob Galliers; Sumantra Ghoshal (courtesy of the London Business School); Albert Humphrey (courtesy of TAM plc); Joseph Juran (courtesy of the Juran Institute Inc.); Milton Friedman (courtesy of the University of Chicago News Office); Warren Bennis (courtesy of Warren Bennis and Buffalo University); David Teece (courtesy of the Berkeley Research Group LLC); Frederick W. Taylor (courtesy of Frederick Winslow Taylor Collection/Samuel C. Williams Library/Stevens Institute of Technology/Hoboken, NJ/USA); Robert Tannenbaum (courtesy of the UCLA Anderson School of Management); Peter Checkland.

The authors and publishers are also grateful to the companies who kindly permitted us to use their logos or associated images, and in some cases to write about them in case studies: Unilever (reproduced with kind permission of Unilever, from an original in Unilever Archives); Oxfam (the Oxfam logo is reproduced with the permission of Oxfam GB, Oxfam House, John Smith Drive, Cowley, Oxford, OX4 2JY, UK www.oxfam.org.uk. Oxfam GB does not necessarily endorse any text or activities that accompany the materials); British Airways (© British Airways); Morrisons (courtesy of Wm Morrison Supermarkets plc); Toyota (courtesy of Toyota); Wikimedia; Google; Xerox (courtesy of the Xerox Corporation); EFQM (for EFQM Award image © EFQM); Levi's (courtesy of Levi's®); Sony (Sony is a registered trademark of Sony Corporation); Virgin (courtesy of Virgin Media); ACN (courtesy of ANC Inc.); Shell; Global Reporting Framework; Mattel (Barbie and associated trademarks and trade dress are owned by and used under licence from Mattel, Inc. © 2010 Mattel. All Rights Reserved. Mattel makes no representation as to the authenticity of the materials contained herein. All opinions are those of the authors and not of Mattel); Diageo; Eurotunnel (logo courtesy of Groupe Eurotunnel. Copyright Eurotunnel); The Open University (courtesy of The Open University); One Laptop Per Child; The Linde Group; NHS Scotland; Starbucks.

Finally, for their permission to reproduce figures, tables, images, screenshots and extracts of text, the authors and publishers are grateful to the following:

Alibaba (screenshot courtesy of www.alibaba.com).

Miniwatts Marketing Group (graph of internet users © Miniwatts Marketing Group and www.internetworldstats.com).

IBM (Map of Social Networks © IBM).

Six Sigma (screenshot courtesy of iSixSigma.com, http://www.isixsigma.com/DMAICroadmap).

BCG (text in the Guru guide and the product portfolio matrix © 1970, The Boston Consulting Group).

McKinsey and Company (text in Guru guide).

Long Range Planning Journal for Figure 5.1 The cultural web. Reprinted from *Long Range Planning*, 1992, 25(1): 28–36, Gerry Johnson, 'Managing strategic change: strategy, culture and action', with permission from Elsevier.

John Wiley & Sons, Inc. for Table 7.1 Potential applications of strategic information systems. Adapted from Turban, McLean and Wetherby (2004) with permission of John Wiley & Sons, Inc.

McGraw-Hill for Table 7.2 from Daniels and Daniels and Table 17.3, D. McGregor and J. Cutcher-Gershenfeld, *The Human Side of Enterprise*, annotated edition © The McGraw-Hill Companies, Inc.

Free Press for Table 17.4 adapted from Stephen R. Covey, *Principle-Centered Leadership*, Free Press, New York. Figure 10.2 from *Competitive Strategy: Techniques for Analysing Industries and Competitors* by Michael E. Porter, copyright © 1980, 1998 by The Free Press and Figure 13.1 from *Competitive Advantage: Creating and Sustaining Superior Performance* by Michael E. Porter, copyright © 1985, 1998 by Michael E. Porter. Adapted with the permission of Free Press, a Division of Simon & Schuster Inc. All rights reserved.

Penguin for Figure 14.1, adapted from Ansoff, and Figure 14.2.

John Oakland for Figure 19.1 adapted from Oakland, 2003, 2004.

EFQM for Figure 19.2 The EFQM excellence model.

Global Reporting Initiative for Figure 6.1, GRI G3 Reporting Guidelines, p. 3. © Global Reporting Initiative (2006) www.globalreporting.org.

NHS Scotland for the text of the case study.

Dreamstime for the image of Ryanair © Tommy Beattie/Dreamstime.com.

iStockphoto for the remaining images in the book.

Pearson for Figure 11.1 from Yip, George S., *Total Global Strategy II*, 2nd edn, © 2003, p. 10. Adapted by permission of Pearson Education Inc., Upper Saddle River, NJ.

Every effort has been made to trace all the copyright holders but if any have been inadvertently overlooked the publishers will be pleased to make the necessary arrangements at the first opportunity.

LIST of abbreviations

B2B	business-to-business	IS	information systems
B2C	business-to-customer/consumer	IT	information technology
BCG	Boston Consulting Group	KM	knowledge management
C2C	customer-to-customer/	KPI	key performance indicator
	consumer-to-consumer	M&A	mergers and acquisitions
CAD	computer-aided design	MBO	management buyout
CAM	computer-aided manufacturing	MIS	management information systems
CBI	Confederation of British Industry	MLM	multi-level marketing
CRM	customer relationship management	NAFTA	North American Free Trade Area
CSF	critical success factor	PBIT	profit before interest and tax
CSR	corporate social responsibility	PDA	personal digital assistant
DP	data processing	P/E ratio	price/earnings ratio
DSS	decision support systems	P&L	profit and loss
EPS	earnings per share	R&D	research and development
ERP	enterprise resource planning	RFID	radio frequency identification
EU	European Union	RSS	rich site summary or really simple
FG	finished goods		syndication
GATT	General Agreement on Tariffs and Trade	SBU	strategic business unit
GDSS	group decision support systems	SIS	strategic information systems
GIS	geographic information systems	TPS	transaction processing systems
HR	human resources	Wi-Fi	wireless fidelity
ICT	information and communications	WIP	work-in-progress
	technology	WTO	World Trade Organization

PART 1

AN INTRODUCTION TO THE STRATEGY PROCESS

We often refer to business strategy as a 'process'. Some authors refer to a cyclical approach to strategy with multiple starting points, others to a linear process. Our approach in this book is to recognize that business strategy is a complex art and often multiple stages are conducted in parallel, but to understand and study strategy, we need a degree of order. So we adopt a linear approach to explaining business strategy but would ask the reader to remember that, in real life, things are not that simple.

Business strategy is never a once and for all event – it goes on and on. There is a need to continually review strategic objectives because the environment is always changing. Depending on the stance a company adopts, the purpose of strategy is either to make a business 'fit' into its environment or to use the resources of the business to 'change the rules of the game' or reshape the environment. By achieving this, the probability that the organization will survive and prosper are enhanced.

In Chapters 1 and 2, we set out the philosophy that underpins strategy and the business strategy process. In **Chapter 1**, we explore what we mean by the term 'strategy' and the difference between a deliberate or prescriptive approach and an emergent approach to strategy. We examine the different elements associated with business strategy and then profile the various schools of strategic management before developing our framework for understanding business strategy.

Chapter 2 examines the implications of adopting different strategic approaches, and determines the main features of competitive positioning strategy and core competence strategy. Strategic thinking is then explored and types of strategic decisions are analysed.

Chapter 1
Strategy and strategic management

Introduction and chapter overview

Strategic thinking and strategic management are the most important activities undertaken by any organization. How effectively and skilfully these activities are carried out will determine the eventual long-term success or failure of the business. In this chapter, we introduce the basic concepts of business strategy by defining what we mean by strategy, examining the key elements of strategy and profiling the different schools of strategic thought. We close the chapter with a presentation of our strategy process framework and thus set the foundations for the chapters that follow.

Learning objectives

After studying this chapter, you should be able to:

- define what is meant by the word 'strategy'
- explain Mintzberg's '5 Ps' framework
- distinguish between deliberate (prescriptive) and emergent strategy
- describe the different elements associated with business strategy
- explain the different schools of strategy and their implications
- profile a framework that allows strategy to be analysed and better understood

1.1   What is strategy and who cares?

At the beginning of a book on business strategy, the question, 'what is strategy?' seems to be the most obvious starting point. The answer to the question is rather more complicated than it might at first appear.

This is because we use the word 'strategy' in many ways. You may have heard people talk about a strategy for a business, a strategy for a football match, a strategy for a military campaign or a strategy for revising for a set of exams. It was this multiplicity of uses of the term that led Henry Mintzberg at the McGill University in Montreal (Mintzberg, 1987; Mintzberg and Westley, 2007) to propose his '5 Ps' of strategy, rather than simply creating a single definition.

Henry Mintzberg was born in Montreal, Canada in 1939. He graduated in 1965 with an MA in management from the MIT Sloan School of Management and a PhD in 1968. His teaching career has been at McGill University since 1968, although he was a visiting professor at the European Institute of Business Administration (INSEAD) in Fontainebleau, France from 1991 to 1999. He is currently the Cleghorn Professor of Management Studies at the Desautels Faculty of Management of McGill University in Montreal.

Mintzberg is an internationally renowned academic and author on business and management and is the two-time winner of the McKinsey award for the best *Harvard Business Review* articles, a winner of the George R. Terry Book Award for best management book (1995) and a fellow of the Royal Society of Canada.

While Mintzberg has been influential in his work on what managers do with their time, and how organizations design themselves, his main contributions to business strategy centre around how strategy is formulated, reconceptualizing organizational structures or configurations and reconsidering the various types of strategy and strategic schools that exist.

Mintzberg's 5 Ps

Mintzberg suggested that nobody can claim to own the word 'strategy' and that the term can legitimately be used in several ways. A strategy can be:

- a plan
- a ploy
- a pattern of behaviour
- a position in respect to others
- a perspective.

Indeed, Mintzberg identified 10 schools of strategy divided into three groups: prescriptive, descriptive and configuration (see Mintzberg et al., 1998). However, the 5 Ps allow us to better understand different views of strategy. It is important not to see each of these Ps in isolation from each other. One of the problems of dividing ideas into frameworks like the five Ps is that they are necessarily simplified. The 5 Ps are not mutually exclusive; it is possible for an organization to show evidence of more than one interpretation of strategy. Indeed, business in the 21st century may demand it, as companies or organizations are required to innovate, reinvent themselves and 'live on the edge of chaos'. Each P is now described in a little more detail.

Plan strategies

A plan is probably the way in which most people use the word strategy. It tends to imply something that is intentionally put in train and its progress is monitored from the start to a predetermined finish. Some business strategies follow this model. 'Planners' tend to produce internal documents that detail what the company will do for a period of time in the future, say, five years. It might include a schedule for new product launches, acquisitions, financing (to raise funding/money), or human resource changes.

Ploy strategies

A ploy is generally taken to mean a short-term strategy. It tends to have limited objectives and it may be subject to change at short notice. One of the best examples of a ploy strategy is that employed in a football match. If the opposing team has a particularly skilful player, the team manager may use the ploy of assigning two players to mark him for the duration of the game. However, this tactic will only last for the one game, or even part of the game, and the next game will have a completely different strategy. Furthermore, the strategy will only operate for as long as the dangerous player is on the pitch. If he is substituted or gets injured, the strategy will change mid-game.

Mintzberg describes a ploy as 'a manoeuvre intended to outwit an opponent or competitor' (Mintzberg , 1987, p. 14). He points out that some companies may use ploy strategies as threats. They may threaten to, say, decrease the price of their products simply to destabilize competitors. A boss may threaten to sack an employee if a certain performance standard is not met – not because the boss intends to carry out the threat, but because he wants to effect a change in the subordinate's attitude.

Pattern strategies

A 'pattern of behaviour' strategy is one in which progress is made by adopting a consistent form of behaviour. Unlike plans and ploys, patterns 'just happen' as a result of the consistent behaviour. On a simple level, small businesses like scrap dealers follow pattern strategies. They are unlikely to produce elaborate plans – they simply buy as much scrap metal as they can. If there is a batch of old scaffolding, they buy it up without thinking about it. However, they would not buy old plastics because that would be outside their pattern of business behaviour. Eventually, following this consistent behaviour makes the scrap dealer a wealthy person, thus it has been a successful strategy.

Such patterns of behaviour are sometimes subconscious, meaning that they do not even realize that they are actually following a consistent pattern. Nevertheless, if it proves successful, it is said that the consistent behaviour has *emerged* into a success. This is in direct contrast to planning behaviour and reflects the strategic 'intent' perspective of strategy.

Position strategies

Positioning is discussed later in the chapter. In essence, positioning means locating the organization in a specific area of market space or within a specific 'environment'. The location or position is deemed to be the best 'fit' between organization and environment, or between the internal and external contexts.

A position strategy is appropriate when the most important thing to an organization is how it relates to, or is positioned in respect of, its competitors or its markets (or customers). In other words, the organization wishes to achieve or defend a certain position. We see this a lot in sport. When a new boxing champion is crowned, their only objective is to remain the champion, to retain their superior position. Accordingly, all their efforts are invested in examining their future opponents and keeping in shape for the next defence of the title.

In business, companies tend to seek such things as market share, profitability, superior research, reputation and so on. It is obvious that not all companies are equal when one considers such criteria. Some car manufacturers have enviable reputations for reliability and quality, while others are not so fortunate. The competitors with a reputation to defend will use a position strategy to ensure that the reputation they enjoy is maintained and strengthened. This may even include marketing messages that point out the weaknesses in competitors' products, while pointing out the strengths of their own.

Perspective strategies

Perspective strategies are about changing the culture, that is, the beliefs and the 'feel', the way of looking at the world, of a certain group of people – usually the members of the organization itself. Some companies want to make their employees think in a certain way, believing this to be an important way of achieving success. They may, for example, try to get all employees to think and act courteously, professionally or helpfully.

Religious groups like the Church of England operate something approximating to this strategy. They have a number of core religious beliefs that they encourage all members to adopt. Then, it is argued, these beliefs will outwork themselves in actions. To be a good member of the Church of England, people must adopt the worldview of the church. The purpose of preaching, teaching, worship and other practices is, in large part, concerned with further embedding Christian beliefs into the personalities of the believers. Success is achieved when all members think in the same way, they all believe in the core doctrines and work them out in their lives through good works.

Clearly, as strategy has evolved and developed as a subject and area of study, strategy as a 'process' has become more prominent and thus the area of Mintzberg's work relating to pattern strategies and configuration has become more mainstream. You will explore such a perspective more when you study the resource-based view of strategy.

There is a key difference between Mintzberg's plan and pattern strategies, which is to do with the source of the strategy. He drew attention to the fact that some strategies are deliberate, while others are emergent.

KEY CONCEPTS

Deliberate strategy, sometimes called planned or prescriptive strategy, is meant to happen. It is preconceived, premeditated and usually monitored and controlled from start to finish. It has a specific objective.

Emergent strategy has no specific objective. It does not have a preconceived route to success but it may be just as effective as a deliberate strategy. By following a consistent pattern of behaviour, an organization may arrive at the same position as if it had planned everything in detail.

Defining the key terms

Organizations exist to serve particular purposes and to achieve related goals. While businesses are usually concerned with providing goods and services and seeking profitability and competitive advantage over their rivals, 'not-for-profit organizations', like the health service, education and charities, focus on providing the best quality service with the efficient and effective use of resources.

Earlier, we explored some of the definitions of strategy (using Mintzberg's 5 Ps model) and we learned that there is no universally agreed definition of strategy. At the most fundamental level, an organization's strategy can be regarded as the means (plans, policies and actions) by which it seeks to achieve its long-term goal or goals. In many organizations, strategy also includes the determination of the goals and objectives themselves, as well as the means of achieving them. These goals and objectives are often referred to as the vision, mission, values,

Values are the underlying principles, perspectives and beliefs that guide action and behaviour in the organization.

The **strategic aim** is a statement of organizational intent specified in terms of where the organization wishes to 'go' and when it wishes to get there.

strategic aims and objectives. They are often influenced by and influence the stakeholders of the organization.

Several terms are used interchangeably in the strategy literature. In order to avoid confusion, we will define some of the fundamental terms used:

- *Strategic management* can be viewed as a set of theories, frameworks, tools and techniques, designed to explain the factors underlying the performance of organizations and to assist managers in thinking, planning and acting strategically. In simple terms, it is a vehicle through which a business can review past performance and, more importantly, determine future actions geared towards achieving and sustaining superior performance.

- *Strategic thinking and leadership* relate to the ability of the leaders of an organization to look into its future and think creatively about its potential development. This thinking, vision and leadership are essential to the longer term development of the organization. Prahalad and Hamel (1990) stressed the need for leaders to think beyond current operations so as to develop a 'strategic intent', which, they argued, shapes the organization's future strategy and development, 'stretching' it beyond its past and present achievements.

- Strategic thinking is based on strategic learning. *Strategic learning* is concerned with the processes by which leaders, managers and organizations learn about themselves, their business and environment. Strategic learning is vital to the development of the strategic knowledge on which superior performance is based (Senge, 1990; Nonaka, 1991).

- *Strategic planning* centres on the setting of organizational objectives, as well as developing and implementing the plans designed to achieve these objectives. Rather unfortunately, strategic planning is often associated with a highly prescriptive approach to strategic management (Mintzberg et al., 1995). In many situations, a prescriptive or deliberate approach will be inappropriate. While the uncertainty of the modern business environment means that detailed and prescriptive long-term planning may be of little value, some form of broad long-term planning, related to strategic thinking and vision, is necessary if strategic intent is to be translated into action.

1.2   Elements of strategy

To understand strategy better, it is useful to look at what the elements of strategy are. We start with a definition and then explore the components of that definition.

Given the above definitions by Mintzberg, we might think that writers in business strategy are unable to agree on a single definition of the word 'strategy'. This is partly true, given the range of philosophical stances adopted. However, some have tried to sum it up succinctly to make it easier for students to understand. One such definition, still widely quoted, was offered by Professor Chandler of Harvard Business School in 1962. Given that Chandler predates Mintzberg, it is not surprising that it is rather more simplistic than Mintzberg might have accepted; nevertheless, its beauty is its simplicity:

> Strategy can be defined as the *determination of the basic long-term goals* and objectives of an enterprise, and the *adoption of courses of action* and the *allocation of resources* necessary for carrying out these goals. (Chandler, 1962, p. 13, emphasis added)

GURU GUIDE

Alfred Chandler was born in Guyencourt, Delaware in 1918. He gained a BA from Harvard in 1940 and then joined the United States Navy. In 1945 he returned to Harvard to study history. He graduated with an MA in 1947 and a PhD in 1952.

His professional career began at the Massachusetts Institute of Technology (MIT) in 1950 as a research associate and then a member of faculty; he remained at MIT until 1963. He then undertook a series of consultancy and research roles before becoming a visiting fellow at Harvard. He remained at Harvard as the Strauss Professor of Business History in the Graduate School of Business, until 1989. He was also a visiting fellow at All Souls, Oxford, and a visiting professor at the European Institute of Washington. His awards include the Pulitzer and Bancroft prizes in 1978, and he was a member of the American Philosophical Society and fellow of the American Academy of Arts and Sciences. In 1977–78, he served as president of the Business History Conference.

Chandler was a renowned business historian and author, who studied major US companies between 1850 and 1920 when modern capitalism was shaped. He believes his work contributed to a nationwide restructuring of corporations, with the multi-divisional form becoming standard for large organizations. Indeed, it is said that AT&T pursued his ideas in its 1984 restructuring of the company and indeed industry. He died in 2007.

Three components of strategy

Chandler's definition is a good one because it shows the scope of what 'good' strategy is. The italics in the quote show the three important contents of strategy:

- The *determination of the basic long-term goals* concerns the conceptualization of coherent and attainable strategic objectives. Without objectives, nothing else can happen. If you do not know where you want to go, how can you act in such a way as to get there? And how do you know when you have arrived?
- The *adoption of courses of action* refers to the actions taken to arrive at the objectives that have been previously set. If your objective is to be in France, the actions you would take would include arranging transport. You might do this by ringing travel agents, servicing your car, or using the internet to book.
- The *allocation of resources* refers to the fact that there is likely to be a cost associated with the actions required to achieve the objectives. If the course of action is not supported with adequate levels of resource, and the resources aligned to the business, the objective will not be accomplished.

Hence, strategy contains three things. In order to achieve your objective of being in France, you would take the actions of booking or arranging travel, taking leave from work and actually making the journey that will take you to France. However, these actions would not be possible if they could not be resourced. You need the resources of a plane, train, car or similar, with a suitably qualified pilot or driver, money to pay for your travel and other such 'inputs'. If any one of these is missing, you will be unable to meet your objective.

Resource inputs (sometimes called factors of production) are essential inputs that are central to the normal functioning of the organizational process. We can readily appreciate that human beings rely on certain vital inputs such as air, water, nutrition, warmth, shelter and so on, but organizations have similar needs. An organization's resource inputs fall into four key categories, described below.

Strategic objectives often form the strategy road map for an organization. They are 'stepping stones' to achieving the strategic aim and should be SMART in nature, that is, specific, measurable, achievable, relevant and time bound.

Resource inputs (sometimes called factors of production) are essential inputs that are central to the normal functioning of the organizational process.

Financial resources comprise money for capital investment and working capital. Sources include shareholders, banks, bondholders.

Human resources comprise appropriately skilled employees to add value in operations and to support those who add value, which may include supporting employees in marketing, accounting or personnel functions. Sources include the labour markets for the appropriate skill levels required by the organization.

Physical (tangible) resources comprise land, buildings (offices, warehouses and so on), plant, equipment, stock for production, IT and so on. Sources include estate agents, builders and trade suppliers.

Intellectual (intangible) resources comprise inputs that cannot be seen or felt but which are essential for continuing business success. Included here are elements of tacit knowledge such as technical know-how, legally defensible patents and licences, brand names, registered designs, logos, 'secret' formulations and recipes, business contact networks or databases.

1.3   Schools of strategy

Strategic management emerged as a discipline in the USA in the 1950s (Drucker, 1954; Selznick, 1957) and through the 1950s and 60s was characterized by the drive for efficiency gains through planning and control. This resulted in an emphasis on forecasting and cost control with value gained through scale economies. These early developments were often driven from the perspective of market or industry fit, with market/industry structure influencing conduct (the strategy adopted by organizations) resulting in performance (profit). In turn, this process results in strategic groups that impact on future market/industry structure, and therefore require a new conduct, and the cycle continues. This is called the S-C-P paradigm (structure-conduct-performance) and is at the centre of much of the work from Harvard Business School. In our book, we term this view of strategy the 'positioning school'.

An alternative to this are the Austrian and Chicago Schools, with alternative perspectives in value creation, innovation and competitiveness, which, when combined with the experiences of globalization (1980s) and ever more complex environments, required a more flexible and dynamic perspective based on the ability to change and innovate using available resources, competences and talent available to the organization (1990/2000s). This resulted in the 'resource-based view' or value school of strategy.

The resource-based view or value school of strategy is founded on the development of core competences that allow for quick, agile and innovative approaches to business which create and manage complexity and seek to renew value at every opportunity.

So, we have two distinct schools of thought, although some authors would claim as many as eight schools exist – the positioning school and the resource-based view.

Market/industry fit is the matching of an organization's resources to the industry and market structure within which it operates.

Strategic groups are collections of firms operating in the same strategic space trying to compete for premium share of profit.

Peter F. Drucker was born in Vienna in 1909. He was educated in Austria and England. During his lifetime he worked in various roles as a newspaper correspondent, professor, historian, economics commentator, teacher of religion, philosophy, political science and Asian art and throughout his career he acted as a management consultant to the government, public sector and corporations; he published 39 books and had his work translated into more than 20 languages, with over six million copies sold. His work has had a major influence on modern organizations and their management over the past 60 years.

Drucker is credited with developing most of the thinking in management theory of the 1900s; central to his philosophy was the belief that an organization's most valuable resource is a highly skilled workforce and that a manager's job is to prepare and allow people to perform at their best. He explored and proposed ideas around management by objectives, privatization, customer focus/orientation, decentralization, and the roles of chief executives. He stimulated debate around whether structure followed strategy and the virtues of 'sticking to the knitting' as well as pioneering the influences of the information age.

1

The positioning school

The first school we address is the positioning school. This perspective is founded on 'positioning' the organization in the 'best' place in the market or industry 'space' based on the structure-conduct-performance paradigm (Scherer, 1980). The model has it that *performance* is dependent on the *conduct* (activity, tactics or strategy) displayed by buyers and sellers in any given market, based on a range of criteria such as prices, investment, advertising, technological development, firm collaboration and so on. In turn, such conduct is dependent on the *structure* of each given market, defined by the number, size and distribution of sellers and buyers, the degree of product differentiation, entry barriers, cost structures, integration and diversification, and the resulting attractiveness of the industry/ market. This school can be seen to be at the heart of much strategic management work and evidenced by the work of Learned et al. (1965), Andrews (1971), Porter (1979, 1980, 1985, 1996, 2001), Ghemawat (2002) and the consultants from McKinsey and the Boston Consultancy Group.

The resource-based view

In contrast, the second prominent school can be seen to be the resource-based view (RBV), latterly to evolve into the value school. With its origins in the Chicago School, it views superior performance as resulting from the better use of underlying assets deployed by a firm. This school tended to dominate the area of strategic thinking from the 1980s (Prahalad and Hamel, 1990; Grant, 1991; Eisenhardt and Martin, 2000) through to the current day, with an emphasis on innovation, creativity, value chains, knowledge and talent and, more recently, dynamic capabilities. In essence, the RBV was developed to more fully reflect the broad range of resources available to organizations in their quest for competitive advantage, including the intangible, firm-specific resources (or assets) such as the skills, expertise, experience and knowledge that workers possess. Therefore, these 'assets' are deemed to provide not only the industry threshold competences but core competences, making competitive advantage more difficult to copy and potentially more sustainable, especially if the advantage is embedded in the skills, knowledge, networks and processes of the organization.

So, in effect, the positioning school has an 'outside-in' perspective (outside – external environment, in – influences organization strategy), while the resource-based view has an 'inside-out' perspective (inside – use of resources and competences, out – influences environment and performance).

The development of business strategy

Table 1.1 summarizes the development of business strategy management thinking since the 1950s. We have split these into phases to show how the field has developed. It is worth noting that organizations across the globe can find themselves at different phases and, as such, all phases of development currently exist in one form or another.

Table 1.1 Phases of business strategy development

	Phase 1 1950s	Phase 2 1960s–70s	Phase 3 1970s–80s	Phase 4 1990s	Phase 5 Present
Strategy approach	Business contexts	Control and planning	Positioning	Resource-based view	Dynamic capabilities
Themes	Budgetary control	Economies of scale	Economies of scope	Economies of expertise	Innovation and creativity
Emphasis	Budgets and control	Mergers and acquisitions, diversification	Industry leadership	Value creation and capability building	Agility and speed
Frameworks/ techniques	Financial control, forecasting, budgeting	Forecasting, synergy, BCG	Environmental analysis, industry structure analysis, SWOT, globalization	Competences, core competence, knowledge management, value chain, learning organization	Innovative capabilities, adaptive capabilities, adoptive capabilities, collaboration, knowledge management

---

CASE STUDY   ACN Inc.

ACN Inc. provides a range of discounted utilities and support services to the business and domestic markets. Founded in Chicago in 1989, it has grown to establish a presence in the USA and Canada, 18 countries in Western Europe and Australia. The company headquarters is in Chicago, and it has regional headquarters in Amsterdam and Sydney. Revenues for last year were $32m, of which $28m came from its US activities, $3m from Australia, and just over $1m from Western Europe. At present, the markets and products/services are as follows:

- North America: telecommunications, gas, electricity and water
- Australia: telecommunications

- Western Europe: telecommunications, mainly landline but with some mobile telecommunications in some countries.

In particular, ACN entered the Western European markets so as to take advantage of the opportunities presented by privatization and deregulation.

The core product and service is landline telecommunications. For all products and services, the basis for business (the stated strategy) is to acquire capacity at wholesale prices from the particular utilities providers, and then sell this capacity on to individual consumers at rates immediately below the local provider's prices and charges. For example:

- in France, ACN acquired the right to sell landline telecommunications capacity from France Telecom at 1 cent per minute. France Telecom sells to customers at 2.5 cents per minute, so ACN will sell at 2.2 cents per minute

- in the USA, ACN acquired the right to sell electrical supply capacity from the electricity generating companies at 0.5 cents per kilowatt hour (kWh); the rate charged to customers by other providers is 1.5 cents per kWh, so ACN sells to customers at 1.3 cents per kWh.

The products and services are sold as a niche brands immediately below the mass-market and established provider rates.

This approach to the business gained initial momentum through taking advantage of the deregulation of the US telecommunications and energy markets. When the position was replicated in these sectors in the UK and elsewhere, ACN thought itself well positioned to take advantage. For example, in the UK telecommunications sector, BT was ordered to give up part of its landline monopoly to competitors and alternatives. ACN entered the UK telecommunications market in 2002, buying capacity from BT and selling it on at its own preferred charge levels, coming in, as usual, at just below BT rates.

ACN entered the French telecommunications market in early 2004. ACN followed its usual pattern of buying capacity from the national monopoly, in this case France Telecom (FT). ACN then set about selling the proposition to the French population.

The sales method used was multi-level marketing (MLM). Throughout its existence, ACN has always used a form of MLM. MLM is a method of product and service distribution that relies on one individual finding a number of customers to sell to, these customers then find another number of customers to sell to, and these customers then find another number of customers to sell to, and so on. A web or network is created. This method has been used in various sectors to distribute a variety of products and services. Some have been successful and are well established in different locations and cultures. For example:

- Avon has a high reputation and well-established network of this form of selling in the UK
- Tupperware used this form of selling and distribution, and only failed or began to lose its position of pre-eminence because supermarkets and other retail outlets started selling equivalent products.

Others have been less successful and more contentious. Some have led to accusations of 'pyramid selling'. Pyramid selling is a similar process, especially when products and services have to be bought and paid for in full by individuals who are then faced with sole and independent responsibility for selling on. This is strictly illegal in the UK.

ACN uses an adopted format. The difference between ACN and other MLM (or pyramid selling) companies is that there are no products or inventories to hold. ACN's people are all independents, associates. Individual rewards are gained from finding new customers, signing them up, and from their subsequent volume telephone usage. Further rewards are additionally gained when the first person's customers then sign up customers of their own. Each level of customers thus contributes to their own prosperity, and especially to the prosperity of those above them. In France, ACN adopted the strategy of using the large English expatriate community in the south and west to be the associates, reasoning that they would be able to sell easily to the French population at large.

In spite of deregulation, however, the main providers of telecommunications services have remained the big national companies – AT&T, BT, FT. Deregulation has forced each to improve their product and service quality, and alter their approaches to charging, and to the actual prices and charges made. In general, each has been able to use its dominant market position and enduring familiarity to do this effectively in response to the new entrants. At the margins, however, new providers have been able to grow successful, profitable and effective business; the sheer volume, size and service usage in the telecommunications sector makes this possible and, for good providers, highly profitable.

ACN targets the core markets, those served by BT/FT, rather than attempting to get people already with other providers to change again. In France, 95% of landline traffic is still carried by FT, so the prospects for ACN look good.

Case study questions

1 To what extent does ACN have a strategy, and does it matter?
2 Comment on the proposition to sell products/services to customers at prices immediately below the main providers' charges. What are the barriers that have to be overcome in order for this to be effective?
3 Comment on the use of English expatriates to sell a range of US products and services to the French population. What factors ought to have been addressed before this decision was taken?
4 What other opportunities could ACN have explored as alternatives to expansion overseas?

1.4   The business strategy framework

As we have seen, strategy, strategic management and business strategy can be a complex and difficult to define area. To help us make sense of strategy and to better understand what organizations do, how they do it, and why, it is useful to have a frame of reference or some kind of guiding framework.

Figure 1.1 provides a framework and is intended to bring some order to what is often a messy subject. The framework can be used to help analyse an organization, strategy or context (case study), or it can be used to assist in formulating a strategy for an organization. Given our previous discussion, an emphasis on the right-hand side of the framework (external environment dominant) in terms of strategy process would highlight a positioning perspective to strategy development, while an emphasis on the left-hand side (internal environment dominant) would indicate more of a resource-based view. In this book, we use this framework to help structure our discussions.

Business strategy is often recognized as having three key stages. These stages are repeated and refined through the use of continual learning or the feedback loop. Stage 1 is strategic analysis, followed by development of the business strategy and finally the implementation of the strategy:

1 *Strategic analysis (internal and external analysis):* The internal and external environmental analysis results in identification of the organization's strengths, weaknesses, opportunities and threats (SWOT). These can then be used to align core competences to either create market value (the value creation school) or to understand the structure of the market/industry and the required resources and critical success factors (CSFs) to position the organization in the strategic space that provides best fit and profit potential (the positioning school).

2 *Development of the business strategy:* This is the generation, evaluation and selection of potential strategies that could be adopted by the organization to gain and sustain competitive advantage or provide best value/impact if a charity or public sector organization.

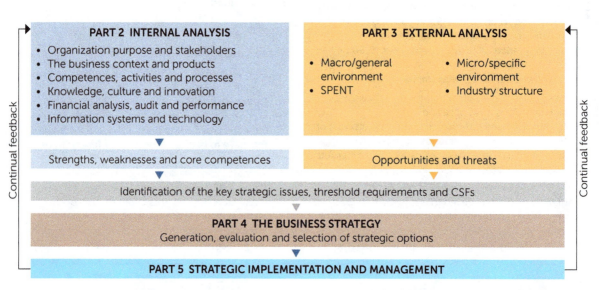

Figure 1.1 **The business strategy framework**

3 *Strategic implementation and management:* This stage explores issues associated with implementing a business strategy and examines the changing nature of the business world. The focus is on leadership, culture, change management issues and the emerging shape of future economies.

Finally in the framework, there is a feedback loop to allow continual reflection and refinement.

1

This is a helpful chapter to read before starting your report using the **Strategic Planning Software** (www.planning-strategy.com).

For test questions, extra case studies, audio case studies, weblinks, videolinks and more to help you understand the topics covered in this chapter, visit our companion website at www.macmillanihe.com/companion/business/campbell.

VOCAB CHECKLIST FOR ESL STUDENTS

Audit	Frontier	Patents	Pyramid selling
Bondholders	Know-how	Personnel	Road map
Contentious	Manoeuvre	Pre-eminence	Sack (to fire)
Deregulation	Market share	Preconceived	Synergy
Encapsulate	Momentum	Premeditated	Tacit
Enterprise	Monopoly	Privatization	Working capital
Expatriate	Niche	Profiling	
Forecasting	Paradigm	Public sector	

Definitions for these terms can be found in the 'Vocab Zone' of the companion website, which provides free access to the Macmillan English Dictionary online at www.macmillanihe.com/companion/business/campbell.

REVIEW QUESTIONS

1 Explain the difference between each of the Ps in Mintzberg's view of strategy.
2 Comment on the appropriateness of Chandler's definition of strategy.
3 Evaluate the differences in perspective between the positioning view of strategy and the resource-based view.

DISCUSSION TOPIC

Positioning strategies are simply not sustainable in the 21st century. Discuss.

HOT TOPICS – Research project areas to investigate

For your research project, why not investigate ...

■ ... how the evolution of strategic management thinking has impacted on organization strategy.
■ ... to what extent Mintzberg's 5 Ps of strategy hold true for public sector organizations.
■ ... what approaches to strategy are adopted by third sector/social enterprise organizations.
■ ... whether companies based in emerging/transition economies have different perspectives on the strategy process than those in established/mature economies.

Recommended reading

Argyris, C. (1977) 'Double loop learning in organisations', *Harvard Business Review*, 55: 115–25.

Grant, R.M. (1996) 'Prospering in dynamically-competitive environments: organizational capability as knowledge integration', *Organization Science*, **7**(4): 375–87.

Jacobson, R. (1992) 'The "Austrian" school of strategy', *Academy of Management Review*, **17**(4): 782–807.

Kay, J. (1995) 'Learning to define the core business', *Financial Times*, 1 December.

McKiernan, P. (1997) 'Strategy past; strategy futures', *Long Range Planning*, **30**(5): 790–8.

Mintzberg, H. (1990) 'The design school: reconsidering the basic premises of strategic management', *Strategic Management Journal*, 11: 171–95.

Newbert, S. (2005) 'New firm formation: a dynamic capability perspective', *Journal of Small Business Management*, **43**(1): 55–77.

Nonaka, I., Toyama, R. and Konno, N. (2000) 'SECI, Ba and leadership: a unified model of dynamic knowledge creation', *Long Range Planning*, **33**(1): 5–34.

Prieto, I.M. and Easterby-Smith, M. (2006) 'Dynamic capabilities and the role of organizational knowledge: an exploration', *European Journal of Information Systems*, **15**(5): 500–10.

Teece, D.J., Pisano, G. and Shuen, A. (1998) 'Dynamic capabilities and strategic management', *Strategic Management Journal*, **18**(7): 509–33.

Wenger, E. and Snyder, W. (2000) 'Communities of practice: the organizational frontier', *Harvard Business Review*, **78**(1): 139–45.

Chapter references

Andrews, K.R. (1971) *The Concept of Corporate Strategy*, Homewood, IL: Dow Jones Irwin.

Chandler, A.D. (1962) *Strategy and Structure*, Cambridge, MA: MIT Press.

Drucker, P.F. (1954) *The Practice of Management*, New York: Harper Row.

Eisenhardt, K.M. and Martin, J.A. (2000) 'Dynamic capabilities: what are they?', *Strategic Management Journal*, **21**(10/11): 1105–21.

Ghemawat, P. (2002) Competition and business strategy in historical perspective', *Business History Review*, **76**(1): 37–74.

Grant, R. (1991) 'The resource based theory of competitive advantage: implications for strategy formulation', *California Management Review*, **33**(3): 114–35.

Learned, E.P., Christensen, C.R., Andrews, K.R. and Guth, W.D. (1965) *Business Policy: Text and Cases*, Homewood, IL: Irwin.

Mintzberg, H. (1987) 'The strategy concept 1: five Ps for strategy', *California Management Review*, **30**(1): 11–24

Mintzberg, H. and Westley, F. (2007) 'Cycles of organizational change', *Strategic Management Journal*, **13**(S2): 39–59.

Mintzberg, H., Ahlstrand, B. and Lampel, J. (1998) *Strategy Safari: A Guided Tour Through the Wilds of Strategic Management*, New York: Free Press.

Mintzberg, H., Quinn, J.B. and Ghoshal, S. (1995) *The Strategy Process: Concepts, Contexts and Cases*, Englewood Cliffs, NJ: Prentice Hall.

Nonaka, I. (1991) 'The knowledge-creating company', *Harvard Business Review*, **6**(8): 96–104.

Porter, M.E. (1979) 'How competitive forces shape strategy', *Harvard Business Review*, **57**(2): 137–45.

Porter, M.E. (1980) *Competitive Strategy: Techniques for Analysing Industries and Competitors*, New York: Free Press.

Porter, M.E. (1985) *Competitive Advantage*, New York: Free Press.

Porter, M.E (1996) 'What is strategy?', *Harvard Business Review*, **74**(6): 61–78.

Porter, M.E. (2001) 'Strategy and the internet', *Harvard Business Review*, **79**(2): 63–78.

Prahalad, C.K. and Hamel, G. (1990) 'The core competence of the corporation', *Harvard Business Review*, **68**(3): 79–91.

Scherer, F.M. (1980) *Industrial Market Structure and Economic Performance* (2nd edn), Chicago, IL: Rand McNally.

Selznick, P. (1957) *Leadership in Administration: A Sociological Interpretation*, Evanston, IL: Row Peterson.

Senge, P. (1990) 'The leader's new work: building learning organizations', *Sloan Management Review*, **32**(1): 7–23.

Chapter 2
Perspectives on strategy

Introduction and chapter overview

This chapter helps to set business strategy and strategy making in context. We explore in more detail the key perspectives on strategy and in doing so examine deliberate and emergent strategy, and competitive positioning and competence perspectives. We follow this up with a discussion of the nature of strategic thinking and the competences needed for supporting such ideas. The chapter then examines the different sources of strategy before clarifying the types of strategy decisions required by organizations.

Learning objectives

After studying this chapter, you should be able to:

- discuss the implications of adopting an emergent versus a deliberate strategy
- determine the main features of the competitive positioning and core competence strategies
- explain what strategic thinking is and outline the components of strategic thinking
- profile the different sources of strategy, including the planning approach, competitive positioning approach, emergent approach, core competence approach and knowledge-based strategy
- explain the different types of strategic decisions, different levels of strategy and where strategy is carried out

2.1 Perspectives on strategy

The developing nature of strategy as a coherent academic discipline is reflected in two related debates revolving around what constitutes the most appropriate approach to strategic management (Figure 2.1). There is some disagreement among strategists on the best way of understanding the determinants of competitive advantage. Some writers advocate an approach to strategic management that is deliberate (sometimes called planned or prescriptive), while others argue that the emergent approach is better (strategy that evolves

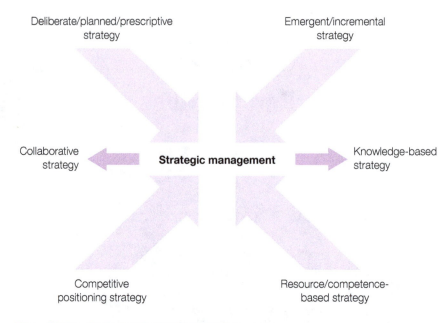

Figure 2.1 **The development of strategic management**

incrementally) (see Chapter 1). A parallel debate centres on whether competitive advantage stems primarily from the competitive position of the business in its industry or from business-specific core competences. These themes are explored in the following sections.

The debate surrounding the development of strategic management can be summarized under two broad headings:

1 The deliberate/planned versus emergent/incremental controversy.
2 The competitive positioning versus core competence/resource-based strategy controversy.

We began our discussion of these debates in Chapter 1 and will continue in various contexts throughout this book. Here, we summarize the main features of these approaches and briefly explore their advantages and disadvantages (see Table 2.1). To do so, it is useful to read the case study on the Virgin group of companies and then to reflect on how the group has developed.

The deliberate versus emergent strategy debate

Deliberate (planned or prescriptive) strategy

The deliberate (planned or prescriptive) approach views the formulation and implementation of strategic management as a logical, rational and systematic process. After analysis of the business and its environment, strategists must set well-defined corporate and business objectives and formulate, select and implement strategies that will allow these objectives to be achieved. This may be seen to be the case in many organizations that flourished in the 1970s, including General Electric, Ford and public utility companies (nationalized industry). Such an approach has been criticized on the grounds that there is often a major discrepancy between planned and realized strategies (Mintzberg, 1987) and whether systemic approaches are possible at all (Stacey, 2007; Stacey and Griffin, 2009). It is also argued that the increasing turbulence and chaos of the business

CASE STUDY Virgin

Richard Branson started what has become the Virgin empire in 1967. The first products and services were student magazines. Branson then diversified into a mail-order record business, specializing in buying and selling second-hand records. At the time, a large volume of the public bought records (especially popular music and rock) on a regular basis, and the prices of both single and long-playing albums (LPs) started to rise. Branson offered an alternative by selling second-hand records, based on the assumption that many records were of limited value and duration. He offered a guaranteed minimum price for those wishing to sell to him, so as to ensure that he could undercut the sales of new records to a point at which people would have to take notice of the prices that he was charging.

Branson moved into the music recording and recording studio business in 1971. The proposition was to offer good quality and good value facilities to those who would not otherwise get the chance, or those who the mainstream music business were unable or unwilling to sign up. His first major artists were the Sex Pistols (a punk rock band who had gained notoriety for bad behaviour and riots at their concerts) and, at the other end of the music spectrum, a composer called Mike Oldfield, who produced a major rock/alternate composition called 'Tubular Bells'. 'Tubular Bells' became the soundtrack to *The Exorcist*, a major, iconic film that came out in 1975. The revenues and royalties from the music ventures and the use of 'Tubular Bells' on the film transformed the Virgin organization. The money from each gave Branson the capital backing, cash flow assurance and business credibility to raise the funds, expertise and resources necessary to expand his business interests.

The result has been the growth of the Virgin empire into a family of over 300 companies. At present, Virgin has a presence in the following major industries and sectors:

- Transport, including airlines, railways and holiday resorts
- Clothing and textiles, including wedding and bridal wear
- Leisure, including publishing, films and videos, computer games, cinemas and theatres
- Mobile phones
- Financial services (including credit cards and insurance).

The standard model is either for the company to approach other companies in the sector under consideration to develop a partnering agreement and arrangement, or to review and evaluate business propositions and ideas that are presented to them. The partnering is undertaken with a view to putting the Virgin brand on whatever is chosen, and alongside this to partner the financial commitment so that the risk and the rewards are shared.

All new ventures and propositions, and the intended partners as well as the external and internal conditions surrounding them, are carefully evaluated, as are the markets, locations, unique selling propositions and products and services themselves. The result is that Branson and the organization collectively arrive at a view of whether or not they want to pursue the venture, and how much they are prepared to put in. Those who have dealt with Branson when negotiating and agreeing the structure of a venture state that normally, once he has made up his mind what something is worthwhile, he cannot be persuaded to change.

'The Branson test'

Everything under consideration has additionally to satisfy the 'Branson test'. The Branson test requires that new ventures involve existing products and services. Virgin does not normally do inventions or pioneering, it takes existing products and services and puts its own distinctive 'take' on them. Additionally, the products and services must be non-contentious and 'ethical' – Virgin does not do tobacco, alcohol or armaments (though it does publish 'adult literature').

The markets too must already exist – Virgin does not undertake product testing or market development from scratch. The markets must at the outset be under-served or badly served by existing providers, so that there is room for a distinctive quality and high brand entrant to come in and take a share. The markets must be capable of further development and exploitation; it must not be stagnant or in sharp decline. The stated aim in each case is to develop and sustain a quality based niche of between 2 and 15% of the total market; a niche that seeks a distinctive quality of service, and for which they are prepared to pay medium to high prices relative to the rest of the sector.

Finally, everything must be capable of being 'Bransoned' – there must be a sense of fun and cheekiness to which he can bring his own very distinctive PR approach. For example, for the original launch of Virgin Airlines, he dressed as a pirate and gained full international media coverage sitting astride one of British Airways' iconic Concorde airliners, and for the launch of Virgin Brides, he grew his beard longer and bushier, dressed in one of the bridal gowns, and jumped into a swimming pool while wearing it. The media coverage of these and other exploits has always given an enormous boost to the brand.

Once agreement is reached with the partners, the products and services are then given the Virgin brand. The Virgin brand values are: good quality products and services at reasonable prices; fast and effective customer service; universality of product and service access; and a clear sense of identity with Branson himself.

A clear statement of the order of priority of key stakeholders supports the brand and its values. The staff come first, because it is impossible to deliver top quality service if the staff are not well trained and motivated. The customers come second, because their business and confidence are needed in order to keep the business viable and profitable. The financiers and backers come third, because without the first two groups, no financial interests can be satisfied.

Case study questions

1 To what extent does the Virgin approach clarify the organization's strategic thinking; and to what extent could the approach become restrictive?

2 What are the main pressures that organizations such as Virgin have to address when considering their sources of strategy and competitive advantage, when they follow a distinctive approach such as this?

3 What problem is the Virgin organization going to have to address for the future, in order to preserve and secure its sources of competitive advantage?

environment makes highly prescriptive planning a nonsense. Rigid plans prevent the flexibility that is required in an environment of volatile change. Being over-prescriptive, it is argued, also stifles the creativity that often underpins successful strategy.

On the other hand, it is argued that systematic planning makes it possible to organize complex activities and information, align business objectives, set targets against which performance can be evaluated, and generally increase the degree of control which can be exercised over the operation of the business. The deliberate or prescriptive approach is often linked to the competitive positioning approach.

Emergent or incremental strategy

The emergent or incremental view of strategy adopts the position that strategy evolves incrementally over time, a result of 'muddling through' (Lindblom, 1959). This view is based on the premise that businesses are complex social organizations operating in rapidly changing environments. Under these circumstances, strategy will tend to evolve as a result of the interaction between stakeholder groups and between the business and its environment. Examples of this type of strategy are clear in the way Virgin developed and in the way companies

such as Sony, Honda and Adidas have evolved and adapted. It is argued that an emergent approach has the advantages of increased organizational flexibility (Bower, 1970; Burgelman, 1980). It can form a basis in organizational learning and can provide an internal culture for managers to think and act creatively rather than having to act within the rigid framework of deliberate strategy. The danger is that an emergent approach may result in a lack of purpose in strategy and it can make it difficult to evaluate performance – because if an organization has no explicit objective, performance against it cannot be measured.

To counter the criticisms of emergent strategy, Quinn (1978) and Quinn and Voyer (1994) see a role for some planning in the context of emergent strategy, advocating 'purposeful incrementalism'. This approach places a strong emphasis on organizational learning (see later in this chapter) and strategy as an ongoing, never-ending process (Markides, 1999), perhaps championing a need for a mixture of deliberate and unplanned approaches (Moncrieff, 1999; Lovallo and Mendonca, 2007).

The competitive positioning versus resource/core competence approach

In Chapter 1 we explored the different schools of strategic thought and found that two key schools have emerged as dominant in strategic thinking – the positioning school and the resource-based view (or core competence approach). In this section, we explore these two perspectives a little more fully to understand the foundations of any strategic directions or decisions.

Competitive positioning

We established that this school of thought dominated strategic management in the 1980s and still had considerable significance in the 1990s. Although the approach was widely criticized in the 1990s, the analytical frameworks devised by Porter in the 1980s are still widely used by both managers and academics. The major strength of the approach lies in the ready applicability of these frameworks to analysis of the business and its environment. The approach to strategy is essentially 'outside-in' (McKiernan, 1997) to establish a competitive position for the business in its environment which results in it outperforming its rivals.

In terms of procedure, the process of analysing competitive position begins with the five forces framework. This is used to analyse the attractiveness of an industry, the configuration of demand and supply, and the nature of competition in the organization's industry. This is followed by selection of the appropriate

GURU GUIDE

Michael E. Porter was born in Ann Arbor, Michigan in 1947 and is C. Roland Christensen Professor of Business Administration at Harvard. He is generally recognized as the father of the modern strategy field, and his ideas are taught in virtually every business school in the world. His work has redefined thinking about competitiveness, economic development and the role of corporations in society. Porter founded three major non-profit organizations and is one of the founders of the Monitor Group. In addition to his research, writing and teaching, he acts as a strategy adviser to business, government and the social sector. He has advised numerous leading US and international companies, including Caterpillar, Procter & Gamble, Scotts Miracle-Gro, Royal Dutch Shell and Taiwan Semiconductor. Porter also plays an active role in US economic policy with the executive branch and Congress, and has led national economic strategy programmes in numerous countries. He is currently working with the presidents of Rwanda and South Korea. He serves on two public boards of directors as well as on the board of trustees of Princeton University.

His honours and awards include the David A Wells Prize in Economics, six McKinsey awards for best *Harvard Business Review* articles, Richard D. Irwin Outstanding Educator in Business Policy and Strategy from the Academy of Management, the Adam Smith Award from the National Association of Business Economists, and the International Academy of Management's first ever Distinguished Award for Contribution to the Field of Management.

Porter is a leading authority on company strategy and the competitiveness of nations and regions, and his contributions are often seen as central to strategic management programmes. He advanced thinking in the area of strategic groups and clusters, articulated approaches to analysing industry attractiveness and industry structure, developed a means of examining the competitiveness associated with different countries, industries and regions, and provided an approach to understand the value creation of processes in organizations.

Porter has authored over 125 articles and 18 books and was described in Business Week (1990) as 'a business phenomenon in his own right'.

generic strategy together with value chain analysis to ensure that the business configures its value-adding activities in such a way as to support a strategy based on either differentiation or cost leadership.

In the 1990s, this approach was criticized for its overemphasis of the role of the industry in determining profitability and its underestimation of the importance of the individual business (Rumelt, 1991). Porter's frameworks have also been criticized as being too static, although Porter argues that they must be applied repeatedly to take account of the dynamism of the environment. The reality is that without Porter's work, strategic management would be devoid of many of its most practical and applicable analytical tools.

Table 2.1 **Approaches to strategic management**

Approach	Theory	Advantages	Criticisms
Deliberate (prescriptive or planned) strategy	Strategic management is a highly formalized planning process Business objectives are set and strategies are formulated and implemented to achieve them	Clear objectives provide focus for the business Objectives can be translated into targets against which performance can be measured and monitored Resources can be allocated to specific objectives and efficiency can be judged The approach is logical and rational	There are often major discrepancies between planned and realized strategy Rigid planning in a dynamic and turbulent business environment can be unproductive Prescriptions can stifle creativity Rigid adherence to plans may mean missed business opportunities
Emergent or incremental strategy	Strategy emerges and develops incrementally over time in the absence of rigid planning	Emergent strategy increases flexibility in a turbulent environment, allowing the business to respond to threats and exploit opportunities Changing stakeholder interactions can mean that strategy is often, of necessity, emergent	There is a danger of 'strategic drift' as objectives lack clarity It is more difficult to evaluate performance as targets are less well defined
Competitive positioning statgey	Competitive advantage results from an organization's position in respect to its industry The business analyses the strength of the competitive forces in its industry and selects an appropriate generic strategy. The business configures its value-adding activities to support this generic strategy The approach to strategy is 'outside-in'	Well-developed analytical frameworks like Porter's five forces, value chain and generic strategies Structured approach helps to simplify the complexity of business and the business environment Good for identifying opportunities and threats in the environment	Neglects the importance of business-specific competences as opposed to industry-wide factors Some of the analytical frameworks, for example generic strategies, have been widely criticized
Resource or competence-based strategy	Organizations must identify and build core competences or distinctive capabilities that can be leveraged in a number of markets The approach to strategy is 'inside-out'	The approach emphasizes the importance of the individual business in acquiring competitive advantage Strategic intent, vision and creativity are emphasized	Analytical frameworks are in their infancy and are currently poorly developed The importance of the environment in determining competitive advantage is underestimated

Resource-based view or core competence-based strategy

The 1990s witnessed the rise of resource or core competence-based strategic management (Prahalad and Hamel, 1990; Kay, 1993; Heene and Sanchez, 1997). The major difference to the competitive positioning approach is that the importance of the individual business in achieving competitive advantage is emphasized rather than the industry. The approach is therefore 'inside-out'. Although this approach came to prominence in the 1990s, its origins lie in the work of Penrose (1959), who emphasized the importance of the business and its resources in determining its performance. Interest in the approach was revived by Prahalad and Hamel's 1990 work 'The core competence of the corporation'. A core competence is some combination of resources, skills, knowledge and technology that distinguishes an organization from its competitors in the eyes of customers. This distinctiveness results in competitive advantage. An example of such advantage may be a local taxi firm using telephone recognition technology to know where calls are made from and thus providing the additional service of suggesting where customers would be picked up from. This sense of personalization adds value and build customer loyalty. In much the same way, customer relationship management systems are used to build intelligence about customers and so personalize services for them.

The approach also emphasizes organizational learning, knowledge management and collaborative business networks as sources of competitive advantage.

GURU GUIDE

Coimbatore K. Prahalad was born in Coimbatore, India in 1941. He graduated from Loyola College, Chennai, with a BSc in physics before being recruited as an industrial engineer with Union Carbide in 1960. He graduated from Harvard with a DBA in 1975 before returning to India to teach management. He continued as a visiting research fellow at Harvard while in India. Prahalad was appointed to the position of the Paul and Ruth McCracken Distinguished University Professor of Corporate Strategy at the Stephen M. Ross School of Business at the University of Michigan. He has been honoured for his contributions with a Lifetime Achievement Award from the Ross School of Business. He received honorary doctorates from the University of London (Economics), Stevens Institute of Technology (Engineering) and University of Abertay, Dundee (Business). He was a member of the UN Blue Ribbon Commission on Private Sector and Development. He died in 2010.

Gary P. Hamel was born in 1954. He graduated from Andrews University, Berrien Springs, Michigan in 1975 and undertook his PhD at the Ross School of Business in the University of Michigan, graduating in 1990. He is the founder of Strategos, an international management consulting firm based in Chicago and a visiting professor at London Business School and the University of Michigan. Dr Hamel has won two McKinsey awards for *Harvard Business Review* articles and is a fellow of the World Economic Forum and the Strategic Management Society.

Prahalad and Hamel made a major contribution to reshaping strategic thinking by introducing the notion of core competences. This helped to rekindle debate around the competitive basis of organizations and the sustainability of competitive advantage.

The resource/core competence approach has focused the search for competitive advantage on the individual business, but its critics argue that it lacks the well-developed analytical frameworks of the competitive positioning school and, perhaps, understates the potential importance of the business environment in determining success or failure.

2.2   Strategic thinking

Strategic thinking is distinct from the prescriptive processes associated with strategic planning. Graetz (2002, p. 456) captures this well when claiming that 'strategic thinking and planning are distinct, but interrelated and complementary thought processes'.

Graetz (2002, p. 457) claims that the role of strategic thinking is 'to seek innovation and imagine new and very different futures that may lead the company to redefine its core strategies and even its industry'. In this respect, strategic thinking is about combining strategic knowledge, context and organizational awareness to shape, reshape and redefine the business boundaries, direction and resources in order to gain a competitive advantage, be it short, medium or longer term. An example of this is the repackaging of the product Lucozade by GlaxoSmithKline, who redefined a product traditionally used as a tonic drink for aged and ailing people, which was a shrinking market, poor for return custom and not particularly easy to brand, to a sports and energy drink, now a well-known and flourishing product.

> **Strategic thinking** is about combining strategic knowledge, context and organizational awareness to shape, reshape and redefine the business boundaries, direction and resources in order to gain a competitive advantage, be it short, medium or longer term.

Liedtka (1998) argues that strategic thinking differs from strategic planning, in that:

- The future cannot be predicted, only the shape of the future, therefore detailed planning is fruitless
- Strategy formulation and implementation are interactive processes and therefore dynamic and complex. As such, they cannot be treated as sequential or discrete activities
- All managers play a key role in strategy formulation and implementation and control, so they need to operate with strategic intent, flexibility and an understanding of the 'bigger picture'
- As strategy and change are inescapably linked, finding new strategic options and implementing them successfully is harder and more important than evaluating the options
- Finally, the planning process itself is seen as a critical value-adding element, rather than the actual resulting objectives.

Thus strategic thinking is focused very much on the process and the talent associated with such a process. This raises the question as to what attributes are required for such a process.

Liedtka (1998) proposed five major attributes of strategic thinking in practice:

- a *systems perspective:* or the ability to understand the implications of strategic actions
- *intent focused:* the ability to allow individuals to focus on the overall goals of the organization and not get 'bogged down' in details
- *thinking in time:* being able to hold the past, present and future in mind at the same time (scenario planning is an excellent tool for this)

- being *hypothesis driven:* to ensure that critical and creative thinking are embedded in strategy development
- *intelligent opportunism:* being sensitive and responsive to real opportunities, not every opportunity.

Scenario planning has often been used in the modelling of war games. In a business sense, it is probably best known as the methodology or approach used by Royal Dutch Shell and was designed by Wack in 1971. In essence, scenario planning involves exploring the critical dimensions of a market or industry and the elements of the environment that have potential impacts to change and shape that market. Once understood, these can be manipulated to create different potential futures and to guesstimate the potential impacts of such futures. The organization is then in a position to begin to form contingency plans to deal with the range of potential futures and provide a more rapid response should such changes actually occur.

2.3   Sources of strategy

Strategic management is a relatively young discipline and its immaturity is reflected in the ambiguity of some of its terminology and the fact that there is no single agreed approach to the subject. McKiernan (1997) identified four stands to strategy theory, planned strategy, competitive positioning strategy, competence-based strategy and emergent strategy (as discussed above), and the knowledge-based approach is sometimes subsumed into core competence or resource-based strategy. We believe, however, that knowledge-based strategy has its own distinctive characteristics, at the same time as providing a fundamental underpinning to all the other theories of strategic management, and so we consider it as an approach in its own right.

While the literature of strategic management sometimes presents these five approaches as discrete and even in conflict with each other, it is more useful to view them as interdependent and, in many ways, complementary and mutually enriching. Each approach represents a different perspective and provides analytical frameworks through which managers can gain greater understanding of the strategic capabilities of their organizations.

Here, we consider the four approaches already discussed and the knowledge-based approach and their contribution to strategic thinking.

The planned approach

The prescriptive, deliberate or planned approach is based on long-term planning that seeks to achieve a 'fit' between organizational strategy and the environment in which it operates. As we have seen, this approach views strategic management as a highly systematized and deterministic process (Ansoff, 1965; Argenti, 1974; Andrews, 1987). The prescriptive paradigm of strategic management has been criticized as being unrealistic, particularly in times of rapid and turbulent change. Nevertheless, the need to set long-term objectives and to formulate broad plans and policies is necessary for the survival and progression of any organization. Detailed and inflexible long-term planning is, on the other hand, unnecessary and often counterproductive. Competitive advantage can be gained by being opportunistic and taking advantage of unforeseen opportunities.

The competitive positioning approach

The competitive positioning paradigm, drawing largely on the work of Porter (1980, 1985) dominated strategic management in the 1980s. It also emphasizes the idea of 'strategic fit' between the organization and its environment so as to achieve competitive advantage, referring to this as 'competitive positioning'. The approach is often described as 'outside-in', as the initial emphasis is on analysis of the environment before determining how to achieve a strategically desirable position. Porter's frameworks, the five forces (used for analysing the organization's competitive environment; Chapter 10), generic strategy (used to identify sources of competitive advantage; Chapter 13) and the value chain (used to analyse the activities and resources of the organization; Chapter 13) still provide some of the most useful tools of strategic analysis. There are apparent limitations to Porter's tools but, as long as these limitations are recognized, they are valuable to managers seeking to make sense of complex organizations and their environments.

The emergent or learning approach

As we established, an alternative to the strategic planning movement is the emergent or learning approach (Lindblom, 1959; Mintzberg and Waters, 1985; Mintzberg et al., 1995). This is based on the view that the modern dynamic and hypercompetitive business environment will inevitably mean that there will be a gap between 'planned' and 'realized' or actual strategies. A rapidly changing environment means that organizations must incrementally change and adapt strategy on the basis of organizational learning. This does not preclude 'deliberate' strategic planning completely but implies that strategic plans must be flexible, guiding the overall direction of the organization, but adapted when changing circumstances dictate.

The core competence approach

In the 1990s, a strong movement developed which suggested that competitive advantage arises from an organization's internally developed core competences or distinctive capabilities rather than from its environment (Stalk et al., 1992; Hamel and Prahalad, 1994; Teece, 2007). Whereas Porter (1980, 1985) stressed the importance of the industry in determining competitive advantage, this approach suggests that the core competence of the organization is of far greater importance (Rumelt, 1991; Baden-Fuller and Stopford, 1992). The approach is 'inside-out', suggesting that businesses seeking competitive advantage must first examine and develop their own distinctive resources, capabilities and competences before exploiting them in their environment. Clearly, some organizations in the same industry are more successful than others, lending support to the view that competitive advantage is largely internally developed. Equally, however, there is a danger of ignoring the environment, as customers and their needs, competitors and changes in technology can play an important role in determining competitive success, as happened with companies such as IBM, Amstrad and Sony, which had to change rapidly or die.

Knowledge-based strategy

What is required is a holistic view of strategy that embraces all facets of the organization, its resources, capabilities, core competences and activities, and its interactions with the environment – customers, suppliers, competitors, government, legislation, technology and so on. This holistic approach is embraced by the knowledge-based approach to strategic management, which has developed in recent years (Roos, 2005). In essence, this approach suggests that competitive advantage depends on the development of new and superior knowledge through the processes of organizational learning.

In fact, Prahalad and Hamel (1990) recognized the relationship between core competences, knowledge and organizational learning, defining core competences as, 'the collective learning of the organization'. Later research also suggested that businesses cannot afford to be internally or externally driven. Instead, competitive advantage depends on the ability of the organization to develop knowledge-based core competences, which are essentially market-driven strategies that are sensitive to customer needs, based on organizational learning. Such an approach encompasses the use of any conceptual frameworks that assist in the processes of learning and the creation of new knowledge. As Mintzberg et al. (1995, p. 28) suggested, the various approaches to strategic management can be regarded as 'complementary, representing two different forms of analysis both of which must be brought to bear for improving the quality of strategic thinking and analysis'.

So, the knowledge-based view of competitive advantage is based on the assumption that knowledge is the most important resource in complex, dynamic and uncertain environments, where knowledge is viewed as being at the centre of wealth-creating/value-adding activity. Strategy formulation depends on deciding what knowledge is vital for competitive advantage and whether that knowledge should be core. The organization is then designed around identifying, developing and managing that core knowledge. Therefore, while it is still necessary to scan the external environment and undertake a SWOT analysis, organizations cannot take advantage of opportunities that have been identified unless they have the core capabilities to do so.

This book adopts a holistic approach to the subject and draws on the theories and frameworks developed within all these perspectives. Essentially, however, competitive advantage is seen as arising from new knowledge, which is, in turn, created through organizational learning. In a rapidly changing world, competitive advantage can only be sustained if the process of learning is both continuous and continual. Organizations must learn by gathering information about their business, their activities, their resources, their core competences, their customers and their needs, their competitors, and other aspects of the business environment. This information must then be analysed to develop new strategic knowledge, which will act as the basis of new core competences and strategies that will produce superior performance.

The **knowledge-based view** of competitive advantage is based on the assumption that knowledge is the most important resource in complex, dynamic and uncertain environments, where knowledge is viewed as being at the centre of wealth-creating/value-adding activity.

2.4   Types of strategic decisions

Different 'levels'

It is useful at this stage to understand what characterizes strategic decisions. Management decisions within any organization can be classified in three broad (and sometimes overlapping) categories: strategic, tactical and operational. These can be illustrated as a hierarchy, in which higher level decisions tend to

Figure 2.2 **Levels of strategic decision-making**

shape those at subordinate levels (Figure 2.2).

Strategic, tactical and operational decisions within an organization differ from each other in terms of:

- focus
- the level in the organization at which they are made
- scope
- time horizon
- degree of certainty or uncertainty
- complexity (Table 2.2).

The three levels are now explored in more detail:

1 *The strategic level:* Strategic decisions are concerned with the acquisition of sustainable competitive advantage, which involves the setting of long-term corporate objectives and the formulation, evaluation, selection and monitoring of strategies designed to achieve those objectives. Strategic decisions are made by senior managers (usually directors), they affect the whole organization, are long term in nature, complex and are based on uncertain information. Managers at the strategic level require multiconceptual skills – the ability to consider the effects of multiple internal and external influences on the business and the possible ways in which strategy can be adjusted to account for such influences.

Table 2.2 **Comparing strategic, tactical and operational decisions**

	Strategic	Tactical	Operational
Focus of decision	Achieving sustainable competitive advantage	Implementation of strategy	Day-to-day operations
Level of decision-making	Senior management, board of directors	Head of business unit or functional area	Supervisory
Scope	Whole organization	Business unit or functional area, for example marketing	Department
Time horizon	Long term (years)	Medium term (months to years)	Short term (days, weeks, month)
Certainty/ uncertainty	High uncertainty	Some uncertainty	High certainty
Complexity	Highly complex	Moderately complex	Comparatively simple
Examples	Decision to launch new product, enter new market, investment decision and so on	Decision to advertise, alter price and so on	Decision to reorder stock, scheduling of jobs

The decision early on in easyJet's history to operate as a low-cost, no-frills airline is an example of a strategic decision, as is Dyson's commitment to continual innovation. Such decisions were taken at the most senior level, and affect the whole competitive position of the business, and all members of the business.

2   *The tactical level:* Tactical decisions are concerned with how corporate objectives are to be met and how strategies are implemented. They are dependent on overall strategy and involve its fine-tuning and adjustment. They are made at the head of business unit, department or functional area level and affect only parts of the organization. They are medium term in timescale, semi-complex and usually involve some uncertainty but not as much as at the strategic level.

3   *The operational level:* Operational decisions are concerned with the shorter term objectives of the business and with its day-to-day management. They are dependent on strategy and tactics. These decisions are made at junior managerial or supervisory level, are based on a high degree of certainty, and are not complex. The procedures in a sales office are typical operational activities – processing orders that have a tactical purpose in pursuit of the overall strategy.

Congruency and 'fit'

The success of strategy rests on an important, but rather obvious principle. Once the strategic level objectives have been set, the tactical and then the operational objectives must be set in such a way that they contribute to the achievement of the strategic objectives. In other words, all three levels must 'agree' or 'fit' together. This introduces the concept of 'congruence'.

We can visualize the decision-making framework as a pyramid (Figure 2.2). The top, where the strategic decisions are made, is thin, while the bottom (operational decisions) is fatter. This representation is intended to show that strategic decisions are taken infrequently, while operational decisions are taken often. Strategic decisions are few and far between, while operational decisions are taken weekly, daily or even hourly. For every one strategic decision, there will be more tactical decisions and possibly hundreds of individual operational decisions.

Where is a strategy actually carried out?

Although we have identified the top level in an organization's decision-making as strategic, we must not confuse this with the strategy itself, which is carried out at all levels of the organization. Strategy exists at all levels and it is useful to distinguish between the different levels as well as considering the relationships between them.

Network strategy

Many organizations and most businesses operate within a network of suppliers, distributors, customers and, sometimes, competitors. Although there may be no explicit strategy at this level, it is likely that the organizations will share certain objectives and information, and that aspects of strategy will be devised collaboratively. Collaborative advantage through networks, strategic alliances and joint ventures can be an important source of competitive advantage. For example, collaboration between Japanese car manufacturers like Toyota and their

component suppliers, which involves the sharing of information and objectives, is at the heart of just-in-time management, which, in turn, contributes significantly to their competitive edge.

Corporate strategy

Corporate strategy is at the level of the whole organization. Many organizations (especially larger ones) consist of a number of businesses linked together to varying degrees in terms of ownership, objectives, products, management, marketing, finance and so on. The degree of linkage can vary significantly from corporation to corporation. In terms of strategy, the degree of integration, coordination and commonality between the individual businesses can also vary enormously. It will depend on the extent to which knowledge and core competences can be shared across the various businesses that comprise the organization. For example, Ferrari's Formula One team is heavily reliant on the financial resources of the sports car manufacturing part of the business. At the same time, the sports car manufacturing benefits from technological developments made through Formula One racing, and the marketing effort benefits from the publicity the racing team attracts. Thus there is a sharing of knowledge and core competences across the business and there are synergies between activities.

In some organizations, strategic decision-making takes place at the level of the business or strategic business unit (SBU). In cases where businesses within a corporation have little relationship with each other, strategic decision-making occurs largely at the level of the business or SBU. The strategic level of the organization may do little other than set broad policies and objectives, together with performance targets.

Business strategy

Much strategic decision-making takes place at the level of the business or SBU. This will be within a context set by the strategic level but which may allow considerable strategic autonomy (or not), according to whether or not there is potential for synergy and economies of scale and scope. Core competences in marketing, finance, sourcing and distribution can be shared across the whole corporation, but each business is likely to require certain distinctive competences particular to its own local geographic, competitive or industry conditions. For example, Virgin's various activities share the same brand name but different businesses demand different competences.

Functional strategy

Within the strategy of the business, each area of value-adding activity or functional area (design, procurement, production, marketing, distribution, finance, information systems and so on) will need to design and implement a strategy that supports, that is, is congruent with, the overall strategy of the organization. Functional strategy is of considerable importance in the successful implementation of business strategy and in its fine-tuning or tactical management.

For test questions, extra case studies, audio case studies, weblinks, videolinks and more to help you understand the topics covered in this chapter, visit our companion website at www.macmillanihe.com/companion/business/campbell.

VOCAB CHECKLIST FOR ESL STUDENTS

Advocate	Discrepancy	Hypothesis	Procurement
Aerospace	Dynamism	Incrementalism	Prominence
Autonomy	Facets	Interdependent	Sequential
'Bogged down'	Financier/backer	Interrelated	Stagnant
Commonality	Fine-tuning	Leveraged	Subsume
Conceptual	Forum	'Muddling through'	Turbulence
Congruency	Fruitless	Non-contentious (see	Underpinning
Contingency	Generic	'contentious')	Volatile
Counterproductive	Guesstimate	Notoriety	
Determinant	Holistic	Opportunism	
Deterministic	Hypercompetitive	Phenomenon	

Definitions for these terms can be found in the 'Vocab Zone' of the companion website, which provides free access to the Macmillan English Dictionary online at www.macmillanihe.com/companion/business/campbell.

REVIEW QUESTIONS

1   Outline the potential implications for managers of adopting an emergent rather than a deliberate approach to strategy.
2   Outline the key factors that differentiate a positioning strategy from a core competence-based approach.
3   Define strategic thinking and explain how you would encourage it in an organization.
4   Discuss the difference in perspective between the different levels of strategic decision-making (strategic, tactical and operational).

DISCUSSION TOPIC

Organizations often have three levels of strategic decision-making – strategic, tactical and operational. Discuss what tensions may exist between the levels of the organization in terms of their priorities and propose what criteria you would use to decide on which level takes precedence.

HOT TOPICS – Research project areas to investigate

If you have a project to do, why not investigate ...

- ... the competences and characteristics required of managers to exercise effective strategic thinking.
- ... the effectiveness of scenario planning in knowledge-intensive industries.
- ... the approaches adopted by organizations to formulating strategy across the three levels of strategic decision-making.

Recommended reading

Abraham, S. (2005) 'Stretching strategic thinking', *Strategy & Leadership*, **33**(5): 5–12.

Ambrosini, V. and Bowman, C. (2009) 'What are dynamic capabilities and are they a useful construct in strategic management?' *International Journal of Management Reviews*, **11**(1): 29–49.

Barney, J.B. (1991) 'Firm resources and sustained competitive advantage', *Journal of Management*, **17**(1): 99–120.

Easterby-Smith, M., Lyles, M.A. and Peteraf, M.A. (2009) 'Dynamic capabilities: current debates and future directions', *British Journal of Management*, **20**: S1–8.

Heracleous, L. (1998) 'Strategic thinking or strategic

planning', *Long Range Planning*, **30**(3): 481–7.

King, A.W. (2007) 'Disentangling interfirm and intrafirm causal ambiguity: a conceptual model of causal ambiguity and sustainable competitive advantage', *Academy of Management Review*, **32**(1): 156–78.

Mintzberg, H. (1990) 'The design school: reconsidering the basic premises of strategic management', *Strategic Management Journal*, 11: 171–95.

Nonaka, I., Toyama, R. and Konno, N. (2000) 'SECI, ba and leadership: a unified model of dynamic knowledge creation', *Long Range Planning*, **33**(1): 5–34.

Pemberton, J. and Stonehouse, G. (2000) 'Organisational learning and knowledge assets: an essential partnership', *The Learning Organization*, **7**(4): 184–94.

Quinn, J.B. (1992) *The Intelligent Enterprise*, New York: Free Press.

Rumelt, R.P. (1984) 'Towards a strategic theory of the firm', in R.B. Lamb (ed.), *Competitive Strategic Management*, Englewood Cliffs, NJ: Prentice Hall.

Schoemaker, P.J. (1995) 'Scenario planning: a tool for strategic thinking, *Sloan Management Review*, **36**(2): 25–40.

Stacey, R. (2007) *Strategic Management and Organisational Dynamics: Challenge of Complexity to Ways of Thinking about Organisations*, Harlow: Pearson Education.

Stonehouse, G., Pemberton, J. and Barber, C. (2001) 'The role of knowledge facilitators and inhibitors: lessons from airline reservations systems', *Long Range Planning*, **34**(2): 115–38.

Teece, D.J., Pisano, G. and Shuen, A. (1997) 'Dynamic capabilities and strategic management', *Strategic Management Journal*, **18**(7): 509–33.

Chapter references

Andrews, K. (1987) *The Concept of Corporate Strategy*, Homewood, IL: Irwin.

Ansoff, H.I. (1965) *Corporate Strategy: An Analytical Approach to Business Policy for Growth and Expansion*, New York: McGraw-Hill.

Argenti, J. (1974) *Systematic Corporate Planning*, Sunbury-on-Thames: Nelson.

Baden-Fuller, C. and Stopford, J. (1992) *Rejuvenating the Mature Business*, London: Routledge.

Bower, J.L. (1970) *Managing the Resource Allocation Process*, Boston, MA: Harvard Business School Press.

Burgelman, R. (1980) Managing innovating systems: a study in the process of internal corporate venturing, PhD dissertation, Graduate School of Business, Columbia University.

Graetz, F. (2002) 'Strategic thinking versus strategic planning: towards understanding the complementarities', *Management Decision*, **40**(5): 456–62.

Hamel, G. and Prahalad, C.K. (1994) *Competing for the Future*, Boston, MA: Harvard Business School Press.

Heene, A. and Sanchez, R. (eds) (1997) *Competence-based Strategic Management*, London: John Wiley.

Kay, J. (1993) *Foundations of Corporate Success*, Oxford: Oxford University Press.

Liedtka, J.M. (1998) 'Linking strategic thinking with strategic planning, *Strategy and Leadership*, **26**(4): 30–5.

Lindblom, C.E. (1959) 'The science of muddling through', *Public Administration Review*, **19**: 79–88.

Lovallo, D. and Mendonca, L. (2007) 'Strategy's strategist: an interview with Richard Rumelt', *McKinsey Quarterly*, 4: 56–67.

McKiernan, P. (1997) 'Strategy past; strategy futures', *Long Range Planning*, **30**(5): 790–8.

Markides, C.C. (1999) 'In search of strategy', *Sloan Management Review*, **40**(3): 6–7.

Mintzberg, H. (1987) 'Five Ps for strategy', *California Management Review*, **30**(1): 11–24.

Mintzberg, H. and Waters, J.A. (1985) 'Of strategies, deliberate and emergent', *Strategic Management Journal*, **6**(3): 257–72.

Mintzberg, H., Quinn, J.B. and Ghoshal, S. (1995) *The Strategy Process: Concepts, Contexts and Cases,* Englewood Cliffs, NJ: Prentice Hall.

Moncrieff, J. (1999) 'Is strategy making a difference?', *Long Range Planning Review*, **32**(2): 273–6.

Penrose, E. (1959) *The Theory of the Growth of the Firm*, Oxford: Oxford University Press.

Porter, M.E. (1980) *Competitive Strategy: Techniques for Analysing Industries and Competitors*, New York: Free Press.

Porter, M.E. (1985) *Competitive Advantage*, New York: Free Press.

Prahalad, C.K. and Hamel, G. (1990) 'The core competence of the corporation', *Harvard Business Review*, **68**(3): 79–91.

Quinn, J.B. (1978) 'Strategic change; logical incrementalism', *Sloan Management Review*, **20**(1): 7–21.

Quinn, J.B. and Voyer J. (1994) *The Strategy Process*, Englewood Cliffs, NJ: Prentice Hall.

Roos, G. (2005) 'Intellectual capital and strategy; a primer for today's manager', in P. Coate (ed.) *Handbook of Business Strategy*, Bradford: Emerald.

Rumelt, R. (1991) 'How much does industry matter?', *Strategic Management Journal*, 12: 167–85.

Stacey, R. (2007) 'The challenge of human interdependence: consequences for thinking about the day to day practice of management in organizations', *European Business Review*, **19**(4): 292–302.

Stacey, R. and Griffin, D. (2009) *Complexity and the Experience of Values, Conflict and Compromise in Organisations*, New York: Routledge.

Stalk, G., Evans, P. and Shulmann, L.E. (1992) 'Competing on capabilities: the new rules of corporate strategy', *Harvard Business Review*, **70**(3): 57–69.

Teece, D.J. (2007) 'Explicating dynamic capabilities: the nature and micro foundations of (sustainable) enterprise performance', *Strategic Management Journal*, **28**(13): 1319–50.

PART 2

INTERNAL ANALYSIS

In Part 1, we examined what strategy is and what different schools or perspectives exist in the field. Now, to understand an organization's strategic position, stance and perspectives, it is necessary to examine and evaluate the environment within which an organization operates. The 'environment' is usually divided into two types, the internal environment, that is, everything that happens within the boundary of the organization, and the external environment, or everything that happens outside the boundary of the organization itself. Part 2 is concerned with the internal environment.

When examining the internal environment, we term this 'internal analysis'. The internal analysis forms the basis of understanding what a business is about. It often deals with soft issues of business context, stakeholder expectation, culture, processes, people and management style. In addition, the harder issues are also examined in terms of products, IT systems and organizational structure.

Figure 2 highlights internal analysis and where it fits into the overall business strategy process.

Figure 2 Internal analysis and the business strategy process

In terms of strategic development, if an organization adopts more of a resource-based (or value school) view of strategic development, the process will have a greater emphasis on internal analysis and an understanding of the organization's strengths, weaknesses and core competences.

Chapter 3 sets the scene by explaining the role and importance of different business contexts. It examines business models and establishes the characteristics of products, markets and services. This is then related to product life cycle and portfolio theory. The end result is a greater appreciation of what business context is all about and how it can influence business strategy.

The core areas of competences, activities and processes are explored in **Chapter 4**, mainly through the application of value concepts and the analysis of resources and core competences.

Chapters 5, 6 and **7** focus on key areas of resource and process. They examine knowledge, culture and innovation, before focusing on financial analysis, and information systems and technology.

Chapter 8 draws together the key points of the internal analysis, namely the development and understanding of an organization's strengths, weaknesses and strategic capabilities.

Chapter 3

The business context and products (goods and services)

Introduction and chapter overview

The purpose of the organization drives its strategic development and the way in which it views its place in society. This purpose is often articulated through the vision and mission statements and enacted through products and strategy. The combination of business context, products and strategy gives rise to a range of business models that are employed as important aspects of competitive strategy.

In this chapter, we discuss the purpose of the organization and profile the different types of business models before examining what we mean by products and the need for a balanced product portfolio. The chapter provides the first stage or foundations for understanding what organizations are all about, and sets the context within which the internal environmental analysis can be undertaken.

Learning objectives

After studying this chapter, you should be able to:

- explain how to determine the purpose of an organization
- identify different types of business models
- define what is meant by a product and describe Kotler's five levels of product benefit
- describe and criticize Copeland's product typology
- understand the stages in, and uses of, the product life cycle
- explain the concept of 'portfolio'
- describe the composition and limitations of the BCG matrix and the GE matrix

3.1 Business purpose, context and models

The purpose of a business or organization is reflected in the vision and mission statements. These are then translated into strategic intent, strategic aims, objectives and, ultimately, action and direction. As such, the purpose of the organization is central to its strategic development.

The **vision** is an attempt to articulate what the organization should be like in the future. It is what the organization is seeking to become.

The vision tends to be long term in nature and defines the desired future state of the organization in terms of its contributions to stakeholders, society and its strategic direction. Examples of vision statements include PepsiCo, which claims

The **mission statement** provides direction for the organization by defining what the organization is and its reason for existing. As such, the mission statement often encapsulates the vision and values.

'Our vision is put into action through programs and a focus on environmental stewardship, activities to benefit society, and a commitment to build shareholder value by making PepsiCo a truly sustainable company', and Oxfam, which claims 'that diverse communities of women and men living in poverty will exercise their rights to a decent and secure standard of living in a rich industrialized society'.

The **mission statement** is a short, succinct statement of the purpose or reason for existence of the organization. Google's mission is to 'organize the world's information and make it universally accessible and useful', while Nike claims 'To bring inspiration and innovation to every athlete in the world. If you have a body, you are an athlete.'

This purpose is also influenced by the business context within which the organisation operates. Commonly, business context can be divided into for-profit organizations, non-profit organizations (commonly public sector) and not-for-profit organizations (voluntary or charity sector). It is the context that will influence what the organization seeks to achieve and how it measures success. The context will also influence the business model.

What is a business model? According to Slywotzky (1996, p. 52), a business model is:

> the totality of how a company selects its customers, defines and differentiates its offerings, defines the tasks it will perform itself and those it will outsource, configures its resource, goes to market, creates utility for customers, and captures profits. It is the entire system for delivering utility to customers and earning a profit from that activity.

So business models are fundamental to the design of the organization. Business models also reflect the technological and other environmental changes that occur at the time the business is operating or is formed or evolved.

Business models can be built around:

- *an advertising model*, where revenues (or rents) are earned by adverts, promotions or, in the case of websites, redirecting consumers
- *a brokerage model*, where the business acts as an agent. This includes market exchanges, auctions or classifieds
- *a utility model*, which represents a charge for using the product or service
- *a subscription model*, where revenues come from membership of some 'protected' user group or market
- *a community model*, clearly evident in the use of Web 2.0 technologies and social networking, such as Bebo, Friends Reunited and so on
- *an affiliate model*, where organizations work together to increase market scope or share
- *a manufacturer model*, which represents the classic economic conversion of raw materials into higher value products (goods or services)
- *a merchant model*, either in virtual form, mail order or physical presence
- *an infomediary model*, where information is provided as the core product offering, often combined with other business models.

So there are many different and interrelated or overlapping business models. For the purpose of business strategy, it is useful for us to understand 'what business the organization is in' and what form of business model it is using. We can then better appreciate and understand what the organization is doing, will do, and why.

CASE STUDY Gate Security Systems Ltd

For the past seven years, Gate Security Systems Ltd (GSS) had provided the technology and staffing for all of the security check-in activities demanded by busy airports in the UK and elsewhere. By 2009, GSS was providing and delivering these services at six airports in Europe as well as three in the UK.

This work is extremely lucrative. All airports have to have state-of-the-art security, so as to be able to pick up any wrongdoing on the part of members of the travelling public. As well as the high-profile attention to 'the terrorist threat', airport security has to be able to detect the smuggling of drugs, firearms and illicit jewellery, gold and silver. Airport security also has to be able to try and relate mismatches and lack of fit in passports, travel documentation and other identity. Airport security has also to be able, when necessary or required, to provide instant tracking for financial transactions and credit card fraud. Airport security systems and technology have to be capable of scanning all kinds of luggage and detecting any explosives, contraband or firearms without any failure or lapse at all.

The airports themselves have to be secure from incursions of any sort. This means that there has to be a system for the checking of vehicle access and egress when people are being set down and picked up, and when they are being ferried to and from the car parks and hotels, which in many cases are many hundred metres from the terminals and points of arrival and departure. This also applies to all deliveries of everything, both to the public and also the secure areas.

GSS undertook to provide all these services, and the company gave guarantees over the absolute integrity of its staff and systems. However, because of the combination of political, media and public pressure for total security in all aspects of air travel and transport operations, a series of hasty, costly and ineffective decisions were taken.

Like many others providing these services around the world, GSS fell foul of what was called 'the rush for technology', which would make all air travel and transport totally secure in the wake of the 9/11 attacks in New York and the 7/7 attacks in London. Again like many others, GSS upgraded its scanning and information processing technology very quickly, only to find that in common with over 150 airports around the world, the equipment could not distinguish fully between solid objects and liquids, if these were in packaging. To be fully effective, therefore, meant that, in practice, every item of hand baggage and checked-in luggage had to be opened and searched. The technology also had difficulty with accurately identifying other substances and items, including clothing made out of nylon or terylene.

Accordingly, this technology had to be discarded shortly after its installation, and then replaced with something that had been better designed and more state of the art. This cost GSS £700m. However, the new technology was also found to be lacking; in particular, some of the most common and notorious faults were:

- it could not distinguish between substances of a similar consistency; in particular, it could not distinguish between semtex explosives and toothpaste
- it could not distinguish between different liquids; although it could identify liquids as being liquids, it could not, for example, distinguish between coffee and paraffin.

These and other faults and shortcomings led to global, international and regional directives on what could and could not be carried in hand luggage and what had to be checked in and placed in the luggage holds of airlines.

There were then additional problems with the security of the airport facilities themselves. Following a small and isolated (but nevertheless very serious) terrorist attack on one of the airports supposedly protected by GSS, a full strategic review was ordered by BAA, the owner and operator of three airports for which GSS provided the security service and technology. The review was scheduled for the first week in September 2009, and it was to take place at Stansted, one of London's airports.

On the day the review was supposed to start, the airport had to be closed because environmental protesters breached the perimeter fence and then staged a sit-in on the main runway. When the review did finally get underway, the following quickly became clear:

- the company had failed to invest in technology upgrades and staff training. Following the £700m loss, it bought the cheapest options that it could find, rather than either searching for the best, or commissioning its own technology
- the need to upgrade security checks and tighten the ability to spot suspicious objects and people as they passed through the airport was undermined by the lack of adequate staffing levels or staff training
- the speed at which people moved through the security check-in processes, especially at busy times, was unacceptable, and following a series of media exposés, the government ordered BAA to improve throughput speeds at all times. When BAA tried to shift the blame on to GSS, the government ignored this, stating that it was up to BAA to sort the matter out immediately.

2

Because of the environmental protest and demonstration, it had become absolutely clear to the review body that there was a priority need to check the security of airport premises.

Case study questions

1   What is the context in which GSS is carrying out its activities?
2   What is the key business model present, and where do the fundamental strengths and weaknesses of the approach lie?
3   What is the product/service portfolio on offer here, and to whom? What are the product life cycle problems that have to be addressed in industries, sectors and circumstances such as these?
4   What options are open to the various parties as the result of the review findings indicated above?

3.2   Defining product and services

A **product** is anything that is offered for sale.

A **good** is tangible and is something that can be owned.

A **service** is something that is done on the buyer's behalf and is intangible in nature.

Most organizations will offer their main purpose or 'value proposition' as a product. We can define a product as anything that is offered for sale. Hence, a product might be a physical good, such as a car, a service, such as a lawyer, or a mixture of both, such as a restaurant. A good is tangible and is something that can be owned. A service is something that is done on the buyer's behalf and is intangible in nature. Some products contain both a good and a service element, such as when we purchase hairdressing services from a barber or hairdresser (the service) who then also washes and blow-dries the hair using hair care products (such as shampoo – goods). The totality of the hairdressing product contains both goods and services.

In product strategy, it is useful to think how value might be added to the product from the customer's point of view. To do this, it can be helpful to consider the product's features and benefits in a number of levels. Different approaches can give different numbers of levels. Here we consider Kotler's five-benefit model (1997):

1   *The core benefit* provided by the product. In a car, for example, this would be the ability to transport. Since all the products on the market will provide this benefit, this will rarely be the level on which companies compete.
2   *The generic product*, which includes everything that would be necessary to make the product function. For the car, this might include the seats, appropriate controls and legal safety equipment.
3   *The expected product*, which is all that the customer has come to expect in a product. In our example of a car, this might include a radio, comprehensive guarantee and certain levels of performance.
4   *The augmented product* goes beyond the customer's expectations to provide something extra and desirable, for example air conditioning and on-board satellite navigation in a car.
5   *The potential product* is the product level that encompasses all that the product might ultimately become, but currently does not incorporate. The ownership of a certain car, for example, may confer on the owner a certain status in society, provide them with opportunities that would otherwise not present themselves or even assist in the attraction of a sexual partner.

In mature markets, competition is normally at the augmented product level or above, and the basic product is taken for granted. What is in the expected product in one market may be in the augmented product in another. Air conditioning in a car might be a bonus in a temperate climate, but a necessity in a tropical one. Thus, a car company that had gained a competitive advantage by superior reliability would lose that advantage once all cars had become reliable. It then has to be able to offer something else or face a lack of competitiveness. Over time, the augmented product becomes the expected product, so there has to be a continuous search for something extra to offer.

Augmentation adds to costs, and the company has to consider whether the customer will be willing to pay for the extra costs in the final price. Sometimes, after a period of rivalry, where competitors try to compete by adding more and more features and cost, a market segment emerges for a basic stripped-down, low-cost version that just supplies the expected benefits.

GURU GUIDE

Philip Kotler was born in 1931 in Chicago and received his MA from the University of Chicago and his PhD from MIT. His initial study was in economics and his postdoctoral work was in mathematics at Harvard University and behavioural sciences at University of Chicago. He is currently the SC Johnson & Son Professor of International Marketing at Kellogg School of Management, Northwestern University.

Professor Kotler has extensive consulting experience and has been a member of several boards, including the advisory board of the Drucker Foundation, and he was also the chairman of the College of Marketing of the Institute of Management Sciences. He has several honorary doctorates, most notable among them Stockholm University, the University of Zurich and the University of Economics and Business Administration in Vienna. Professor Kotler has received several best article awards, and other prestigious awards, including the American Marketing Association's Distinguished Marketing Educator Award and the European Association of Marketing Consultants Marketing Excellence Award.

Professor Kotler is a distinguished figure in marketing management. His work has been influential in understanding theories and concepts related to marketing and his work is often considered as seminal in marketing management. He has published extensively in a range of areas of marketing and continues to push forward thinking in the field. Most recently, his work has contributed to debates around social marketing, ethics and 'negative' image.

Copeland's product typology and strategy

There is a commonly held view that different types of products need to be managed and brought to market in different ways. Services, for example, cannot be stored, must be consumed at the point of production, are intangible, and it is difficult to judge quality in advance. As a result of these factors, we might anticipate off-peak pricing offers, the need for supplier credibility, and difficulties in advertising not experienced by physical products. Industrial products are less likely to be sold direct to the end user than consumer products, with advertising being relatively more important for consumer products and high-quality personal contact being relatively more important for industrial products, hence the use of sales representatives to speak directly to industrial buyers.

There have been a number of attempts to build on product characteristics to produce classification systems for products that will serve as a comprehensive guide. A system based on dividing consumer products into convenience, shopping and specialty goods (Copeland, 1923) has endured and is one of the most popular product classification systems used at the present time:

Convenience goods are products where purchase is relatively frequent, at low prices, and the customer sees little interest or risk in the purchase.

Shopping goods are those that are typically more expensive, of more interest to the purchaser, and some risk is seen in the purchase.

Specialty goods are seen as products that are so differentiated from others, often carrying considerable prestige, that customers may insist on only one brand.

- *Convenience goods:* **Convenience goods** are products where purchase is relatively frequent, at low prices, and the customer sees little interest or risk in the purchase. Examples would include low-price confectionery, batteries and carbonated drinks. As a consequence, the customer will typically buy the product available in the most convenient outlet, and the supplier will have to make the product available in as many outlets as possible. Point of sale display and simple reminder advertising with little information content are likely to be important.

- *Shopping goods:* **Shopping goods** are those that are typically more expensive, of more interest to the purchaser, and some risk is seen in the purchase. Examples would include cars, PCs and cameras. The customer will typically 'shop around' to make comparisons and gather information. These goods do not, therefore, have to be available in all possible outlets, and promotional material will usually have a high information content. In some categories of shopping goods, such as PCs, customers can demonstrate a high level of technical knowledge that assists them in their purchase and producers must usually satisfy customers on a technical level before a sale is made.

- *Specialty goods:* **Specialty goods** are seen as products that are so differentiated from others, often carrying considerable prestige, that customers may insist on only one brand. High prices, high levels of service and restricted distribution would be appropriate. An example would be that of Hasselblad cameras, which dominate certain parts of the professional photography market. There is no need or benefit for the products to be available in every camera shop, but they would tend to appear in shops where customers would expect a high level of service and expertise.

Specialty goods: Belgian chocolates

Limitations of Copeland's framework

The use of classification systems is widely accepted by managers and academic researchers. It is easy to show how they work in practice, and many examples can be produced to show how appropriate they are. A strong argument against their slavish adoption is that they can exhibit circular logic. In other words, we examine how a product is marketed, and on this basis assign it to a particular classification. We then use that to say how it *should* be marketed. This is a recipe for maintaining the status quo, and companies adopting this practice, even if implicitly, will never lead with new product strategies. Over time, many products will gradually change from shopping goods to convenience goods. Thus, some watches will be speciality goods, some will be shopping goods, and now the lowest priced watches on the market will effectively be convenience goods.

Changes in technology and customer taste or fashion may also create opportunities for things to be done differently, and there will always be part of a market that will respond to an approach that is different from the norm. Some organizations recognized that technology, in reducing transaction cost, could make telephone banking viable. Avon was built on the basis that some customers would be prepared to buy cosmetics from people selling them on their doorsteps as opposed to buying in conventional retail outlets.

Product type may be a useful starting point to guide management thinking, but it is not a substitute for creativity and analysis.

3.3 The product life cycle

The **product life cycle** is the complete 'life' of a product or service from its inception and growth, through shake-out and maturity, to its eventual decline and death.

The **product life cycle** concept is based on the analogy with living things, in that they all have a finite life. All products would be expected to have a finite life, whether it be long or short. The life cycle can operate at an individual product level, a product type or a product class level, where arguably a market life cycle would be a more appropriate title. At the individual product level, the product life cycle is a useful tool in product planning, so that a balance of products is kept in various stages of the life cycle.

At the product class level, we can use the product life cycle concept to analyse and predict competitive conditions and identify key issues for management. It is conventionally broken into a number of stages, as shown in Figure 3.1. We shall explore the key issues posed by the different stages.

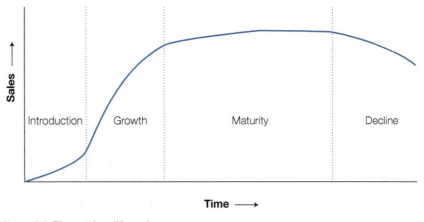

Figure 3.1 The product life cycle

The introduction stage

The introduction stage follows the product's development. It is new to the market and will be bought by 'innovators', a term used to describe a small proportion of the eventual market. The innovators may not be easy to identify in advance and there are likely to be high launch and marketing costs. Because production volumes are likely to be low (because it is still at a 'pilot' stage), the production cost per unit will be high.

The 'price elasticity of demand' will strongly influence whether the product is introduced at a high 'skimming' price, or a low 'penetration' price. Price skimming is appropriate when the product is known to have a price inelastic demand, such as new pharmaceuticals or defence equipment. Penetration is appropriate for products with price elastic demand and when gaining market share is more important than making a fast recovery of development costs.

Pioneer companies – those that are first to the market with a particular product – are usually forced to sell the product idea in addition to an existing brand, and the early promotion may help competitors who enter the market later with 'me too' versions of the product idea.

Entering the market at an early stage is usually risky. Not only will the company be incurring a negative cash flow for a period, but many products fail at this stage. Against this risk is the prospect of increasing market share in the new product area faster than the 'me toos', such that the first product may become the industry standard in future years.

Pioneer companies are those that are first to market with a particular product.

The growth stage

During the growth stage, sales for the market as a whole increase and new competitors typically enter to challenge the pioneer for some of the market share. The competitors may develop new market segments in an attempt to avoid direct competition with the established pioneering market leader.

The market becomes profitable and funds can be used to offset the development and launch costs. This is an important time to win market share, since it is easier to win a disproportionate share of new customers than to get customers to switch brands later on. As new market segments emerge, key decisions will need to be made as to whether to follow them or stay with the original. It has been shown that in the electronic calculator market, for example, demand was initially concentrated among scientists and engineers (Brown, 1991). Then businesses starting using them, then university students and finally the market reached its height when demand was found among schoolchildren. A pioneer wishing to stay in all these markets would have to make the brave decision to move out of organization-to-organization business into a mass consumer market.

The maturity stage

Maturity is reached when a high proportion of people who will eventually purchase a product have already purchased it once. It is likely to be the longest stage, but depending on the market, this could range from days or weeks to many decades. It is important at this stage either to have achieved a high market share, or to dominate a special niche in the market. It can be expensive and risky to achieve large market share changes at this time, so that some companies prefer to concentrate their competitive efforts on retaining existing customers, and competing hard for the small number of new customers appearing.

It has been pointed out that market share among leading competitors is often stable over extremely long periods of time (Mercer, 1993), and this may be used as a criticism of the product life cycle concept. However, over the time of maturity in the market, companies have to be vigilant in detecting change in the market, and be ready to modify or improve products and to undertake product repositioning if necessary.

The decline stage

It is part of product life cycle theory that all markets will eventually decline, and therefore companies have to be ready to move to new markets when decline seems to be inevitable, or to be ready with strategies to extend the life cycle if this is felt to be feasible. Appropriate extension strategies could include developing new uses for the product, finding new users, and repositioning the product to gain a presence in the parts of the market that will remain after the rest of the market has gone. Even where markets have reached an advanced stage of decline, particular segments may remain that can be profitable for organizations able to anticipate their existence and dominate them.

Companies that succeed in declining markets usually adopt a 'milking' strategy, wherein investment is kept to a minimum, and take up any market share that may be left by competitors that have left the market because of the decline. There is a certain recognition that death will come eventually and thus any revenues that can be made in the interim are something of a bonus.

2

Example   The human life cycle metaphor

The concept of life cycle does not just apply to products, it also applies to humans. Human beings undergo a life cycle that has a huge bearing, not just on our biological changes, but also on behaviour.

We undergo introduction when we are conceived and grow inside our mother. After birth, we begin to grow – a process that continues until, after puberty, we reach our full height and weight. Our maturity phase is the longest. For most people, it will last from our mid-teens until the time when our faculties begin to fail us – perhaps in our sixties or seventies. When we reach old age, we begin to decline. Our eyesight may begin to deteriorate, we slow down and we may lose some of our intellectual sharpness. Finally, when decline has run its course, life is no longer viable, and we die.

Criticisms of the product life cycle

The product life cycle appears to be widely understood and used as a tool for strategic analysis and decision-making (Greenley and Bayus, 1993). Despite this, some important criticisms have been made. While it is easy to go back into history and demonstrate all the features of the concept, it is hard to forecast the future and, in particular, it is hard to forecast turning points. Not to try to do so at all, however, would seem to avoid confronting hard strategic issues.

Another criticism is that life cycles may sometimes not be inevitable as dictated by the market, but created by the ineptitude of management. If management assume that decline will come, they will take the decision to reduce investment and advertising in anticipation of the decline. Not surprisingly, decline does come, but sooner that it otherwise would have done had the investment not been withdrawn.

In a large-scale survey of UK companies, Hooley (1995) confirmed the existence of the familiar bell-shaped pattern of sales in many markets. The study challenged the widely held view that profits would be low or negative in the early stages of the life cycle, and found that the market position of organizations could quickly move to profit in the growth stage of the life cycle. This trend has been observed many times in industries such as creative technology, games and fashion. In essence, life cycles are shorter and need to provide returns quicker.

3.4   Product portfolio theory

Given that products represent the main output of an organization, it is essential to ensure that what is offered to the market allows for a sufficient range of products as well as products at different stages of development or maturity. The range of products offered is termed the **product portfolio**. The challenge for organizations is to balance the portfolio to provide a degree of sustainability and return for **stakeholders**.

The **product portfolio** is the range of products offered.

Stakeholders are the people who can influence or are influenced by the organization. They can be primary (active) stakeholders, such as customers, suppliers, labour, financial institutions, or secondary (passive) such as government, local community, lobby groups.

The notion of portfolio exists in many areas of life, not just for products. Underpinning the concept is the need for a business to spread its opportunity and risk. A broad portfolio signifies that a business has a presence in a wide range of product and market sectors. Conversely, a narrow portfolio implies that the organization only operates in a few (or even one) product or market sectors.

A broad portfolio offers the advantage of robustness in that a downturn in one market will not threaten the whole company. Against this advantage is the problem of managing business interests that may be very different in nature – the company may be said to lack strategic focus. An organization operating with a narrow portfolio (perhaps just one sector) can often concentrate solely on its sector but it can become vulnerable if there is a downturn in demand in the one sector it serves.

The BCG matrix

The Boston Consulting Group matrix offers a way of examining and making sense of a company's portfolio of product and market interests. It is a way of viewing the entire product range to see a company's products as a collection of items in a similar way that a holder of shares in several companies might consider the decisions on what to do with the shares.

GURU GUIDE

The **Boston Consulting Group** (BCG) was founded in 1963 by Bruce D. Henderson as the management and consulting division of the Boston Safe Deposit and Trust Company, itself a subsidiary of the Boston Company.

Henderson, a former Bible salesman, had gained an engineering degree from Vanderbilt University before attending Harvard Business School (HBS). He left HBS 90 days before graduation to work for Westinghouse Corporation, where he became one of the youngest vice presidents in the company's history. He left Westinghouse to head Arthur D. Little's management services unit before accepting an improbable challenge from the CEO of the Boston Safe Deposit and Trust Company to start a consulting arm for the bank.

Source: Adapted from the BCG website. See http://www.bcg.com for full details.

One way of looking at the products in a portfolio is to consider each product in its position in the product life cycle and aim to have a balance of products in each stage. A more sophisticated approach is based on the idea that market share in mature markets is highly correlated with profitability, and that it is relatively less expensive and less risky to attempt to win share in the growth stage of the market, when there will be many new customers making a first purchase. This is the approach taken by the BCG matrix. It is used to analyse the product range with a view to aiding decisions on how the products should be treated in an internal strategic analysis. Figure 3.2 shows the essential features of the Boston matrix.

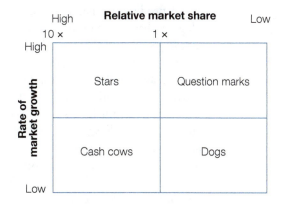

Figure 3.2 **The Boston Consulting Group matrix**
Source: Product Portfolio Matrix, © 1970, The Boston Consulting Group

The two axes of the matrix are:

- *The market share measure:* The horizontal axis is based on a particular measure of market share – share relative to the largest competitor. A product with a share of 20% of the market, where the next biggest competitor had a share of 10%, would have a relative share of 2, whereas a product with a market share of 20%, and the biggest competitor also had 20%, would have a relative share of 1. The cutoff point between high and low share is 1, so high market share products in this analysis are market leaders. This arrangement of scale is sometimes described as being 'logarithmic' in nature.
- *The market growth measure:* The vertical axis is the rate of market growth, with the most relevant definition of the market being served. A popular point used to divide high and low growth in the market is 10% year-on-year growth, but the authors have found it useful in practical situations to use growth that is faster than the rate of growth in the economy as a whole, which, after inflation, is usually between 1% and 2.5% a year.

The following is a description of the matrix:

- *Cash cows:* A product with a high market share in a low growth market is normally both profitable and a generator of cash. Profits from this product can be used to support other products that are in their development phase. Standard strategy would be to manage conservatively, but to defend strongly against competitors. This product is called a 'cash cow' because profits from the product can be 'milked' on an ongoing basis. This should not be used as a justification for neglect.

- *Dogs:* A product that has a low market share in a low growth market is termed a 'dog', in that it is typically not very profitable. To cultivate the product to increase its market share would incur cost and risk, not least because the market it is in has a low rate of growth. Accordingly, once a dog has been identified as part of a portfolio, it is often discontinued or disposed of. More creatively, opportunities might be found to differentiate the dog and obtain a strong position for it in a niche market. A small share product can be used to price aggressively against a large competitor as it is expensive for the large competitor to follow suit.

- *Stars:* Stars have a high share of a rapidly growing market, and therefore rapidly growing sales. They may be the sales manager's dream, but they could be the accountant's nightmare, since they are likely to absorb large amounts of cash, even if they are highly profitable. It is often necessary to spend heavily on advertising and product improvements, so that when the market slows, these products become cash cows. If market share is lost, the product will eventually become a dog when the market stops growing.

- *Question marks:* Question marks (sometimes termed 'problem children') are aptly named as they create a dilemma. They already have a foothold in a growing market, but if market share cannot be improved, they will become dogs. Resources need to be devoted to winning market share, which requires bravery for a product that may not yet have large sales, or the product may be sold to an organization in a better position to exploit the market.

The matrix does not have an intermediate market share category, but there are large numbers of products that have large market share, but are not market leaders. They may be the biggest profit earners for the companies that own them. They usually compete against the market leader at a disadvantage that is slight, but real. Management need to make efficient use of marketing expenditure for such products and try to differentiate them from the leader. They should not normally compete head on, especially on price, but attempt to make gains if the market changes in a way that the leader is slow to exploit.

Accurate measurement and careful definition of the market are essential to avoid misdiagnosis when using the matrix. Critics, perhaps unfairly, point out that there are many relevant aspects relating to products that are not taken into account, but it was never claimed by The Boston Consulting Group that the process was a panacea and covered all aspects of strategy. Above all, the matrix helps to identify which products to push or drop, and when. It helps in the recognition of windows of opportunity, and is strong evidence against simple rules of thumb for allocating resources to products.

A composite portfolio model: the GE matrix

The limitations of the BCG matrix have given rise to a number of other models that are intended to take a greater number of factors into account, and to be more flexible in use. A leading example is the General Electric (GE) matrix, developed by McKinsey & Company in conjunction with the General Electric company in the USA. It is mainly applied to strategic business units (SBUs) such as the subsidiaries of a holding company. The model rates market attractiveness as high, medium or low, and competitive strength as strong, medium or weak. SBUs are placed in the appropriate category, and although there is no automatic strategic prescription, the position is used to help devise an appropriate strategy.

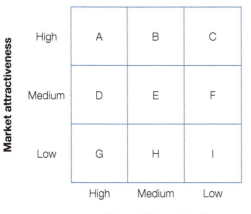

Figure 3.3 The GE matrix

Source: C.W. Hofer and D. Schendal, *Strategy Formulation: Analytical Concepts*, copyright 1978 West Publishing

Market attractiveness criteria will be set by the user, and could include factors such as market growth, profitability, strength of competition, entry/exit barriers, legal regulation and so on. Competitive strength could include technological capability, brand image, distribution channel links, production capability and financial strength. The flexibility to include as many variables as required is useful, but could lead to oversubjectivity. Most users of the model recommend that the variables be given a weighting to establish their relative importance, which will, in turn, reduce the potential for bias. In practice, managers tend to be aware that the tool is likely to be used as a basis for resource allocation and, consequently, they may attempt to influence the analysis in the favour of their own product or SBU. The analysis gives rise to a three-by-three matrix (Figure 3.3).

The GE matrix can be described as follows:

- For products in cell A, the company would invest strongly, as this is potentially an attractive strategic position, where distinctive competences can be harnessed to good opportunities.
- In B, the company could be aggressive and attempt to build strength in order to challenge, or it could build selectively.
- In C, there are real dilemmas, in that there is the difficulty of competing well against stronger competitors – most plausible options would be to divest, as the opportunity might be attractive to others, or to specialize around niches where some strength could be built.
- D would indicate investment and maintenance of competitive ability.
- E and F would indicate risk minimization and prudent choices for expansion.
- G and H would indicate management for earnings.
- I would require divestment or minimizing investment.

Extreme care is required in the judgements that would place products or SBUs into any one category, and the model does not directly take into account synergies between different products or business. The astute reader will recognize that the model represents a means of relating competences to the external environment, and that it is also a means of taking SWOT a stage further.

Multinational market portfolio analysis

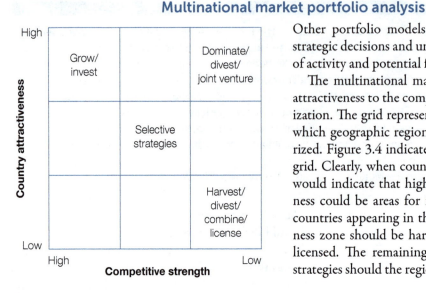

Other portfolio models can be used to help inform strategic decisions and understand both current balance of activity and potential futures.

The multinational market portfolio relates country attractiveness to the competitive strengths of the organization. The grid represents nine potential positions by which geographic regions can be analysed and categorized. Figure 3.4 indicates the options arising from the grid. Clearly, when countries or regions are mapped, it would indicate that high strength and high attractiveness could be areas for investment and growth, while countries appearing in the low strength/low attractiveness zone should be harvested, divested, combined or licensed. The remaining boxes indicate the potential strategies should the region be plotted in them.

Figure 3.4 **Multinational market portfolio**
Source: Adapted from Harrell and Kiefer, 1993

STRATEGIC
PLANNING SOFTWARE

www.macmillanihe.com
Companion Website

This is a helpful chapter to read before starting your report using the **Strategic Planning Software** (www.planning-strategy.com).

For test questions, extra case studies, audio case studies, weblinks, videolinks and more to help you understand the topics covered in this chapter, visit our companion website at www.macmillanihe.com/companion/business/campbell.

VOCAB CHECKLIST FOR ESL STUDENTS

Affiliate	Illicit	Repositioning
Analogy	Incursion	'Rule of thumb'
Astute	Ineptitude	Seminal
Auction	Innovators	'Sit-in'
Augment	Logarithmic (see 'logarithm')	Slavish
Brokerage	Lucrative	Smuggling
Classifieds	Merchant	State of the art
Confectionary	Misdiagnosis	Stewardship
Contraband	Mission statement	Subsidiary
Distribution channel	Panacea	Temperate climate (see
Divestment	Perimeter	'temperate')
Egress	Pharmaceuticals	Typology

Definitions for these terms can be found in the 'Vocab Zone' of the companion website, which provides free access to the Macmillan English Dictionary online at www.macmillanihe.com/companion/business/campbell.

REVIEW QUESTIONS

1 Explain how the purpose of the organization can impact on its strategic priorities.
2 Define what is meant by a business model and give examples of different types of business models in the retail sector.
3 Explain what is meant by the term 'product' and how products provide benefit to users.
4 Using theory related to the concept of 'portfolio', explain why it is important for an organization to have a balanced portfolio.

DISCUSSION TOPIC

All organizations, private, public or voluntary, need an effective business model. Discuss.

2

HOT TOPICS – Research project areas to investigate

If you have a project to do, why not investigate …

- … the critical success factors of business models for delivering online trading of sports goods.
- … the effectiveness of the BCG matrix as a framework for portfolio management in creative industries such as computer gaming.
- … how perceptions of managers change towards customer values, as organizations move through the product life cycle.

Recommended reading

Aaker, D.A. (1995) *Strategic Market Management* (4th edn), New York: John Wiley & Sons.

Coates, N. and Robinson, H. (1995) 'Making industrial new product development market led', *Marketing Intelligence and Planning*, **13**(6): 12–15.

Doyle, P. (1994) *Marketing Management and Strategy*, Englewoods Cliffs, NJ: Prentice Hall.

Jobber, D. (1995) *Principles and Practice of Marketing*, New York: McGraw-Hill.

Lancaster, G. and Massingham, L. (1993) *Marketing Management*, London: McGraw-Hill.

Sowrey, T. (1990) 'Idea generation: identifying the most useful techniques', *European Journal of Marketing*, **42**(5): 20–9.

Von Hippel, E. (1978) 'Successful industrial products from customer ideas', *Journal of Marketing*, **42**(1): 39–49.

Chapter references

Brown, R. (1991) 'The S-curves of innovation', *Journal of Marketing Management*, **7**(2): 189–202.

Copeland, M.T. (1923) 'Relation of consumers' buying habits to marketing methods', *Harvard Business Review*, 1: 282–9.

Greenley, G.E. and Bayus, B.L. (1993) 'Marketing planning decision making in UK and US companies: an empirical comparative study', *Journal of Marketing Management*, 9: 155–72.

Harrell, G.D. and Kiefer, R.O. (1993) 'Multinational market portfolios in global strategy development', *International Marketing Review*, **10**(1): 60–72.

Hooley, G.J. (1995) 'The lifecycle concept revisited: aid or albatross?', *Journal of Strategic Marketing*, 3: 23–39.

Kotler, P. (1997) *Marketing Management Analysis, Planning, Implementation, and Control* (9th edn), Englewood Cliffs, NJ: Prentice Hall International.

Mercer, D. (1993) 'Death of the product life cycle', *Adman*, September: 15–19.

Slywotzky, A. (1996) *Value Migration: How to Think Several Moves Ahead of the Competition*, Boston, MA: Harvard Business School Press.

Chapter 4

Business competences, processes and activities

Introduction and chapter overview

In Chapter 1 we considered the different schools of strategic thought and established that there has been, and continues to be, considerable debate in the academic literature as to the sources of competitive advantage. We recognized that the debate centres around the question 'how do organizations achieve superior performance?' and that two positions have emerged as the most prominent potential answer to this question.

The competitive positioning school of thought, based primarily on the work of Michael Porter (1980, 1985), stresses the importance of how the organization is positioned in respect to its competitive environment or industry, and the resource-based or competence school (Prahalad and Hamel, 1990; Heene and Sanchez, 1997) argues that it is the competences (abilities) of the business and the distinctive way that it organizes its activities which determine the ability to outperform competitors. As with most controversies, we suggest that both schools of thought have their merits – both are partial explanations of the source of competitive advantage.

This chapter concentrates on a key element of the internal analysis, the organization's competences or strategic capabilities. To do this, we develop an understanding of the dynamics of the organization and in particular the concepts of competences, processes and 'value-adding' activities.

Learning objectives

After studying this chapter, you should be able to:

- explain the concepts of core competences, competences, resources and the relationships between them
- determine the relationship between core competences and core activities
- explain how the configuration of value-adding activities can improve business performance
- explain the concept of the value chain and the value chain framework
- explain how the value chain framework 'works'

4.1   Identifying business processes

A key part of the internal analysis of an organization is an understanding of how the business does things, in other words, how the organization manages, deploys and aligns its resources and capabilities in order to deliver its products and supporting activities.

The concept of business processes is not new, indeed Adam Smith (1776) referred to them in an attempt to explain the stages of production for making a pin. What is significant is that business processes lie at the heart of what a business does and how it does it. The result is that processes can be directly related to the production process or may be used to support it, they may be what is termed 'upstream', that is, at the early stages of the construction of the product, or 'downstream', that is, at the end stages of the product, and they may be supported in a physical way or an intangible way. The nature of business processes has made them the subject of many studies, mainly in attempts to improve efficiency (lean production, business process redesign) or effectiveness (customer-centric approaches, value-based processes).

2

KEY CONCEPT

Lean production (or lean manufacturing) is often known simply as lean. The approach works from the perspective of value creation and the consumer, or user of the system. Value is any process or activity that the consumer will pay for and, as such, all other elements are deemed wasteful, and thus targeted for elimination.

What is clear is that the form, sustainability and effectiveness of an organization's business processes rely on the organization's available resources, competences and configuration of activities. We shall explore each of these in turn.

4.2   Resources, competences and core competences

The terms 'competence' and 'capability', 'core competence' and 'distinctive capability' are often used interchangeably in textbooks on business strategy. Although some writers (Stalk et al., 1992) argue that there are significant differences between the terms 'competence' and 'capability', we will use the terms to mean broadly the same things based on the following definitions:

A **competence** is an attribute or collection of attributes possessed by all or most of the companies in an industry.

- A competence is an attribute or collection of attributes possessed by all or most of the companies in an industry. Such attributes are commonly termed 'threshold competences'. Without such attributes, a business cannot enter or survive in the industry. Competences develop from resources and embody skills, technology or know-how. For example, in order to operate in the pharmaceuticals industry, it is necessary to possess the ability to manufacture medicines (by using specially designed factory equipment) and, importantly, a detailed understanding of how medicines work on the human body. Every successful survivor in the industry possesses both areas of competence.

A **core competence** is an attribute, or collection of attributes, specific to a particular organization that enables it to produce above-average performance.

- A core competence or *distinctive capability* is an attribute, or collection of attributes, specific to a particular organization that enables it to produce above-average performance. It arises from the way in which the organization has employed its competences and resources more effectively than its competitors. The result of a distinctive capability is an output that customers value higher than that of competitors. It is based on one or more factors – superior organizational knowledge, information, skills, technology, structure, relationships, networks and reputation.

■ A *resource* is an input employed in the activities of the business. Success rests in large part on the efficiency by which the business converts its resources into outputs. Resources fall into four broad categories – human, financial, physical (buildings, equipment or stock) and intangible (know-how, patents, legal rights, brand names or registered designs).

KEY CONCEPT

Competitive advantage is often seen as the overall purpose of business strategy. Some texts use the phrase 'superior performance' to mean the same thing. Essentially, a business can be said to possess competitive advantage if it is able to return higher profits than its competitors. The higher profits mean that it will be able to commit more retained profit to reinvest in its strategy, thus maintaining its lead over its competitors in an industry. When this superiority is maintained successfully over time, we refer to it as a 'sustainable' competitive advantage. Competitive advantage can be lost when management fail to reinvest the superior profits in such a way that the advantage is not maintained.

Core competences tend to be both complex and intangible, so it is necessary to explore the nature of the resources and competences that underpin them before exploring the concept further. The purpose of such analysis is to allow managers to identify which resources and competences act as the foundation of existing or potential core competences (Figure 4.1). It is extremely important to note that not all the competitors in an industry will possess core competences or distinctive capabilities (Kay, 1995). It is only those players who are producing above-average performance who can be considered as possessing core competences. Those with only average or below-average performance possess competences and resources, without which they could not compete in the industry at all, but not core competences. This can be expressed as follows:

Core competence (distinctive capability) = superior acquisition and employment of resources + superior development of 'general' competences.

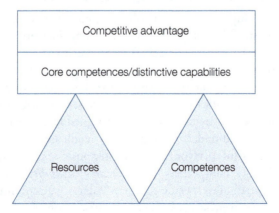

Figure 4.1 **The twin sources of core competences**

2

GURU GUIDE

John Kay was born in 1948 in Edinburgh. He was educated at Edinburgh University and Nuffield College, Oxford University. In 1971, he became one of the youngest lecturers to teach economics at Oxford University. In 1979, he become the first research director of the Institute of Fiscal Studies, and was soon its director. In 1986, he accepted a chair at the London Business School, and founded the renowned consultancy firm London Economics. In 1991 he became a visiting professor at London Business School, and in 1996, he took a directorship at the newly created Said Business School in Oxford.

Professor Kay has been a director with Halifax plc. He was also a member of the task force set up to revive Lloyds insurance market and a member of the steering group for the government's review of company law. He is an elected fellow of the Academy of Management. Since 2007 he has been a member of the Scottish government's Council of Economic Advisers.

He is renowned economist, and has written several influential texts on economics, and has written a column in the *Financial Times* since 1995. Kay's work embraces the concept of adding value and allows us to better understand how business strategy can add value. Much of his work opened up issues that are currently being grappled with. These include sustainability, innovation and distinctive competence.

4.3   Resource analysis

Tangible assets include stocks, materials, machinery, buildings, human resources, finance and so on.

Intangible assets include skills, knowledge, brand names, goodwill and patent rights.

Resources can be both 'tangible' and 'intangible'. They are the inputs that enable an organization to carry out its activities. Tangible assets include stocks, materials, machinery, buildings, human resources, finance and so on. Intangible assets include skills, knowledge, brand names, goodwill and patent rights (see Coyne, 1986; Hall, 1992). Intangible resources are often produced within the organization but tangibles are obtained from outside organizations. Such resources are obtained in resource markets in competition with businesses from within and outside the industry. Relationships with the suppliers of resources can form an important part of the organization's core competence, for example its ability to attract the most appropriately skilled human resources in the job market.

When we analyse a company's resources as part of an internal analysis, three frameworks can be employed to provide a comprehensive review:

1   We might consider them by *category* – human, financial, production technology, information and communications technology, and materials. These resources are then evaluated quantitatively (how much or how many) and qualitatively (how effectively they are being employed). Physical resources like buildings and machinery will typically be audited for capacity, utilization, age, condition, contribution to output and so on. Materials and stocks can be assessed on the basis of quality, reliability, availability, number of suppliers, delivery times and unit costs. Human resources are considered in terms of numbers, education, skills, training, experience, age, motivation, wage costs and productivity in relation to the needs of the organization.

2   We can analyse resources according to their *specificity*. Resources can be specific or non-specific. For example, skilled workers tend to have specialized and industry-specific knowledge and skills. Some technology, for example computer software, is for general (non-industry-specific) business use, like word-processing, database and spreadsheet software. Other computer

software applications, like airline computer reservation systems, are written for highly specialized uses. Whereas non-specific resources tend to be more flexible and form the basis of competences, industry-specific resources are more likely to act as the foundations of core competences, for example the specialized knowledge of scientists in the chemical industry.

3   Resources can be evaluated on the basis of how they contribute to internal and external *measures of performance*. Internal measures include their contribution to:

- business objectives and targets – financial, performance and output measures
- historical comparisons – measures of performance over time (such as against previous years)
- business unit or divisional comparisons.

External measures can include:

- comparisons with competitors, particularly those who are industry leaders and those who are the closest competitors and are in its strategic grouping
- comparisons with companies in other industries.

By employing these techniques of analysis, an organization is able to internally and externally benchmark its performance as a stimulus to improving performance in the future. Performance, however, is based on more than resources and competences.

4.4   Core competences

Core competences are distinguished from competences in several ways:

- they are only possessed by those companies whose performance is superior to the industry average
- they are unique to the company
- they are more complex
- they are difficult to emulate (copy)
- they relate to fulfilling customer needs
- they add greater value than 'general' competences
- they are often based on distinctive relationships with customers, distributors and suppliers
- they are based on superior organizational skills and knowledge.

In the motor industry, for example, all manufacturers have the competences and resources required to build motor vehicles, but a company like BMW has core competences in design, engine technology and marketing that are the basis of its reputation for high-quality, high performance cars. These core competences make it possible for BMW to charge premium prices for its products. In this way, core competences are the basis of an organization's competitive advantage.

Kay (1993) presents a slightly different explanation, arguing that competitive advantage is based on what he terms 'distinctive capability'. **Distinctive capability** can develop from reputation, architecture (internal and external relationships), innovation and strategic assets. Marks & Spencer's competitive advantage can be explained in terms of its reputation for quality, its special relationships with its suppliers and its customers. Marks & Spencer has exacting but mutually

Distinctive capability can develop from reputation, architecture (internal and external relationships), innovation and strategic assets.

profitable relationships with the businesses that supply its products. It demands high quality at reasonable cost, and flexibility in return for large volumes of business. Its relationship with customers is based on its reputation for good service, refunds and exchanges of goods, and high-quality products. The end result is that it has a performance that is superior to most of its high-street competitors.

Core competence arises from the unique and distinctive way that the organization builds, develops, integrates and deploys its resources and competences. An existing core competence can be evaluated for:

- *customer focus:* does it adequately focus on customer needs?
- *uniqueness:* can it be imitated by competitors, and if so, how easily?
- *flexibility:* can it be easily adapted if market or industry conditions change?
- *contribution to value:* to what extent does it add value to the product or service?
- *sustainability:* how long can its superiority be sustained over time?

Competences can also be judged against these criteria in order to evaluate their potential to form the basis on which new core competences can be built.

Core competences can never be regarded as being permanent. The pace of change of technology and society are such that core competences must be constantly adapted and new ones cultivated. A good example of the need to adapt comes from an examination of IBM. In the 1980s, IBM had core competences in the design, production, marketing and sales of PCs. The value that customers attached to these competences was lost in the late 1980s and early 1990s because competitors were able to match IBM's competences in design and production of PCs and at a lower price. IBM had failed to adapt its core competences so that they became merely industry-wide competences. Its superiority was eroded because it failed to sustain its advantage.

The aim of an analysis of resources, competences and core competences is, therefore, to:

- understand the nature and sources of particular core competences
- identify the need for and methods of adaptation of existing core competences
- identify the need for new core competence building
- identify potential sources of core competence based on resources and competences
- ensure that core competences remain focused on customer needs.

Resources, competences and core competences are obviously closely related to the ways that a business organizes and performs its value-adding activities. In the resource-based view of strategy, the concept of 'dynamic capabilities' has emerged as a term to encapsulate these areas.

Dynamic capabilities
represent the ability of
organizations to innovate,
adapt and adopt in terms of
their tangible and intangible
resources.

Dynamic capabilities represent the ability of organizations to innovate, adapt and adopt in terms of their tangible and intangible resources, and are the foundation of many forms of competition in today's business environment. It is therefore necessary to analyse the way in which value-adding activities are configured and coordinated (Teece, 2007).

David J. Teece has a PhD in economics from the University of Pennsylvania, and has held teaching and research positions at Stanford University and Oxford University. He has previously held the position as Mitsubishi Bank chair, and has been director of the Institute for Management, Innovation, and Organization at the University of California at Berkeley. He has received four honorary doctorates. He is Thomas W. Tusher Professor in Global Business and director of the Institute of Management, Innovation, and Organization at the Haas School of Business, University of California, Berkeley. Dr Teece was a co-founder and chairman of the Law and Economics Consulting Group, and co-founded the Berkeley Research Group in 2010.

Dr Teece has over 30 years' experience as an active consultant, engaged in economic, business, and financial consulting services to businesses and governments around the world. He has worked on matters in industries ranging from music recording to DRAMS, software, lumber and petroleum, and has testified in both federal and state courts, before Congress, and before the Federal Trade Commission, as well as in several international jurisdictions.

He is the author of more than 200 books and articles. According to *Science Watch* (November/December 2005), he is the lead author of the most cited article in economics and business worldwide, 1995–2005. He is also one of the top 10 cited scholars for the decade, and has been recognized by Accenture as one of the world's top 50 business intellectuals.

KEY CONCEPTS

Competence leveraging refers to the ability of a business to exploit its core competences in new markets, thus meeting new customer needs. It can also refer to the ability of the business to modify and improve existing core competences.

Competence building takes place when the business builds new core competences, based on its resources and competences. It is often necessary to build new competences alongside existing ones when entering new markets, as it is unlikely that existing competences will fully meet new customer needs.

4.5   Analysis of value-adding activities

Value chain analysis seeks to provide an understanding of how much value an organization's activities add to its products (goods and services) for its consumers compared to the costs of the resources used in their production (the value margin).

Value chain analysis (Porter, 1985) seeks to provide an understanding of how much value an organization's activities add to its products (goods and services) for its consumers compared to the costs of the resources used in their production (the value margin). A given product can be produced by organizing activities in a number of different ways. Value chain analysis helps managers to understand how effectively and efficiently the activities of their organization are configured and coordinated. The acid test is how much value is added in the process of turning inputs into final products. Value is measured in terms of the price (or emotional commitment) that customers are willing to pay for the product (Figure 4.2).

From Figure 4.2, it can be seen that when the market price (MP) has been set, it still results in a section of consumers who have a reserved price (RP) in excess of the MP. In other words, they are prepared and able to pay more than the MP for the product. The implication of this (beyond market segmentation and fencing) is that they may be made to part with higher than MP if additional value or urgency can be portrayed (real or perceived).

CASE STUDY Northern Rock

On the morning of 6 September 2007, people in the UK switching on their televisions to see the early news bulletins were astounded to see pictures of hundreds of Northern Rock bank customers queuing hours before the bank opened to get their money out.

This was because Northern Rock had had to declare a cash flow crisis, and a loss of institutional, customer and consumer confidence. A chapter of accidents, a lack of key resources, and an attitude of collective and individual vanity that caused a small provincial UK bank to consider itself a truly global player in its industry had brought this about.

Northern Rock was (and remains) a small regional UK bank, specializing in lending mortgage money to people in mid to low income brackets who wished to buy their own homes. The company had found itself under great pressure to increase its lending volumes and enhance its customer base, using finance available on the global financial markets to underwrite these activities. Now it was faced with ruin.

The problems of Northern Rock (and indeed many of the UK retail banks and mortgage lenders) had roots set deeply in the past. All the UK retail banks had found themselves under great pressure to expand the volumes of credit available, the bases on which this credit would be made available, and the range of people to whom credit would be made available. Taking people's homes as the security against which loans and mortgages were made available, the availability of, and volumes of, credit were greatly increased. The results were a property boom, in which houses were bought and sold for ever increasing prices, and a consumer credit boom, in which the money released from the housing market was used to purchase home improvements, holidays, cars and other retail items.

Over the past 15 years, the UK property market had therefore grown greatly in all parts. House sales and values were at record highs. All parts of the retail sector had also grown over the same period, especially the home furnishings, home improvements and garden sectors. However, it became apparent that this could not be sustained over the long term, and in 2003, the British Retail Consortium first drew attention to some of the problems and issues that might come up, declaring that the UK 'do it yourself' (DIY) sector was overprovided by 25%, that is, that one of the four main providers in this sector would either be taken over by one of the others, or else one of them would go bankrupt.

Nevertheless, property values continued to rise. There then was a boom in off-balance, self-certificated and subprime lending in the UK, in which homeowners on otherwise modest incomes, that is, the core customer base of Northern Rock, could remortgage their properties to a stated, notional or alleged value, and draw out the residue as cash. This cash would then be used on consumer goods and other purchases, as above. Some of the finance houses started to lend not just to the full value of the property, but to a maximum of 125% of the stated value.

Over the 15-year period, the banking sector had been able to source short- and medium-term funds from anywhere in the world. The banking sector had also, in common with many others, been able to buy and sell credit and debts as assets. These assets became a commodity themselves, to be traded between banks, finance houses and other cash and credit providers located anywhere in the world. Northern Rock had become an enthusiastic player in this practice, and for a short time had been able to raise as much money as it wanted through the purchasing and sale of what came to be known as 'bundles of assets'.

The bundles were being traded on the basis of less than full information, and in many cases banks were buying and selling to each other on the basis of valuations that were dreamed up on the spot, purely in order to meet the present obligations.

The Frankfurt brokers drew the attention of the financial institutions to this, and the national banks and financial regulatory bodies in the UK, the USA, Japan and the EU conducted their own investigations. They too became worried, and now faced the problem of having to do something about this without completely destabilizing the property and financial markets. The extent of the problem initially emerged very slowly. However, it became clear that this was indeed a major problem for the international banking sector, which resulted in a widespread loss of confidence and certainty across the world.

The results were cataclysmic for the whole sector, and many banks in the USA, the UK and elsewhere were forced to close or else merge with others. For Northern Rock, the outcome was ruin by any other name, although it was saved from bankruptcy by being taken into government ownership.

Case study questions

1 What resources did Northern Rock need in order to develop its strategy to be a global organization in its sector? What resources did the company lack?
2 How should the problems of 'bundling of assets' have been addressed?
3 What further lessons are there for managers who seek a resource-based strategy for their organizations?

2

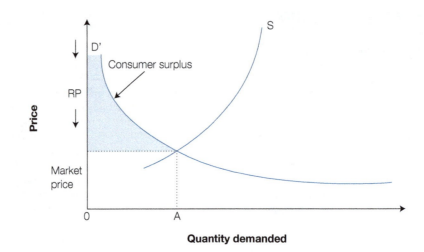

Figure 4.2 **Price and value added**

There are six common types of value (real or perceived) that can be created for the consumer and used as tools for differentiating a 'product'. These are:

- *Economic value:* best expressed in terms of wealth, resources or the economic conversion process
- *Physical value:* associated with a person's wellbeing, health, comfort or rest
- *Emotional value:* linked to a person's emotions and includes fear, joy, contentment or excitement
- *Social value:* reflecting the interpersonal and relationship dimension of society
- *Cognitive value:* in relation to the quest for knowledge and, ultimately, wisdom
- *Political value:* relates to influence, control and power.

Physical value: first class

Value can be increased by:

1 Changing customer perceptions of the product so that they are willing to pay a higher price for a product than for similar products produced by other businesses

2 Reducing production costs below those of competitors.

These two ways of increasing value relate to the concepts of efficiency and effectiveness:

Efficiency is the ability to accomplish a task with minimum, time, effort or use of resources.

Effectiveness is the ability to deliver the expected result or value for the user or consumer.

Efficiency is the ability to accomplish a task with minimum, time, effort or use of resources.

Effectiveness is the ability to deliver the expected result or value for the user or consumer.

KEY CONCEPT

The **value added** to a good or service is the difference in the financial value of the finished product compared to the financial value of the inputs. As a sheet of metal passes through the various stages in car production, value is added so that a tonne of metal worth a few hundred pounds becomes a car worth several thousand pounds. The rate at which value is added depends on how well the operations process is managed. If the car manufacturer suffers a cost disadvantage by, say, holding a high level of stock or working with out of date machinery, then the value added over the process will be lower.

2

There are clear linkages between value-adding activities, core competences, competences and resources. Resources form the inputs to the organization's value-adding activities, while competences and core competences provide the skills and knowledge required to carry them out. The more that core competences can be integrated into value-adding activities, the greater will be the value added.

These forms of value adding tend to represent the basis of competitive advantage, that is, lower cost or differentiation.

The value-adding process

Businesses can be regarded as systems that transform inputs (resources, materials and so on) into outputs (goods and services). This is illustrated in Figure 4.3.

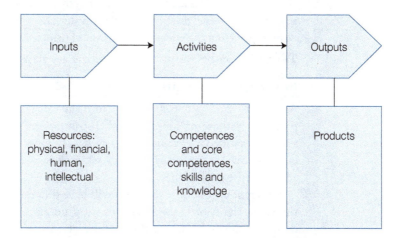

Figure 4.3 A simplified schematic of the value-adding process

The activities inside the organization add value to the inputs. The value of the finished goods is equivalent to the price that a customer is willing to pay for the goods. The difference between the end value and the total costs is the 'margin' – the quantity that accountants would refer to as the 'profit margin', before interest, taxation and extraordinary items.

The value chain can be used to analyse the value created by the economic conversion of the raw materials into products (primary activities) or by additional value created by factors that can impact on such a process (secondary activities).

The value chain

The activities of the organization can be broken down into a sequence of activities known as the 'value chain', as described by Porter in 1985 (see Figure 4.4).

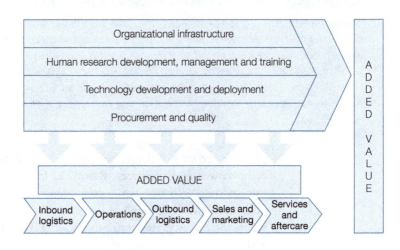

Figure 4.4 The value chain
Source: Adapted from Porter, 1985

The activities within the chain may be classified as primary activities and support activities:

- *Primary activities* are those which directly add value to the final product.
- *Support activities* do not directly add value themselves but indirectly add value by supporting the effective execution of primary activities.

Table 4.1 describes the primary and secondary activities.

Analysis of the value chain

An organization's value chain links into the value chains of other organizations, particularly those of suppliers and distributors. This 'chain' of value chains is sometimes called the 'value system' or 'total supply chain'. Linkages with suppliers are known as 'upstream' linkages, while those with distributors and customers are 'downstream' linkages.

Different types of organization will have different value chains. For example, the value chain of Dixons, the electrical goods retailer, does not include the design and manufacture of the products it sells. Marks & Spencer's value chain does include some design but does not include manufacturing.

Table 4.1 A summary of the activities in the value chain

Primary activities	Inbound logistics	Receipt and storage of materials (inputs) Stock control and distribution of inputs
	Operations	Transformation of inputs into final product
	Outbound logistics	Storage and distribution of finished goods
	Sales and marketing	Making the product available to the market and persuading people to buy
	Service	Installation and after-sales support
Support activities	Procurement	Purchasing of resources
	Technology development	Product, process and resource development
	Infrastructure	Planning, finance, information systems, management
	Human resource management	Recruitment, selection, training, reward and motivation

Similarly, not all of an organization's activities are of equal importance in adding value to its products. Those which are of greatest importance can be considered as 'core activities' and are often closely associated to core competences. Thus in a fashion house like Calvin Klein, design activities are of the greatest importance in adding value and the organization's core competences are concentrated in this area.

Analysis of value-adding activities helps to identify where the most value is added and where there is potential to add greater value by changing the way in which activities are configured and by improving the way in which they are coordinated. It is important to note that an organization's value chain is not analysed in isolation but that it is considered in conjunction with its external linkages to suppliers, distributors and customers.

A value chain analysis would be expected to include:

- a breakdown of all the activities of the organization
- identification of core activities and their relationships to core competences and current organizational strategies
- identification of the effectiveness and efficiency of the individual activities
- examination of linkages between activities for additional added value
- identification of blockages that reduce the organization's competitive advantage.

A useful technique in value chain analysis involves comparison with the value chains of competitors to identify the benefits and drawbacks of alternative configurations.

The aim of value chain analysis is to identify ways in which the performance of the individual activities and the linkages between them can be improved. This may involve identification of improved configurations for activities or improved coordination of them. It is particularly important to consider the extent to which value chain activities support the current strategy of the organization. For example, if the current strategy is based on high quality, then the activities must be configured so as to ensure high-quality products. On the other hand, if the organization competes largely on the basis of price, then activities must be organized so as to minimize costs.

The onset of the internet and the emergence of a range of e-businesses have resulted in a new version of the value chain, basically depicting the different form of business processes and the virtual nature of many businesses. In this respect, the traditional primary activities of inbound logistics, operations, outbound logistics, sales and marketing, and after-sales support are replaced with attracting customers, selecting services, organizing information, distributing and supporting. While new technology has impacted and will continue to impact on the business landscape, the value chain is still a useful model to use to understand what a business does and how it does it. However, this does not imply that a business must itself undertake all the activities they require, as they can outsourced to other organizations for whom the activity is core.

STRATEGIC PLANNING SOFTWARE

This is a helpful chapter to refer to when completing 1.2.2 Value Chain within the Internal Analysis section in Phase 1 of the **Strategic Planning Software** (www.planning-strategy.com). For more information on the value chain, also see Chapter 13.

Companion Website

For test questions, extra case studies, audio case studies, weblinks, videolinks and more to help you understand the topics covered in this chapter, visit our companion website at www.macmillanihe.com/companion/business/campbell.

VOCAB CHECKLIST FOR ESL STUDENTS

Astounded	Eroded	Specificity
Benchmark	Fencing	Steering group (see 'steering
Cataclysmic	Infrastructure	committee')
Configuration	Installation	Subprime lending (see
Cultivated	Leveraging	'subprime')
Deploy	Networks	Sustainability
E-businesses	Outperform	Threshold
Elimination	Qualitatively	
Emulate	Quantitatively	

Definitions for these terms can be found in the 'Vocab Zone' of the companion website, which provides free access to the Macmillan English Dictionary online at www.macmillanihe.com/companion/business/campbell.

REVIEW QUESTIONS

1 Explain the difference between competence and core competence.
2 Explain each element of the value chain and how organizations can create value through efficient and effective activities.
3 Evaluate how value-adding activities can be configured to improve business performance in the banking sector.

It is important to create value for consumers. This value needs to be real and tangible in order to be attractive. Discuss.

HOT TOPICS – Research project areas to investigate

If you have a project to do, why not investigate ...

- ... the appropriateness of the value chain as a tool for a not-for-profit organization.
- ... how organizations decide to configure their resources during times of financial crisis.
- ... perceptions of managers as to whether outsourcing is the best way to gain competences quickly.

Recommended reading

Barney, J.B. and Clark, D.H. (2007) *Resource-based Theory: Creating and Sustaining Competitive Advantage*, Oxford: Oxford University Press.

Jarillo, J.C. (1993) *Strategic Networks: Creating the Borderless Organization*, Oxford: Butterworth-Heinemann, Chapters 4–5.

Petts, N. (1997) 'Building growth on core competences: a practical approach', *Long Range Planning*, **30**(4): 551–61.

Porter, M.E. (1985) *Competitive Advantage*, New York: Free Press.

Chapter references

Coyne, K.P. (1986) 'Sustainable competitive advantage: what it is, what it isn't', *Business Horizons*, **29**(1): 54–61.

Hall, R. (1992) 'The strategic analysis of intangible resources', *Strategic Management Journal*, **13**(2): 135–44.

Heene, A. and Sanchez, R. (1997) *Competence-based Strategic Management*, London: John Wiley.

Kay, J. (1993) *Foundations of Corporate Success*, Oxford: Oxford University Press.

Kay, J. (1995) 'Learning to define the core business', *Financial Times,* December 1.

Porter, M.E. (1980) *Competitive Strategy: Techniques for Analysing Industries and Competitors*, New York: Free Press.

Porter, M.E. (1985) *Competitive Advantage*, New York: Free Press.

Prahalad, C.K. and Hamel, G. (1990) 'The core competence of the corporation', *Harvard Business Review*, **68**(3): 79–81.

Smith, A. (1776) *An Enquiry into the Nature and Causes of the Wealth of Nations*, London: Strachan and Cadell.

Stalk, G., Evans, P. and Shulmann, L.E. (1992) 'Competing on capabilities: the new rules of corporate strategy', *Harvard Business Review*, **70**(3): 57–69.

Teece, D.J. (2007) 'Explicating dynamic capabilities: the nature and micro foundations of (sustainable) enterprise performance', *Strategic Management Journal*, **28**(13): 1319–50.

2

Chapter 5

Knowledge, culture and innovation

Introduction and chapter overview

Human resources, and knowledge in particular, are undoubtedly one of the key resource inputs to any organizational process. Without human input, there would be no creativity, innovation, enterprise, skills or intellectual work effort.

In this chapter, we examine the idea of knowledge management and define culture. We then go on to explain the importance of culture to an organization and explore the cultural web, a model used to examine the way that the features of culture influence the organization. The chapter concludes by introducing the concepts of creativity and innovation and highlighting their importance to the resource-based view of strategy.

Learning objectives

After studying this chapter, you should be able to:

- explain the importance of human resources
- explain what knowledge management is
- explain the importance of collaborative networks
- define culture and explain its determinants and why it is important
- explain the components of the cultural web and the nature of paradigms
- describe two typologies of cultural types
- explain the difference between creativity and innovation

5.1 The importance of human resources

This section explores the key resource of most organizations, people. We will examine the importance of human resources (HR), and the identification of human resources as critical success factors (CSFs).

People are an important, if not the most important, resource to most organizations. Decisions about the future strategy of the organization are made by people and strategies are implemented by people. The success or failure of a current strategy will depend not only on decisions made in the past but also on how those decisions are being implemented now by people employed by the organization. It is therefore important to ask questions about who, how and why people are doing what they are doing and what they should do in strategic implementation. In short, human resources add value, manage the business and can contribute to strategic success, while, conversely, they can make spectacular errors that can be costly to the organization. Just recall how a simple speech by CEO Gerald Ratner to the Institute of Directors on 23 April 1991 resulted in the value of the business plummeting by £500m and a complete rebranding and name change of the business. What did he say? Two key things:

> We also do cut-glass sherry decanters complete with six glasses on a silver-plated tray that your butler can serve you drinks on, all for £4.95. People say 'How can you sell this for such a low price?' I say, because it's total crap.

Ratner also said that some of the earrings sold at Ratners were 'cheaper than a M&S prawn sandwich but probably wouldn't last as long'.

An understanding of the capabilities of individuals and groups in terms of attitudes, abilities and skills, as well as how individuals relate one to another, is an important part in the preparation and development of strategy, as people are often at the heart of any organizational core competence.

Identifying human resources as critical success factors

It can be useful to establish which, if any, employees or groups of employees are critical to strategic success. These are the people that the organization's success may have been built on in the past and it is likely that the existing structures are centred around them.

In some organizations, people who are critical to strategic success may be found on the board of directors, giving strategic direction to the company as a whole. In others, they might be found in research, developing the new products on which future success will be built. Marketing people or operations management might also be critical in some businesses. It follows that a key part of the resulting HR strategy will be to protect and retain such key people.

It is usually the case that there are one or more reasons why superior performers in an industry are in the positions that they are. These key reasons for success are **critical success factors** (CSFs). Some companies have uniquely skilled employees, such as particularly important computer programmers or research scientists. In this case, the CSF is a human resource. In other businesses, the CSF might be a unique location, a brand image, an enviable reputation, a legally protected patent or licence, a unique production process or technology, or any combination of these. This is not to say that other parts of the organization are unimportant, but merely that the CSF is *the* most important cause of the success.

In terms of competitive strategy, the approach to a CSF is to defend it – in some cases at whatever cost. This usually takes to form of 'locking it in' to ensure that the advantage is maintained or that competitors are prevented from gaining the same advantage.

Critical success factors (CSFs) are those human factors that would help achieve the desired level of an organization's goal.

5.2   Knowledge management

Throughout the late 1990s and into the 2000s, the attention of many strategists was drawn to the concept of knowledge (or talent) management. In this section, we explore knowledge management (KM) emerging from organizational learning, and then examine the keys to successful KM.

Organizational learning and knowledge management

Closely related to the rational/logical approaches to strategy, such as the prescriptive and competitive positioning schools of thought, is the notion that organizations must continually learn about themselves and their environment. At the same time – and here this point is in agreement with the core competence approach – it is widely acknowledged that organizational knowledge underpins many core competences. Accordingly, organizational learning and KM have been the subject of considerable recent research and theorization (see for example Argyris, 1992; Grant, 1997; Demarest, 1997). Grant (1997, p. 452) argues that 'the knowledge-based view represents a confluence of a number of streams of research, the most prominent being "resource-based theory" and "epistemology"'.

Explicit and implicit knowledge

Organizational learning and KM are concerned with the creation, development and dissemination of knowledge within an organization. This 'knowledge' can be either explicit or implicit:

- **Explicit knowledge** is knowledge whose meaning is clearly stated, details of which can be recorded and stored, such as important formulations, procedures or ways of acting.
- **Implicit or tacit knowledge** (Demarest, 1997) is often unstated, based on individual experience and difficult to record and store. Implicit knowledge is often a vital source of core competence and competitive advantage, as it is difficult for competitors to emulate, such as experience in a given sector, an understanding of a particular technology or the multiple contact networks that have been built up over many years by managers and salespeople.

Both forms of knowledge begin as individual knowledge but, to substantially improve performance, they must be transformed into organizational knowledge. This is a particularly difficult transformation for implicit knowledge. It is the role of KM to ensure that individual learning becomes organizational learning.

Explicit knowledge is knowledge whose meaning is clearly stated, details of which can be recorded and stored, such as important formulations, procedures or ways of acting.

Implicit or tacit knowledge is often unstated, based on individual experience and difficult to record and store.

Implicit or tacit knowledge: an IT technician

Types of organizational learning

Argyris (1978, 1992) argues that organizations must develop 'double loop learning'. In other words, learning is not just a case of learning how to solve an immediate problem but must also aim at developing principles that will inform and determine future behaviour. It must also result in the ability to generalize from specific learning. Such learning takes place when individual solutions are reached and then generalized to apply in other circumstances.

Senge (1990) identifies two types of learning found in leading organizations: 'adaptive learning' and 'generative learning'. Adaptive learning centres on changing in response to developments in the business environment. Such adaptation is often necessary for business survival. Generative learning is about building new competences or identifying or creating opportunities for leveraging existing competences in new competitive arenas. For example, Marks & Spencer's entry into financial services was based on leveraging its existing competences in retailing and adding new competences, based on learning about the nature of financial services, initially through its store card operations.

Adaptive learning centres on changing in response to developments in the business environment.

Generative learning is about building new competences or identifying or creating opportunities for leveraging existing competences in new competitive arenas.

2

GURU GUIDE

Chris Argyris was born in Newark, New Jersey in 1923. He graduated from Clark University in 1947 with a BA in psychology and from Kansas University with an MA in economics and psychology in 1949. He gained his PhD in organizational behaviour from Cornell University in 1951. In a distinguished career, Professor Argyris has been a faculty member at Yale University (1951–71), where he served as the Beach Professor of Administrative Science and chairperson of the department; and the James Bryant Conant Professor of Education and Organizational Behavior at Harvard University (1971–). He is also a professor emeritus at Harvard Business School, a director of the Monitor Company and a fellow of the National Academy of Human Resources.

He was one of the most distinguished figures in the HR movement of the 1970s, and one of most recognized, respected figures in the area of organizational behaviour and organizational learning. Professor Argyis is widely regarded as the founding father of the learning organization and has received numerous awards, including honorary doctorates and the Irwin award for lifetime contribution to the discipline of management. His articles have received best article prizes from various publishers including *Harvard Business Review*.

Successful knowledge management

Knowledge management incorporates organizational learning but it is also concerned with the management of existing stocks of knowledge. Effective KM must overcome:

- barriers to learning and knowledge creation
- difficulties in storing and sharing knowledge, particularly tacit knowledge
- difficulties in valuing and measuring knowledge (Demarest, 1997).

Knowledge management is, therefore, primarily concerned with the creation of new knowledge, the storage and sharing of knowledge and the control of knowledge. Knowledge management is an important element in building core competences that must be distinctive and difficult to imitate.

The often intangible nature of knowledge tends to make it distinctive and difficult to copy. In the case of a company like Microsoft, it is evident that its core competences are largely knowledge based. Quinn (1992, p. 28) argued

Knowledge management is primarily concerned with the creation of new knowledge, the storage and sharing of knowledge and the control of knowledge.

that 'most successful enterprises today can be considered intelligent enterprises' as they focus on building knowledge-based core competences. Similarly, Grant (1997, p. 450) pointed out that 'companies such as Dow Chemical, Anderson Consulting, Polaroid and Skania are developing corporate-wide systems to track, access, exploit and create organizational knowledge'. Now, many organizations have such systems both in the public and private sectors. Within such organizations, questioning and creativity are encouraged, as are trust, teamwork and sharing. At the same time, they have created infrastructures that support learning, assist in the storage and controlled diffusion of knowledge, and coordinate its application in creating and supporting core competences.

There is some way to go in understanding the role of knowledge and its management in strategy. This has prompted some thinkers to provide a means of navigating KM through its evolution. Adopting the perspective of von Krogh et al. (2000), as well as Nonaka and Takeuchi (1995), that KM is determined by the view of knowledge has resulted in a number of high-level generations (Snowden, 2002; McElroy, 2003). However, there seems to be little agreement as to the generations, prompting Firestone and McElroy (2003) to talk of the

Table 5.1 **Three generations of knowledge management**

	Generation		
	1st	**2nd**	**3rd**
	Supply-driven KM	Supply and demand-driven KM	Complex KM
Approaches	Knowledge is captured and codified, so codification strategies and intellectual capital protection are core	A distributive and networked approach to knowledge sharing is adopted. Innovation is encouraged, organizational learning, communities of practice and holistic strategies are adopted to stimulate KM practices	Knowledge cannot be managed. However, it is possible to recognize patterns and use storytelling to share knowledge
Researcher			
McElroy (1999)	Supply side KM	Supply and demand side KM	
McElroy (2000, 2003) Firestone and McElroy (2003)	Supply side KM	Supply and demand side KM and complexity	
Skyrme (2001)		Segmentation and integration	
Deakin and Pratt (1999)	Teams and communities	Knowledge discovery	Business transformation
Knight and Howes (2002)	Potential of new technologies	How people know and learn	Building individual productivity and aligning to strategy
Koenig (2002)	Internet out of new technologies	Human relations	Content and reliability
Laszlo and Laszlo (2002)	Intellectual capital	Organizational learning and business innovation	Societal learning, ethical social innovation, evolutionary development
Snowden (2002)	Information for decision support	The SECI cycle (socialization, externalization, combination, internalization)	Complexity
Tuomi (2002)	Information storage and access	Knowledge construction	Link knowing and action in social systems

'knowledge wars'. The basis for these wars is a disagreement surrounding two main areas: the number of generations in existence, and what constitutes each generation. Regarding the former, the main debate is between those who advocate two generations and those identifying a shift towards a third. Concerning the latter, Table 5.1 highlights the differences between the various thinkers and the elements of disagreement. The former highlights the different views of the evolution of knowledge management, with each subsequent generation subsuming the one before it.

The third generation subsumes the former generations and so allows for an embedded knowledge of the values, beliefs and culture of the organization to be held and maintained, as opposed to buying a host of 'new players' who then have to undergo either a change management process or an orientation period. Therefore, a knowledge management system must be worked into the business strategy and implemented in daily processes throughout the company as a whole. It cannot be left solely to the HR department to attract and retain employees, but must be practised at all levels of the organization, with line managers responsible for developing the skills of their immediate subordinates and successors.

5.3   Collaborative networks

In recent years, considerable research and theorization has focused on the extent to which collaboration between businesses (as opposed to competition) may contribute to the attainment of competitive advantage.

The competence-based approach suggests that businesses should concentrate on developing core competences so as to achieve competitive advantage. Any activities not seen as core can be outsourced to other organizations for which those activities are core. Most networks centre on a focal business whose strategy drives the operation of the network. Quinn et al. (1990, p. 83) suggest that such are the changes in service technologies that they now

> provide sufficient scale economies, flexibility, efficiency and specialization potentials that outside vendors [sellers] can supply many important corporate functions at greatly enhanced value and lower cost. Thus many of those functions should be outsourced.

Rather than abandoning control to outside vendors, it is sometimes best to form some sort of alliance or network with them. Collaborative networks potentially provide several advantages by:

- allowing businesses to concentrate on their core competences and core activities
- allowing businesses to pool core competences, thus creating synergy between them
- reducing bureaucracy and allowing flatter organizational structures
- increasing efficiency and reducing costs
- improving flexibility and responsiveness
- making it difficult for competitors to imitate.

The formation of a collaborative network will involve:

- identification of the core competences of the organization

CASE STUDY Barley Engineering

Barley Engineering is a software design and manufacturing firm that produces and installs specialist components and software for the computer industry. Much of the company's work consists of working as a subcontractor and specialist provider to large industrial and commercial software projects. Barley Engineering has also carved out a specialist niche in designing music and lighting software for the entertainment, nightclub and theatre sectors.

Barley Engineering is heavily dependent on maintaining its high level of reputation in both sectors in order to continue to secure work for the future. Barley's profit margins in each of these sectors are good, but volumes of work are limited by the specialist nature of the work. If it loses contracts, this can and does lead to loss of work in other places, and damages its credibility in pitching for further contracts.

In the industrial and project subcontracting part, the work is steady state and assured. There is a large pool of main contractors who call on Barley for an understood range of products and services, for a known price and deadline and delivery schedule. Barley always meets deadline, price and quality criteria, and to date the company has never had a contract dispute.

In the entertainment sector, the work is unpredictable and highly volatile. This is understood by everyone. Prices and charges are high, in return for short-term turnaround times, adjustments and changes – and of course the success of the concert or presentation.

Both parts feed the effectiveness, success and reputation of the other. Those in the industrial sector are impressed by the 'wow' factor that Barley's demonstrations of entertainment technology always bring out. The entertainment sector needs the assurances from the industrial sector that the technology is foolproof, reliable, fully backed up and serviced at short notice whenever necessary. Because of the immediate nature of the entertainment industry, and the critical nature of light shows, theatre lighting and presentation, nothing can go wrong without ruining the whole presentation, and so nightclubs, concert and theatre producers need this absolute assurance for each contract, event and design.

Barley has a large pool of talent on which to draw, both for steady-state employment and for the short-term work and turnaround for the entertainment sector. Barley employs a total of 150 staff, of whom 120 work full time on design, implementation, installation, maintenance and troubleshooting, and they also have a pool of six small software designer companies on whom they can draw at any time, and to whom they pay a fixed-fee retainer to ensure availability on demand.

The culture of Barley is best summarized as fragmented, although there is a strong core of 'work hard/play hard'. There is an inherent cultural inclusiveness within the industry and the sector – everyone has worked for everyone else, everyone knows everyone else and their work. There is regular movement of staff within the sector; people make their reputation quickly and so can command high salaries and fees, at least until the next real or perceived genius comes along.

This part of the software design industry is dominated by four companies, of which Barley is one. Each has about 15% of the total work available. Small companies in the sector do the rest, which is normal for any sector that is constantly moving, changing and developing.

Audrey Aitken is national sales manager for Barley and her work is very specialized. Anyone who works in sales in this sector has to be quick and alert, and they have to be able to almost guess at what is required of potential clients. She now has to sort out a major problem with one of Barley's most prestigious, and most valuable and profitable potential clients – Wembley Stadium.

The entry into Wembley Stadium had been secured two years ago by Ben Foster, Barley's club sales representative, when he had successfully pitched for the contract to supply lighting and audio software for the nightclub next door. During a follow-up visit, by chance, the marketing director of Wembley Stadium was present, and the conversation led to Foster being asked to pitch for Wembley Stadium's entire entertainment software provision. The contract would be huge and prestigious, and would gain a colossal reputational advantage in the sector, as well as being profitable for Barley for a long period of time. Prices, costs, charges and service levels (with especial reference to back-ups being in place for all events) were agreed, and the contract would be worth many millions of pounds over a 10-year period. Foster arranged with the Wembley authorities to bring along

Daniel Cook, his CEO, to take personal charge of the contract.

Then the problems started. Ignoring Foster's pleas that Wembley had agreed the deal in all but signature, Cook had harangued the Wembley authorities about the complexities of the contract. Instead of endorsing the prices, charges and service levels that Foster had agreed, Cook now asserted that these were estimates only and that it was impossible to make the sort of commitments that Wembley wanted and needed. Cook proceeded to harangue the Wembley authorities about the complexities of the software supply industry. The Wembley marketing director then stated that the contract was lost; and he went on to ring the nightclub manager, who has now given Barley three months' notice of termination of contract. Cook now demands that Aitken sack Foster.

Aitken also knows that when the news gets out that Barley has lost the Wembley contract, it is likely to have a huge adverse effect on the industrial and entertainment parts of the business.

Case study questions

1 Where do Barley's sources of competitive advantage lie? What else might it do to ensure its competitive position?

2 What are the problems with knowledge and expertise management as stated or implied in this case? What might companies do in order to be as effective as possible in the management of knowledge and expertise?

3 What options are open to Aitken in trying to resolve this issue?

- identification and focus on activities that are critical to the core competence of the organization and outsourcing those which are not
- achieving the internal and external linkages in the value/supply chain that are necessary for effective coordination of activities and which enhance responsiveness.

Collaboration can be:

- *horizontal:* partners are at the same stage of the value system and are often competitors
- *vertical:* partners are at different stages of the value system, which includes collaboration with suppliers, distributors and customers.

Collaboration can provide benefits including the linking of core competences (of the two parties in the relationship), access to resources and technology, risk reduction, greater control over supplies, betters access to customers and reduced competition. For example, oneworld is an alliance that brings together 11 of the world's biggest and best airlines and allows them to pool resources, enter code-sharing agreements and provide a better customer service. Partners in the alliance benefit from the sharing of complementary competences and their unity prevents competitors from gaining market share.

Collaboration, however, can create problems, which include conflicting objectives between the participating businesses, cultural differences, changing requirements among the partners, and coordination and integration problems.

Virtual organizations

Developments in information and communications technology (ICT) have greatly increased the potential for collaboration between businesses by making it much easier to integrate and coordinate network activities. These changes in technology have made possible the development of 'virtual' organizations. A virtual organization is a network of linked businesses that coordinate and integrate their activities so effectively that they give the appearance of a single business organization.

There is considerable potential for such virtual organizations to enhance

A **virtual organization** is a network of linked businesses that coordinate and integrate their activities so effectively that they give the appearance of a single business organization.

competitive advantage. ICT linkages greatly increase flexibility and efficiency, and make it difficult for competitors to replicate the activities of the network. Linkages to suppliers and customers are greatly improved, as are flows of the information required for strategic decision-making. The net result is that the virtual corporation is more flexible, more responsive and better able than its non-virtual rivals to compete on the basis of time and customer satisfaction.

5.4   Organizational culture

Culture is 'the collective programming of the mind which distinguishes the members of one organization from another'.

Hofstede (1997, p. 180) defines culture as 'the collective programming of the mind which distinguishes the members of one organization from another'. He argues that the core of culture is an individual's values, of which rituals, heroes, symbols and practices are manifestations. Values are primarily learned from an individual's social environment, family, school and workplace. Furthermore, he comments that culture is at a national, regional, ethnic or religious, linguistic, social class, generation or organizational level. Culture is therefore the organizational equivalent of a human's personality. One of the better definitions is that by Stacey (1996, p. 41):

> The culture of any group of people is that set of beliefs, customs, practices and ways of thinking that they have come to share with each other through being and working together. It is a set of assumptions people simply accept without question as they interact with each other. At the visible level the culture of a group of people takes the form of ritual behaviour, symbols, myths, stories, sounds and artefacts.

In simpler language, culture can be explained in terms of the 'feel' of an organization or its 'character'. Definitions can be a bit inaccessible, but the importance of an organization's culture lies in the fact that it can be 'felt' whenever it is encountered. It is the way 'things are done' in a given setting.

Organizations are as individual as people and, in many ways, there are as many cultures as there are organizations – each one is unique. This is not to say, however, that we cannot identify common features between organizational cultures. Table 5.2 provides some descriptions of culture.

Table 5.2 Culture explained

Author	Description
Schein (1997)	'Cultural understanding is desirable for all of us but it is essential to leaders if they are to lead'
Spencer-Oatey (2000)	'Culture is a fuzzy set of attitudes, beliefs, behavioural norms, and basic assumptions and values that are shared by a group of people, and that influence each member's behaviour and his/her interpretations of the "meaning" of other people's behaviour'
Trompenaars and Hampden-Turner (1997)	Seven cultural values: universalism v particularism, communitarianism v individualism, neutral v emotional, defuse v specific cultures, achievement v ascription, human–time relationship, human–nature relationship

Geert Hofstede is a native and resident of the Netherlands. He was born in Haarlem in 1928 and graduated with an MA in mechanical engineering from Delft Technical University in 1953 and a Doctorate in social psychology from Groningen University in 1967. After military service in the Dutch army, he worked in Dutch as well as international business companies in roles varying from production worker to HR director. In the period 1965–71, he founded and managed the personnel research department of IBM Europe. After that he taught and researched at IMD (Lausanne, Switzerland), INSEAD (Fontainebleau, France), the European Institute for Advanced Studies in Management (Brussels, Belgium) and IIASA (Laxenburg Castle, Austria). His teaching languages are Dutch, English, French and German. He joined the University of Maastricht in 1985 as a professor of organizational anthropology and international management, and became an emeritus professor in 1993. Since then he has held visiting professorships in Hong Kong, Hawaii, Australia and New Zealand, and he was active as an extramural fellow of the CentER for Economic Research at Tilburg University.

Hofstede's dissertation made him into a founding father of behavioural accounting. Through his scholarly book *Culture's Consequences* (1980, rewritten 2nd edn, 2001), he became a founder of comparative intercultural research; his ideas are used worldwide. He specifically studied the interactions between national and organizational cultures and noted their link in the behaviour of societies and organizations. His popular book *Cultures and Organizations: Software of the Mind* (1991) has appeared in 18 languages so far; revised editions were published in 2005 and 2010, co-authored with Michael Minkov. In a *Wall Street Journal* ranking of May 2008, Hofstede was listed among the top 20 most influential management thinkers of today, as the only Continental European. He is a fellow of the Academy of Management in the USA, and a doctor honoris causa of universities in the Netherlands, Bulgaria, Greece, Sweden, Belgium, Lithuania and Hungary.

His website is http://www.geerthofstede.nl.

The determinants of culture

The reason why an organization has a particular type of culture is as complicated a question as asking why a human has a particular personality. It has many possible influences, the net effect of which forges culture over a period of time. Any list would be necessarily incomplete, but the following are some of the most important features:

- the philosophy of the organization's founders, especially if it is relatively young
- the nature of the activities in the business and the character of the industry it competes in
- the nature of the interpersonal relationships and of industrial or employee relationships
- the management style adopted and the types of control mechanism, for example the extent to which management style is autocratic or democratic
- the national or regional character of the areas in which the organization's activities are located (Schein, 1985). This, in turn, can affect the power distance, which also influences culture
- the structure of the organization, particularly its 'height' and 'width'
- the dependency the organization has on technology and the type of technology employed, for example the growth of email has had an influence on the culture of some organizations.

Why is culture important?

Culture is important because it can and does affect all aspects of an organization's activities. The metaphor of human personality may help us to understand this. Some people's personality means they are motivated, sharp or exciting to be with. Others are dull, tedious, apathetic or risk averse. These personality features will affect all aspects of their lives.

The same is true of an organization's 'personality'. Culture is important because of the following (not exhaustive) reasons. Culture can have an influence on:

- employee motivation
- the attractiveness of the organization as an employer and hence the rate of staff turnover
- employee morale and 'goodwill'
- productivity and efficiency
- the quality of work
- the nature of the employee and industrial relations
- the attitude of employees in the workplace
- innovation and creativity.

The point to make after such a list is simply that culture is important. It is essential that management understand the culture of the organization in analysing strategic position and implementing strategy.

The **cultural web** is a schematic representation of the elements of an organization's culture so that we can see how each element influences the paradigm.

The cultural web

One of the most commonly used ways of making sense of an organization's culture is to use the cultural web (Johnson, 1992). It is a schematic representation of the elements of an organization's culture so that we can see how each element influences the paradigm (Figure 5.1).

The main elements of the cultural web are described as follows:

- *Stories*: Stories are those narratives that people within the organization talk to each other about, what they tell new recruits and outsiders about the organization. The stories typically recount events and people from the past

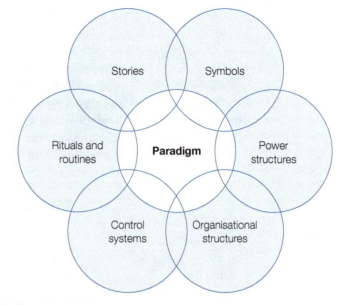

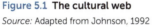

Figure 5.1 The cultural web
Source: Adapted from Johnson, 1992

and present – stories of famous victories and defeats. They tend to highlight what is considered important to the members of the organization.

- *Routines and rituals:* Routines are the procedures for doing things within the organization. They are repeated on a regular basis to the extent that they are taken to be 'the way things are done'. Rituals have a longer time frame and can be formal or informal. Formal routines and rituals are a part of the organization's practice, such as the 'long service award' or the company Outward Bound course that work teams might go on from time to time. Informal routines and rituals might include the way that people behave at the annual Christmas party or the extent to which colleagues do (or do not) go for a drink together after work.

- *Symbols:* Symbolic aspects of organizational life concern those things that symbolize something to some people – a certain level of promotion, the company car they drive, the position of their office, their job title. In some companies, these symbols have no apparent importance at all, while in others, they matter a great deal. The way that employees respond to these symbols can tell us a great deal about the culture.

- *Structure:* The structure of an organization can mean more than just those formal relationships that are shown on an organization diagram. Informal structures can also exist through interpersonal relationships that transcend the formal structures. Some organizations have highly developed informal structures, while others do not.

- *Control systems:* The way in which activities are controlled, whether 'tight' or 'loose', is closely aligned to culture. This has a strong link to power distance and the nature of the activities the organization is engaged in. Control systems, by definition, gauge performance against a predetermined standard, and the methods of setting standards and monitoring performance vary significantly according to culture.

■ *Power structures:* The core assumptions that contribute to the paradigm are likely to be made by the most powerful management groupings in the organization. In some companies, this power resides in the research department, in others it will be the production people. In some organizations, there may be arguments between one or more groupings about what is important.

Each component of the cultural web exerts its own influence on the organization's paradigm. The paradigm describes the aggregate effects of all the cultural influences on the way the organization's members look at the world. This can apply to regions of the world just as it applies to organizations. People indigenous to one region of the world are often thought to have a different view of the world to the citizens of another. This difference is because of the influence that each component of the cultural web exerts on the national or regional paradigm.

We can also use the components of the cultural web to help us to understand a paradigm. In this case, we are using the six 'peripheral' factors as manifestations of, rather than contributors to, the paradigm. If we want to understand the central beliefs of a company (its paradigm), we should examine the cultural web factors. By examining each one, just as we might examine the externalities of a human personality, we can gain clues as to the 'real personality' or culture that is at the centre (the paradigm).

| Example | **The cultural web of a recently privatized public sector organization** |

The company in question is a major player in the Scottish facilities management scene. It was a public sector department charged with providing facilities and care services to the general population of Scotland. It is now a limited liability company and is in the process of implementing a change management programme. The cultural web produced here was adapted from the original work done by MBA students of a Scottish university during a site visit to witness the change management programme in action.

Stories:
Importance of care
Focus on welfare
Old days
Innovators
Office politics
Lack of professionalism

Symbols:
A pointing finger/hand
    logo
Logos highly visible in
    utility vehicles
Job titles displayed
    prominently
Logos pointing to former
    public sector heritage

Power structures:
Medium power distance
Councillors in the board
Prevalent bureaucracy
Influence of unions

Organizational structures:
Grades and pay bands
Subcultures
Distinct groups with agendas
Lack of integration

Control systems:
Formal reporting systems
Legislation associated with care
    given to elderly
Budgets

Rituals and routines:
Heavy workload associated with
    care activities
Annual awards
Meetings and sub-boards

Paradigm:
Care, facilities and catering
    experts
Innovators
Influence of city council
Organization in transition
Ambitious

5.5 Cultural typologies

A number of writers in organizational theory have attempted to group culture types together. The thinking behind such attempts at typology is that if organizations can describe their cultures by type, this would help in strategic analysis. We will briefly consider two of these attempts.

Handy's culture types

Handy (1993) suggested that organizational cultures can be divided into four broad types: power cultures, role cultures, task cultures and person cultures.

Power cultures

This type of organization is dominated by either a powerful individual or a small, dominant group. It is typified by an organization that has grown as a result of entrepreneurial flair. Strategic decisions and many operational ones are made by the centre and few decisions are devolved to other managers. As the organization is dependent on the abilities and personality of the powerful individual, the ability of the organization to change in response to changes in the environment is sometimes limited by the centre. Power cultures are common in small entrepreneurial (owner-managed) companies and in some notable larger organizations with a charismatic leader.

Power cultures are common in small entrepreneurial (owner-managed) companies and in some notable larger organizations with a charismatic leader.

Role cultures

This type of culture is found in many long-established organizations that have traditionally operated in stable environments. They tend to be hierarchical and rely on established procedures, systems and precedent. They often respond slowly to change, as it takes time for change to be recognized through the reporting mechanisms. Delays are also encountered in decision-making processes.

Role cultures are common in traditional bureaucracies, such as the civil service, banks, insurance companies and in some newer business types such as call centres. The task of management in a role culture is to manage procedure. There is usually a high degree of decentralization and the organization is run by rules and laid-down procedures. It is important, however, that this cultural classification is not viewed as inefficient or as a term of derision, as it is a highly suitable cultural type for many organizations.

Role cultures are common in traditional bureaucracies, such as the civil service, banks, insurance companies and in some newer business types such as call centres.

Task cultures

Task cultures are found in organizations engaged in activities of a non-repetitive nature, often high value, one-off tasks. Activities are normally based around flexible multidisciplinary teams containing expertise in the major disciplines required to complete the project. Teams tend to be small but flexible and find change easy to identify and adjust to. Strategic planning tends to concentrate on the task in hand.

As their name suggests, task cultures can be found in organizations that are dedicated to a particular task. Consortia that work on large civil engineering projects may demonstrate task culture, as might missionary teams that work together on a medical project in the developing world.

Task cultures are found in organizations engaged in activities of a non-repetitive nature, often high value, one-off tasks.

2

Person cultures

Person cultures are those that exist primarily for the benefit of the members of the organization itself, hence they tend to be rare in commercial businesses. They can have a very different 'feel' to the other cultures, as all members of the organization work for the benefit of themselves and the other members. Person cultures can be found in learned professional societies, trade unions, cooperatives, some charities and some religious organizations.

In reality, few organizations fit perfectly into one just classification and they may demonstrate elements of two or more. Some diversified organizations may have divisions that fall into all the categories and the cultures may change over time. Many start as power cultures and then tend towards a role culture as size increases.

> **Person cultures** can be found in learned professional societies, trade unions, cooperatives, some charities and some religious organizations.

GURU GUIDE

Charles Handy is often considered as Britain's greatest visionary and is one of the world's foremost thinkers in advanced management. He was born in Kildare, Ireland, in 1932, the son of a Protestant vicar, and studied at Oriel College, Oxford. He started his professional career working for Shell in London and later on in Southeast Asia. However, the prospect of a posting to Liberia caused Handy to leave Shell in favour of a career in academia. In 1966 he joined MIT Sloan School of Management as an international faculty fellow. On his return to the UK he played an important role in shaping the way management was taught in Britain, co-founding the London Business School in 1967.

He has written several books and articles on organizational behaviour and culture and his work is noted for its insightful and innovative ideas about the future of work, business and management. In *The Gods of Management* (1978) he identified four different management cultures which he likened to four Greek gods: Apollo, Athena, Dionysus and Zeus. He is also famous for proposing the 'shamrock organization' as a business model. His vivid use of metaphor and his accessible writing style have made his books extremely popular. He was a chairman of the Royal Society of Arts in London from 1987 to 1989 and has been a regular contributor to *Thought for the Day* on BBC Radio 4.

Miles and Snow's culture types

Miles and Snow (1978) categorized cultures into four types, based on how they tend to react in strategic terms.

Defenders

These organizations tend to seek a competitive advantage in terms of targeting niche markets through cost reduction and specialization. They tend to operate in stable, mature markets and, as the name suggests, they favour defending their current market share by service improvements or further cost savings. Defenders tend to be centralized, have rigid control systems and a hierarchical management structure that does not respond well to sudden change.

Prospectors

These organizations enjoy the challenge of developing and introducing new products to the marketplace. They actively seek out new markets for their products. These strategies require organizations to constantly monitor the environment and be willing and able to respond quickly to changes that may occur. To that end, they are decentralized and flexible.

Analysers

These organizations are 'followers' and are conservative in nature. Steady growth through market penetration is the favoured option, as this can be achieved without radical changes to structure. Moves into new markets and products only occur after extensive evaluation and market research. They learn from the mistakes of others and tend to balance power between the centre and divisions with complex control systems.

Reactors

Reactors are a bit like analysers in that they tend to follow rather than innovate. They differ from analysers in that they are less conservative and sometimes behave impulsively, having failed to fully consider the implications of their actions. These organizations may lack proper control systems and typically have a weak but dominant leader. We discuss leadership as part of the implementation of strategy in Chapter 17.

2

5.6   Creativity and innovation

Innovation is the commercialization or exploitation of creativity and is often represented by a degree of novelty – novelty being relative to the organization, the situation or the process.

Creativity is a human activity that allows for new and novel solutions to problems. Innovation is the commercialization or exploitation of such creativity and is often represented by a degree of novelty – novelty being relative to the organization, the situation or the process.

Joseph Schumpeter (1942) is seen as the father of innovation. He constructed the concept of the 'entrepreneur with innovation' in order to present it as a process of 'creative destruction' essential to the economic growth of a country. However, innovation extends beyond this view: it can be incremental or radical in nature; it can be across product, process, position, users, environments or even ways of thinking, for example new markets, new technologies, new rules, new business models, unthinkable events and so on.

In essence, the architecture of innovation is 'knowledge', knowledge about the components of the business, its market and industry, and how the components can and do fit together. Innovation is often part of a continuous process composed of a range of innovations and, as such, will emerge as the organization's strategy evolves and develops.

Innovation is often categorized as product innovation or process innovation. Product innovation represents the development of new technologies and products as well as new uses for existing products, while process innovation reflects more of an attempt to re-engineer or design the flow of work activity in the organization.

Therefore, it can be seen that innovation has product, process and service development at its core, and in the workplace, it tends to be about examining the way things are currently done with a view to finding new and better ways of doing them. It can be applied to any element of the business/organization, throughout the value chain, and does not have to be original or groundbreaking in nature. Innovation can simply be the extension, modification or combination of already existing ideas in a way that improves existing functions. Indeed, in many ways innovation is relative.

We explore innovation more in Chapter 7 when we look at the resource-based view of strategy.

For test questions, extra case studies, audio case studies, weblinks, videolinks and more to help you understand the topics covered in this chapter, visit our companion website at www.macmillanihe.com/companion/business/campbell.

VOCAB CHECKLIST FOR ESL STUDENTS

Aggregate	Conversely	Novelty
Artefacts	Decanter	Particularism (see
Bureaucracy	Endorsing	'particularize')
Codification	Entrepreneurial	Plummeting
Colossal	Epistemology	Schematic
Confluence	Harangued	Status symbols
Consortia	Individualism	Universalism

Definitions for these terms can be found in the 'Vocab Zone' of the companion website, which provides free access to the Macmillan English Dictionary online at www.macmillanihe.com/companion/business/campbell.

REVIEW QUESTIONS

1   Explain what knowledge management is.
2   Giving examples, explain what the cultural web is.
3   Explain the difference between creativity and innovation.

DISCUSSION TOPIC

It is not possible to manage knowledge, so knowledge management does not exist. Discuss.

HOT TOPICS – Research project areas to investigate

If you have a project to do, why not investigate …

■ … to what extent an organization of your choice exhibits the characteristics of Handy's cultural typologies.
■ … what approaches universities use for managing knowledge.
■ … the role that stories and symbols play in shaping an organization's culture.

Recommended reading

Allee, V. (1999) 'The art and practice of being revolutionary', *Journal of Knowledge Management*, **3**(2): 121–31.

Barney, J. (1991) 'Firm resources and sustained competitive advantage', *Journal of Management*, **17**(1): 99–120.

Bennet, A. and Bennet, D. (2001) 'Exploring relationships in the next generation knowledge organization', *Knowledge and Innovation: Journal of the KMCI*, **1**(2): 91–109.

Campbell, A. and Goold, M. (1987) *Strategies and Style*, London: Basil Blackwell.

Campbell, A., Goold, M. and Alexander, M. (1994) *Corporate Level Strategy*, London: Wiley.

Chandler, A. (1962) *Strategy and Structure*, Cambridge, MA: MIT Press.

Goold, M. (1996) 'Parenting strategies for the mature business', *Long Range Planning*, **29**(3): 358–69.

Kay, J. (1993) *Foundations of Corporate Success*, Oxford: Oxford University Press.

Lynch, R. (1997) *Corporate Strategy*, London: Pitman.

Skyrme, D.J. (1999) *Knowledge Networking: Creating the Collaborative Enterprise*, Oxford: Butterworth-Heinemann.

Snowden, D.J. (2000) 'The ASHEN Model: an enabler of action', *Journal of Knowledge Management*, **3**(7): 14–17.

Stacey, R.D. (2001) *Complex Responsive Processes in Organizations: Learning and Knowledge Creation*, New York: Routledge.

Starovic, D. and Marr, B. (2002) *Understanding Corporate Value: Managing and Reporting Intellectual Capital*, London: CIMA.

Stewart, T.A. (1991) 'Brainpower: how intellectual capital is becoming America's most important asset', *Fortune Magazine*, 3 June: 44–60.

Teece, D.J., Pisano, G. and Shuen, A. (1997) 'Dynamic capabilities and strategic management', *Strategic Management Journal*, **18**(7): 509–33.

Chapter references

Argyris, C. (1978) *Organizational Learning: A Theory of Action Perspective*, Addison-Wesley: Reading, MA.

Argyris, C. (1992) *On Organizational Learning*, London: Blackwell.

Deakin, R. and Pratt, K. (1999) 'Mapping and tracking ', *Knowledge Management*, October: 14–17.

Demarest, M. (1997) 'Understanding knowledge management', *Long Range Planning*, **30**(3): 374–84.

Firestone, J.M. and McElroy, M. (2003) *Key Issues in the New Knowledge Management*, Oxford: Butterworth-Heinemann/Elsevier.

Grant, R.M. (1997) 'The knowledge-based view of the firm: implications for management practice', *Long Range Planning*, **30**(3): 450–4.

Handy, C.B. (1993) *Understanding Organizations* (4th edn), London: Penguin.

Hickson, D.J. and Pugh, D.S. (1995) *Management Worldwide*, London: Penguin.

Hofstede, G. (1967) *The Game of Budget Control: How to Live with Budgetary Standards and yet be Motivated by them*, Assen: Van Gorcum.

Hofstede, G. (1991) *Cultures and Organizations: Software of the Mind*, London: McGraw-Hill.

Hofstede, G. (1997) 'The Archimedes effect', in M.H. Bond (ed.) *Working at the Interface of Cultures: 18 Lives in Social Science*, London: Routledge.

Hofstede, G. (2001) *Culture's Consequences: International Differences in Work-related Values* (2nd edn), Newbury Park, CA: Sage.

Johnson, G. (1992) 'Managing strategic change: strategy, culture and action', *Long Range Planning*, **25**(1): 28–36.

Knight, T. and Howes, T. (2002) *Knowledge Management: A Blue Print for Delivery*, Oxford: Butterworth-Heinemann.

Koenig, M.E. (2002) 'The third stage of KM emerges', *KMWorld*, **11**(3): 20–1, 28.

Laszlo, K.C. and Laszlo, A. (2002) 'Evolving knowledge for development: the role of knowledge management in a changing world', *Journal of Knowledge Management*, **6**(4): 400–12.

McElroy, M. (1999) 'The second generation of KM', *Knowledge Management*, **2**(10): 86–8.

McElroy, M. (2000) 'Integrating complexity theory, knowledge management, and organizational learning', *Journal of Knowledge Management*, **4**(3): 195–203.

McElroy, M. (2003) *The New Knowledge Management: Complexity, Learning, and Sustainable Innovation*, Boston, MA: Butterworth-Heinemann.

Miles, R.E. and Snow, C.C. (1978) *Organisational Strategy, Structure and Process*, New York: McGraw-Hill.

Nonaka, I. and Takeuchi, H. (1995) *The Knowledge-creating Company: How Japanese Companies Create the Dynamics of Innovation*, Oxford: Oxford University Press.

Quinn, J.B. (1992) *The Intelligent Enterprise*, New York: Free Press.

Schein, E.H. (1985) *Organisational Culture and Leadership*, San Francisco: Jossey-Bass.

Schein, E.H. (1997) *Organisational Culture and Leadership* (2nd edn), San Francisco: Jossey-Bass.

Schumpeter, J.A. (1942) *Capitalism, Socialism and Democracy*, London: Allen & Unwin.

Senge, P. (1990) 'The leader's new work: building learning organizations', *Sloan Management Review*, **32**(1): 7–23.

Skyrme, D. (2001) 'Online knowledge markets', in D. Skyrme, *Capitalizing on Knowledge: From E-business to K-business*, Oxford: Butterworth-Heinemann.

Snowden, D. (2002) 'Complex acts of knowing; paradox and descriptive self-awareness', *Journal of Knowledge Management*, **6**(2): 1–14.

Spencer-Oatey, H. (2000) *Culturally Speaking: Managing Rapport through Talk across Cultures*, London: Continuum.

2

Stacey, R. (1996) *Strategic Management and Organisational Dynamics* (2nd edn), London: Pitman.

Trompenaars, F. and Hampden-Turner, C. (1997) *Riding the Waves of Culture*, New York: McGraw-Hill.

Tuomi, I. (2002) *Networks of Innovation: Change and Meaning in the Age of Internet*, Oxford: Oxford University Press.

Von Krogh, G., Ichijo, K. and Nonaka, I. (2000) *Enabling Knowledge Creation: How to Unlock the Mystery of Tacit Knowledge and Release the Power of Innovation*, Oxford: Oxford University Press.

Chapter 6
Financial analysis, audit and performance

Introduction and chapter overview

The ability to measure performance and make sense of an organization's financial situation is an important part of strategic analysis and strategic implementation. In order to carry out a financial analysis of a company's situation or of an industry, it is necessary to understand some of the fundamentals of finance and its sources. This chapter begins with a discussion of the sources of corporate finance and then goes on to discuss the costs of the various types of capital. This information helps you to make sense of a company's financial structure and performance before the tools of conventional financial analysis are discussed. The various 'tools' for financial analysis are introduced and, finally, the important concepts of social audit and benchmarking are explained.

Learning objectives

After studying this chapter, you should be able to:

- understand what is meant by financial analysis
- identify the sources of funds available to companies and the relative advantages and disadvantages of each
- understand the cost and non-cost issues involved in raising and using various forms of capital
- understand the importance of the cost of capital
- understand the limitations of a company report and accounts as a source of data for financial analysis
- describe the major tools that can be used to analyse a company's financial position
- explain the importance of audit and understand the concept of social audit

6.1 An introduction to financial analysis

Most university business courses have some accounting and finance content. Readers may consequently be familiar with some of the content of this chapter and this will be to their advantage. This chapter takes the material from the other units and develops the material into the context of strategic analysis.

Money, or the lack of it, is central to the strategic development of all organizations, large or small. It is one of the key resource inputs and cannot be ignored. The most original strategies and the most complex plans for the future of a business are meaningless unless management have considered the financial position of the organization at the onset and during the period covered by the strategy. The ability of a company to finance current and future strategies is vital to any analysis of the company's position. A central theme of this chapter is the ability of the company to finance current strategies and to raise the funding required for future developments.

The success or failure of the organization is judged by its ability to meet its strategic objectives. The financial information (in the form of annual corporate reports) produced by companies provides a quantifiable means of assessing success. It is important to recognize, however, that other quantifiable information, such as efficiency and productivity data, and non-quantifiable data, such as the company's image, can also be used to make such judgements. In this chapter, we will examine the value of information extracted from corporate reports as a source from which judgements can be made.

Corporate reports are just one source of information about a company's financial state. Managers have a number of ways of gathering information about their own and competitors' finances and we will discuss these later in the chapter.

It is also important to bear in mind, however, that financial performance is only one way of measuring success in strategy. Depending on the company's objectives, more immediate measures of success might include market share increase, enhancement of reputation, share price improvement, reductions in complaints, and improvement in the ability to attract a key resource input such as human resources. It is thus short-termist and myopic to suggest that financial performance is the only measure of success. It is important, but not necessarily the most important measure at a given point in time.

Sources of corporate funding

Financial resources are an essential input to strategic development. Capital for development can be raised from several sources and these are summarized here.

KEY CONCEPTS

Revenue is money that is earned through normal business transactions – sales, rents or whatever the company does in its normal activities.

Capital is money that is used to invest in the business – to buy new equipment, new capacity, extra factory space and so on. The investment of capital enables the business to expand and, through that expansion, increase its revenue and profits in future years. Capital can be raised from shareholders, through retained profits, rights issues, loan capital or the disposal of assets.

Shareholders are the financial owners of the company.

Share capital has, historically, comprised the majority of capital for a limited company's start-up and subsequent development.

Share capital

In most limited companies, a sizeable proportion of capital is raised from shareholders (the financial owners of the company) in the form of share capital.

Share capital has, historically, comprised the majority of capital for a limited company's start-up and subsequent development. In return for their investment, shareholders receive a return in accordance with the company's performance in a given year in the form of a dividend. The dividend per share is taken as an important measure, by shareholders, of the company's success in its chosen strategy. Shares also confer on their holders a right to vote on company resolutions at annual or extraordinary company meetings pro rata with the size of their holding. It follows that a shareholding in excess of 50% of voting shares confers total control over a company's strategy.

Under normal circumstances, share capital is considered to be permanent – it is not paid back by the company. It is thus unlike other forms of capital (for example loan capital), as the shareholders only 'payback' is in the form of dividends and through capital growth – an increase in the value of the shares. Shareholders who wish to divest their shares in a company must usually sell them via a stock exchange (in the case of shares in a public limited company) or through a private sale (in the case of a private company). In exceptional circumstances, some companies offer a 'buy-back' of their own shares in order to increase the board's strategic control over the company.

Shareholders can be individuals or 'institutional shareholders'. Some individuals hold their personal share portfolio but the vast majority of shares are held by

institutional shareholders, such as pension funds, life assurance companies and investment trusts. One large UK company, BOC Group plc (now part of the Linde Group), reported in 1999 that 92% of its ordinary share capital was held by institutional shareholders, with only 19 institutions holding these shares. BOC no longer has its own shareholders, but the Linde Group reported in 2009 that 77% of its share capital was held by institutional investors, with one major shareholder, Allianz, holding a 4% stake in the group. This is not untypical – a concentration of shareholding in the hands of a relatively small number of large investors. The profile of shareholders, however, does vary between companies.

KEY CONCEPTS

Share value is the price of a company's shares at a given point in time. Like any other commodity, their value is determined by the forces of supply and demand. In normal circumstances, the supply is fixed over the short to medium term, so price is determined by how many people want to buy shares. If the market has confidence in a company's prospects, demand for shares will rise and so, accordingly, will their price. If a company's prospects are considered poor, investors will sell their shares, fewer will want to buy them and the price will fall.

Share volume is the number of shares issued by a company in total. This is usually determined at the foundation or flotation of a company, although rights issues and similar events can increase the share volume. It is generally true that larger companies have higher share volumes than smaller concerns.

Rights issue capital

From time to time, a company may seek to increase its capital for expansion or debt reduction by means of a **rights issue**. This is when a company issues new shares to the stock market, normally giving its own shareholders the first refusal pro rata with their current proportion of the company's share volume.

A **rights issue** is when a company issues new shares to the stock market.

The decision to go for a rights issue may well be a strategic decision for management because it can impact on the ownership and hence control of the company. If existing shareholders do not exercise their right to buy, it is likely that ownership will be diluted, that is, shareholders will find that they own a lower percentage of share volume than they did prior to the rights issue.

Those shares not taken up by shareholders, who may be unable or unwilling to buy them, are normally covered by underwriters (institutional investors) at a price agreed, in advance. Underwriting is an important technical feature of new share issues and, as such, is a cost in the process.

A **placing** involves the selling of shares directly to a small number of investors, usually large financial institutions.

A variation on a rights issue is placing. A placing involves the selling of shares directly to a small number of investors, usually large financial institutions. This may be marginally cheaper (to the company) than a rights issue, but its major advantage is its flexibility in enabling new shareholders significant and possibly strategic holdings. Placings take place, for example, as a part of a joint venture agreement, whereby the two companies exchange placed shareholdings as a sign of their mutual commitment to the alliance.

Retained profit as a source of capital

Retained profit, that element of operating profit not paid to shareholders in the form of a dividend, is the most common method of funding strategic developments.

Shareholders provide other funds for development by agreeing not to receive all the company's profits in a given year. Retained profit, that element of operating profit not paid to shareholders in the form of a dividend, is the most common method of funding strategic developments, particularly if the company is quite old in terms of years. By using this form of funding, organizations save on the costs involved in using alternatives, such as fees to merchant banks, lawyers and accountants. It also means that management do not have to reveal nor justify their strategies to others and risk their plans becoming known to competitors.

It should be recognized that retained profits do not constitute a loss to shareholders as such, because the value of the organization and consequently the share price is normally increased when these funds are used for reinvestment. It is, however, important that companies recognize the need to balance the proportion of profits distributed and retained in order to satisfy those shareholders who need regular funds flow themselves (such as insurance and pension companies).

KEY CONCEPTS

The recent introduction of international financial reporting standards has changed the names of some long-standing accounting terms. The most important of these are given here:

Non-current assets used to be known as fixed assets (plant, machinery, real estate) – distinguishes them from current assets, which are assets used to manage the business in the short term in the form of working capital.

Payables used to be known as creditors – reminds us that creditors are those a company owes money to.

Receivables used to be known as debtors – reminds us that debtors are those who owe money (usually customers on account).

Inventory used to be called stock.

Loan capital

An important consideration in the use of retained profits to fund corporate development is the ability of the company to actually make a profit that can be, at least in part, distributed to shareholders as dividends. While a company may make a profit from its normal activities after taxation, some profits are required to meet the cost of other forms of debt finance or loans.

Debt finance is shown in the balance sheet under two headings, 'Payables: amounts following within one year' and 'Payables: amounts falling due after more than one year'. The form of borrowing with most impact on strategic development is that falling due after more than one year – long-term debt. This can take a number of forms. In addition to the use of long-term bank loans, a company can use debentures, convertible loan stocks or corporate bonds.

Debt finance is normally for a set period of time and at a fixed or variable rate of interest. The interest must be paid every year, regardless of the level of profit (referred to as 'servicing the debt'). The interest rate for this source is normally less than the cost of share capital when the typical dividend payable on the shares is taken into account.

Comparing share capital and loan capital

Each of the types of capital described above has its pros and cons. Share capital has the advantage that the amount paid on the capital is dependent on company results. A company can decide not to pay a dividend if profits are poor in any given year. Loan capital, by contrast, must be serviced regardless of results, in much the same way that a mortgage on a house must be repaid regardless of other commitments.

Offsetting this advantage is the fact that share capital is permanent. As long as the company exists, it has an obligation to repay a dividend to its shareholders. Loan capital has the advantage to the company that it is time limited. Servicing the capital is restricted to the term of the loan (like a mortgage on a house) and when it is finally repaid in full, the business has no further obligation to the lender.

The fact that the repayment of debt finance takes precedence over dividends on shares means that shareholders bear an increased risk. If the company performs badly, their return on investment will be small or non-existent in a given year. Against this possibility, they usually expect to receive higher returns compared to providers of loan capital in the years when profits are good.

In practice, business profits can vary significantly over time. In some years, it is preferable to use loan capital, especially when interest rates are low and profits are high. In other years, when profits are lower and interest rates are higher, share capital works out cheaper. The fact that the benefits are so finely divided means that most companies opt to use an element of both. The relationship of debt capital to shareholder capital is referred to as the company's 'gearing ratio'.

Gearing is an indication of how the company has arranged its capital structure. It can be expressed as either:

Gearing is an indication of how the company has arranged its capital structure.

$$\frac{\text{borrowed capital, that is, debt}}{\text{total capital employed, that is, borrowings plus shareholders' capital}}$$

or as:

$$\frac{\text{borrowed capital, that is, debt}}{\text{shareholders' capital, that is, equity.}}$$

Both are usually expressed as percentages by simply multiplying the quotient by 100. It is not important which one is used unless we are comparing the gearing of two or more companies.

Other sources of capital

While the foregoing are the most common mechanisms of raising capital for development, others are available in some circumstances.

One such method is to dispose of existing non-current (fixed) assets. This can range from the selling of equipment or a factory to selling a subsidiary to a third party. Asset sales can offer the benefit of reducing liabilities (if the facility is loss-making) or of selling off non-core activities. The realizable price for the asset will depend on the timing of its sale.

Finally, marginal improvements in a company's capital situation can be achieved by improving the management of working capital. Over the course of a financial year, small savings can accumulate to significant proportions, increasing both profitability and capital for reinvestment. This can be achieved by:

- extending the time taken to pay payables (creditors)
- getting receivables (debtors) to pay sooner
- controlling inventories more efficiently.

KEY CONCEPT

Working capital is the amount of money a company has tied up in the normal operation of its business. Working capital comprises money tied up in inventories, receivables (money owed to the business), payables (money the company owes), and cash or current bank deposits. A company's objective is usually to minimize this figure.

6.2   Cost of capital

Availability of capital (where to get it from) is one issue when examining a company's capital funding, but another equally important consideration is its cost. We learned above that providers of loans or share capital (equity) both require a return on their investment. Management therefore need to know what return (profit) they need to make in order to meet the minimum requirements of capital providers. Failure to achieve this minimum will make the raising of future funds all the more difficult. The cost of capital can be seen as the minimum return required on the company's assets, which in turn, may influence the objectives of the company.

> The **cost of capital** can be viewed as the annual amount payable (as a percentage) against the principal amount of money.

At its simplest, the **cost of capital** can be viewed as the annual amount payable (as a percentage) against the principal amount of money. Most of us will be aware that the return payable on such things as loans varies between lenders and over time as interest rates and risk profiles vary. The cost of loans on a credit card, for example, is much higher than a mortgage loan, where the security against the loan is mainly responsible for the difference.

Cost of capital: loans on a credit card

Costs of debt capital

The costs of debt capital are relatively easy to calculate as they tend to correspond closely to the prevailing rate of interest. If the loan is to be repaid at a fixed rate, the calculation is even more straightforward. It is generally the case that the rate of interest attached to a loan will be strongly influenced by the risk of default. Unsecured loans attract the highest rates, while those that can be recovered by the sale of the asset against which the loan is taken out, such as a property, will attract a lower rate. The history of the business in dealing with lenders (its credit rating) will also be a factor.

Costs of share capital

Calculating the cost of share capital is slightly more complex as it contains more variables. Accounting academics have discussed at length what should and should not be included in this calculation and how each component should be weighted. Reasons for this complexity include the indefinite nature of the funding, the opportunity cost of undistributed profits and shareholders' expectations. In addition, some models try to include components for inflation, industry averages and attitudes towards risk.

At its simplest, the cost of share capital can be calculated as follows:

$$\text{Cost of share capital (equity) as a percentage} = \left(\frac{\text{current net dividend per share}}{\text{current market price of share}}\right) \times 100 + \text{average percentage annual growth rate.}$$

Example   Cost of share capital

If the market price is 400p per share and the annual dividend per share is 20p, and the growth in profits average 10% per annum, this gives:

$$\text{Cost of share capital} = \frac{20}{400} \times 100 + 10\% = 15\%$$

Models of capital costing

The CAPM model

The capital asset pricing model (CAPM) is a more complex but widely used model for calculating the cost of share capital:

$$\text{Cost of share capital} = Ri + \beta\,(Rm - Ri)$$

The model takes into account the competitor financial products available to potential investors. These range from the percentage return on virtually risk-free government bonds (Ri) to a component covering the average interest for the share (equity) markets overall (Rm). The final element of the model represents the company itself or, more correctly, its position relative to the market overall. The β coefficient is a measure of the volatility of the company's financial returns.

The CAPM model does have a number of drawbacks. First, the shares of the company need to be traded on a stock market. This means that the cost of equity in private companies cannot be calculated using this model. Second, the volatility of share prices in recent years causes problems in arriving at a date for 'acceptable' returns. The dynamic and complex nature of many industries and markets also suggests that historical data has limited value.

Example   **CAPM model**

Assume that risk-free government bonds were trading at 4% and the average return on the market was 10%. Also assume that the volatility of the company had been calculated at 1.1, meaning the shares fluctuated slightly more than the market average:

Cost of share capital (equity) = 4% + 1.1 (10% − 4%) = 10.6%

The WACC model

Whereas the CAPM model is used to calculate the cost of share capital, the weighted average cost of capital (WACC) can be used to determine the overall cost of funding to a company. The calculation of this information is relatively simple:

$$\text{WACC} = \left(\begin{array}{c} \text{proportion of} \\ \text{loan finance} \end{array} \times \begin{array}{c} \text{proportion of} \\ \text{shareholders' funds} \end{array} \right) + \begin{array}{c} \text{proportion of} \\ \text{shareholders' funds} \end{array} \times \begin{array}{c} \text{cost of} \\ \text{shareholders' funds} \end{array}$$

Example   **WACC model**

Assume that a company has £30m of loan capital and £70m equity funding, and the cost of each has been calculated as 5% and 15% respectively, the calculation would be as follows:

Type of capital	Proportion	Cost (after tax)	Weighted cost
Loan finance	0.3	5%	1.5%
Shareholders' funds	0.7	15%	10.5%
Total	1.0		12.0%

Why calculate the cost of capital?

The cost of capital is usually an important figure to calculate because if it works out to be too high, the strategy it is intended to fund may not be viable. Given that both debt and share capital attract servicing costs, the profit returns must exceed these servicing costs to the extent that the proposal is economically attractive.

If the projected returns on a strategic development, such as a new factory facility, are little more than the projected servicing costs, then management will have to make a judgement as to whether the investment is actually worth the risk.

The whole situation is rendered more complex if debt capital is obtained at a variable rate of interest. Interest rates can vary substantially throughout an economic cycle and depend on such things as government inflation targets, the currency exchange value and the national rate of capital investment.

There are no guidelines as to the ideal capital structure – the balance between debt and equity finance. The optimal structure will vary from company to company, from industry to industry and from year to year. Some companies will calculate their WACC and include factors that are difficult to quantify, such as the degree of risk faced by the industry, trends in interest rates and even the cost and availability of funds to competitors.

6.3   Financial analysis and performance evaluation

We would usually employ an analysis of a company's financial situation as part of an internal strategic analysis. We may wish to understand a company's finances in order to make an assessment of its 'health' or its readiness to undertake a phase of strategic development.

There are three areas of financial analysis:

- longitudinal analysis, sometimes called trend analysis
- cross-sectional analysis, or comparison analysis
- ratio analysis.

A comprehensive analysis of a company's financial situation would normally involve an element of all three of these analyses. The one thing to bear in mind when looking at accounting statements is that they contain numbers in isolation. An accounting number on it own is just that – a number. In order to make any sense of it, we must compare it with other accounting numbers.

Longitudinal analysis

The simplest means of assessing any aspect of a company's finances is to compare the data for two or more years and see what has increased and what has decreased over that time period, and by how much. It goes without saying that the longer back in time we look, the better idea we will get as to its current position in its historical context. Many company corporate reports provide a 5- or 10-year record and this can help us in constructing a longitudinal analysis.

The easiest way to perform this analysis is to conduct an initial scan of the figures to identify any major changes between the years. This involves simply looking along each line in turn, and highlighting any larger than normal increases or decreases, for example a scan along five years of inventory figures from a balance sheet (indicated below) clearly indicates something happened in year 4. Not only did the figure more than double against year 3, it reverted to the 'normal' trend the following year:

Year	1	2	3	4	5
Inventory	300	330	370	800	450

Anomalies like these may need further investigation. Questions need to be asked or rather answers found to the reasons for such an increase. The impact of the 'blip' on the year's performance must be assessed as must its impact on current performance. Further investigation of the balance sheet or profit and loss account, together with any notes to the accounts, may provide some clues. It may be important to discover how such an increase was financed, why there was a need to carry such high levels of inventory and the impact of such levels on suppliers and customers.

The initial scan may need to be followed by a more detailed analysis, which calculates the year-on-year increase/decrease in percentage terms. It is sometimes helpful to plot trends on a graph against time. This can help to highlight changes at particular points in time.

The identification of trends, in terms of, say, turnover or costs of some items on a balance sheet (such as inventories), can be valuable in our financial analysis. Such trends should, however, be seen in their context. An organization operating in a static or slow growth market may judge a 1% year-on-year increase in turnover as a great success, whereas a company in a buoyant market would judge a 1% increase as a failure.

Cross-sectional analysis

While longitudinal analysis helps us to assess performance against a historical trend, it tells us nothing of the company's performance against that of competitors or companies in other industries. If, for example, in a longitudinal analysis of Company A's financial statements, we identified strong sales growth of 10% a year, we might be tempted to think that the company was performing well. If we then compared this company with one of its competitors and found that the industry average rate of growth was 15%, we would wish to modify our initial assessment of Company A's performance.

KEY CONCEPT

The audited **annual report and accounts** has five compulsory components, as set out in the UK in the Companies Act 1985 (as amended): chairman's statement, auditor's report, profit and loss (P&L) statement, balance sheet and cash flow statement. All limited companies are required to file these. The accounting rules by which they are to be constructed are prescribed in International Financial Reporting Standards to ensure that all companies mean the same thing when they make an entry in one of the financial statements. When they are completed, following the company's financial year end, they become publicly available. Each shareholder has the right to receive a copy, and a copy is lodged at UK Companies House in Cardiff or London (or Edinburgh if it is a Scottish company).

It is for the purposes of comparisons of this nature that cross-sectional analyses are important. As well as comparing accounting numbers like turnover, it is often helpful to compare two or more companies' ratios, such as return on sales or one of the working capital ratios.

Ratio analysis

The third important tool in the analysis of company performance is ratio analysis. A ratio is a comparison (by quotient) of two items from the same set of accounts. Given that there are a lot of numbers in a set of accounts, it will not come as a surprise to learn that a large number of ratios can be drawn – some of which are more useful than others.

Ratio analysis is an area of some academic debate and so the way in which ratios are expressed may vary between accounting and strategy textbooks. It is therefore important to employ a consistent approach to ratio analysis.

For most purposes, we can divide ratios into five broad categories:

1   Performance ratios
2   Efficiency ratios
3   Liquidity ratios
4   Investors' ratios
5   Financial structure ratios.

Performance ratios

Performance ratios test to see how well a company has turned its inputs into profits.

As their name suggests, **performance ratios** test to see how well a company has turned its inputs into profits. This usually involves comparing return (profit before interest and tax, PBIT) against either turnover or capital. This is because the rates of tax and interest payable vary. Using profit after interest and tax would distort the performance figure because it would include an element of cost beyond the company's direct control (the rate of tax and the interest rate).

Here are three examples:

- *Return on capital employed* (ROCE) is perhaps the most important and widely used measure of performance. It indicates the return being made compared to the funds invested. At its simplest, this figure tests the gains of investing in a business as opposed to simply placing capital on return in a bank. Where an organization can break down its figures by divisions or subsidiaries, individual performances can be measured and decisions relating to continued ownership made.
- *Return on equity* (ROE), or return on ordinary shareholders' funds, gives an indication of how effectively the share capital has been turned into profit (it does not take account of loan capital). This ratio should be used carefully as the capital structure of the company can affect the ratio.
- *Return on sales*, or profit margin, either net or gross, is a popular guide to the profitability of a company. This ratio assesses the profit made per pound sold. Return on sales tends to vary from industry to industry and between companies within an industry. Food retailers typically make between 5 and 12%, while companies in the pharmaceuticals sector rarely make less than 20%.

Example   Performance ratios

Each can be expressed as a percentage by multiplying the ratio by 100.

$$\text{Return on capital employed} = \frac{\text{profit before interest and tax (PBIT – from P\&L account)}}{\text{total capital employed (that is, one side of the balance sheet)}}$$

$$\text{Return on shareholders' funds} = \frac{\text{PBIT}}{\text{shareholders' funds (from balance sheet)}}$$

$$\text{Return on sales} = \frac{\text{PBIT}}{\text{total sales (also called turnover or revenue)}}$$

$$\text{Gross margin} = \frac{\text{gross profit}}{\text{total sales}}$$

Note: Gross profit is the profit after direct costs, that is, conversion costs, have been deducted from sales, but before indirect, that is, administrative, costs. Gross margin is an indication of how effectively a company has managed its direct wages, energy and inventories.

Efficiency ratios

Efficiency ratios show how efficiently a company has used its assets to generate sales. We can use any one of a number of a company's inputs to test against sales or profits. Common efficiency ratios include *sales per employee* and *profit per employee*, both of which test the efficiency with which a company uses its labour inputs.

Other commonly used efficiency ratios are *asset turnover* and a variant of this, *non-current (fixed) asset turnover*. A high level of asset turnover indicates that

Efficiency ratios show how efficiently a company has used its assets to generate sales.

the company is using its assets efficiently, while a low level may indicate that the company is suffering from overcapacity. Stock turnover gives an indication of how well the company controls its inventories. A company that keeps stock moving will have a higher stock turnover than one that has piles of unsaleable or obsolete materials. Stock residence time has a cost implication and so a low stock turnover indicates inefficient and costly stock management.

Example   Efficiency ratios

The term 'efficiency' is used in many ways – not just in accounting. We may speak of an efficient engine or the efficiency of a heating system in a house. Efficiency is a comparison of a system's output to its inputs, with a view to testing how well the input has been turned into output. It follows that a more efficient system will produce more output for a given input than a less efficient one.

Efficiency can be expressed mathematically as a quotient:

$$\text{Efficiency} = \left(\frac{\text{work output}}{\text{work input}}\right) \times 100 \text{ (to arrive at a percentage)}$$

These are some efficiency ratios:

$$\text{Sales per employee (£)} = \frac{\text{total sales (from P\&L)}}{\text{number of employees (usually found in the notes to the accounts)}}$$

$$\text{Profit per employee (£)} = \frac{\text{PBIT}}{\text{number of employees}}$$

$$\text{Stock turnover} = \frac{\text{cost of sales (from P\&L)}}{\text{value of stock (from balance sheet)}}$$

It is measured in times, that is, the number of times the total stock is turned over in a given year.

Liquidity ratios

Liquidity ratios test the company's ability to meet its short-term debts, an important thing to establish if there is reason to believe the company is in trouble. Essentially, they ask the question, 'has the company enough available funds to pay what it owes?' These are two liquidity ratios:

Liquidity ratios test the company's ability to meet its short-term debts.

- The *current ratio* is the best-known liquidity ratio. It is a measure of a company's total liabilities in comparison to its total assets and is thus calculated entirely from balance sheet figures. It is used to assess the company's ability to meet its liabilities by the use of its assets such as stock, receivables and cash.
- The *acid test ratio* is a variant of the current ratio and tests the company's ability to meet its short-term liabilities using its cash or 'near cash' assets. Many textbooks suggest a ratio of 2:1 should be a target for the current ratio and a target of 1:1 should be sought for the acid test ratio. These are simple guides and should not be taken as the norm for all industries. For example, many companies in the retail industry have few receivables, high stock turnover but still have payables as a result their current ratio being below 2:1.

Investors' ratios

This family of ratios tests for things that are important to a company's investors – usually its shareholders or potential shareholders. There are three that are widely used:

Earnings per share (EPS) is calculated by dividing profit after interest and tax (called earnings) by the number of shares.

The **price/earnings ratio** (P/E) is calculated by dividing the current market price of the company's ordinary shares by its EPS.

Dividend yield is calculated by dividing the dividend per share at the last year end by the current price.

- **Earnings per share** (EPS) is calculated by dividing profit after interest and tax (called earnings) by the number of shares. It shows how much profit is attributable to each share.
- **The price/earnings ratio** (P/E) is calculated by dividing the current market price of the company's ordinary shares by its EPS at the last year end; it follows therefore that the P/E varies with the share price. Broadly speaking, it is a way of showing how highly investors value the earnings a company produces. A high P/E ratio, where the price is high compared to the last declared EPS, usually indicates growth potential, while a low P/E suggests static profits. The P/E ratio for quoted companies is regularly published in the financial press.
- *Dividend yield* is the third widely used investors' ratio. Potential shareholders often want to know what the most recent return on the share was in terms of percentage. **Dividend yield** is calculated by dividing the dividend per share at the last year end by the current price, and then multiplying by 100 to arrive at a percentage.

2

Example   Investors' ratios

$$\text{EPS} = \frac{\text{earnings (that is, profit after interest and tax)}}{\text{share volume}}$$

$$\text{P/E} = \frac{\text{price of share (as of 'today')}}{\text{EPS at most recent year end}}$$

$$\text{Dividend yield} = \left(\frac{\text{gross dividend per share}}{\text{current price of share}}\right) \times 100$$

Financial structure ratios

We encountered financial structure above when we discussed the relative merits of loan and share capital. The way in which a company 'mixes' these forms of capital is referred to as its financial (or capital) structure. Two ratios are used:

- The *gearing ratio* looks at the relationship between all the borrowings of the company (including short-term borrowings), and all the capital employed by the company. This provides a view of the extent to which borrowing forms part of the total capital base of the company and hence the risk associated with rising interest rates.
- The *debt/equity ratio*, a variation on the gearing ratio, uses the shareholders' funds in the calculation rather than the total capital employed. This ratio provides a more direct comparison between the funds attributed to shareholders and liability of the company to loan providers.

Example   Financial structure ratios

$$\text{Gearing ratio} = \frac{\text{debt capital (typically borrowings due after one year)}}{\text{debt capital plus shareholders' funds}}$$

$$\text{Debt/equity ratio} = \frac{\text{debt capital (borrowings due after one year)}}{\text{shareholders' funds}}$$

Limitations of financial information

For most purposes in strategic analysis, we can accept the proposition that the data we collect from a company's annual accounts is accurate and provides a truthful statement of its financial position. From time to time, however, we may need to qualify our analysis for one or more reasons.

First, while the financial statements are audited for accuracy, other parts of the annual report are not. If our financial analysis consists of an examination of the entire document and not just the accounting sections, we would need to be aware of this. Additional disclosures made in corporate reports may serve a number of purposes. Some commentators have suggested that such disclosures may be something of a public relations and marketing exercise.

Second, we should remember that the financial information in a corporate report is historical, sometimes published months after the period they describe. While this historical information can be used to judge past performance, it may have limited use in predicting future performance. The balance sheet shows the financial position at 'a moment in time' (at the year end). Unlike the P&L account, it does not summarize a full year's trading and things can sometimes change quickly after the year end.

In an attempt to avoid this potential problem, stock exchange quoted companies are required to produce interim reports, normally half-yearly and unaudited, which show their profit and turnover for that period. Quoted companies are also required to provide the stock exchange with information that may have a significant impact on its prospects, such as changes on the board or anything that gives rise to a 'profits warning'.

Third, the financial accountants who prepare a company's financial statements sometimes have cause to 'hide' bad news so as to avoid alarming the company's investors. It is possible to employ legal financial restructuring so as to make some figures appear better than perhaps they are. A year-on-year increase in the value of non-current assets, for example, may appear at first glance to be healthy, but it may be that the company has accumulated a high amount of debt to finance it. It is for this reason that we sometimes need to examine all parts of a company's financial statements to spot any countervailing bad news that has been obscured by the company in its reporting.

6.4 Balanced scorecard as a performance measurement tool

It is important to recognize that, despite the importance of financial indicators to a business, financial success is only one way to measure a business. A number of non-financial indicators of success can also be examined when analysing a business. These are useful because they are predictors of future cash flows, perhaps in several years' time. The point is that it is short-termist to only measure current and historic financial health and a range of non-financial measures can help to predict future success or failure.

The idea of the balanced scorecard was introduced in the early 1990s by Kaplan and Norton (1992). The **balanced scorecard** is a management tool for managers to 'balance' the various indicators of success (or 'perspectives') for a given business. Four measures comprise the balanced scorecard:

The **balanced scorecard** is a management tool for managers to 'balance' the various indicators of success (or 'perspectives') for a given business.

- *Financial indicators:* financial results
- *Behaviour and loyalty of customers:* customers are an indication of how sustainable, in financial terms, a given financial performance is
- *Internal business processes:* these are vital because they indicate the 'health' of the business and its long-term viability
- *Learning and growth:* the ability of the business to learn and grow helps to measure the longer term prospects in terms of innovation, creativity and entrepreneurship.

The scorecard works by assigning a value or weighting (hence the 'balanced' part) to each area of the scorecard and then gathering the information needed to populate each one. It may be, for example, that the strategically important measure for one business is short-term business performance, perhaps to meet a particular measure imposed by a parent company or shareholder. In others, however, the growth of market share (a 'customer' measure) is seen as more important than short-term financial measures. In this case, the balance would weight the 'customer' measure more than the financial.

2

GURU GUIDE

Robert S. Kaplan is an eminent figure in the field of accounting and a prolific author who has published extensively in the fields of strategy and management accounting. He is the co-creator of the balanced scorecard system with David Norton. Born in New York in 1940, he graduated from MIT with an MS in electrical engineering and a PhD in operational research from Cornell University. He started his academic career as dean at the Tepper Business School at Carnegie Mellon University, Pittsburgh. He is presently the Baker Foundation Professor at Harvard Business School. He has received numerous accolades and awards for his research and contribution towards management accounting. In 2006, Kaplan was inducted into the Accounting Hall of Fame and in 2008, the Institute of Management Accountants selected him for a Lifetime Contribution Award for Distinguished Contributions to Advancing the Management Accounting Profession. The *Financial Times* included him in its 2005 list of Top 25 Business Thinkers. He currently serves on several corporate and non-profit boards including Acorn Systems and Evergreen Energy, and speaks globally on performance and cost management systems.

David Norton is a distinguished strategist and management guru. He is founder and director of Palladium Group, an international organization specializing in systems and processes to improve the execution of business strategy. He holds a doctorate in business administration from Harvard Business School, and with Robert Kaplan, Dr Norton has co-authored five books and has co-written several influential articles, including eight in the *Harvard Business Review*. In 2007, he was voted as one of the world's most influential management thinkers and in 2008 was honoured with the Champion of Workplace Learning and Performance Award by the American Society for Training and Development. The work on the balanced scorecard has had a significant impact on the way organizations measure their contributions to achieving market goals and, more recently, the environmental/green agendas. The approach broke the mould from the more inward-looking approaches to performance management to being more outward looking and measuring what 'matters'. Norton is alleged to have coined the phrase 'the balanced scorecard', after a round of golf with an IBM executive who mentioned to Norton that what he needed to measure his company's performance was a scorecard like the one used during a game of golf.

The balanced scorecard has been developed to enabled businesses to use each of the four areas as useful measures in themselves. It is assumed that success in all areas is as important as financial success, and this has given rise to 'management by KPIs' (key performance indicators). Each measurement area is broken down into a number of KPIs and these are then used to control activities within the business in a similar way that budgetary control has been used in the past.

6.5   Other analysis tools

While the majority of situations can be made sense of using the above 'tools', two others are sometimes useful and these are discussed here.

Financial benchmarking

Inter-company comparison or benchmarking is a variation on cross-sectional analysis. It usually involves an analysis of similar companies in the same industry but it can occasionally be an inter-industry analysis.

KEY CONCEPT

Benchmarking is a process where an organization compares elements of its business, processes or performance against the industry norms, best practice or 'best in class'. The metrics can include quality, time or cost. Benchmarking involves management identifying the best firms in their industry, or any other industry where similar processes exist, and mapping how well they perform against them.

In order to make the benchmarking analysis meaningful, the company selection should usually be guided by similarity by:

- company size, that is, they should be comparable in terms of turnover, market value or similar
- industry, in that the companies produce similar products
- market, that is, the companies share a similar customer base.

In practice, the sample selection for a benchmarking study always involves some compromise because no two companies are in all respects directly comparable. Many companies, for example, operate in more than one industry and this may render problematic any comparisons with another company that operates in only one industry.

The practice of inter-company (cross-sectional) analysis using financial data has been undertaken by accountants for many years. Benchmarking, however, can be used to compare financial and, importantly, non-financial information between two or more companies.

Benchmarking is now used to compare the effectiveness of various processes, products and procedures against others. The objective is to identify where superior performance is found in whatever variable is being used for comparison. Once the company with the highest performance is identified, the exercise is to explore the reasons behind the superior performance and learn from best practice.

The benchmarking process involves decisions on:

- what to benchmark (financial or non-financial data)?

- who to benchmark against (sample selection)?
- how to get the information?
- how to analyse the information?
- how to use the information?

The value of benchmarking is in identifying not only which company has the superior performance in a sector but also why this is the case. An analysis might, for example, show that Company X enjoys a return on sales significantly higher than the other companies in the sector. Company X thus occupies the profitability benchmark in the sector. The other companies may then wish to examine the practices within Company X that give rise to this level of performance.

For non-financial indicators, an analysis may highlight the fact that Company Y is able to attract the best qualified people within a key category of personnel, for example the best scientists or computer programmers. In this case, Company Y demonstrates the benchmark in successful recruitment. Other companies who are unable to attract the best personnel would then examine Company Y to see why it is so successful in this regard.

Common-size accounts

Common-size accounts are particularly useful in cross-sectional analyses but can also be used to analyse the same company's accounts from year to year. If we were, for example, to examine the P&L accounts or balance sheets of two companies in the same industry, at first we may be unable to make sense of differences between the two. We can sometimes make sense of the two separate accounts by making the totals of both equal 100 and then dividing each entry by the resultant quotient. A simplified example of common-size accounts is shown in Table 6.1.

Table 6.1 Simplified example of common-size accounts

| | Company A | | Company B | |
	£m	Common size	£m	Common size
Sales	113.4	100	224.6	100
Cost of sales	65	57.32	112	49.87
Gross profit	48.4	42.68	112.6	50.13
Administrative costs	33.7	29.72	67	29.83
Operating profit	14.7	12.96	45.6	20.3

We can make comparisons between the cost structures of the two companies despite the fact that Company B has approximately twice the turnover of Company A. We can tell, for example, that, overall, Company B is better at controlling costs that Company A, evidenced by the fact that its operating profit is 20.3 compared to Company A's figure of 12.96 (both common-sized). We could draw comparable conclusions from other common-size components of the accounts.

6.6 Audit and social audit

The audit of final 'year end' company accounts is a condition of being granted limited liability in law and is also an assurance to shareholders that the figures reported are a 'true and fair view' of the state of the company at the time of the report. The audit (sometimes called 'assurance' or 'verification') is conducted by qualified auditors (accountants qualified to conduct audits) and each annual report contains an audit report to the shareholders.

One of the major areas of growth in recent years has been the growth of social auditing. While a financial audit is the statutory (required by law) verification of a company's financial performance, a social audit measures the company's social performance. Unlike a financial audit, social audits are not required in law (are voluntary) and there is no agreed standard against which to conduct the audit.

As with the concept of the balanced scorecard, which implicitly supports the notion that business success cannot be reduced to financial numbers, many believe that it is important to measure the social (and environmental) impact of a business. The importance of stakeholders and the ethical assumptions underpinning social audits are discussed in Chapter 20.

Essentially a means of measuring the impact on a range of stakeholders, a social and environmental audit measures and records performance against a predetermined set of metrics. Importantly, the audit process means that an external independent body provides a report on how well the business has done against those measures. The independent audit, as with a financial audit, provides a much more robust reassurance of actual performance against target. Once the audit has been conducted, companies may then choose to voluntarily report on social and environmental impact in an external report.

One of the notable developments in recent years has been the emergence of audit and reporting standards for social and environmental information. Because there is no statutory 'list' of items that should be included, a number of organizations have attempted to develop frameworks that companies can use. These tend to be relatively ambitious in nature, mainly because of the personal agendas of those devising the frameworks.

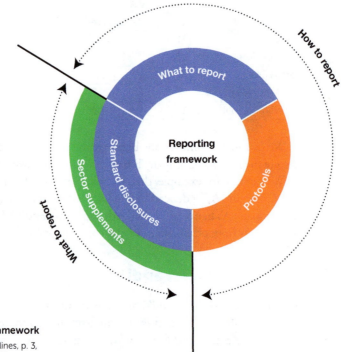

Figure 6.1 GRI reporting framework

Source: GRI G3 Reporting Guidelines, p. 3,
© Global Reporting Initiative, 2006

CASE STUDY   Hamilton Cars and World Motor Corp. Inc.

For several years, it had seemed inevitable that there would be a merger of some sort between Hamilton Cars, the exclusive, top brand sports car company, and World Motor Corp. Inc. (WMC), one of the largest mass manufacturers of cars, trucks and vans in the world. Both are public companies; however, the founding families (the Hamilton family at Hamilton and the Coor family at WMC) still retain seats on the boards of their respective companies, and while neither has a controlling interest, the Coors at WMC still carry great influence.

Hamilton makes its cars at two factories in Germany; and while the technology is adequate, the company sets great store by the expertise of the craft staff, and the individual hand-made content in each of their cars. WMC has factories in 13 countries on every continent of the world, each of which is fully equipped with state-of-the-art, mass production technology.

The original proposal, five years ago, was for Hamilton to take over WMC, although on the face of it, Hamilton was (and remains) a much smaller company. However, because of its perceived brand value, there seemed to be no problem in raising private finance and other equity to complete a takeover. WMC resisted this, and the proposal was dropped. Two years later, the position reversed. Now, WMC went to Hamilton to try and take it over. This was a much more assured bid and was not dependent on private finance, but could be resourced from shareholders' funds (for key data, see table).

Hamilton resisted. But, with the downturn in all car markets, in practice both parties started to find it difficult to manage on their own, and both were looking for additional sources of funds and organizational strength. Both had had to raise substantial loan capital over the past year, and there was now a feeling that they would be better off together than apart. More accurately, Hamilton found that it needed the backing of a much larger company rather than relying on the vagaries of the private capital market; and WMC wanted a premium brand to go with its otherwise mass-market offerings.

So lawyers, accountants and consultants were engaged and a full review of the state and status of both companies and their marques and brands was carried out, which included due diligence and full capital, revenue and market audits. The legal, financial, audit and evaluation teams all duly reported back to the boards of both companies. The findings were wholly favourable; and a strategy for the merger was drawn up.

This strategy took full account of new product development for the future, and it was here that the greatest synergies and economies of scale were envisaged. WMC expected to benefit from the design expertise in the luxury market to gain a leading edge in producing and presenting the next wave of models to the mass motor vehicle markets. Hamilton expected to be able to take advantage of the mass-market production technology to reduce its very high unit production costs, and to improve its output per member of staff statistics. There was an early agreement to share distribution outlets, customer and client lists, and sales networks.

To maximize the return on the merger, design and manufacturing premises and locations would be streamlined. In particular, Hamilton's specialist factories would be closed within three years, and additional capacity would be generated at WMC's state-of-the-art manufacturing facilities in China and Poland, so as to be able to produce the Hamilton range of cars more cost-effectively, and with a much greater precision than at present.

The intangibles were harder to pin down. Hamilton staff worked shorter hours for more pay than WMC, although they received fewer holidays (six weeks at WMC, four weeks at Hamilton). There was a pension scheme at WMC and none at Hamilton. There were lifetime employment guarantees and a no-strike deal at Hamilton, while WMC had a very traditional approach

Key data	WMC		Hamilton	
	Last year	This year	Last year	This year
Capital $ billion	38	44	0.9	1.1
Percentage loan capital	15	40	30	55
Turnover $ billion	130	133	3.9	3.7
Profit $ billion	19	11	0.8	0.7
Staff numbers (000)	130	134	6,000	6,000
	WMC		Hamilton	
Cost per car (manufacturing) $	800		6,500	
Output (cars) per member of staff	93		30	

to employee relations, relying heavily on formal processes, works councils, consultation and negotiating bodies across all the company's sites. However, there seemed to be no point in making a big issue out of these things – the families would come to terms with the new status quo, and the new organization set itself five years to generate a common corporate culture and unified terms and conditions of employment.

There was, however, some debate over the continuing role of the founding families in the future merged company. The Coors in particular wanted to continue to exert influence over policy and direction for the future. Now in its fourth generation in the motor industry, the Coors regarded themselves as a dynasty. They expected to maintain this position for many generations to come, and had already promised their three daughters and two sons that they could

always work for the family firm. They were not ready to share this influence with a family they regarded as being at the dilettante part of the industry. For their part, the Hamiltons were used to independence. They also wanted their son to lead the firm and so they too appeared to be struggling to come to terms with the new organizational structure, culture and intended ways of working.

Case study questions

1 What are the main drivers, pressures and restraints in this case?
2 Where are the strengths of the new company expected to lie?
3 Which areas need further examination, in order for this venture to stand any chance of lasting success?

With the United Nations Environment Programme as its partner, the Global Reporting Initiative (GRI) is the steward of the most widely used reporting framework for performance on human rights, labour, environmental, anti-corruption and other corporate citizenship issues. The GRI framework (Figure 6.1) is the most widely used standardized sustainability reporting framework in the world. It sets out to achieve these goals by offering a framework of disclosure items that can be measured, audited and then reported on. This, it is argued, provides a more complete picture of an organization's performance than mere financial performance (see www.globalreporting.org).

This is a helpful chapter to refer to when completing 1.2.2 Value Chain within the Internal Analysis section in Phase 1 of the **Strategic Planning Software** (www.planning-strategy.com). For more information on the value chain, also see Chapter 13.

For test questions, extra case studies, audio case studies, weblinks, videolinks and more to help you understand the topics covered in this chapter, visit our companion website at www.macmillanihe.com/companion/business/campbell.

VOCAB CHECKLIST FOR ESL STUDENTS

Anomalies	Inventory	Quantifiable
'Blip'	Liquidity	Quotient
'Buy-back'	Longitudinal	Ratio
Countervailing	Obsolete	Receivables
Cross-sectional	Offsetting	Underwriters, underwriting
Dividends	Payables	
Flotation	Pro rata	

Definitions for these terms can be found in the 'Vocab Zone' of the companion website, which provides free access to the Macmillan English Dictionary online at www.macmillanihe.com/companion/business/campbell.

1   Explain what we mean by a financial analysis.
2   Explain the limitations of a company report when used for financial analysis.
3   Evaluate the alternative options for funding a company's developments based on current position, future prospects and past performance.
4   Describe the main tools used to analyse a company's financial position.

DISCUSSION TOPIC

Organic growth through company cash reserves is the best form of funding growth. Discuss.

2

HOT TOPICS – Research project areas to investigate

If you have a project to do, why not investigate ...

- ... the approaches to social auditing adopted by knowledge-intensive firms.
- ... how carbon trading may influence the approach to financial practices of organizations of the future.
- ... perceptions of managers as to the most appropriate financial ratios for not-for-profit organizations.

Recommended reading

Allen, D. (1997) *An Introduction to Strategic Financial Management*, London: CIMA/Kogan Page.

Camp, R.C. (1994) *Business Process Benchmarking*, Milwaukee, WI: ASQC Quality Press.

Department of Trade and Industry (1992) *Best Practice Benchmarking*, London: DTI.

Ellis, J. and Williams, D. (1993) *Corporate Strategy and Financial Analysis*, London: Pitman.

Franks, J.R. and Broyles, J.E. (1979) *Modern Managerial Finance*, Chichester: John Wiley.

Higson, C. (1995) *Business Finance*, Oxford: Butterworth-Heinemann.

Mott, G. (1991) *Management Accounting for Decision Makers*, London: Pitman.

Chapter reference

Kaplan, R.S. and Norton, D.P. (1992) 'The balanced scorecard: measures that drive performance', *Harvard Business Review*, **70**(1): 71–9.

Chapter 7

Information systems and technology

Kevin Grant[1]

Introduction and chapter overview

Business professionals play a key role in planning, organizing, leading and controlling organizational resources for the achievement of organizational goals and objectives. In today's turbulent and uncertain world, modern mangers from private, public and voluntary sectors have to deal with more diverse and far-reaching challenges than ever before. Managers need to keep pace with ever advancing technologies and incorporate the most appropriate and relevant of these into their strategies and business models, while continually seeking enterprising and innovative solutions to achieve and sustain a competitive advantage.

Information systems are having a dramatic impact on organizations and the way business is conducted. This chapter seeks to explore the area of information systems from a strategic and business, rather than a technical, perspective.

Learning objectives

After studying this chapter, you should be able to:

- distinguish between data and information and explain how the information age presents new challenges to managers
- explain what attributes make information useful to managers
- classify the types of information systems that now exist
- introduce and discuss the nature of strategic information systems and demonstrate how they can add value to the business
- appreciate how to infuse the technical infrastructure with the strategic intent and aspirations of the business via IT/IS alignment

7.1 Why managers need to embrace information systems

Contemporary managers need to be able to recognize and exploit the benefits of technology. Information systems-based technology has grown to become an essential area of study over the past 30 years, and an integral part of everyday

1 Caledonian Business School, Glasgow Caledonian University. Email Kevin.Grant@gcu.ac.uk

Google™

work and personal life. Organizations have become inextricably intertwined with information, systems, information technology (IT) and information systems (IS). Every business function uses information systems across every business sector. Technology is no longer exclusively the domain of the IT department – just think of systems like YouTube, Twitter, Facebook, Google Docs and Google Groups.

IT/IS has been evolving since the 1950s. Historically, the discipline has been a vocational and applied area of study and practice, formed from the 'nexus of computer science, management and organization theory, operations research and accounting' (Davis and Olson, 1985, p. 13).

Information systems
are the systems that deliver information and communication services, and the organizational function that plans, develops and manages the information systems.

For modern organizations, the term **information systems** refers to the systems that deliver information and communication services, and the organizational function that plans, develops and manages the information systems. The UK Academy of Information Systems (UKAIS, 2010) defines information systems as 'the means by which people and organisations, utilising technologies, gather, process, store, use, and disseminate information'. The domain of study 'involves the study of theories and practices related to the social and technological phenomena, which determine the development, use and effects of information systems in organisations and society' (UKAIS, 2010).

2

Information systems comprise the following generic categories:

1 Theoretical underpinnings of information systems
2 Data, information and knowledge management
3 Information in organisational decision making
4 Integration of information systems with organisational strategy and development
5 Information systems design
6 Development, implementation and maintenance of information systems
7 Information and communication technologies (ICT)
8 Management of information systems and services
9 Organisational and social effects of ICT-based information systems
10 Economic effects of ICT-based information systems (UKAIS, 2010).

As IS/IM is a relatively new field of enquiry in practice, there are a number of conflicting schools of thought. There are those who emphasize the technological (IT) component of an information system – the hardware and software and the design methods used to bring the technology into production. This group overall consider themselves as scientists and technologists and adopt the methods of the sciences. A second group regards an information system as a social system, which focuses on using technology; this group includes those using science as the foundation and those who look to the humanities as their basis. A third group stresses the systemic nature of an information system and derives both analysis and design from systems theory and soft systems (Checkland, 1981).

Given the former, information management (IM) represents the management and strategic use and alignment of information systems as a corporate resource. However, the difference between information systems and information management is often semantic, rather than fundamental. Such a distinction is necessary for a meaningful discussion and helps in clarifying many of the important issues regarding alignment of business and information strategies. The differentiation between IS and IT is essential when developing IS/IT strategies, since the technology structure is never enough to ensure the successful alignment of IS/IT and business strategies. The definitions used for IS and IT stem from Ward and Peppard (2003):

1 *Information systems* (IS) refer to how information is gathered, processed, stored, used and disseminated by the organization. The IS strategy defines the organization's requirement for information and systems to support the overall strategy of the business

2 **Information technology** (IT) refers to hardware, software and telecommunications networks technology. The IT strategy is concerned with how the organization's demand for information and systems will be supported by technology.

Information technology (IT) refers to hardware, software and telecommunications networks technology.

To help to unpack these complex areas, the area of horse racing will be initially used to illustrate the differences. IT can be viewed as the horse, as it is the 'kit' that runs around the racecourse until it is told to stop. It is also given direction and is controlled by another system. This system is IS. In our example, IS is represented by the jockey. The jockey, using the IT 'horse', plans to run the race in a particular way, using the reins and the stirrups to communicate with the horse when it needs to go faster, slow down and so on. In this analogy, IM (information management) is the owner and trainer of the horse, who develops a business plan, determining when to run the horse, in which race, and using which jockey. Business tactics are used to determine what 'odds' or business value can be secured from the knowledge of what the horse can do, what the jockey can do, and who else is running in the race, 'the competitors', and other external conditions such as the track and the weather conditions.

GURU GUIDE

Peter Checkland was born in 1930 in Birmingham, England. He graduated with an MA in chemistry from St John's College, Oxford and joined ICI in 1955. After 15 years as a manager in the synthetic fibre industry, he joined the department of systems engineering at Lancaster University and led a team in developing solutions to problem situations faced by managers. He is an emeritus professor of systems at Lancaster University Management School and is the developer of the soft systems methodology. He is a distinguished figure in systems thinking and is a foremost proponent of action research.

Professor Checkland has honorary doctoral degrees from the Open University, the Czech University of Economics, City University and Erasmus University in the Netherlands. He was awarded the Beale Medal by the Operational Research Society in recognition for his outstanding contribution to operational research, and the Gold Medal of the UK Systems Society. He was also awarded a special award by USA's Systems Engineering Honor Society and the Pioneer Award by the International Council on Systems Engineering.

Modern professional business managers need to take responsibility for effectively deploying technology to add value, and exploit strategic opportunities as part of their day-to-day activities. Managers should have awareness and insight into the different technologies available, how technology could be best integrated into their spheres of influence and take responsibility to bring about meaningful transformational change. They need to keep abreast of current technologies such as enterprise resource planning (ERP) systems, emerging technologies such as radio frequency identification (RFID) tags and Web 2.0/3.0, and computer-supported business practices such as customer relationship management (CRM), e-supply chains, IT service management, vendor management and information innovation.

Historically, the use and perception of strategic information management was connected with IT and IS as tools to help managers to become more efficient, enhance communication and improve decision-making. As the technology matured and enterprises developed knowledge of managing technology and information, the focus shifted from day-to-day activities to a long-term strategic view. This trend was connected with adopting technologies and information to redesign existing ways of working to ensure consistency, uniformity and direction. As a greater understanding of the enterprise developed, managers were able to recognize that new ways of working are possible.

However, it is worth noting that technology and systems are essentially business tools. As such, the IT and IS dimensions of an enterprise tend to reflect underlying strategic developments and priorities. This is seen in two core areas, the drive for efficiency, and the need to differentiate for effectiveness. The early use of IT and IS was geared towards streamlining organizations, managing scale economies, coping with globalization, global communications and making processes more efficient. More recent trends have emerged around knowledge management, intellectual capital management, customer relationship management, innovation, social networking, bringing about change and business transformation and managing complex adaptive systems that concentrate on local interactions rather than grand, enterprise-wide systems. All these approaches are designed to gain competitive advantage and provide value-adding or service improvements by the adoption and implementation of systems and technology. In this respect, developments in IT and IS exploitation can be seen to be aligning, driving and sustaining the critical business strategy of the enterprise.

7.2   What is IT?

IT is, without doubt, transforming the nature of business. Wysocki and Young (1991) provide these examples of companies that have developed strategic information systems and achieved a competitive advantage:

- American Hospital Supply (AHS): connects customers with corporate computers at AHS, giving customer control over supply and reorder of medical supplies and the ability to maximize stock levels and reduce working capital tied up in stock.
- American Airlines: SABRE (semi automated business research environment) leads the market in airline reservation systems and creates a powerful barrier to entry into the airline business, which links and locks travel agents to and with particular airline operators.
- Otis Elevator: uses computer systems for corporate elevators to diagnose faults, allowing more efficient engineer callouts and better/faster repairs and the ability to 'sell' to the customer a 365, 24 hours a day elevator service.

IT is changing the way a business reacts, thinks about and develops its products, services, processes, management, staff and industry.

IT is the collective name for all the technologies that acquire, transmit, process, disseminate, store (if necessary) data and information. There are hundreds and thousands of examples of information technologies, which affect our lives every day. Some examples are the telephone, personal computer, photocopier, networks, database, calculator, ATMs, barcodes, RFID tagging, PDAs, mobile phones, smartphones, smart dust, digital tattoos, and decision support systems.

One thing that is often misunderstood is the difference between data and information. Data is facts, numbers in their recorded but unprocessed state. Data is continually created by all business activities. Some of this data will be collected where it is seen as being of some potential use to someone, but it is not information until it has been processed into an acceptable form and used by someone. Information is data that has been processed to make it meaningful to the person who receives it. Let us use an example. Take the number 37. To me, standing in a supermarket, it is a just a number, a piece of data. Change the context to a doctor in their surgery, and it is the body's natural temperature. If that number was 39, however, to the doctor it means something is wrong and the patient needs to be taken to hospital immediately, but it is still only 39 to me in the supermarket doing my shopping.

Having received the data, we then need to communicate it to another person. Effective communication is usually viewed as being the right person(s) receiving the right data via the right channel at the right time. Information should be specific, accurate and relevant, detailing only the information necessary for the person, in a usable format, which is appropriate and relevant to their purpose(s). The final attribute is that of completeness, as complete data can help to give confidence in the usage and exploitation of information to support decision-making, improve communication and to provide a sustainable competitive advantage.

What do information systems do? In simple terms, they convert 'raw' data into information. In this respect, data (or 'facts') is the raw material (input) for an information system, which is processed (or transformed) into 'information' – the output of the system. The processing of data into information can be via a number of techniques (Davenport and Prusak, 2000) such as:

1 *Contextualization:* by examining why the data was collected and for whom
2 *Categorization:* by units of analysis, such as product, process, application or shop
3 *Calculation:* by analysis using mathematical or statistical techniques or judgement
4 *Correction:* by removing errors from the data, via feedback and control mechanisms
5 *Condensing:* by summarizing or condensing the data for another more senior person or function within the organization.

So information systems can be formal or informal, computer based or not.

7.3   Taxonomy for information systems

Ward and Peppard (2003) identify three different eras in the evolution of the role of information systems and technology in organizations:

(Sidebar)

Data is facts, numbers in their recorded but unprocessed state.

Information is data that has been processed to make it meaningful to the person who receives it.

- Data processing (DP) – from the 1960s onwards
- Management information systems (MIS) – from the 1970s onwards
- Strategic information systems (SIS) – from the 1980s onwards.

The three eras overlap as they mature. Some organizations are still at the MIS stage, while others have entered and maximized their 'value adding' in the SIS era. IS can add value if the organization is mature enough to handle the effective strategic alignment of technologies to their business strategy. However, SIS are different and are often misunderstood in relation to this taxonomy.

The typical classes of information systems are as follows (Oz, 2004; Stair and Reynolds, 2010):

Transaction processing systems (TPS) are the building blocks for a company's information management policy.

- **Transaction processing systems** (TPS) are the foundation stones on which all other organizational systems are based. They are the building blocks for a company's information management policy. These include sales orders, hotel reservations, payroll or record keeping. TPS tend to concentrate on data capture of routine tasks, and are designed to handle high volumes of data, operating 24/7/365.

Management information systems (MIS) are integrated information systems that connect different levels of management for the sharing of information.

- **Management information systems** (MIS) support management across all levels of the organization. A MIS is an integrated information system that connects different levels of management for the sharing of information. A MIS is:

  > a system to convert data from internal and external sources into information and to communicate that information, in an appropriate form, to managers at all levels and all functions to enable them to make timely and effective decisions for planning, directing and controlling the activities for which they are responsible (Lucey, 2004)

  At the heart of the MIS is the processing of data into useful information.

Decision support systems (DSS) support middle and senior managers, and focus on facilitating decision-making.

- **Decision support systems** (DSS) support middle and senior managers, and focus on facilitating decision-making. DSS have been used to assist humans to make decisions (structured, semi-structured and unstructured) about courses of action in particular problem areas. They are 'open packages', as there are no predetermined solutions and human judgement has to be used in the design, creation and interpretation of the results. DSS provide extensive databases and analytical tools such as spreadsheets, project planning systems, executive support and expert systems, such as online insurance rating systems.

Group decision support systems (GDSS) support the decision-making activities of groups.

- **Group decision support systems** (GDSS) support the decision-making activities of groups. There are, potentially, considerable cost savings to be made by using GDSS-related technologies such as video-conferencing, or the use of Web 2.0 technologies.

Geographic information systems (GIS) are IS that have a 'map' as a key component.

- **Geographic information systems** (GIS) are IS that have a 'map' as a key component. Taxis often use GIS on board to help the driver plan their route:

  > GIS rests on the assumption that different kinds of spatial data have common structure, and are processed in similar ways, and that there is consequently value in creating common spatial data handling and processing systems. (Goodchild, 1995, p. 54)

  Modern GIS present an opportunity 'to solve business problems by providing a capability to process the high proportion of business data that is geographic data' (Grimshaw, 2000, p. 1), as probably 90% of business data is spatial. GIS are good for providing structure and to identify patterns in data.

7.4   Strategic information systems

In their simplest form, SIS include any information system that can change, support and inform the strategic goals and objectives of a business, or can influence its ability to manipulate the environmental relationships it has, for example, with customers or suppliers.

SIS are playing an increasingly significant role in the future direction of organizations and their organizational strategies. Recent years have seen a range of innovative applications, such as RFID, e-CRM, business-to-business (B2B), business-to-customer (B2C) and, most notably, the internet, the World Wide Web and social networking technologies, such as Facebook, YouTube and Twitter. These have led to a change in the nature of many businesses and a shift in consumer expectations and engagements.

Porter (2001) regards the internet as a powerful tool that can provide opportunities for enhancing the competitive position of organizations, although some, such as Tapscott (2003) and Evans and Wurster (2000), disagree, claiming that modern technologies are not an extension of what and how the business can operate, but that they transform the nature of the business. However, the more widely held view is that technologies are enablers to existing thinking, processes and services. Building barriers against new entrants, changing the basis for competition, changing the balance of power in supplier relationships, tying in new customers, raising switching costs, and creating new products and services can all arise from the use of technology (Galliers and Somogyi, 1987).

Strategic information systems can help organizations today in a variety of ways (Table 7.1).

GURU GUIDE

Robert D. (Bob) Galliers graduated with a PhD in 1987 from London School of Economics and Political Sciences (LSE). Professor Galliers was the research director in the Department of Information Systems at LSE, and the dean of Warwick Business School in the UK. He is now the University Distinguished Professor at Bentley University, USA, having served as provost for the period 2002–09. He is well known for his contribution to the study of information systems.

Professor Galliers is an eminent leader in the field of management information systems and has written a number of books and many articles related to information management strategy, strategic information management, and IT-related organizational transformation and innovation. He has been editor-in-chief of the *Journal of Strategic Information Systems* since its inception in 1991.

He is currently a visiting professor at the Australian School of Business, University of New South Wales, Brunel University, LSE, King's College, London, and the University of the Witwatersrand, South Africa. He has also held various consulting positions, and in 1995, was honoured by Turku School of Economics and Business Administration, Finland with an honorary doctorate. He is a fellow of the British Computer Society, the Association of Information Systems and the Royal Society of Arts.

Table 7.1 Potential applications of strategic information systems

Application	Description of application
(A) *Innovative applications*	Create innovative applications that provide direct strategic advantage to organizations
(B) *Competitive weapons*	Information systems themselves are recognized as a competitive weapon
(C) *Changes in processes*	IT supports changes in business processes that translate to strategic advantage
(D) *Links with business partners*	IT links a company with its business partners effectively and efficiently
(E) *Cost reductions*	IT enables companies to reduce costs
(F) *Relationships with suppliers and customers*	IT can be used to lock in suppliers and customers, or to build in switching costs
(G) *New products*	A firm can leverage its investment in IT to create new products that are in demand in the marketplace
(H) *Competitive intelligence*	IT provides competitive (business) intelligence by collecting and analysing information about products, markets, competitors, customers and environmental changes

Source: Adapted from Turban et al., 2004

2

To help illustrate the eight points outlined in Table 7.1, an example is given below. It shows what IT/IS can do for an organization and why organizations need to think and manage information, systems and information systems from a strategic perspective.

Example   Online publishing

Let's assume that Kevin and David, authors of *The Tractor and the Farm* series of books, decide that they want to use the internet to help make additional money, as they don't like giving a percentage of each book sold to the publisher, the printer, the book distribution company and the bookshop, the current way authors develop books and get them to the marketplace. Let us also assume that their latest book, *The Big Red Tractor in Farmer Smith's Farm*, retails for £11.50 in bookshops. This cost is made up of the following elements:

1   Bookshops (to cover costs and make a profit) – £3.50 per book
2   Book distribution company (to cover costs and make a profit) – £2.50 per book
3   The printer (to cover costs and make a profit) – £2.50 per book
4   The publisher (to cover costs and make a profit) – £2.00 per book
5   The authors – £1 per book.

The authors are only making 50 pence each per book, with the rest of the supply chain making their living from their work.

After studying SIS, Kevin and David think they can use the internet and websites to sell books differently from what has gone before. This an innovative application of the technology – doing something different that the technology is able and capable of doing. Readers and authors enter a common relationship supported by the technology, which in this case is the World Wide Web (A in Table 7.1). Kevin and David realize that this innovative idea changes the way people buy books and how authors can get their books to the marketplace (C in Table 7.1). Kevin and David set up a website for people interested in tractors

and farms and storytelling. They quickly develop an interactive, dynamic and socially oriented website, which records who visits the website, for how long and what sort of things they look at, known as 'customer intelligence' (H in Table 7.1). As more and more people visit the website, Kevin and David think: How do we build a relationship with these people, in order to sell books? They realize that it is not the technology that is the key, but the interaction and relationship between them and the people who want to read their books (F in Table 7.1).

They get to work, writing two chapters of the next book. But instead of writing the rest of the chapters and trying to convince a publisher to publish their book, they contact, via email, all the people who have visited the website, via their cookies (electronic footprints, mainly their email, which are left when someone visits a website), and attach the first two chapters of the latest adventure of the big red tractor. Interestingly, many of the people they emailed printed out the two chapters. This saved Kevin and David money, as the readers printed out the work on their own printers using their own paper and toner (E in Table 7.1), so the only cost they had occurred was the time to develop the story and the time and money to design and maintain the website. In the email, they also asked if people would email them with comments and views about the two chapters, that is, how the story could be developed, what they would like to see happening to the characters and so on. This is an example of building a relationship with customers (F in Table 7.1) and creating a new product (G in Table 7.1) in the marketplace.

Remember, these readers are keen followers of tractors, who can afford home computers and printers, so they have high disposal incomes to spend on their hobbies. Not all responded but many did, providing lots of feedback direct to Kevin and David (C in Table 7.1) as to how the story and the characters could be developed and so on. So now, Kevin and David have a new email list of people who are very interested in tractor books (H in Table 7.1) as well as many ideas to develop subsequent chapters and finish the book.

This time they write the remaining chapters of the story, using many of the ideas provided to them by the community of practice who provided feedback. But this time, they develop a secure site that can only be accessed by a password, which is needed to access and download the remaining chapters (A and B in Table 7.1), once a fee has been paid using a credit card. They email the second list, the people who responded regarding the first two chapters. The email starts by saying that they had taken on board many of the ideas and that the remaining twelve chapters, which can be accessed via the web for a small subscription fee, incorporate many of the developmental ideas provided to them by the community of practice. Once the fee is paid by credit card, an email is sent to them, which allows access to the new chapters. Kevin and David know that they cannot charge too much for the remaining chapters, as book publishing is a highly competitive market. They decide to sell the book for £4.50, as a way of securing demand and sales. They anticipate a good response from people wanting a password, as they know they would be interested to see if any of their original ideas and suggestions had been incorporated in the story and the remaining chapters (F and G in Table 7.1).

Having sent the email, they are inundated with requests for passwords and people paying the £4.50, which, given the fact that they are saving £7, they feel is great value. Remember, they receive PDF files and print the chapters out themselves, so Kevin and David do not incur any printing and reproduction costs. As you would expect in this new relationship (A and B in Table 7.1), Kevin and David are also very happy, as before they used to only get £1 per book, now they receive £4.50, which is a return of over 400%. The people who lose out are intermediaries, who, given the technology and the customer interaction and relationship, are no longer needed as much as they once were, as they failed to deliver added value to the needs of the authors and the readers of the books.

Then they have another great idea, maybe their readers would be interested in buying a model of the big red tractor so they email Click It All Together (the model makers) and suggest that they pay them a fee, and they can put a link on their secure, password-only accessible website to buy a model kit of the big red tractor; an example of A and D in Table 7.1.

Kevin receives an email from his friend Bob in the USA, who asks if he can have a copy of the chapters, so that he can read them. Kevin and David then realize they can sell the book to the Americans the same way they had sold it in the UK, without physically having to go to America, and they realize the cycle starts all over again, subject to regional legal, technological and cultural variations.

Kevin and David are now talking about setting up a blog for their legions of fans and a Google Group page to create a community of practice of red tractor fans to share and swap ideas, thoughts and experiences, which Kevin and David hope to capitalize on again to inform their planned new book.

Now we can see how information systems, in this case the internet, can be used as a strategic tool or weapon. The example also highlights that you need to have a decent selling proposition that is valued by the consumer, and a solid business plan, model and clear revenue streams (something many of the casualties of the dot-com crash did not ensure). The technology and IS can then facilitate processes and enhance operations.

Once an organization achieves a competitive advantage from an innovative application of relevant and appropriate technologies, keeping it can be difficult. This is because the technology is often available to all and can therefore be used by a new business in the same way – second mover. If they do it correctly and better, they too will gain a competitive advantage, and the cycle will continue. Therefore, the technology is not a barrier to entry, unless it is patented or protected in some form.

From the example above, it can be seen that organizations can build relationships with clients and develop strategic networks that allow for external as well as internal efficiencies and effectiveness, in essence, using technology to improve and support the demand side (internet) and supply side (supply chain) of the operation. Two key areas that lend themselves to the pursuit of competitive advantage through efficiency and effectiveness are how IS are used as part of the internet revolution (see Chapter 18) and how the organization develops IS throughout its supply (or value) chain, in its business processes.

The strategic use and management of information, systems and information systems has never been so popular and much needed by businesses, the public sector, small and medium-sized enterprises and social enterprise organizations. All operate within a dynamic and complex business context and an environment that changes rapidly, requires more agility, must be cost-effective and responsive to the needs of the consumer, the marketplace and the economic and political environment.

Table 7.2 charts the impact technology has had, thus far, on business and society.

Table 7.2 **The change in business**

Before the strategic era of IT/IS	After the strategic era of IT/IS
Geographic concept	Business concept
Concerned about functionality	Processes and adding value
Mechanistic	Holistic
Functional activity	Cross-functional activity
Managers – controllers	Managers – connectors
Vertical communication – key	Communication to and from all levels

Source: Adapted from Daniels and Daniels, 1993

One thing that is emerging is the utilization of technology to bring about innovation within business. Innovation can be incremental or radical in nature, it can be across products (OECD/Eurostat, 2005), processes (Edquist, 1997), position (Pedersen and Dalum, 2004), users (von Hippel, 1988, 2005), social networks (Rogers, 1983), environments (Tushman, 1997) or even paradigms (Popadiuk and Choo, 2006), and it is based on concepts or sources of discontinuity, such as new markets, new technologies, new rules, new business models or unthinkable events.

Product innovation
represents the development
of new technologies and
products as well as new
uses for existing products.

Process innovation reflects
an attempt to re-engineer
or design the flow of activity
in the organization.

What is clear is the need to distinguishing between product innovation and process innovation. **Product innovation** represents the development of new technologies and products as well as new uses for existing products, while **process innovation** reflects more of an attempt to re-engineer or design the flow of activity in the organization. However, each have an IT/IS and technological dimension to them.

So innovation includes product, process and service development at its core. It tends to be about examining the way things are currently done with a view to finding new and better ways of doing them. It can be applied to any element of the business, throughout the value chain and does not have to be original or groundbreaking in nature, just 'new' in relative terms to the context. So, innovation can simply be the extension, modification or combination of existing ideas in a way that improves existing functions or creates opportunities for the organization.

Table 7.3 provides some ideas as to how technology (IT/IS) can support and enable innovation.

Table 7.3 Technology enabling innovation

Innovation type/ category	Example of technology/IT/IS
Product	New Apple iPod or Blackberry, an example of technologies converging, or the developing market of domestic robots
Process	Use of robots in the car and manufacturing industry, manufacturing resource planning (MRP II) systems, B2B, B2C
Organizational	New division, business unit, team, for example call centre, customer support, voice over internet protocol, or the unit that manages service-level agreements for outsourced IT functions, such as the purchase, maintenance and cleaning of computer hardware
Management	New management systems/philosophy, for example total quality management/business process re-engineering, ERP systems, enterprise-wide systems
Commercialization	New approach to marketing/selling, for example internet selling, digital cash or subscription-based websites of communities of practice
Service	New type of service-related business, for example online insurance, social networking, community of practice, blogs, RSS (rich site summary or really simple syndication) feeds or podcasts

S-curves

To help forecast what technologies are emerging, 'S' curves (or growth curves) are used. If an 'S' curve was to be drawn today for emerging technologies that could influence the strategic potential of an organization, the following technologies would be highlighted:

- Use of gaming for staff development, learning and development
- Podcast and downloadable PDF
- Web 2.0 and mobile web
- Customer, supplier and staff profiling technologies
- Mobile and wireless technologies
- Nanotechnologies and digibots
- Location and activity-based IT services

- Digital tattoos
- Autonomic computers
- Service-oriented architecture
- Open standards and software (including web services)
- Green IT/sustainability
- Quantum cryptography
- Wireless sensor networks
- Injectable tissue engineering
- Nano solar cells.

However, for any of the above to feature as a strategic weapon in the future, they will need to exhibit all of the following features:

- Satisfy a real user requirement
- Do it the way users want and understand
- Easy to use
- Adequate response and speed
- Reliable and quality solutions
- Benefit justifies the cost.

Managing information, systems, information systems and technologies requires a balance between IT leadership and IT governance, which, in IT terms, addresses the following questions: knowing who is responsible for making decisions; knowing how decisions are made; and knowing who is responsible for ensuring that decisions are implemented.

7.5   Business IT/IS alignment

Business IT/IS alignment is critical for the strategic use of IT/IS. Alignment is about achieving a purposeful connection between strategy, organization, processes, technology and people (Henderson and Venkatraman, 1996).

The notion of strategic IT/IS alignment centres on three arguments (Hirschheim and Sabherwal, 2001):

1 Organizational performance depends on structures and capabilities that support the successful realization of strategic decisions.
2 Alignment is a two-way process, where business and IS strategies can act as mutual drivers.
3 Strategic IS alignment 'is not an event but a process of continuous adaptation and change' (Henderson and Venkatraman, 1993, p. 477).

So, in terms of information, systems and information systems, the first logical step for alignment is to ensure that working on the right things is a precondition to creating value. In order to deliver value, systems have to be implemented in an efficient and effective manner, but to do so, the right priorities need to be identified in the first place (how will systems support the overall strategy?).

The second stage is then to use alignment to gain a competitive edge by influencing the strategic position of the organization.

The business benefits of achieving strategic IT/IS alignment are (Grant and Gardner, 2010):

- *Organizational agility:* if IT/IS develop in an iterative manner without holistic consideration of current or future business needs, systems are likely to become diverse and incapable of scaling or adapting over time. In contrast, where systems are planned to align with business needs, agility is much improved. This improvement comes not only through standardization, but also from confidence and success in reusing mature components.

- *Operational efficiency:* modern business relationships are complex, involving a blend of customers, suppliers, service providers and other third parties. By effective alignment of IT/IS to the needs of these relationships, for example in the management and integration of the supply chain, businesses can improve their operational efficiency, with consequent competitive advantage.
- *IT cost reduction:* where IT/IS are developed in an iterative manner without focus on the organization's wider alignment needs, multiple solutions may be developed or procured for similar business needs, increasing IT capital costs and providing fragmented solutions that are more difficult and expensive to support. Business costs may also increase, as staff work around the systems to compensate for their shortcomings. Alignment facilitates standardization and consolidation, with consequent reductions in cost.
- *Risk management:* the discipline of alignment planning forces an organization to consider the effectiveness of its systems against a diverse range of factors. This highlights potential commercial or legal compliance risks and promotes thorough system revisions. By improving visibility, alignment also eases the ongoing management of risk.

7.6 Strategic information systems management

The area of strategic information systems management is still emerging and there is some confusion as to definitions, terms and perspectives. Some organizations see the technology base as a way of improving the efficiency of what they are already doing in relation to information provision and communication in general, while others take technology developments as opportunities to rethink and fundamentally challenge what they are doing and how they do it.

Information has emerged as a recognized 'resource', which needs to be managed precisely to achieve organizational objectives, goals and policies. Drucker (1988) suggested that, in the 21st century, the typical organization will be information based. He argued it will be flatter, having dramatically slimmed down its management size and level, and will be staffed mainly by 'knowledge workers'. Everyone will be responsible for meeting their own information needs, and the organization as a whole will need to have a unified vision and abandon former parochial views on information and its role.

So, strategic information systems management attempts to bridge the particular 'business' of the organization with the technology relevant to data processing and the communication needs of the business. Information and its management must be driven by the needs of the organization and not by the novelty of the available technology; in effect, aligning business needs with the technological opportunities available and ultimately satisfying these needs. Such needs are increasingly moving towards supporting innovation, knowledge management and reducing or managing complexity.

CASE STUDY NHS Scotland

NHS Scotland, founded in 1948, forms the cornerstone of the publicly funded healthcare system in Scotland. NHS Scotland is a huge healthcare provider – there are more than 4,000 GPs and over 80% of the population are registered with NHS dentists. The figures highlight the scale and scope of its undertakings. For example, in 2009, NHS Scotland estimates that more than 23 million patients had face-to-face contact with its GPs and practice-based nurses, and consultant clinics treated more than 4 million outpatient visitors, an increase of 2.8% from the previous year's figures. This is a typical slice of NHS Scotland activities in 2009 (http://www.isdscotland.org/isd/810.html):

- The number of staff employed was 168,976
- A total of 974,000 inpatient and day case procedures were carried out
- Operating costs were £9.3bn for the financial year ending March 2009
- It pays over £4bn a year in staff wages
- £1.3bn was spent by NHS boards on prescription drugs
- It is a major administrator of immunization programmes in Scotland. For example, the overall uptake of human papillomavirus immunization among girls in the second, fifth and sixth years of secondary school in Scotland in 2008/09 was 93.5% for the first dose, 92.4% for the second dose and 87.7% for the third dose
- It performed over 450,500 cervical smears in the year ending March 2009.

Since its inception, NHS Scotland has been a pioneer in the use of technology to enhance the delivery of its services. For example, the world's first kidney transplant was done in Edinburgh in 1960, while the Caithness General Hospital in Wick became the world's first whisky-powered hospital (via a biomass, wood-burning power source at the malt whisky distillery). Advances have also been made in the adoption of IT and now NHS Scotland is considered a leader in developing patient-centred care services. The role of information systems in NHS activities became more prominent in 1998, when the Department of Health commissioned a report to study the use of information systems in enhancing the delivery of patient care and services. The report *Information for Health* (DH, 1998) outlined the need for providing lifelong electronic health records for clinical use and making available the information regarding best clinical practices for treatment and care. The aim was to provide on-demand access to electronic patient records and offer a platform whereby best clinical practices are shared by all in the NHS. The culmination of this study and further ratifications laid the foundations for the formation of NHS Connecting

for Health, a directorate within the Department of Health in 2005. The primary role of this directorate is in supplying information and IT systems needed in the delivery of patient-centred care services in England.

In Scotland, the information and IT systems delivery is provided by National Information Systems Group (NISG), an arm of National Services Scotland (NSS), a non-departmental public body that provides support services to NHS Scotland. NISG supports the delivery of information management and technology products and specialist services that enable clinical processes and improve efficiency across NHS Scotland. NISG has been involved in many of NHS Scotland's IT initiatives, and an examination of two examples highlights the transformation and benefits brought about by the adoption and implementation of information and related communication technologies in healthcare.

Scottish Care Information

Scottish Care Information (SCI) is an initiative to connect the primary healthcare services with secondary care systems using the internet. Primary care systems are the first points of contact in patient care; they include services like GP practices, opticians, dentists, pharmacists, walk-in centres and NHS Direct. These services are connected to secondary care systems, like NHS trust hospitals, ambulance trust, emergency care and so on, by the internet. SCI provides the gateway whereby patient information is seamlessly transferred from primary to secondary care systems and vice versa. For example, the SCI gateway connects approximately 80% of GPs in Scotland. The GPs are connected through the 'general practice administration system' for Scotland and the network allows the sharing of patient records and essential information between different boards and care systems. Further, every registered patient in Scotland receives a unique community index number, which enables NHS clinicians to access patient records across Scotland and, in the case of emergencies, allows quick intervention and delivery of safe and effective treatment. It is estimated that, in any given month, over 15,000 clinical personal and administrators use the system to share patient-related information, ranging from test results to referrals to discharge information.

CLEAR

CLEAR stands for 'clinical enquiry and response' service and provides NHS Scotland professionals with a knowledge base of patient care. It is a repository providing evidence-based information on diagnosis and treatment options for a variety of illnesses. NHS clinical professionals can ask questions relating to prognosis and treatment of patient care through the CLEAR

2

website and can get evidence-based answers from a variety of sources including NHS 24, the medicines information service and health management library. In short, it is an online medical database, which can provide specific responses to queries relating to clinical diagnosis and treatment. The responses are published online and are categorized into domains for clarity and easy reference. The growing database is expected to increase knowledge sharing within the NHS Scotland community and contribute to the overall improvement in delivery of care services.

There are numerous other NHS Scotland IT initiatives, and all have been implemented with a view to increasing efficiency and providing a world-class health service to the people of Scotland. Further initiatives are planned, using the latest technologies to make available superior patient-centred services.

NHS Scotland is ushering in a groundbreaking era and its initiatives have laid the foundations for a truly advanced e-health society.

Case study questions

1 From an organizational perspective, what are the advantages of developing IT-led services?
2 There has been a lot of criticism in the popular press of NHS IT investments. What are the pros and cons of large-scale IT investments?
3 What are the legal and ethical issues in sharing patient information?
4 NHS Scotland is moving towards an e-health platform, where information will be held from 'cradle to grave'. What are the implications of such initiatives? Do you think it is 'big brother' in action?

STRATEGIC
PLANNING SOFTWARE

This is a helpful chapter to refer to when completing 1.2.2 Value Chain within the Internal Analysis section in Phase 1 of the **Strategic Planning Software** (www.planning-strategy.com). For more information on the value chain, also see Chapter 13.

Companion Website

For test questions, extra case studies, audio case studies, weblinks, videolinks and more to help you understand the topics covered in this chapter, visit our companion website at www.macmillanihe.com/companion/business/campbell.

VOCAB CHECKLIST FOR ESL STUDENTS

Data processing	Nano solar cells (see	RSS feed
Digital cash	'nano' and 'solar cells')	Semantic
Disseminate	Nanotechnology	Stockpiles
Inextricably	Nexus	Taxonomy
Iterative	Parochial	
Mechanistic	Quantum cryptography (see	
Mercantile	'quantum' and 'cryptography')	

Definitions for these terms can be found in the 'Vocab Zone' of the companion website, which provides free access to the Macmillan English Dictionary online at www.macmillanihe.com/companion/business/campbell.

REVIEW QUESTIONS

1 Explain the difference between data and information.
2 Define a knowledge worker and the challenges they face in the information age.
3 Describe the different types of information systems that exist and how an organization can use them for competitive advantage.
4 Explain why it is important to align IT/IS to the business purpose, needs and aspirations.

DISCUSSION TOPIC

Organizations using the most current technologies will always gain first mover competitive advantage. Discuss.

HOT TOPICS – Research project areas to investigate

If you have a project to do, why not investigate ...

- ... the role of technology in creating customer value in the banking sector.
- ... the decision factors used by managers when determining which technologies to employ in their organizations.
- ... approaches to IT/IS alignment in shared service provider organizations.

Recommended reading

Andriole, S.J. (2007) 'The 7 habits of highly effective technology leaders', *Communications of the ACM*, **50**(3): 67–72.

Armbrust, M., Fox, A., Griffith, R. et al. (2009) *Above the Clouds: A Berkeley View of Cloud Computing*, Technical Report No. UCB/EECS-2009-28, Electrical Engineering and Computer Sciences, University of California Berkeley, CA, http://www.eecs.berkeley.edu/Pubs/TechRpts/2009/EECS-2009-28.html [accessed 27 March 2009].

Bannister, F. and Remenyi, D. (2005) 'Why IT continues to matter: reflections on strategic value of IT', *Electronic Journal of Information Systems Evaluation*, **8**(3): 159–68.

Bannister, F., Berghout, E.W., Griffiths, P.P. and Remenyi, D. (2006) Tracing the eclectic (or maybe even chaotic) nature of ICT evaluation, in D. Remenyi and A. Brown (eds) *Proceedings of the 13th European Conference on IT Evaluation*, Reading: Academic Conferences Ltd.

Bernoff, J. and Li, C. (2008) 'Harnessing the power of the oh-so-social web', *MIT Sloan Management Review*, **49**(3): 35–43.

Binney, D. (2001) 'The knowledge management spectrum: understanding the KM landscape', *Journal of Knowledge Management*, **5**(1): 33–42.

Chan, Y.E. and Reich, B.H. (2007) 'IT alignment: an annotated bibliography', *Journal of Information Technology*, **22**(4): 316–96.

Christensen, C.M. (1997) *The Innovator's Dilemma*, Boston, MA: Harvard Business School Press.

Dhillon, G. (2008) 'Organizational competence in harnessing IT: a case study', *Information & Management*, **45**(5): 297–303.

Galliers, R.D., Leidener, D.E. and Baker, B.S. (2003) *Strategic Information Management: Challenges and Strategies in Managing Information Systems*, Woburn, MA: Butterworth-Heinemann.

Garrison, G. (2009) 'An assessment of organizational size and sense and response capability on the early adoption of disruptive technology', *Computers in Human Behavior*, **25**(2): 444–9.

Grant, K., Hackney, R. and Edgar, D. (2010) *Strategic Information Systems Management: Priorities, Procedures and Policy*, Thompson/Cengage.

He Shin, N. (2001) 'Strategies for competitive advantage in electronic commerce', *Journal of Electronic Commerce Research*, **2**(4): 164–71.

Kohli, R. and Grover, V. (2008) 'Business value of IT: an essay on expanding research directions to keep up with the times', *Journal of the Association for Information Systems*, **9**(2): 23–39.

Lucas, H.C. Jr and Goh, J.M. (2009) 'Disruptive technology: how Kodak missed the digital photography revolution', *Journal of Strategic Information Systems*, **18**(1): 46–55.

Luftman, J. (2000) 'Assessing business-IT alignment maturity', *Communications of the AIS*, **4**(14): 1–50.

Luftman, J. and Brier, T. (1999) 'Achieving and sustaining business-IT alignment', *California Management Review*, **42**(1): 109–22.

Schilling, M. (2004) *Strategic Management of Technological Innovation*, New York: McGraw-Hill.

Stacey, R.D. (2005) *Experiencing Emergence in Organisations: Local Interaction and the Emergence of Global Pattern*, London: Routledge.

Tapscott, D. and Williams, A.D. (2006) *Wikinomics: How Mass Collaboration Changes Everything*, New York: Portfolio Hardcover.

Weil, P. and Ross, J. (2004) *IT Governance: How Top Performers Manage IT Decision Rights for Superior Results*, Boston, MA: Harvard Business School Press.

Weill, P. and Woodman, R. (2002) 'Don't just lead, govern: implementing effective IT governance', *CISR Work Papers*, No. 326.

Willcocks, L.P., Feeny, D. and Lacity, M. (2007) Outsourcing, knowledge, and organizational innovation: a study of enterprise partnership, in L. Markus and V. Grover (eds) *Business Process Transformation*, Hershey, PA: Idea Group.

2

Chapter references

Checkland, P. (1981) *Systems Thinking, Systems Practice*, New York: Wiley.

Daniels, J.L. and Daniels, N.C. (1993) *Global Vision: Building New Models for the Corporation of the Future*, New York: McGraw-Hill.

Davenport, T.H. and Prusak, L. (2000) *Working Knowledge: How Organizations Manage What they Know*, Boston, MA: Harvard Business School Press.

Davis, G. and Olson, M. (1985) *Management Information Systems: Conceptual Foundations, Structure, and Development* (2nd edn), New York: McGraw-Hill.

DH (Department of Health) (1998) *Information for Health: An Information Strategy for the Modern NHS 1998–2005 – Executive Summary*, London: TSO.

Drucker, P. (1988) 'The coming of the new organisation', *Harvard Business Review*, **66**(1): 45–53.

Edquist, C. (1997) *Systems of Innovation: Technologies, Institutions and Organizations*, London: Pinter.

Evans, P. and Wurster, T.S. (2000) *Blown to Bits: How the New Economics of Information Transforms Strategy*, Boston, MA: Harvard Business School Press.

Galliers, R.D. and Somogyi, E.K. (1987) 'Applied information technology: from data processing to strategic information systems', *Journal of Information Technology*, **2**(1): 49–55.

Goodchild, M.F. (1995) 'Geographic information systems and geographic research', in J. Pickles (ed.) *Ground Truth: The Social Implications of Geographic Information Systems*, New York: Guilford Press.

Grant, K., Hackney, R. and Edgar, D. (2010) *Strategic Information Systems Management: Priorities, Procedures and Policy*, Thompson/Cengage.

Grimshaw, D.J. (2000) *Bringing Graphical Information Systems into Business* (2nd edn), Chichester: John Wiley.

Henderson, J.C. and Venkatraman, H. (1993) 'Strategic alignment: leveraging information technology for transforming organizations', *IBM Systems Journal*, **32**(1): 472–84.

Hirschheim, R. and Sabherwal, R. (2001) 'Detours in the path toward strategic information systems alignment', *California Management Review*, **44**(1): 87–108.

Lucey, T. (2004) *Management Information Systems* (9th edn), London: Cengage.

OECD/Eurostat (2005) *Oslo Manual: Guidelines for Collecting and Interpreting Innovation Data* (3rd edn), Paris: OECD.

Oz, E. (2004) *Management Information Systems* (4th edn), Boston, MA: Course Technology/Thomson Learning.

Pedersen, C.R. and Dalum, B. (2004) Incremental versus radical change: the case of the digital north Denmark program. International Schumpeter Society Conference, Italy. DRUID/IKE Group, Department of Business Studies, Aalborg University.

Popadiuk, S. and Choo, C.W. (2006) 'Innovation and knowledge creation: how are these concepts related?', *International Journal of Information Management*, 26: 302–12.

Porter, M.E. (2001) 'Strategy and the internet', *Harvard Business Review*, **9**(3): 62–78.

Rogers, E.M. (1983) *Diffusions of Innovations*, New York: Free Press.

Stair, R. and Reynolds, G. (2010) *Principles of Information Systems: A Managerial Approach* (9th edn), Boston, MA: Thomson/Course Technology.

Tapscott, D. (2003) *The Naked Corporation: How the Age of Transparency Will Revolutionize Business*, New York: Free Press.

Turban, E., McLean, E. and Wetherby, J. (2004) *Information Technology for Management*, Chichester: Wiley.

Tushman, M.L. (1997) 'Winning through innovation', *Strategy and Leadership*, **25**(4): 14–19.

UKAIS (UK Academy of Information Systems) (2010) Definition of IS, http://www.ukais.org.uk/about/DefinitionIS.aspx, accessed 3 June 2010.

Von Hippel, E.A. (1998) *The Sources of Innovation*, New York: Oxford University Press.

Von Hippel, E.A. (2005) *Democratizing Innovation*, Cambridge MA: MIT Press.

Ward, J. and Peppard, J. (2003) *Strategic Planning for Information Systems* (3rd edn), New York: John Wiley & Sons.

Wysocki, R.K. and Young, J. (1991) *Information Systems Management Principles in Action*, Chichester: John Wiley & Sons.

Chapter 8

Strengths, weaknesses and strategic competence

Introduction and chapter overview

This chapter completes the internal analysis element of business strategy. Pulling together the previous frameworks, concepts and principles, the chapter presents the idea of strengths, weaknesses and strategic competence. This makes up half of the SWOT analysis (strengths, weaknesses, opportunities and threats), which is often seen as a starting point of developing a business strategy. However, as is evident from Chapters 1–7, there are many elements that lead to a robust and evidence-based justification of an organization's strengths and weaknesses. We will now consolidate this analysis and explain the term 'strategic competence'. This is important, as the strengths, weaknesses and competences often form the basis of any resource-based (or value school) approach to strategy. Once complete, we shall move on to Part 3 of the book and explore the external analysis and the foundations of the opportunities and threats faced by an organization and thus the missing parts of our SWOT jigsaw.

Learning objectives

After studying this chapter, you should be able to:

- define what is meant by an organization's strengths and weaknesses
- determine what is meant by an organization's strategic competence

8.1 Strengths and weaknesses

The strengths and weaknesses emerge from our strategic internal analysis, as shown in Figure 8.1.

From Figure 8.1, it is clear that the uniqueness of an organization's resources and the clarity of purpose and direction are the foundation of a sustainable strength that can be used in gaining and maintaining competitive advantage. First, we define what we mean by strengths and weaknesses.

Strengths (and weaknesses) often come from the same categories of activities or 'sources'. The sources are usually related to systems, innovation, product design and development, leadership, alliances or networks, intangible assets, and the

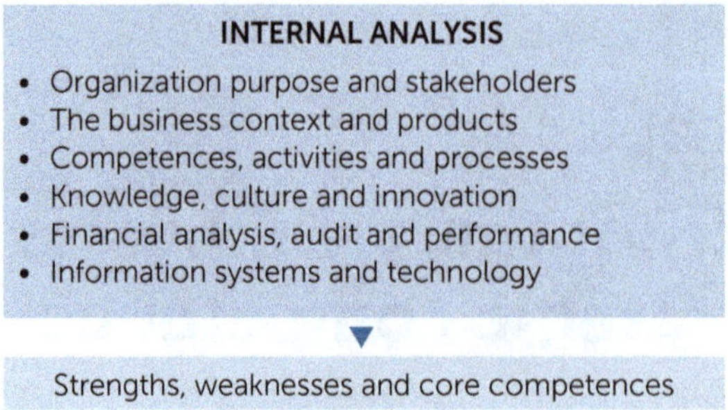

INTERNAL ANALYSIS
- Organization purpose and stakeholders
- The business context and products
- Competences, activities and processes
- Knowledge, culture and innovation
- Financial analysis, audit and performance
- Information systems and technology

▼

Strengths, weaknesses and core competences

Figure 8.1 **The internal analysis**

nature, volume and quality of resources. As such, strengths can often be categorized under two key headings: ability and available resources:

- In terms of *ability*, it is the organization's ability to 'cope with' and exploit the ever changing business environment, the ability to grow the business and the ability to spot, enter and exploit new market opportunities.
- In terms of *resources*, strengths often lie in the quality and availability of resources, and the effective and efficient way in which the resources are deployed.

So, in summary, a strength is something the organization does or owns that contributes to its ability to gain a competitive advantage.

Weaknesses are often found in the same category areas as strengths, but on this occasion, they are areas where the organization is 'not performing'. By not performing, we mean the weaknesses are failures, losses, defeats, or inabilities to meet dynamic situations or situations requiring rapid change. In this respect, weaknesses manifest themselves in key areas:

- *poor quality* of resources, workmanship and relationships
- *inadequate processes or systems*, resulting in poor alignment, 'bottlenecks' and wastage
- *slow response* to market, industry or environmental change
- *resource shortages*, especially of mission critical resources
- *poor managerial and leadership skills*.

Understanding relative strengths and weaknesses

Once the strengths and weaknesses have been identified, it is useful to attempt to quantify them in terms of the 'degree' to which they are a strength or a weakness. Doing this allows for developments and actions to be prioritized and greater impact to be achieved. These issues are discussed in later chapters.

After quantifying the strengths and weaknesses, it is useful to consider them in relative terms to other operators on the industry. This is important, as often an absolute (key) strength or weakness may be a relatively low strength or weakness when compared to competitors. So we can use benchmarking techniques to draw a relative perspective to our own organization's profile (see Chapter 6). Indeed, this can be done across different industries and thus seek to benchmark performance against the 'best in class'. Once a strength has been quantified and benchmarked, it needs to be nurtured and protected in order to allow for sustainable strategic advantage.

CASE STUDY   Bucks Burger Bars Inc.

Bucks Burger Bars Inc. (BBB) is a major international player in the fast-food industry. Steven McCormack, a Canadian entrepreneur, founded BBB 40 years ago. While on holiday in the UK, he found that the fast food on offer was so variable and uncertain in terms of availability and quality that he decided that this was a niche he could fill. Also, he was hoping to get married in the near future and so needed either a job that paid well or (preferably) a company to run.

He started off with a fleet of ice cream vans, selling good quality products to tourists in London and the seaside resorts of the UK. When this proved to be successful, he developed the range of products to include fish and chips and other hot foods. Alongside this he developed a range of outlets to include fish and chip shops, burger bars and ice cream parlours. At the end of five years, McCormack had at least one BBB outlet in every city and large town in England, and many had more than one.

The initial phase of business development had been flexible and fluid. Anyone who wanted to join what had, by now, become known as the 'BBB dream' could do so, more or less on their own terms. Those who wanted to take out franchise arrangements were given full support, subject only to a legally binding contract in terms of the products on sale, the cleanliness and the quality and appearance of the premises, and the terms and conditions under which the franchise staff were employed. Those who wanted to work for McCormack as employees could do so, and those who chose to do this were placed in specific branches and outlets as managers and executives. A full franchisee and management training and development programme supported the whole venture. There were also absolute standards of product and service delivery, training for all staff, and cleaning rotas and schedules.

The whole range of activities was very successful in the UK, and McCormack realized that the idea could be introduced elsewhere, if it could be tailored to suit the different markets and locations. So he looked to North America for his next ventures. He opened his first chain of coffee bars in the US on the twenty-first

anniversary of the first UK opening; and he also opened a range of fast-food outlets, in direct competition with McDonald's, Burger King and Wendy. These ventures were successful, and the US activities quickly expanded so that there was a total of 950 BBB outlets in all. In Canada, McCormack opened a total of 70 BBB outlets in all the big cities, although here they concentrated on selling doughnuts, coffee and breakfasts.

From small beginnings, McCormack had built for himself a major business empire. In particular, his ability to take the strengths of his UK company and adapt these according to the demands of the US and Canadian markets was seen as a major corporate and strategic strength of the company. Having built the company to this present position of strength and reputation, McCormack now sold the company to a management buyout backed by venture capital. By this time, all aspects of the company were fully profitable, and total revenues for the year of the buyout were $90bn, generating a profit of $7.5bn.

The new owners and management of BBB now took stock. Since the departure of McCormack, several issues had come to light. There was a lack of any form of management structure. All branch managers had always reported more or less directly to McCormack himself, or to the four chosen undermanagers who he had employed and who had been with him since the start (known to the rest of the company as 'the four horsemen of the apocalypse'). The managers involved in the buyout quickly came to realize how little they really had had to do with the direction and executive management of the company. They knew little about the plans for the future, and still less about where the revenues came from; they had total figures, but no detailed breakdowns either by product or location.

The venture capitalists backing the buyout also wanted answers. They had been drawn in on the basis of McCormack's success, and they needed and wanted to know what the new executive management team were going to do. Funding was not a problem; however, strategy and direction were needed. Everyone recognized the success of the company to date, now it was time to be moving on to the next stage. Also, because of the reputation of the company, built up by McCormack, it was going to be relatively straightforward to raise funds and additional backing, should this be needed.

Case study questions

1   What are the strengths and weaknesses of Bucks Burger Bars?
2   Where do the priorities now lie?
3   What options are now open to the new management team and the venture capitalists?

Determining strategic competence

In Chapter 4, we explored the concept of competence and core competences. The internal analysis will not only identify the competences and core competences but it will allow us to relate these to our understanding of the organization's strengths and weaknesses to quantify the organization's strategic capabilities and thus give us a better understanding of 'what the organization could do' or 'what is within the organization's means'.

Often, these capabilities are similar between organizations operating in any one industry, with the key challenge being how to use such capabilities to best effect, either to compete more effectively or to 'change the rules of the game'.

These capabilities are usually built on the strengths and relate to operational effectiveness, customer satisfaction, organization flexibility and ability to innovate. Clearly, to build such resource strengths and capabilities requires a strong management team, 'quality' employees, a focus on strategic activities and a willingness to collaborate or outsource to minimize weaknesses. Many of these issues are explored in later chapters.

For test questions, extra case studies, audio case studies, weblinks, videolinks and more to help you understand the topics covered in this chapter, visit our companion website at www.macmillanihe.com/companion/business/campbell.

VOCAB CHECKLIST FOR ESL STUDENTS

'Bottlenecks'	Deployed	Robust
Branch/outlet	Franchise	Workmanship
Consolidate	Nurtured	

Definitions for these terms can be found in the 'Vocab Zone' of the companion website, which provides free access to the Macmillan English Dictionary online at www.macmillanihe.com/companion/business/campbell.

REVIEW QUESTIONS

1   Define what is meant by a strength and a weakness.
2   Explain how to identify a company's strengths and weaknesses.
3   Explain what strategic competence is and how an organization can protect its strategic competences.

DISCUSSION TOPIC

Analysing the strengths and weaknesses of an organization is pointless as it is backward-looking and historical in nature. Organizations need to be more forward thinking. Discuss.

Recommended reading

Brooksbank, R. (1996) 'The BASIC marketing planning process: a practical framework for the smaller business', *Journal of Marketing Intelligence & Planning*, **14**(4): 16–23.

Hill, T. and Westbrook, R. (1997) 'SWOT analysis: it's time for a product recall', *Long Range Planning*, **30**(1): 46–52.

Lee, S.F., Lo, K.K., Leung, R.F. and Sai On Ko, A. (2000) 'Strategy formulation framework for vocational education: integrating SWOT analysis, balanced scorecard, QFD methodology and MBNQA education criteria', *Managerial Auditing Journal*, **15**(8): 407–23.

Panagiotou, G. (2003) 'Bringing SWOT into focus', *Business Strategy Review*, **14**(2): 8–10.

Piercy, N. and Giles, W. (1989) 'Making SWOT analysis work', *Journal of Marketing Intelligence & Planning*, **7**(5/6): 5–7.

Shinno, H., Yoshioka, S., Marpaung, S. and Hachiga, S. (2006) 'Qualitative SWOT analysis on the global competetiveness of machine tool industry', *Journal of Engineering Design*, **17**(3): 251–8.

Valentin, E.K. (2001) 'SWOT analysis from a resource-based view', *Journal of Marketing Theory and Practice*, **9**(2): 54–68.

Weihrich, H. (1982) 'The Tows Matrix: a tool for situational analysis', *Long Range Planning*, **15**(2): 54–60.

2

PART 3

EXTERNAL ANALYSIS

Part 2 explored the elements that lead to identifying the strengths and weaknesses of an organization – the internal analysis of the business environment. Part 3 examines the tools and techniques that are used to understand the opportunities and threats that face an organization. To do this, we examine the external business environment through a process called 'external analysis'. Figure 3 highlights where external analysis fits within the overall business strategy process.

If an organization subscribes to a positioning view of strategy, the external analysis is critical for them to determine how to position themselves and where to position their organization in their respective industry. In effect, the external analysis is the starting point for a positioning view of business strategy.

To undertake an effective external analysis requires three key factors or areas of understanding.

First, we need to be aware of and understand the potential impact of the macroenvironment or the external general environment. The macroenvironment contains a number of influences that affect not only an organization itself, but

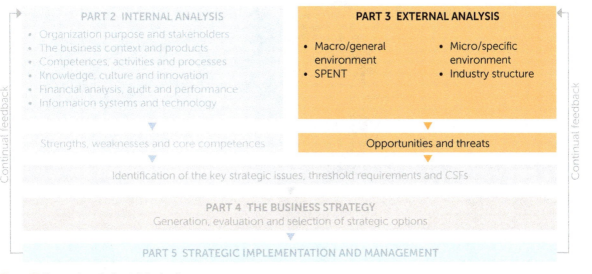

Figure 3 External analysis and the business strategy process

also the rest of the players in the economy. As such, it is essential to scan and understand what factors make up the macroenvironment and how the elements may influence an industry or an organization. **Chapter 9** explains how to do this using a SPENT analysis.

Once we understand the macroenvironment, we can start to explore how changes in an environment can influence organizations and industries. However, to do this we need to examine the microenvironment (or specific environment). The microenvironment is how the industry is organized and structured. This is the sphere in which an organization interacts with others players and shapes the competitive environment of an industry. If we understand how the industry is made up and what influences it, we can then start to see how the changes in the macroenvironment can impact on and shape the industry, and appropriate responses and strategies can be formulated. We examine approaches to understanding the microenvironment in **Chapter 10**.

Chapter 11 focuses on the international and global context. This is useful in providing a wider perspective of the business environment and the conditions facing many organizations.

Chapter 12 draws together the analysis into an identification of opportunities and threats, explaining how the overall SWOT (strengths, weaknesses, opportunities and threats) analysis comes together.

Chapter 9
Analysis of the macroenvironment

Introduction and chapter overview

In Part 3, we explore how the external environment can impact on an organization and therefore the strategy the organization adopts. The environment is anything that influences or impacts on the organization, its markets, its resources or its stakeholders. The outside environment is commonly split into two types, the external general environment (or macroenvironment) and the specific, industry or competitive environment (the microenvironment). This chapter examines the macroenvironment.

Different textbooks tend to adopt their own mnemonic for external general environmental analysis. Basic analysis includes analysis of the STEP/PEST factors – sociodemographic, technological, economic and political factors. Other approaches have attempted to include a category for the analysis of environmental/ecological factors – STEEP analysis. This book takes the view that the extra 'E', in this context, is a bit confusing as the whole process is an analysis of the 'business environment'. Another approach, PESTLE/PESTEL analysis, includes the four PEST factors, the 'E' for environmental factors and 'L' for legislative factors, although most books have taken the view (as does this text) that legislation is a political factor.

Hence, in an attempt to be comprehensive while also avoiding confusion, this textbook suggests a new approach – the SPENT analysis. SPENT includes the four PEST/STEP factors plus 'N' for natural environmental factors. This chapter proceeds to consider how general macroenvironmental analysis can be undertaken and then considers the five SPENT factors.

Learning objectives

After studying this chapter, you should be able to:

- explain what is meant by the macroenvironment
- determine the different types of environmental change
- explain Ginter and Duncan's mechanisms of carrying out macroenvironmental analysis
- describe the components of each of the five SPENT influences
- describe how the SPENT factors are interlinked and interrelated

9.1   The macroenvironment

The **macroenvironment** is the broad environment outside an organization's industry and markets.

We refer to the macroenvironment as the broad environment outside an organization's industry and markets. It is generally beyond the influence of the individual business but can have significant impact on the micro- or specific environment (industry and market) in which the business operates. The macroenvironment is sometimes referred to as the 'general' or 'remote environment' because it tends to exert forces from outside the organization's sphere of influence and usually beyond its control.

Changes in the macroenvironment can be of immense importance to an organization and they tend to impact on all organizations within an industry and sometimes also within the markets served by the industry. They can bring about the birth or death of an entire industry, they can make markets expand or contract, and they can determine the level of competitiveness within an industry. It is essential that managers are alert to actual and potential changes in the macroenvironment and that they anticipate the potential impacts on their industry and markets. Being able to predict changes and acting to take advantage of, or defend against, macroenvironmental changes can, in itself, be a source of competitive advantage. For example, many UK financial institutions either failed or were nationalized during the 2009 economic crisis. They failed to anticipate the changes in the wider macroenvironment and paid the price, either by being forced out of business or being the target of takeovers.

In this respect, the type of environmental change can indicate the type of response required. In general, there are two types of change:

- *Cyclical changes:* such as fashion, seasonality or boom and bust, which require a temporary tactical response
- *Structural changes:* such as advances in technology or changes to infrastructure, which are more permanent in nature and require a permanent response.

Understanding the types of change, the pace of change, and the direction and magnitude of the change can help organizations to develop strategies that are more aligned to both their internal capabilities and their external environment.

We use a macroenvironmental analysis to allow us to better understand the environment and its potential impact.

Conducting macroenvironmental analysis

We still use the work of Ginter and Duncan (1990) as a tool for understanding the environment, as their approach has stood the test of time and is clearly appropriate for our purposes. They stated that 'macroenvironmental analysis involves:

- *scanning* the macroenvironment for warning signs and possible environmental changes that will affect the business
- *monitoring* environments for specific trends and patterns
- *forecasting* future directions of environmental changes
- *assessing* current and future trends in terms of the effects such changes would have on the organization.'

In their paper, Ginter and Duncan gave the example of the sportswear manufacturers Adidas and Converse. Converse failed to adequately analyse the macroenvironment and this, in turn, caused it to miss the opportunity of catering for the premium (upper priced) segment of the running shoe market. Nike, on the other hand, more accurately predicted the strength of demand in the segment and exploited the market opportunities much more successfully, which partly explains why Nike is a better known brand than Converse.

The same authors went on to identify the potential benefits of macroenvironmental analysis as:

- increasing managerial awareness of environmental changes
- increasing understanding of the context in which industries and markets function
- increasing understanding of multinational settings
- improving resource allocation decisions
- facilitating risk management
- focusing attention on the primary influences on strategic change
- acting as an early warning system, providing time to anticipate opportunities, threats and devise appropriate responses.

Limitations of macroenvironmental analysis

We should be careful to note that macroenvironmental analysis has its limitations and pitfalls. The macroenvironment can be extremely complex, and at any one time, there may be conflicting and contradictory changes taking place. The pace of change in many macroenvironmental situations is increasing and becoming more turbulent and unpredictable. This degree of uncertainty has, to some extent, cast some doubt on the value of carrying out a macroenvironmental analysis at all. By the time an organization has come to terms with one major change in the macroenvironment, another change often occurs that requires even more attention and action.

Accordingly, those managers who are concerned with strategic analysis must:

- be aware of the limitations and inaccuracies of macroenvironmental analysis
- understand the complexity of the environment in which they operate and the sources of information on which the analysis is based
- carry out the analysis continuously, because it changes so frequently
- constantly seek to improve sources of information and techniques for its analysis
- use the information as one source of organizational learning, alongside other information-gathering activities (see Chapter 7)
- use the information to inform future strategy.

With these points in mind, macroenvironmental analysis is, nevertheless, a valuable mechanism for increasing the strategic awareness of managers.

9.2 The SPENT factors

The complexity of the macroenvironment makes it necessary to divide the forces at work into the five broad categories we encountered at the start of the chapter. It is important to remember that the five categories are partly interrelated and can interact with each other. It is equally important to identify the relative importance of the influences at work for the business, its industry and its markets. Finally, because of the uncertainty of the effects of macroenvironmental change on the specific or microenvironment (see Chapter 10), it is essential that a range of possible outcomes of the changes are identified and considered. Techniques for this analysis are considered later in this chapter.

Sociodemographic influences

Analysis of the sociodemographic environment is concerned with understanding the potential impacts of society and social changes on a business, its industry and markets.

For most analyses, analysis of the social environment will require consideration of:

- *social culture* (values, attitudes and beliefs)*:* its impact on demand for products and services, attitudes to work, savings and investment, ecology, ethics and so on
- *demography:* the impact of the size and structure of the population on the workforce and patterns of demand
- *social structure:* its impact on attitudes to work and certain products.

Social culture

The cultures of the countries in which a business operates can be of particular importance. The culture of a country consists of the values, attitudes and beliefs of its people, which, in turn, will affect the way they act and behave. There are important cultural differences between all countries (see Chapter 21). Culture can affect consumer tastes and preferences, and attitudes to work, education and training, corruption and ethics, credit, and to the social role of a business in society. Even between similar countries or between regions of the same country, social culture can differ significantly in certain ways. Brewers, for example, are well aware of differences in 'drinking culture' across

Social culture: beer and wine

Europe. Where the British, Germans, Irish and the Czechs on the whole prefer beer, the French, Italians and Spanish tend to prefer wine when relaxing with friends or on a night out. In other countries, religious observance means that the majority don't drink alcohol at all.

Demography

Demography is the social science concerned with the charting of the size and structure of a population of people.

Demographic trends are similarly important. Demography is the social science concerned with the charting of the size and structure of a population of people. The size of the population will obviously be a determinant of the size of the workforce and the potential size of markets. Just as important will be the structure of the population. The age structure will determine the size of particular segments and also the size of the working population. The size and structure of the population will constantly be changing and these changes will have an impact on industries and markets.

Social structure

Social structure is strongly linked to demography and refers to the ways in which the social groups in a population are organized. There are a number of ways of defining social structure, such as by sociodemographic groupings, by age, sex, location, population density in different areas and so on. The social structure will affect people's lifestyles and expectations and so will strongly influence their attitudes to work and their demand for particular product types. For example, the growing middle-class population in India and China is demanding an increase in luxury products, particularly sports cars and luxury watches.

Among the most important general changes in recent years in the social environment has been people's attitudes towards the natural environment (see Chapter 20) and sustainability. Increasing awareness of the problems caused by pollution and the exhaustion of non-renewable resources has made businesses in many industries rethink the way they produce their products and the composition of the products themselves. Similarly, changes in social structure (upward mobility), lifestyle (increased leisure) and demography (ageing populations in developed countries) have significantly altered many market and industry structures.

Political, governmental, legal and regulatory influences

The **political environment** is that part of the macroenvironment that is either under the direct control or influence of the government and/or the state.

The political environment is that part of the macroenvironment that is either under the direct control or influence of the government and/or the state.

'Government' is a loosely defined term and can be considered at three 'levels':

- *national level:* the government of a particular country
- *subnational level:* local government based at town halls, civic centres and so on. In some countries, some policy making is devolved to regions, cantons and so on, such as Scotland and Wales. Some federal countries, such as the USA, Germany and Switzerland, have relatively powerful 'local' (or state) policy-making bodies at subnational government level
- *supranational level:* political bodies that exert influence on several national governments. The European Union (EU), North American Free Trade Agreement (NAFTA) and the United Nations (UN) are examples of supranational political bodies.

Governments (at whatever level) have direct control or influence, to a greater or lesser extent, over:

- *Legislation and regulation:* this covers laws that influence employment, consumer protection, health and safety at work, contract and trading, trade unions, monopolies and mergers, and tax
- *Economic policy:* particularly fiscal policy. Governments usually set policy over the levels of taxation and expenditure in the country
- *Government-owned businesses* (nationalized industries)*:* some governments retain control over key strategic industries and the way in which these are controlled can have knock-on effects to other parts of the country
- *Government international policy:* government intervention to influence exchange rates and international trade.

A government's objectives towards the regulation of business will depend in large part on the political leaning of the governing party. Most governments have, however, sought to construct policy over a number of key areas of business activity. These include:

- control of inflation (so as to improve international competitiveness)
- promotion of economic growth and investment
- control of unemployment
- control of interest rates
- the impact of the 'credit crunch'
- stabilization of exchange rates
- control of balance of payments
- control of monopoly power, both by businesses and trade unions
- provision of public and merit goods, like health, education, defence and so on
- control of pollution and environmental protection
- redistribution of incomes (to varying degrees)
- consumer protection
- regulation of working conditions
- regulation of trade.

To varying degrees, all businesses will be affected by political influences. So it is important for managers to monitor government policy to detect changes early so as to respond effectively.

Another important aspect of the political environment is 'political risk' and its potential effects on business. Political risk is particularly important in international business. While Europe and North America are comparatively politically stable, other parts of the world, like Eastern Europe, South America and parts of the Middle East and Africa, have undergone periods of political instability. It is therefore necessary to monitor closely the political situation in these areas when trading with them as the political risks are large. Even in more stable areas, political uncertainty can be higher at, for example, election times or when other political crises arise.

Economic influences

Analysis of the economic environment centres on changes in the macroeconomy and their effects on business and consumers. It is important to remember that, because governments intervene (to varying extents) in the operation of all countries' economies, many factors classed as political in this chapter will have important economic implications.

Broadly speaking, the regulation of a national economy is brought about by two key policy instruments, fiscal policy and monetary policy. These policy instruments, alongside influences from international markets, determine the economic climate in the country in which a business competes. From these, a number of other vital economic indicators 'flow' and it is these that organizations experience, either for good or ill.

When the effects of fiscal and monetary pressures work themselves out in the economy, they can affect any or all of the following economic factors:

- economic growth rates: the year-on-year growth in the total size of a national economy, usually measured by gross domestic product
- levels of income in the economy
- levels of productivity: output per worker in the economy
- wage levels and the rate of increase in wages

- levels of inflation: the year-on-year rise in prices
- levels of unemployment
- balance of payments: a measure of the international competitiveness of one country's economy against its international competitor countries
- exchange rates: the exchange value of one currency against another.

KEY CONCEPTS

Fiscal policy is the regulation of the national economy through the management of government revenues and expenditures. Each fiscal year, a government raises so much in revenues (through taxation) and it spends another amount through its various departments (health, education and defence). The government is able to influence the economic climate in a country by varying either or both of these sides of the fiscal equation. In the UK, the chancellor of the exchequer is in charge of fiscal policy.

Monetary policy is the regulation of the national economy by varying the supply and price of money. Money supply concerns the volume of money (in its various forms) in the economy and the 'price' of money is the base rate, which determines the interest rate that banks and other lenders charge for borrowings. Since May 1997, monetary policy has been overseen by the Monetary Policy Committee of the Bank of England.

Economic growth, exchange rates, levels of income, inflation and unemployment will all affect people's ability to pay for products and services and hence affect levels and patterns of demand. Similarly, exchange rates and levels of productivity, wages and inflation will affect the costs of production and competitiveness. All these indicators must be monitored in comparison to those faced by competitors abroad to provide indications of changes in international competitiveness.

Natural influences

The natural environment is able to exert significant influence on business in some situations, although for other businesses, it may have no influence at all. As with sociodemographic, political and economic influences, the more widely spread the company's operations are, the more possible natural variables the company will need to be aware of. In this context, natural events include earthquakes, landslides, avalanches, hurricanes, floods, tsunamis (tidal waves), deforestation, droughts, freezes, and volcanic eruptions. There is, however, a debate as to the extent to which human activity has intensified the likelihood of these 'natural' events. On a more day-to-day basis, the weather can determine demand for goods such as ice creams, umbrellas and clothes, and services such as travel.

There are two observations about natural events:

1 Their impact on business activity can be powerful and, in almost all cases, the events are difficult to predict or avoid.
2 The risk of certain natural events occurring varies by geographical location.

Natural influences can occur on any scale, from very small to very large. A rainy spell may trigger an upturn in demand for umbrellas and Wellington boots, while a sunny spell may stimulate demand for ice cream, sunscreen and shorts. A river in flood may cause damage to homes, pubs, farms and other small businesses along its banks. The volcanic eruption on the island of Montserrat in 1997 destroyed valuable property as well as the island's tourism industry, and the volcanic eruptions in Iceland by Eyjafjallajökull affected 20 countries, shut

Natural influence: sunny spells lead to a demand for ice cream

down European airspace and cost the UK economy over £500m. On an even larger scale, earthquakes can destroy entire towns, kill tens of thousands of people and destroy all the businesses previously located there. For businesses affected by a natural disaster (or a manmade natural disaster, of which the latest in a long line is the BP oil spillage in the Gulf of Mexico in 2010, which cost the company an estimated $8bn and much damage to its reputation), the effects can be extremely costly and far-reaching.

Technological influences

Technology has had a major impact on most organizations and will undoubtedly continue to do so into the future, so we have dedicated Chapters 7 and 18 to explore technology in more detail. Here we look at some general developments. Analysis of the technological environment involves developing an understanding of the effects of changes in technology and their impact on all areas of an industry, its members and their activities, including:

- goods and services
- production processes
- information and communications
- transport and distribution
- society, politics and economics.

Changes in technology affect the products available to consumers and businesses, the quality of the products and their functionality. For example, the development of the microprocessor has made possible the development of many new products including PCs, and microprocessors now control the functioning of washing machines and programmable microwave ovens and DVD players. Production processes in many industries have been transformed and automated by wireless technology (Wi-Fi), broadband, computer-aided design (CAD) and computer-aided manufacturing (CAM). This has speeded up design processes, transformed working practices and increased the efficiency of production.

Developments in information and communications technology (ICT), like the development of PCs, iPads, networks, satellite, cable and digital communications, and the internet, together with rapid advances in software, have contributed to revolutionizing the way that business is conducted in many industries. Activities are now better coordinated, research and development (R&D) is speeded up and many businesses are much more flexible, connected and responsive.

Similarly, changes in transport technology have revolutionized business and have changed societies and cultures. It is possible to transport materials, components and products with far greater speed and at much lower cost as a result of developments in road, rail, sea and air transport. These improvements in transport have also increased the amount of personal and business travel that people undertake. Increasing personal travel has had significant influence on the patterns of consumption in many countries. In the UK, patterns of food and alcohol consumption have altered dramatically. In the markets for alcoholic drinks, for example, continental lager consumption has increased, partly as a result of the increased mobility that modern transport systems have brought about.

It is important to note, however, that not all technology is electronic. At is simplest, a technology is an innovation that in some way advances human understanding. In ancient Egypt, for example, the invention of the shadoof, an irrigation tool for transferring water from one location to another, was a technology. The bow and arrow, the invention of gunpowder, the discovery of the forces at work in an arched bridge and innovations leading to the shaping of a modern car are all examples of technology. Chemists work with chemical technologies that lead to the development of new medicines, and plastics, while engineers use different technologies to optimize the design of everything from roads to buildings to aircraft.

As a consequence, it is important that organizations monitor changes in the technologies that can affect their operations or their markets. In most industries, organizations must be flexible and be ready to innovate and to adopt new technologies as they come along. The way in which, and the extent to which, organizations do or do not employ the latest technology can be an important determinant of its competitive advantage.

9.3   The relationships between the SPENT influences

When carrying out a SPENT analysis, it is tempting to think of each influence as separate, when they are, in fact, often interlinked. Increasing concerns about ecology and 'green issues' provide a good example of this. In recent years, there has been an important social trend that has changed people's attitudes towards the effects of products and production processes on the environment. Whereas 20 years ago most consumers showed little concern for the long-term effects of products and processes on the natural environment, today people are increasingly aware of the need to protect it. This has led to pressure on governments to introduce legislation and other measures to control pollution. Consumers' desire for products that are themselves environmentally friendly and have been produced by 'green' methods has resulted in the realization by business that there are profits to be made by being environmentally friendly. This, in turn, has led to R&D aimed at designing products and processes that are less damaging to the environment. Among the numerous examples are aerosols that do not use CFCs, 'green IT', hybrid fuel cars, catalytic converters for automobile engines, unleaded fuel, reduced use of fossil fuels that produce gases which damage the ozone layer and so on. The witnessing of real environmental incidents on television (natural macroenvironmental influences) serves to intensify concern about environmental concerns and this, in turn, puts further societal pressure on businesses.

In this example, the effects of ecological issues (natural influences) on business combined with social factors (increased awareness of environmental issues) have impacted on political factors (legislation) and the three forces together have helped to stimulate technological change – products and processes that are less damaging to the environment. Accordingly, a macroenvironmental analysis should recognize the ways in which the five SPENT factors might be linked to each other.

By way of caution, however, it should be borne in mind that the SPENT framework is a 'prompt' to aid analysis and to ensure a disciplined approach to

CASE STUDY　City and Country Communications

Two years ago, City and Country Communications (CCC), the UK and international telecommunications company, announced a major restructuring of its organization and strategic approach. The announcement was made following a review of activities conducted by Booz Allen Hamilton, the top international consultants, and directed by John Graham, CCC's chief executive.

CCC sell comprehensive, mainly corporate, communications packages at premium prices. The company is a major international player in the field, with activities in 90 countries, and its stated strategic position, which is published each year in annual reports and corporate communications, is that it is 'a major global provider of communications solutions'. Marketing activity is extensive, in terms of attracting new business and servicing existing contracts. CCC ensures that there is always an extensive range of fixed-line and mobile telecommunication and internet/web-based add-ons, which are made available to existing customers at premium prices and charges. CCC has recently agreed a comprehensive contract with Apple to buy mobile-based apps at wholesale prices, and package them and sell them on as individual add-ons to their present product and service ranges.

Revenues last year were £2.5bn, with a profit margin of 6%; the percentage profit margin had changed little over the past decade, even though revenues had exactly doubled over the same period. However, in common with the majority of telecommunications, internet service and satellite providers, in recent years, costs have been rising and revenues falling. Additionally, capital gearing is very high, with loans providing 60% of the capital base of the company. CCC's share price has fallen sharply, declining by 80% over the past seven years. Recently, the share price has risen by about 5%, but the share value and the trading outlook remain uncertain.

Consequently, top and senior management had ordered the review, and had engaged Booz Allen Hamilton to assist in providing clarity and direction, and an independent perspective. After the review was completed, Graham took charge of the changes. The basis of the approach was to take costs out of the business where possible, and to concentrate production and sales efforts where these were most likely to have their greatest effect.

Additionally, the company was to move to high-tech production and sales, and this was in order to gain a stronger foothold on the corporate sectors of Western Europe, North America and East Asia. In support of this, CCC relocated its head office from London to Hong Kong, so as to be closer to the locations of high-tech production and desired business development in East Asia. CCC closed down the London offices in Docklands, and opened a regional office in Manchester, serving the whole of the UK and EU.

Graham also stated that the company was to reduce staff by 3,000, or about 10% of the workforce, with most of the jobs being lost in middle management. Manufacturing, especially of the new high-tech equipment, was to be contracted out to providers in East Asia and the Pacific Rim, and the technology for each corporate package would be put together on an individual and customized basis. The stated aim of the new high-tech products was to be fast, effective, reliable and energy-efficient, and this was to be a key priority of the new marketing efforts, sales pitches and presentations.

Concentrating production and sales efforts meant reducing the customer base. The overwhelming majority of CCC's customers were (and remain) companies and organizations. The stated aim was to reduce the present customer base of 30,000, so as to concentrate on the 3,000 most profitable and valuable customers. This core of 3,000 would form the focus of the new marketing and sales initiatives. As well as concentrating on these large, valuable existing clients, CCC would also identify and target new clients whose revenues and contract values were known, believed or understood to be in the same range as the core clientele.

So in March last year, the company duly cut off the 27,000 customers that it had notified that it no longer needed or wanted; these customers had to find new telecommunications provisions. The projected loss of revenues from these 27,000 customers was £93m, but this was stated to represent only 4% of turnover.

Case study questions

1　What is the strategy of this company? Where do its sources of competitive advantage lie?
2　Comment on the stated intent of the company. What else now needs to happen and why?
3　How would you analyse the environment and the strengths and shortcomings of deciding that you no longer need or want a particular customer base?
4　Where do the company's immediate problems and priorities now lie?

macroenvironmental analysis. The importance of the process is to identify issues that will have an impact on the organization and the industry. Categorizing them correctly between the factors is of secondary importance.

9.4 Using the SPENT analysis

Now that we know what the SPENT influences are and how they are interrelated, we turn to actually using the framework in strategic analysis. We generally think of the analysis as falling into four stages:

1 Scanning and monitoring the macroenvironment for actual or potential changes in social, political, economic, natural and sociodemographic factors.
2 Assessing the relevance and importance of the changes for the market, industry and business.
3 Analysing each of the relevant changes in detail and the potential relationships between them.
4 Assessing the potential impact of the changes on the market, industry and business.

What to analyse

When managers carry out a SPENT analysis as part of a strategic analysis (and the same is true of students examining a case study), they would normally examine how each factor might impact on:

- *the industry in which the organization competes:* the effects of SPENT factors on the five competitive forces (buyer power, supplier power, threat of entry, threat of substitutes, competitive rivalry)
- *an organization's markets:* the effects of SPENT factors on product markets, for example market size, structure, segments, customer wants, and so on, and the resource markets in which organizations gain their inputs
- *the internal parts of an organization:* the effects of SPENT factors on the organization's core competences, strategies, resources, and value systems.

3

Example   **SPENT analysis features**

Social:
- Demographics – market, labour, national, international and so on
- Education/training
- Religion, beliefs, values and attitudes
- Lifestyles
- Pollution, green issues, energy
- Could include war, unemployment, terrorism

Political:
- Government policies – environmental, fiscal, international, grants, competition policy
- Contending party policies
- European/worldwide agreements – EU, WTO
- Political stability, war, terrorism
- Levels of government interference/power

- Anti-trust activities
- Trade barriers
- International 'opinion'
- Defence issues
- Elections/takeovers and so on
- Budget
- Health and safety/fire
- Employment
- Environment
- Criminal and commercial law (UK Competition Commission)
- EC law, for example 2007 EC Package Travel Directive
- International law
- UK Carbon Reduction Commitment scheme

- Unspoken/written regulations – etiquette
- General government company law

Economic:

- Recession/boom
- GDP/GNP national accounting
- Balance of payments/public sector borrowing requirement
- Fiscal issues
- Inflation/interest rates
- Local/regional/national/international market forces
- Labour issues/unemployment
- Pricing
- Issues affecting cost of factors of production
- Purchasing power – income, savings, credit and so on
- Class divide – income
- Monetarism vs Keynsianism
- Monetary union
- Corporate and business tax, relief, costs and so on

Natural:

- Climate change
- Natural disasters
- Weather
- Availability of natural resources

Technological:

- Innovation
- Automation
- Change – speed
- Infrastructure
- New technology and emerging technologies
- Consider – necessity of change, competitive advantage/environment, need for labour, effects of more free time

There is a very close link between social, political and economic factors, with technology facilitating and driving issues, and legislation regulating developments.

This is a helpful chapter to refer to when completing 1.1.1 PEST Analysis within the External Analysis section in Phase 1 of the **Strategic Planning Software** (www.planning-strategy.com). See particularly section 9.2 SPENT analysis.

For test questions, extra case studies, audio case studies, weblinks, videolinks and more to help you understand the topics covered in this chapter, visit our companion website at www.macmillanihe.com/companion/business/campbell.

VOCAB CHECKLIST FOR ESL STUDENTS

Automation
Balance of payments
Biotechnology
Boom
CFCs
Class divide (see 'classism')
Deforestation
Ecology
Economic indicators
Etiquette
Exchange rates
Expenditure

Fiscal policy (see 'fiscal' and 'policy')
Functionality
Gross domestic product
Inflation
Interest rates
Irrigation
Life sciences
Microprocessor
Mnemonic
Monetarism
Monetary policy (see 'monetary' and 'policy')

Ozone layer
Profit margin
Revenue
Sociodemographic (see 'socio-' and 'demographic')
Subnational (see 'sub-' and 'national')
Supranational
Takeovers
Taxation
Trade unions

Definitions for these terms can be found in the 'Vocab Zone' of the companion website, which provides free access to the Macmillan English Dictionary online at www.macmillanihe.com/companion/business/campbell.

REVIEW QUESTIONS

1 Explain what the macroenvironment is and how it can impact on an organization.
2 Explain how different types of change can influence an organization's reaction to environmental shifts.
3 What are Ginter and Duncan's mechanisms of carrying out macroenvironmental analysis?
4 Explain how an organization can use the SPENT analysis to inform its strategy.

DISCUSSION TOPIC

It is not worth monitoring the macroenvironment because all organizations are impacted on, so there is no effect on the competitive position of the organization. Discuss.

HOT TOPICS – Research project areas to investigate

If you have a project to do, why not investigate ...

■ ... how organizations in the financial services sector monitor changes in the business environment.
■ ... which factors of the macroenvironment impact most on fast-food operations.

Recommended reading

3

Albright, K.S. (2004) 'Environmental scanning: radar for success', *Information Management Journal,* **38**(3): 38–45.

Aldehayyat, J. and Anchor, J. (2008) 'Strategic planning tools and techniques in Jordan: awareness and use', *Strategic Change,* **17**(7/8): 281–93.

Chakravarthy, B. (1997) 'A new strategy framework for coping with turbulence', *Sloan Management Review,* **38**(2): 69–82.

Dave, V. (2006) 'Perceptions of strategic uncertainty: a structural exploration', *Journal of Small Business and Entrepreneurship,* **19**(1): 21–35.

Elenkov, D.E. (1997) 'Strategic uncertainty and environmental scanning: the case for institutional influences on scanning behaviour', *Strategic Management Journal,* **18**(4): 287–302.

Fahey, L. and Narayanan, V.K. (1986) *Macroenvironmental Analysis for Strategic Management*, St Paul, MN: West Publishing.

Helms, M.M. and Wright, P. (1992) 'External considerations: their influence on future strategic planning', *Management Decision,* **30**(8): 4–11.

Jian Kang, J., Cheah, C., Chew, D. and Liu, G. (2007) 'Strategic adaptations to environments inside China: an empirical investigation in the construction industry', *Chinese Management Studies,* **1**(1): 42–56.

Levitt, T. (1983) 'The globalisation of markets', *Harvard Business Review,* **6**(3).

Makridakis, S. (1990) *Forecasting, Planning, and Strategy for the 21st Century*, New York: Free Press.

Mintzberg, H. (1991) *The Strategy Process: Concepts, Contexts, Cases*, Englewoods Cliffs, NJ: Prentice Hall.

Sanchez, R. (1993) 'Strategic flexibility, firm organization, and managerial work in dynamic markets: a strategic options perspective', *Advances in Strategic Management,* 9: 251–91.

Sanchez, R. (1995) 'Strategic flexibility in product competition', *Strategic Management Journal,* **16**(5): 135–59.

Stonehouse, G.H., Hamill, J. and Purdie, A. (1999) *Global and Transnational Business: Strategy and Management*, London: John Wiley.

Strebel, P. (1992) *Breakpoints*, Cambridge, MA: Harvard Business School Press.

Thomas, H. (2007) 'An analysis of the environment and competitive dynamics of management education', *Journal of Management Development,* **26**(1): 33–42.

Turner, I. (1996) 'Working with chaos', *Financial Times*, 4 October.

Chapter reference

Ginter, P. and Duncan, J. (1990) 'Macroenvironmental analysis for strategic management', *Long Range Planning,* **23**(6): 91–100.

Chapter 10

The microenvironment: markets and analysis of the competitive environment

Introduction and chapter overview

In this chapter we explore the importance of the microenvironment and the nature and structure of industries and markets. We are then able to determine how elements like market share influence business strategy. We focus attention on the customer and forms of market segmentation, before relating the ideas and concepts to industry analysis, strategic groups and alternative resource-based view approaches to competing.

Learning objectives

After studying this chapter, you should be able to:

- explain what is meant by an industry
- explain the term 'market' and describe three ways in which markets can be defined
- describe market segmentation and explain the three ways markets can be segmented
- explain the importance of industry and market analysis
- describe the construction and application of Porter's five forces framework
- define and distinguish between competitive and collaborative behaviour in industries
- describe and explain the limitations of the resource-based model of industry analysis
- define strategic groups and describe their usefulness in industry analysis

10.1 Industries and markets: the importance of industry and market identification

Some strategic management texts wrongly use the terms 'industry' and 'market' interchangeably. Kay (1995) correctly pointed out that to confuse the two concepts can result in a flawed analysis of the competitive environment and, hence, in flawed strategy. Modern businesses (especially larger companies) may operate in more than one industry and in more than one market. Each industry and market will have its own distinctive structure and characteristics, which will have particular implications for the formulation of business strategy. Kay (1993, p. 127) also pointed out that a distinctive capability, or core competence, 'becomes a competitive advantage only when it is applied in a market or markets'. Industries are centred on the supply of a product, while markets are concerned with demand. It is important, therefore, to understand and analyse both industries and markets to assist in the process of strategy selection.

KEY CONCEPTS

Industries produce goods and services – the supply side of the economic system.
Markets consume goods and services that have been produced by industries – the demand side of the economic system.

The industry

It is sometimes difficult to define a particular industry precisely. Porter (1980) defined an industry as a group of businesses whose products are close substitutes, but this definition can be inadequate because some organizations and industries produce a range of products for different markets. Alternatively, organizations can be grouped according to the similarity of their production processes. Two major official classifications of industries employing this means of grouping are the Standard Industrial Classification of Economic Activities in the UK and the Nomenclature Générale des Activités Économiques dans les Communautés Européennes of the EU. These classifications, mainly used by investors and stock markets, can be extended to define an industry as a group of businesses that shares similar products, processes, technologies, competences, suppliers and distribution channels. Analysis of these features of an industry will inform the process of strategy formulation.

The competitors in a given industry may produce products for more than one market. For example, businesses in the 'white goods' industry produce both washing machines and refrigerators. The materials, technology, skills and processes employed in the manufacture of both products are similar. The materials used are obtained from similar suppliers and the products are sold to consumers through the same distributors (the main electrical retail multiples). Clearly, there is an identifiable 'white goods' industry. Yet both these products (washing machines and refrigerators) satisfy different customer needs, are used for entirely different purposes and are therefore sold to separate markets. One make of washing machines competes with another, while one make of refrigerator competes with another.

The following are usually relevant when analysing an industry:

- Location
- Location of support and resource markets for the industry
- Extent of concentration or fragmentation, that is, industry structure
- Product types produced
- Levels of output, growth and life cycle position
- Ownership issues
- The other activities of industry members.

The market

While an industry is centred on producers of a product (a good or service), a market is centred on customers and their requirements (needs and wants). A particular market consists of a group of customers with a specific set of requirements that may be satisfied by one or more products. Analysis of a market will involve gaining an understanding of customers, their requirements, the products which satisfy those requirements, the organizations producing the products and the means by which customers obtain those products (distribution channels).

As well as selling their products in markets, businesses also obtain their resources (labour, materials, machinery and so on) in markets, referred to as 'resource markets'. Additionally, most businesses are interested in markets for substitute products and they will also be keen to investigate new markets for their products.

The relationship between a business, its industry and markets

The analysis of its industry and markets allows a business to:

- identify other industries where it may be able to deploy its core competences
- understand the nature of its customers and their needs
- identify new markets where its core competences may be exploited
- identify threats from existing and potential competitors in its own and other industries
- understand markets from which it obtains its resources.

Analysis of the competitive environment (industry and market) is as important to the development of an organization's future strategy as is internal analysis (the subject of Part 2). The industry and market context play an important role in shaping an organization's competences and core competences. The core competences of a business must continually be reviewed in relation to changing customer needs, competitors' competences, and other market opportunities.

Defining markets and market share

Economists refer to a market as a system with two 'sides'. The demand side comprises buyers or consumers of a product or resource, while the supply side produces or manufactures a product or resource.

In strategy, we often use the term slightly differently. By market, we usually mean a group of actual or potential customers with similar needs or wants (the demand side). We refer to the supply side as an industry.

The definition and boundaries of an organization's markets represent a key starting point for the formulation of strategy, and provide a basis for measuring competitive performance. The analysis and definition of markets will provide key information concerning threats and opportunities.

> **Market share** is a measure of an organization's performance with regard to its ability to win and retain customers.

Market share is a measure of an organization's performance with regard to its ability to win and retain customers. It can be measured either by volume or by value. Volume measures concern the organization's share of units sold to the market, for example number of barrels of oil sold by an oil company in proportion to the total number of barrels sold. Value measures concern the sales turnover of one company in proportion to the total value of the market.

We can also define the boundaries of markets in different ways. If different companies define a market in different ways, it is not surprising that the sum of their claimed market share may total more or less than 100%. The grocery market, for example, may mean different things to different companies. One might include just the English market for groceries, while another might measure it for the whole UK. It is important that market share measures are stated explicitly, with the market boundaries clearly defined.

There are three ways in which markets are commonly defined: based on product, based on need satisfaction or function performed, or based on customer identity.

We will briefly examine each of these in turn.

Market based on product

If someone working for an organization is asked what market they are in, a common reply will be to describe the products that are produced and/or sold. Thus, we would have examples like 'consumer detergents' or 'industrial machinery'. If the product definition is wide, this type of definition is close to describing an industry. Since government economic statistics are often produced on this basis, markets defined in this way often have the advantage of ease of measurement.

A drawback of this approach is that it sometimes fails to take into account that a product may provide a range of different benefits, and the same need might be met by different products, often derived from completely different technology. This can lead to a failure to recognize threats that may come from a different industry altogether. Cinema and computer games appear to be entirely different products with different markets, but they both may compete for customers' discretionary income and time if they are considered as part of the 'leisure' market.

An advantage of a product-based definition of markets can be that economies of scale of production may be gained by the sharing of a particular production process. Taken to extreme, this can lead to a view of a market as the market for the products that a company happens to make, even where they have little in common apart from a production process. An example of this would be a company using a plastic moulding machine. If the company were to utilize the machine 7 days a week, 24 hours a day, it would be efficient in production terms. However, if the range of products included golf tees, toys and components for the motor industry, the different end customers would make it difficult to sell the products economically. It would have sacrificed marketing synergy for production efficiency, and to analyse its customer base, it would have to recognize that it operated in several markets.

Market based on need satisfaction or function performed

The reason why consumers purchase a good or service is to gain utility. The concept of utility infers that whenever a consumer makes a purchase, they make a cost–benefit calculation, wherein they judge that the benefit they receive from the product is worth more than the price paid. This understanding enables the organization to identify its markets according to customer's perceptions.

While the need satisfaction definition can lead to a more open-minded approach to the formulation of strategy, its weakness can be that broad definitions can lead to a view of markets that does not allow a practical approach to decision-making. A cinema chain, for example, might define itself as being in the

The concept of **utility** infers that whenever a consumer makes a purchase, they make a cost–benefit calculation, wherein they judge that the benefit they receive from the product is worth more than the price paid.

'leisure' market, but it is probably wise for cinema companies to also consider threats and opportunities that might arise from television, bars, computer games, holidays and so on. Opportunities only arise from leisure activities that the company's competences would allow it to enter, and threats would come from activities that would be likely to substitute customers' business.

KEY CONCEPTS

A **want** is a good or service that is desired but is not necessarily essential.
A **need** is a good or service that is deemed essential or is currently lacking.

Market based on customer identity

Groups of customers have requirements in common, and differ from other groups of customers. In this way, the identity of customers can be used to define markets. We could, for example, consider the 'office consumables market' a quite distinct market. The market might be for products as diverse as pencils, pens, envelopes, computer disks and so on, but the market could clearly be seen as being for things that offices in organizations need to buy on a regular basis.

In terms of strategy formulation, the advantage of this approach is that it allows accurate targeting of the customer, so that efficient use can be made of advertising, mailshots, personal selling and so on. Its main disadvantage is that while marketing economies may be made, there is a risk that a number of different technologies need to be employed, so that it would be uneconomic to produce all the items required, and some or all of the products sold would have to be bought in. We can contrast this with the product definition approach in that with this, some marketing may have to be subcontracted, whereas with the customer identity approach, some manufacturing is likely to be outsourced.

Combined definition

In practice, most businesses serve several markets with a range of products. They will define their markets with a combination of the ways listed here, and to the extent that one or another approach is uppermost, the advantages and disadvantages that we have already encountered will apply. A key task for management at the strategic level is to produce combinations that gain synergistic benefits and that enable opportunities to be best chosen and exploited. In cases where changes in aspects of the technology of supply, or the characteristics of markets take place so that synergies previously achievable are no longer there, a case exists for restructuring an organization to divest itself of some activities and/or to acquire new ones.

In terms of working out competitive success in markets, a key concept is that of the 'served market'. This is that part of a market that the company is in. It is on that basis that the measure of market share is most meaningful.

10.2   Market segmentation

Markets are rarely completely homogeneous. Within markets, there are groups of customers with requirements that are similar, and it is this similarity of needs and wants that distinguishes one market segment from another. These 'submarkets' are known as 'market segments'. By considering the extent to which the segments should be treated differently from others, and which ones will be chosen to serve, organizations can develop target markets and gain a focus for their commercial activity.

This process of segmentation represents a powerful competitive tool. It is true to say that a business will prosper by giving the customer what the customer wants. Since not all customers are likely to want the same thing, then identifying subgroups and attending to their requirements more exactly is a way of gaining competitive advantage. We might say that it is better to be hated by half of potential customers and loved by the other half than to be quite liked by them all. The latter is a recipe for being everyone's second choice, and underlines the danger of placing too much reliance on averages in market research.

By identifying a specific market segment and concentrating marketing efforts on the segment, many organizations can build a mini-monopoly in that segment. Organizations that have identified a highly specific segment can succeed and gain reasonable profits by configuring their internal activities to precisely meet the needs and wants of the customer group.

For the most part, we can assume that segments exist naturally in most markets, and it is up to organizations to exploit the differences that exist in the submarkets. We do, however, have to recognize that the activities of companies can also shape segments to some extent. We could expect, for example, that men and women may buy differently. If, in those markets, suppliers offer and promote different products to men and women, then this tendency will be reinforced.

Three broad approaches are recognized in respect of the ways that an organization can approach marketing to market segments (or submarkets):

- *Undifferentiated marketing:* This means that the organization denies that its total markets are segmented at all and relates to the whole market, assuming that demand is homogeneous in nature. The economies of a standardized approach to marketing outweigh any advantages of segmenting the market. Undifferentiated marketing is appropriate when the market the organization serves is genuinely homogeneous in nature. In Chapter 11 we will encounter this concept in the context of internationalization and globalization. Companies like Coca-Cola, Levi's and McDonald's employ this strategy successfully because demand for their products does not vary much from country to country. Organizations that adopt this approach have standard products, standard packaging and advertising, and these differ little or not at all between countries.

- *Differentiated marketing:* Companies that adopt differentiated marketing recognize separate segments of the total market and treat each segment separately. Different segments need not always be different in every respect – it could be that some standard products can be promoted differently to different segments because of certain similarities or common characteristics. In other cases, the product will be substantially or completely different and marketing to each segment will necessitate a distinctive approach to each one.

■ *Concentrated marketing:* An extreme form of differentiated marketing is concentrated marketing, where an organization's effort is focused on a single market segment. In return for giving up substantial parts of the market, an effort is made to specialize in just one niche, and so we may see this referred to as 'niche marketing'. This approach offers the advantage that the organization can gain detailed, in-depth knowledge of its segment, which, in turn, can enable an ever improving match between the product and the customer requirement. The disadvantage relates to the extent to which the company may become dependent on the one segment it serves. Any negative change in the demand pattern of the segment will leave the supplier vulnerable because of the narrowness of its market portfolio.

A company operating with a large product range in many markets will typically use a multifocus strategy – a combination of the above.

Product positioning

Product positioning is the way in which a product or a brand is perceived in relation to preferences of market segments, and in relation to competitive products. Thus, in a particular alcoholic drinks market, attributes thought to be important by customers might be alcoholic strength (weak versus strong) and taste (bitter versus sweet). There may be groups of customers with preferences for any combinations of these attributes, and a range of competing products that by means of the products themselves and their advertising and promotion are seen to occupy a particular position. This can be represented by a product positioning diagram, as shown in Figure 10.1. The oval shapes on the chart represent the preferences of a group of customers and the customer perceptions of existing products are marked by an X.

If an organization finds a group of customers with a particular requirement for a combination not currently offered, it will literally have discovered a 'gap' in the market (see bottom right of the figure). More likely, it will have to make the best of subtle differences in position, since all major combinations may be filled.

> **Product positioning** is the way in which a product or a brand is perceived in relation to the preferences of market segments, and in relation to competitive products.

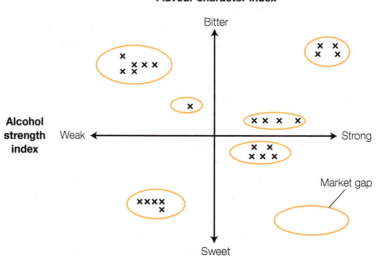

Figure 10.1 The product positioning framework

Bases for segmentation

A segmentation base is a way of distinguishing one customer type from another. There are potentially limitless ways that markets can be divided into segments, and the ultimate segment would be one customer. In practice, a number of criteria typically have to be met before a base for dividing a market can be considered to be commercially viable. The major criteria for establishing market segments are:

- market size
- identifiability of the segment
- measurability of the segment
- accessibility to the segment
- buying behavioural characteristics of the segment.

We will briefly examine these criteria in turn.

Market size criteria

Smaller segments may allow more and more exact matching of customer requirements, but this comes at a cost as marketing and manufacturing economies of scale are lost. If an advertisement is produced, there will be fixed costs of production and design, whether it is run once or several times. In production, separate tooling might be required to produce different versions of a product. Companies can reduce the cost by producing different versions of a product with a large number of common components.

In the 21st century, some of long-held assumptions that limit the smallest segments that can be economically reached are likely to change. Flexible manufacturing technology is reducing the minimum production runs that are economic for a separate product. In advertising, we are used to the concept of broadcasting. In the future, we shall have to become used to the concept of 'narrowcasting', as a revolution in media takes place. At present, if a company advertises on television, and its product is only of interest to city dwellers, it is also unnecessarily paying to reach all the rural viewers. Cable technology allows organizations to direct adverts much more accurately at prospective customers. The same process is taking place in mailshots, where most mailshots can now be accurately targeted and the internet allows people to select what they want to see. The result of this process will be that great rewards will be available to organizations that can come up with sophisticated segmentation strategies, as opposed to straightforward old-style mass marketing.

Identifiability of the segment

Ultimately, whatever base is being used for segmentation, we should still be able to answer the question as to *who* is in the segment, even if this is a bit indistinct. Otherwise, the organization will not be able to reach the segment effectively.

Measurability of the segment

If we cannot measure the size of the segment that using a particular base would create, we would not be in a position to judge its potential. Any organization that adopts a marketing strategy without accurate knowledge of the size of the market segment cannot be sure it has the optimal level of information on which to make important investment decisions.

Accessibility to the segment

Any market segment identified must be reachable by an organization's marketing communications. However, in order for marketing communications to be cost-effective, they must be aimed at the target segment and not at others. This latter issue requires a careful examination of the media and how effectively each medium reaches the target segment within cost constraints.

Buying behavioural characteristics of the segment

Even if all the other criteria can be met, it is pointless to divide a market up in a way that does not represent real or potential differences in buying behaviour. The whole point of market segmentation is to identify subgroups of a market that share commonalities such that their buying behaviour will be similar. If this is not the case for some reason, the exercise is useless.

In consumer markets (as distinct from industrial markets), we use the ways in which people naturally differ to divide markets up. The most commonly used 'people dividers' are:

- *Demographic variables:* such as difference by age, stage of family life cycle, gender, income, occupation, education, race, religion
- *Geographic variables:* such as difference by country, region, type of housing/ neighbourhood (geodemographic)
- *Psychographic variables:* which exploit the lifestyle, personality or intelligence differences between people
- *Behavioural variables:* such as attitudes to brand loyalty, frequency of use (heavy or light usage), or consumption occasion.

KEY CONCEPT

Demographic variables are used to define market segments in consumer markets. It is self-evident that people can be divided from each other in many ways and the more variables that are applied to a total market, the smaller and more homogeneous the segment becomes. The most commonly used demographic variables are those that are readily identifiable. Differences such as sex, age, occupation, type of residence and stage of family life cycle are all easy to identify. Less easy – and therefore less usable – are differences such as religious affiliation, sexual orientation, political persuasion and musical preferences. It is unfortunate, then, that some of this latter category of variables are powerful in respect of their ability to predict patterns of demand for some product types.

10.3   Industry analysis

Industry analysis aims to establish the nature of the competition in an industry and the competitive position of a business with respect to its microenvironment.

Industry analysis aims to establish the nature of the competition in an industry and the competitive position of a business with respect to its microenvironment. Industry dynamics, in turn, are affected by changes in the macroenvironment (see Chapter 9). For example, ageing populations in many developed countries have significantly affected the need to develop drugs suitable for treating the ailments of older people. There is a danger that industry analysis can be seen as a 'one-off' activity, but like all components of the strategic process, it should be undertaken on an ongoing basis. The industry analysis framework developed by Porter (1980) is the most widely used and is explained in this section.

Porter's five forces model of industry analysis

Porter (1980) developed a framework for analysing the nature and extent of competition within an industry. He argued that there are five competitive forces that determine the nature of competition within an industry. Understanding the nature and strength of each of the five forces within an industry assists managers in developing the competitive strategy of their organization.

The five forces are:

- the threat of new entrants to the industry
- the threat of substitute products
- the power of buyers or customers
- the power of suppliers (to businesses in the industry)
- rivalry among businesses in the industry.

By determining the relative 'power' of each of these forces, an organization can identify how to position itself to take advantage of opportunities and overcome or circumvent threats. The strategy of an organization may then be designed to exploit the competitive forces at work within an industry.

3

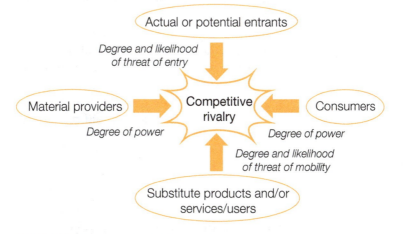

Figure 10.2 Porter's five forces framework
Source: Adapted from Porter, 1998

When using Porter's framework, it is important to identify which of the five forces are the key forces at work in an industry at any given point in time. In many cases, it transpires that one or more of the five forces prove to be 'key forces' and the strategic analysis must focus on these if it is to use the framework fruitfully. The dynamic nature of the competitive environment (meaning that it is constantly changing) means that the relative strength of the forces in a particular industry will change over time. Thus it is important that the five forces analysis is repeated on a regular basis so as to detect such changes before competitors and allow an early adjustment of strategy. Before any conclusions can be drawn about the nature of competition within an industry, each of the five forces must be analysed in detail.

We will now discuss each of the five forces in turn.

Force 1: the threat of new entrants to the industry

The **threat of new entrants** to the industry depends on the 'height' of entry barriers.

The threat of new entrants to the industry depends on the 'height' of entry barriers. As a rule of thumb, the lower the entry barriers to an industry, the more competitors in the industry. Barriers to entry can take a number of forms:

- *The capital costs:* The size of the investment required by a business wishing to enter the industry will be an important determinant of the extent of the threat of new entrants. The higher the investment required, the less the threat from new entrants. The lower the required investment, the greater the threat.
- *Regulatory and legal constraints:* Industry regulation varies. Some, such as energy, pharmaceuticals and defence equipment, are subject to a complex regulatory framework, while others are less so. In some industries, regulation concerns health and safety, product handling, and licences to operate, export, or set up new facilities. Each regulatory or legal permission or restriction is capable of acting as a barrier to entry.
- *Brand loyalty and customer switching costs:* If the players in an industry produce differentiated products and customers are brand loyal, potential new entrants will encounter resistance in trying to enter the industry. Brand loyalty will also be an important factor in increasing the costs for customers of switching to the products of new competitors.
- *Economies of scale available to existing competitors:* If existing competitors are already obtaining substantial economies of scale, it will give them an advantage over new competitors who will not be able to match their lower unit costs of production.
- *Access to input and distribution channels:* New competitors may find it difficult to gain access to channels of distribution, which will make it difficult to provide their products to customers or obtain the inputs required or find markets for their outputs.
- *The resistance offered by existing businesses:* If existing competitors choose to resist strongly, it will make it difficult for new organizations to enter the industry. For example, if existing businesses are obtaining economies of scale, it will be possible for them to undercut the prices of new entrants because of their cost advantage. In some cases, existing competitors may make price cuts or increase marketing expenditure specifically in order to deter new entrants.

If barriers to entry make it difficult for new competitors to enter the industry, this will limit the amount of competition within it. As a result, competitors within the industry will attempt to strengthen the barriers to entry by cultivating brand loyalty, increasing the costs of entry and 'tying up' input and distribution channels as far as possible.

Force 2: the threat of substitute products

A **substitute** can be regarded as something that meets the same needs as the product of the industry.

A substitute can be regarded as something that meets the same needs as the product of the industry. For example, an individual wishing to cross the English Channel can choose to travel by cross-channel ferry, hovercraft or the train service through the Channel Tunnel. These products all provide the benefit to the customer of crossing to France, despite the fact that the ferry and rail services are provided by different industries. The extent of the threat from a particular substitute will depend on two factors:

- *The extent to which the price and performance of the substitute can match the industry's product:* Close substitutes whose performance is comparable to the industry's product and whose price is similar will be a serious threat to an industry. The more indirect the substitute, the less likely the price and performance will be comparable.
- *The willingness of buyers to switch to the substitute:* Buyers will be more willing to change suppliers from one industry if switching costs are low or if a competitor in another industry offers a product with lower price or improved performance. This is also closely tied in with the extent to which customers are brand loyal. The more loyal customers are to one supplier's products (for whatever reason), the less the threat from substitutes will be.

One of the key strategic manoeuvres in maintaining customer loyalty is to increase the cost – to the customer – of changing to a new supplier. If switching costs are high, customers will have an economic disincentive to switch and will tend to stay with the existing supplier. For substitution of products within an industry, switching costs are usually low. It costs nothing in money or effort, for example, to switch brands of coffee or washing powder. For indirect substitutes (those provided by other industries), there are likely to be higher actual or perceived switching costs. If buyers have had to make an investment in order to accommodate one supplier's product, the extra investment involved in switching would act as a disincentive.

Competitors in an industry will attempt to reduce the threat from substitute products by improving the performance of their products, by reducing costs and prices, and by differentiation.

> ### KEY CONCEPT
>
> **Switching costs** refer to substitute products, one of the barriers to mobility in a market. Switching costs are the cost (actual or perceived) of changing from one product or service provider to another. Such costs can be tangible or intangible in nature. Switching costs may be financial, but may also be expressed in terms of lower quality, reduced confidence in the competitor's product or poorer product performance.

Force 3: the bargaining power of buyers

The **bargaining power of buyers** is the extent to which the buyers of a product exert power over an industry. Broadly speaking, the more power buyers exert, the lower the transaction price. This has obvious implications for the profitability of the supplier. The bargaining power of buyers will be influenced by the following factors:

*The **bargaining power of buyers** is the extent to which the buyers of a product exert power over an industry.*

- *The number of customers and the volume of their purchases:* The fewer the buyers and the greater the volume of their purchases, the greater their bargaining power. A large number of buyers, each acting largely independently of each other and buying only small quantities of a product, have comparatively weak power.
- *The number of businesses supplying the product and their size:* If the industry in question is fairly concentrated and its members are large in comparison to the buyers, buying power will tend to be reduced. The degree of concentration has the effect that a few suppliers will tend to reduce the bargaining power of buyers, as choice and the ability to 'shop around' are reduced.
- *Switching costs and the availability of substitutes:* If the cost of switching between substitutes is low, then customers (buyers) will be more powerful because of the inability of industry players to inflate their prices, which will be constrained by the price of the substitute products.

We should bear in mind that buyers are not necessarily those at the end of the supply chain. At each stage of a supply chain, the bargaining power of buyers will have a strong influence on the prices charged and the industry structure. In the supply chain for beer, for example, the buyers include consumers, wholesalers, supermarket chains, pubs and restaurants. The amount of power that each buyer exerts can differ substantially. Supermarket chains can exert far greater pressure on brewers than can individual consumers.

Force 4: the bargaining power of suppliers

Businesses must obtain the resources they need to carry out their activities from resource suppliers. These resources fall into the four categories we encountered in Chapter 1: human, financial, physical and intellectual.

Resources are obtained in resource markets where prices are determined by the interaction between the businesses supplying a resource (suppliers) and the organizations from each of the industries using the particular resource in question. It is important to note that many resources are used by more than one industry. As a result, the bargaining power of suppliers will not be determined solely by their relationship with one industry but by their relationships with all the industries they serve.

The major factors determining the strength of suppliers are as follows:

- *The uniqueness and scarcity of the resource that suppliers provide:* If the resources provided to the industry are essential to it and have no close substitutes, suppliers are likely to command significant power over the industry. If the resource can be easily substituted by other resources, its suppliers will have little power. It is for this reason, for example, that people with rare or exceptional skills can command higher salaries than lesser skilled people.
- *The cost of switching to another resource:* If the resource can be easily substituted, switching costs will be low. If there is high labour turnover or low penalty clauses in debt rescheduling, the power over suppliers of these resources will be increased.
- *How many other industries have a requirement for the resource:* If suppliers provide a particular resource to several industries, they are less likely to be dependent on one single industry. Thus, the more industries to which they supply a resource, the greater their bargaining power.

The **bargaining power of suppliers** will not be determined solely by their relationship with one industry but by their relationships with all the industries they serve.

■ *The number and size of the resource suppliers:* If the number of organizations supplying a resource is small and there are a large number of buyers, the greater their power over the organizations in that industry. If the suppliers are small and there are a large number of them, they will be comparatively weak, particularly if they are small in comparison to the organizations buying the resource from them. For example, most of Marks & Spencer's suppliers are relatively weak because they are small in comparison to the retailer. Marks & Spencer has a number of suppliers and is able to switch suppliers if necessary to gain lower input costs or higher quality.

In short, suppliers to an industry will be most powerful when:

■ the resource they supply is scarce
■ there are few substitutes for the resource
■ switching costs are high
■ they supply the resource to several industries
■ the suppliers themselves are large
■ the organizations in the industry buying the resource are small.

When the opposite conditions apply, suppliers will be weak.

Force 5: the intensity of rivalry among competitors in the industry

Businesses within an industry will compete with each other in a number of ways. Broadly speaking, competition can take place on a price or non-price basis.

Price competition involves businesses trying to undercut each other's prices, which will, in turn, be dependent on their ability to reduce their costs of production. **Non-price competition** will take the form of branding, advertising, promotion, additional services to customers and product innovation. In some industries, competitive rivalry is fierce, while in others, it is less intense or even genteel.

In Figure 10.2 above, we see that the other four forces point in towards this fifth, central force. This is to remind us that the strength of this force is largely dependent on the contributions of the other four that 'feed' it. In particular, the intensity of competition in an industry will depend on the following factors:

■ *The height of entry barriers and the number and size of the competitors in the industry:* If there are a few large competitors in an industry, it is probably due to high entry barriers. Conversely, if an industry comprises many smaller competitors, this is probably the result of lower entry barriers. Competitive rivalry on both a price and non-price basis will be higher in the industry comprising more and smaller competitors.
■ *The maturity of the industry:* If the product is mature and the industry is subject to 'shake-out', competition will be more intense.
■ *The degree of customers' brand loyalty:* If customers are loyal to brands, there is likely to be less competition and what competition there is will be on a non-price basis. If there is little brand loyalty, competition will be more intense.
■ *The power of buyers and availability of substitutes:* If buyers are strong and there are close substitutes available for the product, the degree of competitive rivalry will be greater.

A high degree of rivalry will usually compromise the potential profitability of an industry and will typically result in innovation, which stimulates consumer demand for that industry's products. In recent years, many industries have become more competitive.

Price competition involves businesses trying to undercut each other's prices, which will, in turn, be dependent on their ability to reduce their costs of production.

Non-price competition will take the form of branding, advertising, promotion, additional services to customers and product innovation.

3

As has been discussed, a relationship can be established between a company's position in respect to the five forces and its potential profitability. Table 10.1 shows a summary of how the five forces can help to determine company and industry profitability.

Table 10.1 Summary of Porter's five forces and profitability

Force	Higher profitability	Lower profitability
Bargaining power of suppliers	Weak suppliers	Strong suppliers
Bargaining power of buyers	Weak buyers	Strong buyers
Threat of new entrants	High entry barriers	Low entry barriers
Threats from substitute products	Few possible substitutes	Many possible substitutes
Competitive rivalry	Little rivalry	Intense rivalry

Example   Five force analysis of the UK university sector

The UK university sector has seen vibrant growth in recent years. It is home to several world-class universities like Cambridge, Oxford and St Andrews, which have a long and illustrious history. The university sector is highly regarded and is the preferred destination for local and international students. The sector supports 2.4 million students (2008/09) and is home to more than 150 universities. It had a total income of nearly £24bn in 2007/08, a rise of 10.3% from the previous year's total of £21.2bn (www.hefce.ac.uk/pubs/hefce/2009/). During the past decade, the sector has seen a number of changes and is further consolidating to face future challenges.

The threat of entry

The sector comprises old traditional and modern new universities. Famous names like Cambridge, London School of Economics (LSE), Oxford, Warwick and so on are part of the higher education scenario and are ranked highly in global league tables. The sector is difficult to enter and the barriers are high, for example it is a knowledge-intensive sector, with competences and expertise built over time. Existing universities have developed competences through investments in research, teaching, pedagogical and support activities. Universities have also developed strong expertise in several fields, for example King's College in medicine, LSE in economics and management, and have attained international fame, reputation and recognition. New entrants face a barrier in attaining the required set of competences and face the task of raising the huge finances required for setting up the necessary infrastructure. Other barriers include satisfaction of legal and regulatory requirements and the ability to compete against the differentiation (in provision of market-oriented or specialist degrees, student placements, research excellence and so on) prevalent in the current market.

The threat of substitution

UK university education is of international repute and has attracted students since the 1800s. UK universities are pioneers in the education system and have laid the foundation

for similar systems in the rest of the world. The degree programmes and courses offered in English are innovative and are closely linked to the research strengths of university schools and departments. The threat of substitution is low and for a student looking for an alternative provider, the options are only available from outside the country.

The power of buyers

Porter (1980) theorized that a greater degree of standardization of products allows buyers to easily switch products and therefore increase their bargaining power. In the case of the UK university sector, the bargaining power of customers is relatively mixed. In the undergraduate scenario, buyer bargaining power is low, primarily because students face stiff competition for available places. The success of getting into a preferred university depends on school examinations, performance in interviews and general conduct. On the other hand, in the postgraduate and part-time scenario, the bargaining power is higher, as students have the option to pursue programmes of interest and have a choice of a variety of providers.

The power of suppliers

The university sector's main suppliers are funding bodies, equipment providers (IT and telephony, furniture, paper and so on), facility management providers and publishers. In the supplier list, except for funding bodies, universities have a choice over providers; their size allows them to exert a greater power over their suppliers. Typically, many suppliers would want universities as customers because of the potential higher volume of transactions and multi-year contracts. With respect to funding bodies, for example the Higher Education Funding Council for England, the bargaining power of universities is directly proportional to their performance. The better their performance in terms of research and teaching (noted in league tables), the higher their proportion of funding.

Competitive rivalry

The sector is highly consolidated: the players in the sector account for nearly all the higher education in the country. With universities providing programmes and degrees relating to medicine, biological sciences, social sciences, physical sciences, business studies, engineering and technology, arts, languages and history, the sector is intense and highly competitive. Many institutions operating in the sector have long-standing reputations and are considered as centres of excellence. For example, Warwick University is regarded as the hub for manufacturing research and is well known for its industrial collaborative efforts, while Glasgow University is known for its cancer research and is regarded as a pioneer in health sciences. The strong competition for government-funded resources pushes the universities to outperform one another and provides little room for outside players to enter the market.

Competitive and collaborative arenas

It is not always the case that businesses in an industry compete with each other – they might, from time to time, have reasons to collaborate with each other. Accordingly, in some 'arenas', businesses compete, while in others, they may work together.

At the root of this understanding is the fact that organizations and industries are open systems – they interact with many environments. The arenas in which the organization operates are:

- *the industry:* the industry within which the organization currently deploys its resources and competences in producing products.
- *resource markets:* the markets from which the organization, its competitors and other industries obtain their resources.

- *product markets:* markets where the organization sells its products. These can be divided into markets for the organization's products, markets for substitute products, and new markets into which the organization may be considering entry.
- *other industries:* where businesses possess similar competences to those of the organization. These industries are important for two reasons. First, the business may be considering entry into them, and, second, the organizations in these industries are potential competitors who may enter the business's industry and markets.

Each of these arenas must be analysed as they directly affect an organization's competitive positioning and hence its chances of outperforming competitors. The competitive and collaborative arena framework builds on Porter's five forces framework but explicitly recognizes that the competitive environment is divided into four separate but interrelated arenas.

A further example of the five forces framework is shown in Figure 10.3, where it has been applied to BSkyB. The BSkyB analysis highlights the dominant position of BSkyB and the resulting bargaining power that emerges, while also highlighting the huge potential for growth into domestic homes through building customer loyalty, exploiting scale and infrastructure and using new technology, such as remote recording, playback, HD, 3D TV and connected services. Overall, this industry can be seen to be increasingly dynamic and will be interesting to monitor for the future.

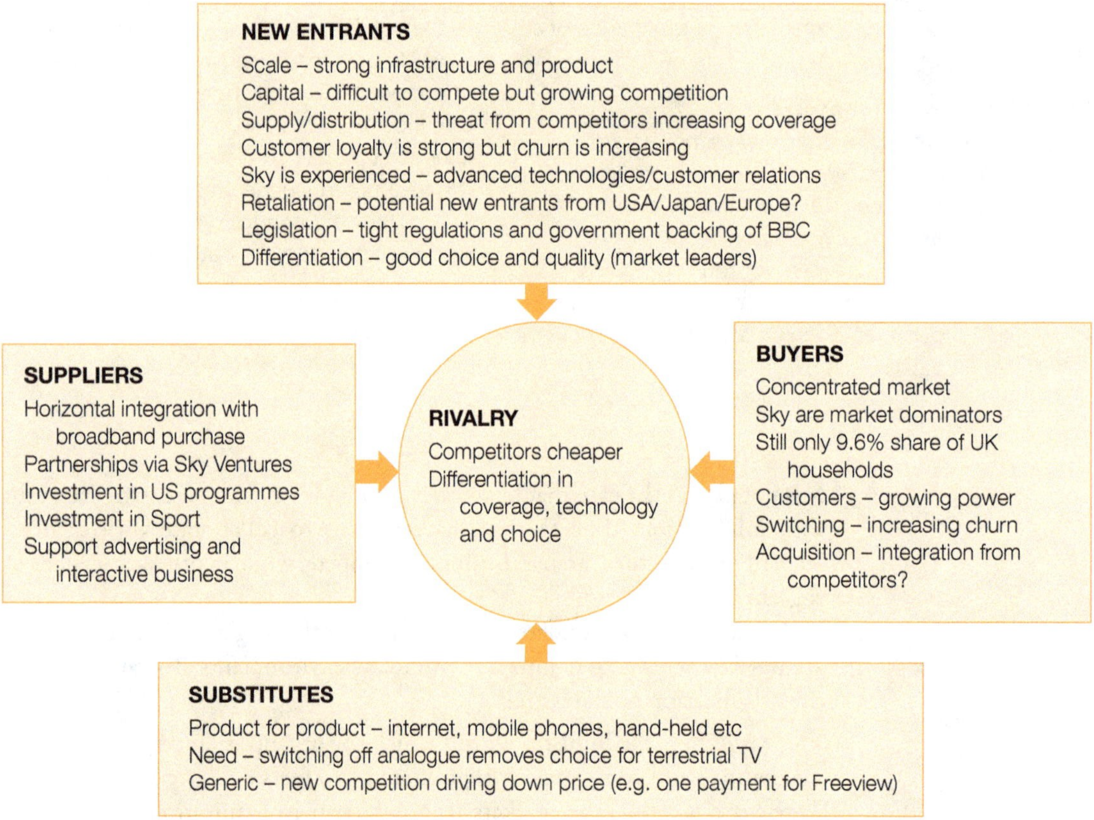

NEW ENTRANTS
Scale – strong infrastructure and product
Capital – difficult to compete but growing competition
Supply/distribution – threat from competitors increasing coverage
Customer loyalty is strong but churn is increasing
Sky is experienced – advanced technologies/customer relations
Retaliation – potential new entrants from USA/Japan/Europe?
Legislation – tight regulations and government backing of BBC
Differentiation – good choice and quality (market leaders)

SUPPLIERS
Horizontal integration with
    broadband purchase
Partnerships via Sky Ventures
Investment in US programmes
Investment in Sport
Support advertising and
    interactive business

RIVALRY
Competitors cheaper
Differentiation in
    coverage, technology
    and choice

BUYERS
Concentrated market
Sky are market dominators
Still only 9.6% share of UK
    households
Customers – growing power
Switching – increasing churn
Acquisition – integration from
    competitors?

SUBSTITUTES
Product for product – internet, mobile phones, hand-held etc
Need – switching off analogue removes choice for terrestrial TV
Generic – new competition driving down price (e.g. one payment for Freeview)

Figure 10.3 Five forces analysis applied to BSkyB

10.4 A resource-based approach to environmental analysis

So far, this chapter has concentrated on explaining the traditional strategic management frameworks employed in the analysis of the competitive environment. The resource-based approach to strategic management, which emphasizes the importance of core competences in achieving competitive advantage, uses a different approach to analyse the competitive environment.

There are several limitations to existing (traditional) frameworks:

- they do not sufficiently integrate external and internal analysis (Heene and Sanchez, 1997)
- they presuppose that businesses are naturally competitive and not collaborative in their behaviour
- they tend to emphasize product markets rather than those where organizations obtain their resources
- they do not adequately recognize the fact that organizations themselves may alter their own competitive environments by their competence-leveraging and competence-building activities
- they do not adequately recognize the fact that organizations currently outside a company's industry and market may pose a significant competitive threat if they possess similar core competences and distinctive capabilities
- they do not recognize that the leveraging of existing competences and the building of new ones may enable businesses to compete outside their current competitive arenas.

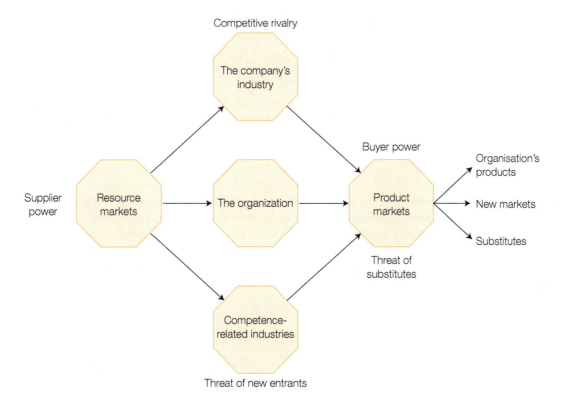

Figure 10.4 The resource-based model of strategy

A resource-based framework for analysis of the business and its competitive environment is shown in Figure 10.4. Analysis is divided into five interrelated areas:

- the organization
- its industry
- product markets – existing markets, markets for substitutes, potential new markets
- resource markets
- competence-related industries – those where businesses possess similar competences to those of competitors.

The significance of each area is considered in more detail.

The organization

'The organization' concerns the configuration of the internal value chain, its competences, resources and core competences (as discussed in Part 2, particularly Chapters 4 and 8). In this context, we are particularly concerned with analysing the organization's value-adding capabilities and its backward and forward value chain linkages.

The organization's industry

The organization's industry consists of the business and a group of companies producing similar products, employing similar capabilities and technology. Analysis of the industry examines, over time, for each player in the industry:

- skills and competences of competitors
- configuration of value-adding activities
- technologies employed
- number and relative size of competitors in the industry
- performance of competitors, particularly in financial terms
- ease of entry to and exit from the industry
- strategic groupings.

The **organization's industry** consists of the business and a group of companies producing similar products, employing similar capabilities and technology.

This analysis will assist the organization in gaining greater understanding of its core competences, its major competitors and their core competences, and competitive and collaborative opportunities and threats.

Product markets

Product markets are those where businesses deploy their competences and sell their products. A business may operate in one or more product markets. In addition, a business will be interested in understanding those markets it is considering entering on the basis of its core competences and also markets for substitute products. Each of these markets will have its own characteristics and each market can be analysed in terms of:

Product markets are those where businesses deploy their competences and sell their products.

- customer needs and motivations
- unmet customer needs
- market segments and their profitability
- the number of competitors in the market and their relative market shares
- the number of customers and their relative purchasing power
- access to distribution channels

- potential for collaboration with customers
- ease of entry
- potential for competence leveraging
- need for new competence building.

Unless an organization's products are sold at a profit, the business will ultimately fail. Market-driven businesses, which set out to meet existing customer needs, anticipate their currently unmet needs and actually seek to shape the needs of their customers, are likely to be the most successful. For example, Apple created a new customer need when it developed and launched the iPod and associated format for digital media.

Market groups

An important part of understanding the market is identifying groups within the market that share common needs. Such shared characteristics will cause specific customer groups to have different needs and to act and behave differently from other customer groups (or segments). Segmentation means dividing the total market into customer groupings, each with their own distinctive attributes and needs. Customer groups are commonly segmented according to demographic variables (or 'people dividers'), although other segmentation instruments are widely used. When customers are other businesses, they can be grouped by the nature of the business, organization type and size. Each segment is then analysed for its size and potential profitability, customer needs and potential demand, based on ability and willingness to buy. Segmentation analysis assists in the formulation of strategy by identifying particular segments and consumer characteristics that can then be targeted.

Customer motivations

Once market segments have been identified, they must be analysed to reveal the factors that influence customers to buy or not buy products. It is particularly important to understand factors affecting customer motivations, such as sensitivity to price, sensitivity to quality and the extent of brand loyalty.

Differences in customer motivations between market segments can be illustrated by reference to the market for air travel, which can be segmented into business and leisure travellers. Customers in each group have different characteristics and needs. Business travellers are not particularly price sensitive but are sensitive to standards of service, scheduling and availability of connections. Leisure travellers are generally much more price rather than service conscious and are less sensitive to scheduling and connections. Market research has an important role to play in building an understanding of customer needs so that they can be targeted by appropriate product or service features.

Potential new markets are those where the product or service bought by customers is based on similar competences to those of the organization or where customer needs are similar to those of customers in a business's market. If conditions are favourable, the organization may consider using its current competences to enter new markets. It may also have to build new competences in order to meet new customer needs.

Resource markets

Resource markets are those where organizations obtain finance, human resources, materials, equipment, services and so on. It is evident that businesses will normally operate in several such markets, each with its own characteristics, depending on the company-specific resources that are required. Resource markets can be analysed in terms of:

- resource requirements
- number of actual and potential resource suppliers
- size of suppliers
- supplier capabilities and competences
- potential for collaboration with resource suppliers
- access by competitors to suppliers
- the nature of the resource and the availability of substitutes.

By analysing each of its resource markets, business managers can identify the extent of the competition they face from resource suppliers, the competition they face from other competitors using the same resources, and the potential for collaboration with suppliers (if appropriate).

Competence-related industries

Other industries containing businesses with similar competences, which often produce products that are substitutes for those of the business in question, must also be analysed. This analysis is necessary for three reasons:

1 The organization may face a threat from other competitors possessing similar competences which may seek to enter its industry and markets.
2 The organization may be able to enter industries where competences are similar to those it already possesses.
3 The organization may be able to enter the markets currently served by competitors in the competence-related industry.

Competence-related industries can be analysed for:

- key competences of businesses in the industry
- number and size of businesses in the industry
- threat from competitors in such industries who may leverage their competences to enter the markets of the business
- opportunities for the business to leverage its existing competences and build new ones in order to enter competence-related industries and their markets
- substitutability of the products of the industry for those of the business – how close the substitute product is to satisfying the same consumer demands as the business's product or service.

The resource/competence-based model is more complex than the five forces framework but offers a more comprehensive analytical framework. It enables an organization to establish the extent of competition within its own industry and market. It also enables the organization to assess the threat of competition from competitors in industries where similar competences to their own are employed. Equally, based on this model, the organization is able to identify other markets which it may be able to enter by leveraging its existing competences and adding new ones.

CASE STUDY   National Bank of Poland

Five years ago, top and senior management at the National Bank of Poland met to try and assess the problems they were having with attracting, recruiting and retaining staff.

Initially, they were at a loss to explain things. After all, they were one of the most prestigious organizations in the country. Poland had joined the EU and was making strong headway. The central banking sector was a highly influential sector, at the heart of national and now international politics. Those who worked in the sector had enormous influence on the future political direction of nations, economies and institutions such as the EU, World Bank and International Monetary Fund (IMF).

Similar problems were being encountered elsewhere in the central banking sector. The Bank of England especially was another institution having great difficulty in attracting and retaining top-quality staff. Indeed, those in top, senior and key positions at the Bank of England wondered how they would ever be able to compete with the commercial banking sector in gaining and keeping expert staff.

The remit of the central banking sector is to advise governments on financial policy, and implement what the political establishments in each country decide. National banks have to be able to attract, recruit and above all retain those with the crucial expertise needed to ensure that the sector continues to deliver its key priorities, which are:

- ensuring price stability and managing inflation and keeping it under control
- managing the money supply of nations and currencies
- maintaining interest rate stability
- implementing government financial policy
- managing everything so that industry, commerce and the financial sectors continue to have confidence in the political and economic direction of the particular countries.

The financial and analytical expertise demanded in the central banking sector and also the commercial banking sector is scarce and very valuable. The best economists, analysts, statisticians, computer programmers and accountants can command high salaries in all sectors, so the public and government-funded sectors, activities and institutions would always be at a fundamental disadvantage.

So the immediate problem was that none of the national banks were able to compete with commercial banks on salary – in any case, they could not afford it, and it was also deemed to be politically unacceptable to spend large amounts of public finance on salaries for what would undoubtedly come to be perceived as an elite group of staff, however expert they may in fact be. There seemed to be an impasse. Many national central banks did indeed try to put up salaries, especially entry-level salaries, but all that happened with this was that the commercial banks put their own salaries up still further.

The problems remained. However, two national banks, the Bank of Poland and the Bank of England, began a radically different approach. Rather than competing purely on salary and terms and conditions of employment, they would look at the things that were valued by particular applicants, and they would look also at the qualities, skills and expertise that the central banking sector needed to remain effective. They would then target those individuals who wanted to work for the central banking sector, who demonstrated these competences and who would make a career based on interest and involvement as well as financial rewards. They also began to question the extent to which financial rewards and high salaries were, in fact, the incentive that people with top qualifications from the world's best universities actually wanted.

The banks of Poland and England carried out analyses of the markets for expert labour and staff and a full analysis of the environment and the basis on which they were competing for this expertise. Two distinct sets of results were found. The first clearly stated that while financial gain and high levels of reward were important to some, this was by no means universal. Many people who went into the commercial banking sector for the high salaries did not in fact stay very long, leaving in search of something more fulfilling. The second set of results demonstrated that highly qualified candidates did not always know or understand what was on offer in the central banking sector; in large part because the central banking sector did not promote itself as an entity and industry, nor as an employer body of great influence and significance.

Working independently, the banks of Poland and England drew up statements of aspirations and expertise. Alongside this, each drew up lists of competences that were required in order to fulfil and deliver this expertise. These competences were to form the basis of a core HR strategy, and would include performance management, career development and the foundation of occupations and professions, as well as being the basis on which staff were to be attracted and (hopefully) retained). Both institutions came to similar conclusions:

- financial rewards, while important, were not the priority for those who wished to work in the central banking sector
- opportunities for progression and advancement were not made clear, and this was what was being sought by those who valued careers in the central banking sector

3

Once adapted, the framework enables managers to:

■ understand the nature of competition within the industry and markets (both product and resource) in which they operate
■ understand the threat from competitors in other industries
■ understand potential opportunities in new industries and markets.

Positioning and strategic groups

A business can rarely confine its analysis to the level of the industry and markets in which it operates. It must also pay particular attention to its closest competitors who are known as its strategic group (Porter, 1980). Strategic groups cannot be precisely defined but they consist of organizations possessing similar competences, serving customer needs in the same market segment and producing products or services of similar quality. Such analysis allows the managers of a business to compare its performance to that of its closest competitors in terms of profitability, market share, products, brands, customer loyalty, prices and so on. In this way, managers are able to benchmark the performance of their organization against their closest rivals.

In the automotive industry, for example, we can observe a number of important strategic groupings. Although Lada and BMW are both car manufacturers – and hence are technically competitors – they operate in quite different strategic groups. They are unlikely to appeal to the same customers and their products, dealership networks, brand identities and prices are quite different. BMW's strategic group includes Lexus, Mercedes-Benz, Jaguar and Audi.

Industry and market critical success factors

In any industry and its associated markets, certain factors are fundamentally important to the success of the businesses operating within that competitive environment. These are known as critical success factors (CSFs). Competitive analysis allows managers to identify CSFs. A business must ensure that its competences and core competences directly address these CSFs.

CSFs differ between individual industries and markets. In the pharmaceutical industry, CSFs will be in the areas of research and development and production. CSFs will differ between the markets for drugs available over the counter and those available only on prescription. CSFs for the over-the-counter market will centre on advertising and linkages to retail pharmacy groups, while those for the prescription market are likely to focus on clinical trials and linkages to governments and doctors. In this way, pharmaceutical companies must develop competences that concentrate on the industry and market CSFs.

This is a helpful chapter to refer to when completing both 1.1.2 Strategic Group Analysis and 1.1.4 Porter's Five Forces within the External Analysis section in Phase 1 of the **Strategic Planning Software** (www.planning-strategy.com). For more information on Porter's five forces, see also Chapter 13, particularly the section on competitive positioning.

For test questions, extra case studies, audio case studies, weblinks, videolinks and more to help you understand the topics covered in this chapter, visit our companion website at www.macmillanihe.com/companion/business/campbell.

VOCAB CHECKLIST FOR ESL STUDENTS

Analogue	Drawbacks	Pioneer
Brewers	Elite	Repute
Commonalities	Genteel	'Shake-out'
Constituent	Homogeneous	'Shop around'
Consumables	Impasse	Statistician
Dealership	Intrinsic	Strata
Discretionary income (see	Mailshots	Subcontract
'discretionary' and 'income')	Outsourcing	Telephony
Disincentive	Pedagogical	

Definitions for these terms can be found in the 'Vocab Zone' of the companion website, which provides free access to the Macmillan English Dictionary online at www.macmillanihe.com/companion/business/campbell.

REVIEW QUESTIONS

1 Explain the difference between an industry and a market.
2 Explain what is meant by market segmentation and profile the different ways in which markets can be segmented.
3 Explain what comprises Porter's five forces framework.
4 Define what is meant by strategic groups.

DISCUSSION TOPIC

It is better to compete against organizations in 'your' industry than to collaborate with them. Discuss.

HOT TOPICS – Research project areas to investigate

If you have a project to do, why not investigate ...

- ... how organizations determine whether to collaborate or not.
- ... whether strategic groups in the airline industry deliver similar financial performance.
- ... how useful Porter's five forces framework is for a not-for-profit organization.

Recommended reading

Ghemawat, P. (2002) 'Competition and business strategy in historical perspective', *Business History Review*, **76**(1): 37–74.

Grant, R.M. (1991) 'The resource based theory of competitive advantage: implications for strategy formulation', *California Management Review*, **33**(3): 114–35.

Grant, R.M. (1996) 'Prospering in dynamically-competitive environments: organizational capability as knowledge integration', *Organization Science*, **7**(4): 375–87.

Jacobson, R. (1992) 'The 'Austrian' school of strategy', *Academy of Management Review*, **17**(4): 782–807.

McKiernan, P. (1997) 'Strategy past; strategy futures', *Long Range Planning*, **30**(5): 790–8.

Newbert, S. (2005) 'New firm formation: a dynamic capability perspective', *Journal of Small Business Management*, **43**(1): 55–77.

Porter, M.E. (1979) 'How competitive forces shape strategy', *Harvard Business Review*, **57**(2): 137–45.

Prahalad, C.K. and Hamel, G. (1990) 'The core competence of the corporation', *Harvard Business Review*, **68**(3): 79–91.

Prieto, I.M. and Easterby-Smith, M. (2006) 'Dynamic capabilities and the role of organizational knowledge: an exploration', *European Journal of Information Systems*, **15**(5): 500–10.

Scherer, F.M. (1980) *Industrial Market Structure and Economic Performance* (2nd edn), Chicago, IL: Rand McNally.

Teece, D.J., Pisano, G. and Shuen, A. (1998) 'Dynamic capabilities and strategic management', *Strategic Management Journal*, **18**(7): 509–33.

Chapter references

Heene, A. and Sanchez, R. (1997) *Competence-based Strategic Management*, London: John Wiley.

Kay, J. (1995) 'Learning to define the core business', *Financial Times*, 1 December.

Porter, M.E. (1980) *Competitive Strategy: Techniques for Analysing Industries and Competitors*, New York: Free Press.

Chapter 11

The international and global context

Introduction and chapter overview

With the advent of the internet and the ability of organizations to communicate and trade globally, independent of size, internationalization and the global context are central to many businesses. One of the most important considerations in the development and implementation of a strategy is the extent to which the organization's activities, products and markets are spread across geographical regions. While some businesses will be predominantly domestically based, others operate in many countries, and others still operate in almost all regions of the world. This chapter is concerned with a discussion of the key issues surrounding the *why* and *how* questions: why do organizations expand in this way and how do they go about it? The *why* questions are covered in a discussion of the factors that drive increased internationalization. The *how* questions are answered in a discussion of the market entry options.

Learning objectives

After studying this chapter, you should be able to:

- define and distinguish between internationalization and globalization
- explain the factors that drive globalization
- describe and demonstrate the application of Yip's framework for analysing the extent of globalization in an industry and market
- explain the major global strategy alternatives
- describe the modes of international market entry

11.1 Defining internationalization and globalization

Business has been international since the days of the ancient Egyptians, Phoenicians and Greeks. Merchants travelled the known world to sell products manufactured in their home country and to return with products from other countries. Initially, international business simply took the form of exporting and importing. The term 'international' describes any business that carries out some of its activities across national boundaries.

Globalization, on the other hand, is more than simply internationalization. A large multinational company is not necessarily a global business. In order for a business to become global in its operations, we would usually expect a number of important characteristics to be in place:

1   Global organizations take advantage of the increasing trend towards a convergence of customer needs and wants across international borders – fast foods, soft drinks or consumer electronics are good examples (see Levitt, 1983).

2   Global organizations compete in industries that are globalized. In some sectors, successful competition necessitates a presence in almost every part of the world in order to effectively compete in its global market.

3   Global organizations can – and do – locate their value-adding activities in those places in the world where the greatest competitive advantages can be made. This might mean, for example, shifting production to a low-cost region or moving design to a country with skilled labour in the key skill area.

4   Global organizations are able to integrate and coordinate their international activities between countries. The mentality of 'home base, foreign interests' that has been so prevalent among traditional multinational companies is eroded in the culture of global businesses. They have learned to effectively manage and control the various parts of the business across national borders and despite local cultural differences.

The development of an organization's global strategy, therefore, will be concerned with global competences, global marketing and global configuration and coordination of its value-adding activities.

Multinational and transnational companies are usually large and have direct investments in one or more foreign countries. The foreign investments may be part-shareholdings, but more usually are wholly owned subsidiaries. The difference is in the degree to which the foreign investments are coordinated.

KEY CONCEPTS

A **transnational company** has a high degree of coordination in its international interests. It usually has a strategic centre that manages the global operation such that all parts act in accordance with a centrally managed strategic purpose.

A **multinational company** is an international company whose foreign interests are not coordinated from a strategic centre.

11.2   Globalization of markets and industries

Levitt and market homogenization

It was Levitt (1983) who first argued that changes in technology, societies, economies and politics were producing a 'global village'. By this he meant that consumer needs in many previously separate national markets were becoming increasingly similar throughout the world. Developments in transport have not only made it easier to move products and materials between countries but they have also resulted in a huge increase in the amount that people travel around the world. This travel educates people to the products available in other countries and, on their return home, they often wish to have access to those products and services from overseas. This trend has been reinforced by changes in IT, particularly those related to cinema and television, which have been important in some aspects of cultural convergence. The development of the WTO (World Trade Organization), and its predecessor GATT (the General Agreement on Tariffs and Trade), has resulted in huge reductions in the trade barriers between countries since the Second World War. Rising income levels and cheaper travel throughout many parts of the world have also given economic impetus to the development of global markets.

It is not only markets that are, in many cases, becoming more global. Industries are also becoming more global. The value chains of businesses in many industries span the globe. In the case of the fashion house Yves Saint Laurent, for example, design and marketing are concentrated in France, while products are mainly manufactured in East Asia. Organizations concentrate some of their activities in locations where they hope to obtain cost, quality or other advantages. Other activities, like distribution, are also often dispersed around the world. The way a business configures its activities across national borders can be an important source of competitive advantage. The spread of an organization's value-adding activities around the world also means that there are important advantages to be gained from effective integration and coordination of activities.

GURU GUIDE

Theodore Levitt was born in 1925 in Vollmerz, Germany. He joined Harvard Business School in 1959.

His influential works were in marketing and his 1975 article 'Marketing myopia' is widely credited as marking the beginning of the modern marketing movement. He is the author of *The Marketing Imagination*, and is a bestselling author whose works have been translated into eleven languages. Professor Levitt is also credited for coining the term 'globalization', although it is more accurate to say he popularized an already existing term. He is the author of numerous articles on various subjects including economics, management, marketing and politics, and was the editor of the *Harvard Business Review* from 1985 to 1989. He won several honours and accolades, including the Academy of Management award for outstanding business book, the George Gallup Award for Marketing Excellence and the William M. McFeely Award of the International Management Council for major contributions to management. He was a four-time winner of the McKinsey award for best annual article in the *Harvard Business Review*. He died in 2006.

Levitt was the first management theorist to emphasize the importance of marketing at a time when budgetary control and productivity were the main factors. The argument that industry should be a customer-satisfying process and not a goods-producing process has changed the way business is conducted and emphasized the role of consumers in ensuring growth for organizations and economies.

Porter and multi-domestic markets

Multi-domestic industries are those where competition in each nation is essentially independent.

Porter (1990) argues that industries can be either global or multi-domestic. Multi-domestic industries are those where competition in each nation is essentially independent. He gives the example of consumer banking where a bank's domestic reputation and resources in one nation have tended to have little effect on its success in other countries. The international banking industry is, Porter agues, essentially a collection of domestic industries.

Global industries are those in which competition is global. The consumer electronics industry is a good example, where companies like Philips, Sony and Panasonic compete in almost all countries of the world. The implication would appear to be that businesses should adopt a global strategy in global industries and a multi-local strategy in multi-domestic markets. Yet the situation is not so simple as this. Even markets like consumer banking are becoming more global.

It is also the case that the degree of globalization of an industry or market may not be uniform. In other words, some aspects of an industry or market may be indicative of globalization, while others may be indicative of localization. The degree of globalization of an industry can be assessed using Yip's globalization driver framework (1992). This is a more useful framework than Porter's because it makes it possible to evaluate both the overall degree of globalization of an industry and which features of the industry are more or less global in nature.

11.3   Globalization drivers: Yip's framework

Yip (1992) argues that it is not simply the case that industries are 'global' or 'not global', rather that they can be global in some respects and not in others. Yip's globalization driver framework (Figure 11.1) makes it possible to identify which aspects of an industry are global and which aspects differ locally. Analysis using this framework can play an important role in shaping the global strategy of a business. A global strategy, according to Yip, will be global in many respects but may also include features that are locally oriented.

Figure 11.1 Globalization driver framework

Source: Adapted from Yip, 2003

Table 11.1 A summary of the globalization drivers

Market globalization drivers	Cost globalization drivers
Common customer needs Global customers Global distribution channels Transferable marketing techniques Presence in lead countries	Global scale economies Steep experience curve effect Sourcing efficiencies Favourable logistics Differences in country costs (including exchange rates) High product development costs Fast-changing technology
Government globalization drivers	**Competitive globalization drivers**
Favourable trade policies Compatible technical standards Common marketing regulations Government-owned competitors and customers Host government concerns	High exports and imports Competitors from different continents Interdependence of countries Competitors globalized

Yip (1992, p. 15) argues that 'To achieve the benefits of globalization, the managers of a worldwide business need to recognize when industry conditions provide the opportunity to use global strategy levers.' Table 11.1 shows a breakdown of the globalization drivers.

Yip's four drivers that determine the nature and extent of globalization in an industry are market drivers, cost drivers, government drivers and competitive drivers (Figure 11.1). We will consider each of these in turn.

Market globalization drivers

The degree of globalization of a market will depend on the extent to which there are common customer needs, global customers, global distribution channels, transferable marketing and lead countries. It is not simply a case of a market being global or not global. Managers must seek to establish which, if any, aspects of their market are global.

Common customer needs

Probably the single most important market globalization driver is the extent to which customers in different countries share the same need or want for a product. The extent of shared need will depend on cultural, economic, climatic, legal and other similarities and differences. There are numerous examples of markets where customer needs are becoming more similar, such as motor vehicles, soft drinks, fast foods, consumer electronics and computers.

The importance of McDonald's, Burger King and Pizza Hut in fast food, Coca-Cola and Pepsi in soft drinks and Sony and Panasonic in consumer electronics are all illustrative of converging customer needs in certain markets. Levitt (1983) refers to this similarity of tastes and preference as increasing 'market homogenization' – all markets demanding the same products, regardless of their domestic culture and traditional preferences.

Common customer need: desktop PC

Global customers and channels

Global customers purchase products or services in a coordinated way from the best global sources. Yip identifies two types of global customers:

1. **national global customers** – customers who seek the best suppliers in the world and then use the product or service in one country, for example national defence purchasers who try to source the highest specification weapons and other military hardware from around the world for use by the domestic armed forces.

2. **multinational global customers** – they similarly seek the best suppliers in the world but then use the product or service obtained in many countries, for example transnational corporations source components for their products globally to ensure optimal quality standards.

National global customers seek the best suppliers in the world and then use the product or service in one country.

Multinational global customers seek the best suppliers in the world but then use the product or service obtained in many countries.

Examples of markets with global customers include automobile components, advertising (advertising agencies) and electronics. Nissan, for example, manufactures cars in a number of different locations around the world including Japan, the UK and Spain, but sources many components for all these locations globally. Businesses serving global customers must 'be present in all the customers' major markets' (Yip, 1992).

3

George Yip was born in Hong Kong in 1948 and grew up in Burma and England. He was a professor of strategic and international management at London Business School and between 2003 to 2006 he was a senior fellow at the Advanced Institute of Management Research. He has also held professorial posts at Cambridge, UCLA and Harvard Business School. His business experience spans marketing and product management, consulting and innovation. He was the vice president and director of research and innovation at Capgemini Consulting and his business experience also includes management stints with Unilever and PricewaterhouseCoopers. He is currently the dean of the Rotterdam School of Management, Erasmus University, the Netherlands.

Professor Yip is a distinguished figure in global strategy and marketing management and his current research interests include internationalization, innovation and global customers. He is a fellow of the Academy of International Business and the International Academy of Management and *The Times Higher Education Supplement* ranked him among the 12 most successful academic consultants in the UK in any discipline (2006).

Alongside global customers, there are sometimes global, or more often regional, distribution channels which serve global customers. Global customers and channels will contribute towards the development of a global market.

Transferable marketing

Transferable marketing describes the extent to which elements of the marketing mix, like brand names and promotions, can be used globally without local adaptations. Clearly, when adaptation is not required, it is indicative of a global market. In this way, brands like McDonald's, Coca-Cola and Nike are used globally. Yet advertising for Nike can be both global and locally adapted, according the popularity of different sports in different parts of the world. If marketing is transferable, it will favour a global market.

> **Transferable marketing** describes the extent to which elements of the marketing mix, like brand names and promotions, can be used globally without local adaptations.

Lead countries

When certain countries lead in particular industries, 'it becomes critical for global competitors to participate in these lead countries in order to be exposed to the sources of innovation' (Porter, 1990). Lead countries are those that are ahead in product and/or process innovation in their industry. These lead countries help to produce global standards and hence global industries and markets. Japan, for example, has leadership in the consumer electronics industry and leads developments within it, while the USA is the lead country in microcomputer and internet software.

Cost globalization drivers

The potential to reduce costs by global configuration of value-adding activities is an important spur towards the globalization of certain industries. If there are substantial cost advantages to be obtained, an industry will tend to be global.

Global scale economies

When an organization serves a global market, it is able to gain much greater economies of scale than if it serves only domestic or regional markets. Similarly, serving global markets also gives considerable potential for economies of scope. Thus businesses such as Procter & Gamble and Unilever, which produce household products like detergents, gain huge economies of scope in research, product development and marketing.

Economies of scale describe the benefits that are gained when increasing volume results in lower unit costs. Although economies of scale can arise in all parts of the value chain, it is probably best understood by illustrating it using purchasing as an example. An individual purchasing one single item will pay more *per item* than a large company buying many of the same item. It is said that the purchaser who is able to purchase in bulk (because of the size and structure of the buyer) enjoys scale economies over smaller organizations who buy in at lower volumes.

Economy of scope describes the benefits that can arise in one product or market area as a result of activity in another. For example, research into material properties for the benefit of the NASA space programme (one area of scope) has resulted in advances in other areas such as fabrics, non-stick pans and coatings for aircraft. Organizations that invest heavily in R&D (such as pharmaceutical companies) are among those who are always seeking economies of scope – seeking to use breakthroughs in one area to benefit another.

Steep experience curve effect

When there is a steep learning curve in production and marketing, businesses serving global markets will tend to obtain the greatest benefits. In many high-tech and service industries, there are steep learning curves yielding the greatest benefits to global businesses.

The idea of the learning curve was first introduced in 1885 by Hermann Ebbinghaus, a German psychologist who pioneered the experimental study of memory. It has been used in many areas of life, not just in business, where it is often termed the 'experience curve'. The learning curve describes the rate at which an individual or an organization learns to perform a particular task. The gradient of the beginning of the curve is referred to as its 'steepness' and is the most important part. The steeper this first part, the quicker the task is being learned. The general shape of a learning curve is described as 'exponential' because the gradient usually decreases along its length as the time taken to perform the task decreases as those performing the task become more accomplished at it.

Let us take an example. When a lecturer sits down to mark a batch of exam papers, he must first familiarize himself with the questions and the answers that are expected. Having done that, the first paper will take the longest of all to mark. When the lecturer has internalized all the questions and answers, the time taken to mark each paper will reduce until the last few papers take the shortest time of all (Figures 11.2a, 11.2b).

The **learning curve** describes the rate at which an individual or an organization learns to perform a particular task.

3

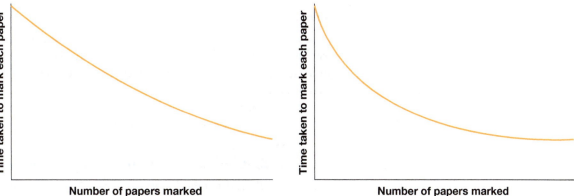

Figure 11.2a Shallow learning curve: a slow learner

Figure 11.2b Steep learning curve: a fast learner

Sourcing efficiencies

If there are efficiency gains to be made by centralized sourcing carried out globally, this will drive an industry towards globalization. Businesses like those in sports apparel and fashion clothing benefit from global sourcing to obtain the lowest prices and highest quality standards.

Favourable logistics

If transportation costs comprise a relatively high proportion of sales value, there will be every incentive to concentrate production in a few large facilities. If transport costs are relatively small, such as with consumer electronic goods, production can be located in several (or many) locations, which are chosen on the basis of other cost criteria such as land or labour costs.

Differences in country costs

Production costs (raw materials and labour) vary from country to country, and, like favourable logistics, this can stimulate globalization. Thus, countries with lower production costs will tend to attract businesses to locate their activities in the country. Many Asian countries have been chosen as centres for production because of their favourable cost conditions. Although countries like Thailand suffered in some respects because of the devaluation of their currency in 1997–98, from the point of view of being chosen as centres for production, they have benefited. Currently, the value of the pound against the euro may have similar effects for Britain.

Fast-changing technology and high product development costs

Product life cycles are shortening as the pace of technological change increases. At the same time, R&D costs are increasing in many industries. These product development costs can only be recouped by high sales in global markets. Domestic markets simply do not yield the volumes of sales required to cover high R&D costs. Thus industries like pharmaceuticals and automobiles face rapidly changing technology and hypercompetition, together with high development costs. As a consequence, they must operate in global markets to ensure the volumes of sales necessary to recoup these costs.

Government globalization drivers

Since the Second World War, many governments have taken individual and collective action to reduce global trade barriers.

Favourable trade policies

The WTO, and its predecessor GATT, has done much to reduce trade barriers, which, in the past, hindered the globalization of many industries. Although there are still significant trade barriers in certain areas, the movement towards freedom of trade has been substantial, thus favouring globalization. The growth of customs unions and 'single markets' such as the European Union (EU) and the North American Free Trade Area (NAFTA) have also made an important contribution in this regard.

Compatible technical standards and common marketing regulations

Many of the differences in technical standards between countries that hindered globalization in the past have been reduced. For example, telecommunications standards, which have traditionally differed between countries, are increasingly being superseded by international standards. Similarly, standards are converging in the pharmaceutical, airline and computing industries, which makes it easier to produce globally accepted products.

There remain important differences in advertising regulations between countries, with UK regulations among the strictest. Generally, however, these differences are being eroded and this is expected to favour greater globalization.

Government-owned competitors and customers

Government-owned competitors, which often enjoy state subsidies, can act as a stimulus to globalization as they frequently compete with other global competitors, thus being forced to become more efficient and global market oriented. On the other hand, government-owned customers tend to favour domestic suppliers, which can act as a barrier to globalization. The privatization of many state-owned businesses in many European countries has reduced this barrier to globalization.

Host government concerns

The attitudes and policies of host government concerns can either hinder or favour globalization. In certain circumstances, host governments may favour the entry of global businesses into domestic industries and markets, which will assist globalization. For example, the UK government has, in recent years, done much to attract inward investment by Japanese and Korean companies. The more governments that espouse such policies, the greater the globalization of an industry. In other cases, host governments will seek to protect industries that they see as strategically important and will attempt to prevent the entry of foreign businesses.

Competitive globalization drivers

The greater the strength of the competitive drivers, the greater the tendency for an industry to globalize. Global competition in an industry will become more intense when:

- there is a high level of import and export activity between countries
- the competitors in the industry are widely spread (they will often be on different continents)
- the economies of the countries involved are interdependent
- competitors in the industry are already globalized.

High exports and imports

The higher the level of exports and imports of products and services, the greater the pressure for globalization of an industry.

Competitors from different continents

The more countries are represented in an industry and the more widely spread they are, the greater the likelihood of globalization.

Interdependence of countries

If national economies are already relatively interdependent, this will act as a stimulus for increased globalization. Such interdependence may arise through multiple trading links in other industries, being a part of a single market or being in a shared political alliance.

Empire Supermarkets (ES) is one of the world's largest supermarket and department store chains, with activities in 11 countries. The company was founded by an agricultural cooperative as an independent outlet for its food products in Atlanta, Georgia, in the southern USA in 1950. ES found that there was a large, ready and more or less assured high-volume market for good food products at reasonable prices. By cutting out the middleman and wholesalers, ES was able to ensure speed of delivery, price advantages and quality assurance from an early stage of development. ES quickly expanded across the whole state of Georgia, and by the mid-1960s, it had stores in every state of the USA.

Now a major force in food retailing, ES started to expand its product range and its locations. The first out-of-country stores were opened in Canada in 1965 and Mexico in 1967. On 1 January 1970, ES opened its 10,000th outlet. Supported by a massive marketing campaign, ES expanded further. Over the next two decades, ES opened over 500 stores in Canada, and 200 in Mexico. ES also began to open town centre stores in the US, under the brand 'ES Central'. The company greatly expanded its product and service ranges, diversifying into clothes, household and garden goods, financial services and even car sales. This meant a major refurbishment of many hundreds of the company's existing stores. The refurbishments cost well over $4bn; however, subsequent results showed that the returns generated were in the order of ten times those that had been projected before the refurbishments went ahead.

However, this did not satisfy the growth demands from the company's major backers. So a new CEO was hired, Francis Belasco, a Canadian national who was recruited from Walmart, where he had made a name for himself as something of a retail guru. Under the leadership of Belasco, ES now looked towards the prosperous markets of Western Europe for further opportunities.

The initiative was given great publicity. The grand strategy was that there was to be a whole new retail world for the people of Europe – good quality food and goods at reasonable prices. This was based on ES's long-standing ability to command the supply side, and use its sheer volumes of demand to be able to guarantee steady long-term business to all its suppliers. It was the assurance of an effective supply side that had given ES its life, as the original cooperative had created it to ensure regular outlets and business volumes for its own produce.

The promise of quality food and a large and expanding range of other goods at affordable prices became the promise on which the customers of Western Europe would be lured away from Tesco and Asda in the UK, and Carrefour, Aldi and Lidl in Continental Europe. After all, all these goods were known to be much more expensive in Western Europe than in North America. ES began a programme of prime site acquisitions in France, Germany and Spain, and building work duly commenced. Belasco and everyone else involved looked forward to the same success that had been enjoyed in North America.

Exactly three years after the first announcement of the venture, ES opened its first 500 European stores on the same day. This was accompanied by a Europe-wide marketing, sales and promotional campaign, which generated major media and public interest. There was a huge, initially favourable response, and success appeared assured. Plans were drawn up for an expansion programme that would make ES a supermarket and department store giant in all the EU countries, and feasibility studies were commissioned for establishing a presence in Japan, Korea, China and India.

However, problems started to appear. ES struggled to gain the promised foothold in the UK and Europe. When they arrived to open their first stores, ES managers found that the main UK and European supermarkets and department store chains were already delivering many of the promises that ES were making. The European companies were themselves expanding all over the EU, establishing their own presence in the major locations of Central and Eastern Europe. Some were opening up new ventures in Asia, the Middle East and even North America. After all, the European companies had been given three years' notice of intent, and so they had plenty of time to prepare a response.

The goods and services on offer at the European supermarkets were also found to be substandard. The European giants had been given plenty of time to develop command of their own major existing and familiar suppliers. ES was therefore faced with having to find alternatives, and when it became apparent that ES was going to need them for a long time, supply side costs on the European venture rose sharply. Matters came to a serious pitch when one of ES's suppliers of plastic goods was caught dumping toxic effluent into the Danube, and another supplier of clothing and textiles was found to be using unpaid child labour. The resulting adverse publicity from both cases all but destroyed the venture.

So after the initial interest, customers and consumers went back to their own familiar outlets. The ES venture persisted for five years, but it never gained any commercially viable foothold, and earlier this year, it was closed down. The sites were sold off and ES returned to America. The European venture had cost a total of $38bn. Belasco was called before ES's major backers, who now demanded an explanation.

Case study questions

1 What has gone wrong with Empire Supermarkets' expansion plans and why? What are the main general lessons for any CEO, company or organization that seeks to become a global or international player?

2 What pressures demanded that ES went overseas? How do you assess and, where necessary, counter these pressures?

3 What other factors need to be taken into account when you do seek to drive into new markets and locations?

Competitors globalized

If a competitor is already globalized and employing a global strategy, there will be pressure on other businesses in the industry to globalize as well. Globalization in the automotive industry is high because of the pressure on organizations to compete globally. An automobile manufacturer will struggle to survive if it only serves domestic markets.

Yip's globalization driver framework provides an extremely useful tool for analysing the degree of globalization of an industry or market. Equally, it makes possible an understanding of which particular aspects of an industry or market are global and which aspects are localized. Each of the drivers must be analysed for the industry and market under consideration and the results of the analysis will play an important role in assisting managers to form the global strategy of their organization. The results will help to determine which features of the strategy are globally standardized and which features are locally adapted. Yip developed the concept of 'total global strategy' based on his globalization driver framework.

Yip's stages in a total global strategy

Yip (1992) argues that a successful global strategy must be based on a comprehensive globalization analysis of the drivers we encountered above. Managers of a global business must, he contends, evaluate the globalization drivers for their industry and market and formulate their global strategy on the basis of this analysis. If, for example, they find that customer demand is largely homogeneous for their product, they can produce a largely standardized product for sale throughout the world. If, on the other hand, they find that there are few cost advantages of global concentration of manufacturing because of unfavourable logistics or adverse economies of scale, they may choose to disperse their manufacturing activities around the world to be close to their customers in different parts of the world. Thus the 'total global strategy' of an organization can be a mix of standardization and local adaptation as market and industry conditions dictate.

Yip goes on to identify three stages in developing a 'total global strategy':

1 *Developing a core strategy:* this will, in effect, involve building core competences and a generic or hybrid strategy that can potentially give global competitive advantage.

2 *Internationalizing the core strategy:* this will be the stage at which the core competences and generic strategy are introduced to international markets and when the organization begins to locate its value-adding activities in

locations where competitive advantages, such as low cost and access to materials or skills, are available. This will include the choice of which markets the business will enter and the means by which it will enter them.

3 *Globalizing the international strategy:* this stage is based on coordinating and integrating the core competences and strategy on a global basis. It will also include deciding which elements of the strategy are to be standardized and which are to be locally adapted on the basis of the strength of the globalization drivers in the industry and market.

Although we have used Levitt, Porter and Yip in this chapter, interested readers should consider reading the work of Bartlett and Ghoshal (1987, 1989), Hamel and Prahalad (1985) and Stonehouse et al. (2000).

11.4   Management across international boundaries

Coordination is of key importance when managing across international boundaries, especially for what are termed 'multinational enterprises' (MNEs). This coordination and control are often achieved through the management structure and aligned with the strategy and resources. Choosing between a multi-domestic strategy or a global orientation has always been a challenge. However, Bartlett and Ghoshal (1992) identify three possible strategic approaches, which are local responsiveness, the transfer of knowledge, and global efficiency. They argued that a focus on one strategy is no longer appropriate and that to succeed, organizations need to combine all three approaches. They termed this the 'transnational solution' (Bartlett and Ghoshal, 1992; Bartlett et al., 2008), an approach that addresses local and global issues as well as knowledge transfer.

11.5   Porter's diamond framework

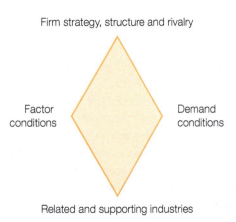

Firm strategy, structure and rivalry

Factor conditions

Demand conditions

Related and supporting industries

Figure 11.3 **Porter's diamond**
Source: Adapted from Porter, 1990

Porter's 'diamond of national advantage' has become something of a classical theory of international trade. The framework provides a practical and systematic approach to understanding the competitive environments that nations create for their established industries and the conditions within which international competition occurs. The argument is that comparative advantage resides in the 'factor endowments' that a country may be fortunate enough to inherit. Factor endowments include land, natural resources, labour, and the size of the local population (see Figure 11.3). In addition to possessing these factor endowments, a nation can create new advanced factor endowments, such as skilled labour, a strong technology and knowledge base, government support, and culture.

The individual points on the diamond and the diamond as a whole affect four factors that lead to a national comparative advantage. These are:

- the pressure on companies to innovate and invest
- the availability of resources and skills
- the information that firms use to decide which opportunities to pursue

Sumantra Ghoshal was born in 1948 in Calcutta, India. He graduated from Delhi University with an undergraduate degree in physics and has doctoral degrees from both MIT and Harvard Business School. His management stints include working for the Indian Oil Corporation and serving as the chairman of the supervisory board of Duncan Goenka. He had an academic spell with INSEAD business school, London Business School and Harvard Business School. He was also on the board of several companies including Mahindra British Telecom Ltd, the Lufthansa School of Business and Swiss Re. He was the founding dean of the Indian Business School in Hyderabad, and a fellow at the Academy of Management, the Academy of International Business and the World Economic Forum.

Professor Ghoshal is a management guru and has written influential articles focusing on the strategic, organizational and managerial issues confronting large and global companies. He has won several prizes, including the George R. Terry Book Award, the Igor Ansoff Award and Management Book of the Year award. He died in 2004.

Christopher Bartlett received an undergraduate degree in economics from University of Queensland in 1964. He graduated with a PhD in business administration from Harvard Business School in 1979 and joined the business faculty in the same year. Professor Bartlett worked as a management consultant with McKinsey's London office and a general manager at Baxter Laboratories in France. At Harvard he has held various distinguished positions including the faculty chair of International Senior Management Program and chairman of Harvard Business School's international executive programme.

Professor Bartlett's interest focuses on managerial challenges in multinational firms and he has published influential books and texts in the areas of strategy, transformational change and leadership. His work is acknowledged internationally and he won the Igor Ansoff Award for best work in strategic management. He is also a fellow at the Academy of Management and the Academy of International Business.

The work of Bartlett and Ghoshal is fundamental in understanding the mindset needed of global matrix managers and the need for local, national and global knowledge and awareness in management.

■ the goals of individuals in companies.

The points of the diamond are described as follows:

■ *Factor conditions:* A country possesses and creates its own key factor conditions such as skilled resources, infrastructure and technological base, and disadvantages in factor conditions will force innovation. Such innovation often leads to a national comparative advantage. Therefore understanding the factor conditions allows for an understanding of current and potential capability.

■ *Firm strategy, structure and rivalry:* Local conditions affect firm strategy, with rivalry forcing firms to move beyond the basic advantages that the home country may enjoy, and seek to exploit other forms of advantage.

- *Demand conditions:* When the market for a particular product is larger locally than in foreign markets, local markets become more expert in production, expected standards and quality are higher, local consumers are more demanding and thus exports are more competitive.
- *Related and supporting industries:* When local supporting industries are competitive, firms enjoy more cost-effective and innovative inputs. The effect of this is strengthened when the suppliers themselves are strong global competitors.

So the diamond can be used to understand the balance and sources of a nation's competitive advantage, although one should consider that many of the elements are self-renewing and interdependent.

11.6   Key strategic decisions

Once a business has developed core competences and strategies that can potentially be exploited globally, the decision must be made as to where and how to employ them. Initial moves into overseas markets will involve market development as these markets and segments can be regarded as new to the business. The initial market development may then be followed by product development and, perhaps, diversification.

When a business enters international and global markets, it will be necessary to build new competences, alongside those which have brought about domestic competitive advantage. These new competences could well be in the areas of global sourcing and logistics, and global management.

The globalization of a business does not happen overnight. It may well involve entry to key countries, with the largest markets first, followed by entry to less important countries later.

In the initial stages of globalization, the key decisions are usually:

- Which countries are to be entered first?
- In which countries are value-adding activities to be located?
- Which market development strategies are to be employed to gain entry to the chosen overseas markets?

Market entry decisions

The decision as to which countries and markets are to be entered first will be based on a number of important factors:

- *The potential size of the market:* is the market for the product likely to be significant? This will, in turn, be determined by the following factors.
- *Economic factors:* are income levels adequate to ensure that significant numbers of people are likely to be able to afford the product?
- *Cultural and linguistic factors:* is the culture of the country likely to favour acceptance of the product to be offered?
- *Political factors:* what are the factors that may limit entry to markets in the host country?
- *Technological factors:* are levels of technology adequate to support provision of the product in the host market and are technological standards compatible?

To begin with, a business will choose to enter markets in those countries where the above conditions are most favourable.

Location of value-adding activities

Managers must determine within which countries they will locate key value-adding activities of their business. They will seek to gain cost, skill and resource advantages. In other words, they will attempt to locate activities in countries where there are production advantages to be gained.

Such advantages depend on:

- *wage levels:* low wage levels will assist in low production costs
- *skill levels:* there must be suitably skilled labour available
- *availability of materials:* suitable materials must be accessible
- *infrastructure:* transport and communications must be favourable to the logistics of the business.

The existence of these conditions within a country will, in turn, depend on:

- *economic factors:* level of economic development, wage levels, exchange rate conditions
- *social factors:* attitudes to work, levels of education and training
- *political factors:* legislation favouring investment and so on
- *technological factors:* levels of technology and transport and communications infrastructure of the country.

Market development methods

Once decisions have been made as to which countries' markets are to be entered and where value-adding activities are to be located, the task for management becomes the determination of which method of development to employ to enter another country. Broadly speaking, a business can choose either internal or external methods for the development of overseas markets. Internal methods are usually slower, but tend to entail lower risk. External methods involve the business developing relationships with other businesses. The choice of method will depend on a number of factors:

- the size of the investment required or the amount of investment capital available
- knowledge of the country to be entered and potential risk involved (political instability)
- revenue and cash flow forecasts and expectations
- operating cost considerations
- control considerations (some investment options will have implications for the parent company to control activity in the host country).

Internal and external development methods are examined in more detail.

Internal development methods

Internal methods are based on the organization exploiting its own resources and competences and involve the organization carrying out some of its activities overseas. This may be exporting its products or setting up some form of production facilities abroad. The advantages of internal methods of development are that they maximize future revenue from sales abroad and they make possible a high degree of control over overseas activities. On the other hand, they can involve significant risk if knowledge of the host country and its markets are limited, and they may require considerable direct investment from the business. The major internal methods of development overseas are direct exporting, overseas production or assembly, and the development of an overseas facility.

Direct exporting

Direct exporting is the transfer of goods (or services) across national borders from the home production facility. Such exporting may simply be shipping a product, or, as sales increase, a sales offices may be set up overseas. Exporting, at its simplest, is the marketing abroad of a product made in an organization's home country. To avoid some of the pitfalls of direct exporting, such as a lack of local knowledge and access to distribution channels, many exporting businesses make use of local agents or distribute their products through locally based retailers, known as a 'piggyback' distribution arrangement.

Overseas production or assembly

Organizations may choose to manufacture or assemble their product overseas. There are a number of reasons for direct investment. Transport costs for the finished product may be so high as to discourage exporting or the business wishes to take advantage of local cost advantages. In some industries, direct investment may be an appropriate option to circumvent import restrictions put in place by host governments.

Development of an overseas facility

Establishing a foreign subsidiary of the business is an option when it is favourable for the parent company to have total control of its overseas operations, decision-making and profits. A subsidiary may carry out the full range of activities of the parent business or it may be only a manufacturing or marketing subsidiary.

External development methods

External methods of development involve the organization entering into relationships with businesses in a host country, which take the form of alliances or joint ventures, mergers and acquisitions (M&A), franchising and licensing. These methods often reflect 'offshoring' and have the advantages of providing local knowledge, potentially reducing risks, reducing operating costs, and reducing investment costs (except in the case of M&A). The major disadvantages (again except in the case of M&A) are reduced revenues and reduced control of activities as optimal income is traded off against the advantage of lower financial exposure.

International alliances and joint ventures

Alliances and joint ventures allow a business to draw on the skills, local knowledge, resources and competences of a locally based company. They reduce the risks of entry to overseas markets by providing local knowledge and they help reduce investment costs.

International mergers and acquisitions

A business may use M&A to enter overseas markets, which give a business access to the knowledge, resources and competences of a business based in the host country, thus reducing some of the risks of market entry.

International franchising

A **franchise** is an
arrangement under which
a franchisor supplies a
franchisee with a tried-
and-tested brand name,
products and expertise in
return for the payment of
a proportion of profits or
sales.

A *franchise* is an arrangement under which a franchisor supplies a franchisee with a tried-and-tested brand name, products and expertise in return for the payment of a proportion of profits or sales. The major advantage to the franchisor is that the risk, investment and operating costs of entering overseas markets are reduced considerably. At the same time, the franchisee can contribute their local knowledge while also benefiting from the lower risks associated with an established business idea. Much of Burger King's expansion overseas has come through franchise development.

International licensing

Licensing involves a
producer transferring
certain rights to a licensee
for the sole use in a host
country of its established
brand, recipe, registered
design or similar piece of
intellectual property.

Licensing is similar to franchising but involves a producer transferring certain rights to a licensee for the sole use in a host country of its established brand, recipe, registered design or similar piece of intellectual property. The licensee pays the licensor a royalty for the use of the intellectual property and, as with franchising, gains from the established market position of the brand. Licensing is widely used in brewing and in some scientific industries.

STRATEGIC PLANNING SOFTWARE

This is a helpful chapter to refer to when completing section 2.3 Development Strategy within Phase 2 of the **Strategic Planning Software** (www.planning-software.com).

For test questions, extra case studies, audio case studies, weblinks, videolinks and more to help you understand the topics covered in this chapter, visit our companion website at www.macmillanihe.com/companion/business/campbell.

3

VOCAB CHECKLIST FOR ESL STUDENTS

Accolades	Gradient	Myopia
Advent	Heralded	Offshoring
Apparel	Hindered	Recouped
Exponential	Homogenization	Superseded
Franchiser, franchisee	Impetus	

Definitions for these terms can be found in the 'Vocab Zone' of the companion website, which provides free access to the Macmillan English Dictionary online at www.macmillanihe.com/companion/business/campbell.

REVIEW QUESTIONS

1 Explain what we mean by internationalization and globalization, and highlight the differences.
2 Explain what factors drive globalization and suggest which are most dominant.
3 Explain how Yip's framework can be used to analyse the extent of globalization in an industry and/or market.
4 Explain the different modes of international market entry.

DISCUSSION TOPIC

It is better to grow and maintain market share in one country than to expand across national boundaries. Discuss.

HOT TOPICS – Research project areas to investigate

If you have a project to do, why not investigate ...

- ... approaches adopted by multinational organizations to meeting the legislation requirements in different countries.
- ... the impact of currency fluctuations on financial institutions operating in the UK.
- ... the competences required of a multinational manager.

Recommended reading

Arora, A., Jaju, A., Kefalas, A.G. and Perenich, T. (2004) 'An exploratory analysis of global managerial mindsets: a case of U.S. textile and apparel industry', *Journal of International Management*, **10**(3): 393–411.

Bartlett, C.A. and Ghoshal, S. (1989) *Managing Across Borders: The Transnational Solution*, Boston, MA: Harvard Business School Press.

Bitzenis, A. (2006) 'Decisive FDI barriers that affect multinationals' business in a transition country', *Global Business & Economics Review*, **8**(1/2): 87–118.

Buckley, P.J. and Casson, M.C. (1998) 'Models of the multinational enterprise', *Journal of International Business Studies*, **29**(1): 21–44.

Chakravarthy, B. and Perlmutter, H.V. (1985) 'Strategic planning for a global economy', *Columbia Journal of World Business*, **20**(3): 3–10.

Douglas, S.P. and Wind, Y. (1987) 'The myth of globalisation', *Columbia Journal of World Business*, **22**(4): 19–29.

Doz, Y. (1986) *Strategic Management in Multinational Companies*, Oxford: Pergamon Press.

Hamel, G. and Prahalad, C.K. (1985) 'Do you really have a global strategy', *Harvard Business Review*, **63**(4): 139–48.

Henzler, H. and Rall, W. (1986) 'Facing up to the globalisation challenge', *McKinsey Quarterly*, 4: 52–68.

Kedia, B.L. and Mukherji, A. (1999) 'Global managers: developing a mindset for global competitiveness', *Journal of World Business*, **34**(3): 230–51.

Porter, M.E. (1980) *Competitive Strategy: Techniques for Analysing Industries and Competitors*, New York: Free Press.

Prahalad, C.K. and Doz, Y.L. (1986) *The Multinational Mission: Balancing Local Demands and Global Vision*, New York: Free Press.

Prahalad, C.K. and Hamel, G. (1990) 'The core competence of the corporation', *Harvard Business Review*, **68**(3): 79–81.

Chapter references

Bartlett, C.A. and Ghoshal, S. (1987) 'Managing across borders: new organisational responses, *Sloan Management Review*, **29**(1): 45–53.

Bartlett, C.A. and Ghoshal, S. (1989) *Managing Across Borders: The Transnational Solution,* Boston, MA: Harvard Business School Press.

Bartlett, C.A. and Ghoshal, S. (1992) 'What is a global manager?', *Harvard Business Review*, **70**(5): 124–32.

Bartlett, C.A., Ghoshal, S. and Beamish, P. (2008) *Transnational Management: Text, Cases and Readings in Cross-border Management* (5th edn), Boston: McGraw-Hill/Irwin.

Hamel, G. and Prahalad, C.K. (1985) 'Do you really have a global strategy?', *Harvard Business Review*, **63**(4): 139–48.

Levitt, T. (1983) 'The globalisation of markets', *Harvard Business Review*, **61**(3): 92–102.

Porter, M.E. (1990) *The Competitive Advantage of Nations*, New York: Free Press.

Stonehouse, G., Hamill, J., Campbell, D.J. and Purdie, A. (2000) *Global and Transnational Business: Management and Strategy,* Chichester: John Wiley & Sons.

Yip, G.S. (1992) *Total Global Strategy: Managing for Worldwide Competitive Advantage*, Englewood Cliffs, NJ: Prentice Hall.

Chapter 12
Opportunities, threats and strategic position

Introduction and chapter overview

The SWOT (strengths, weaknesses, opportunities and threats) analysis is the end point of the strategic analysis. The framework combines the internal analysis, which resulted in the strengths, weaknesses and competences, with the external analysis, which has generated the opportunities and threats. This is shown in Figure 12.1.

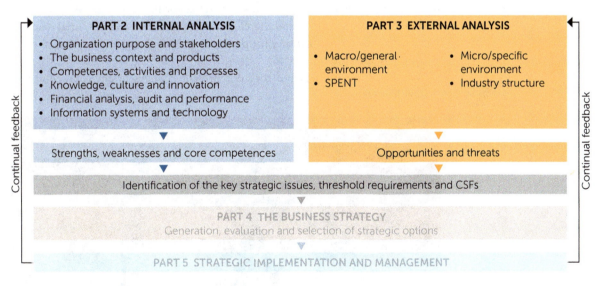

Figure 12.1 **Drawing together the SWOT analysis**

This chapter now explores how to undertake the full SWOT analysis and then examines the strategic position of the organization by exploring the key strategic issues, thresholds and critical success factors (CSFs).

Learning objectives

After studying this chapter, you should be able to:

- define and distinguish between what are deemed opportunities and threats
- explain how to use a SWOT analysis

■ explain what is meant by strategic position and determine the significance of understanding an organization's strategic position

12.1   Opportunities and threats

The SWOT analysis is made up of strengths and weaknesses (see Chapter 8) and opportunities and threats.

The opportunities and threats emerge from our understanding of the external analysis and the analysis of macroenvironments and microenvironments. In this respect, they are composed of what we may term 'environmental factors' (the macroenvironment) and 'competitor factors' (the microenvironment).

Environmental factors cover demographics, economics, policy, legislation, sociological, cultural, environmental and technological shifts (captured using our SPENT framework; Chapter 9).

Competitor factors are captured using Porter's five forces and cover things such as the product life cycle, suppliers, customers, capabilities, resources, new entrants, market segments, prices, new products, substitutes, and distribution (Chapter 10).

The factors themselves are not opportunities or threats, they are categories of things to examine. The opportunities and threats can emerge around each category and relate to the nature of change around each category. As such, an opportunity for one organization can be a threat for another. An example may be the rising price of oil. While this is a threat for bus passenger services (as it pushes diesel prices higher and therefore ticket prices rise and potential demand falls), it may be an opportunity for produces of hybrid and electric cars, as their market may increase.

As such, opportunities and threats represent changes in environmental and competitor factors.

Opportunities and threats: the rising price of oil

CASE STUDY Celands Bank

Five years ago, Celands Bank (CB) began a process of turning itself from a small, specialist merchant bank into a major international player. Based in Iceland, those in charge of the bank set out to run a secure, niche capital management and financing company, expert in funding, underwriting and managing specialist projects and ventures.

CB seemed to have all the advantages necessary to be fully effective in this kind of merchant banking and financial management. A key advantage of the location was that it could conduct its affairs well away from the main money markets and regulatory systems of the world. Journalists rarely came and pried. CB (and other banks also) was (and remains) a major source of well-paid employment and prosperity in Iceland.

Above all, CB was known for its speed of operation, the thoroughness of its work and its absolute security and discretion. Clients came to CB by recommendation or word of mouth. Governments used it when it was necessary to make transfer payments in markets that required discretion and secrecy.

The merchant banking business was especially successful, and CB was able to become involved in mega-projects and ventures that needed ready but discreet sources of capital. It became a major player in the financing of arms' shipments and the strategic management of the arms trade. The arms trade relies on discretion, absolute assurance of funds, and secure, comprehensive and discreet financial transaction management and this CB could provide. Using its discretionary position, CB moved into a position of securing and managing funds for the support of major initiatives in waste recycling and effluent management, and programmes for the development of nuclear energy generation.

Those clients who used CB found that the location, and managerial and financial expertise all contributed to the effectiveness of the working and operational relationships. Above all, they knew that, if need be, they could contact the company at any time of day or night, secure funds at any point of the day or night, and rely on the total discretion of the staff and of the location.

However, there came a point where this was deemed not to be enough. Predators and corporate raiders started to gather round. One market analyst carried out a full-scale evaluation of the strengths and weaknesses of CB, and the opportunities that might be afforded should it restructure, expand its markets, or even go into new ventures and locations.

Then two things happened, one after the other. One of the major armaments companies cancelled its contracts with CB. While the reasons stated were a change of government policy on the use of offshore and discretionary accounts such as those managed by CB, everyone 'on the inside' knew that somewhere there had been a breach of discretion or some other faux pas in relation to the arms industry. The following day, the CEO Anna Grey was dismissed and replaced by Peter Tweed, a nominee of the major shareholders. Grey had spent all her life in this specialist part of the merchant banking sector. She was well known to all the companies and clients that used the bank. She had been the CEO for the past 11 years, and had always enjoyed the full confidence of shareholders, backers and the capital money markets. Now that a breach had occurred, however, the integrity of the sector and of CB itself demanded that she left.

Tweed had 20 years' experience working in corporate, capital, merchant and retail banking, although his only managerial experience was in retail banking and corporate retail strategy. However, he had been successful in everything he had done. He had worked his way through the ranks, and had risen to become deputy CEO of one of the largest US retail banking groups.

Tweed immediately saw the prospects for expansion. He secured the backing of the major shareholders to implement the following strategy:

- use of the company's location as a base for expansion into retail markets
- enlarging the capital and venture arm of the business into retail activity, especially mass-market subprime loans and mortgage lending
- high interest corporate and retail deposit accounts, paying up to three times what would be available in US, UK, EU and Southeast Asia markets.

Seriously alarmed, a group of CB's largest clients, including government officials and diplomats, sought a meeting with Tweed and with representatives of the company's major shareholders. How, they wondered, would the confidentiality, security and discretion survive what Tweed was now going to do? With the volumes of work and with the interest rates on offer, the whole of the Icelandic banking sector would now come under real and continual scrutiny. Tweed replied that he was going to maximize returns to shareholders, and that this could not be done by pursuing the present line of business. There had already been attempts to take the bank over, and he wanted to make sure that this did not happen, or if it did, then shareholders would gain maximum value. There were opportunities out there waiting to be exploited, and if this meant losing one or two clients, then so be it. Tweed then turned to the shareholder representatives for approval, and when this was forthcoming (although with some discomfort), he declared the meeting closed.

3

12.2 Using the SWOT analysis

The SWOT analysis is commonly credited to the Stanford University research team of Dosher, Benepe, Humphrey, Stewart and Lie. The SWOT analysis was developed originally as the SOFT framework (strengths, opportunities, failures and threats) in 1964, resulting from work exploring why corporate planning failed. The outcomes of the research resulted in a 17-stage technique, which started with an identification of issues related to planning categories – product, process, customers, distribution, finance and administration – and required a SWOT analysis to be undertaken for each issue. Each SWOT was then recorded as a 'planning issue' and steps undertaken to resolve or identify actions for each issue. In this process, SOFT or SWOT analysis was born.

GURU GUIDE

Albert Humphrey was born in 1926. He graduated from the University of Illinois with a BSc in chemical engineering, gained a Masters in chemical engineering from MIT and an MBA in business administration from Harvard. His work at the Stanford Research Institute produced a team method for planning that created the SOFT analysis, which was developed into the SWOT analysis. At Stanford Research Institute, he was instrumental in creating the 'International Executive Seminar in Long Range Planning' and the 'stakeholders concept'. The programme was subsequently renamed TAM, Team Action Management, which can be found at http://www.tamplc.com/. Albert Humphrey died in 2005.

It is clear that the SWOT analysis is an extremely useful tool for profiling the perceived capabilities and deficiencies of an organization and how the environment has provided for some opportunities and threats. In fact, the tool is so 'simple' and useful that it often forms the starting point of strategic development for many organizations. However, as we have seen, there are many factors that lead to the SWOT analysis and understanding these provides for a rich use of the tool and what it can bring to the organization.

So, how do we do a SWOT analysis and what do we need to watch out for? Figure 12.2 shows the basic four-quadrant grid that represents the SWOT analysis in its purest form. The grid can be used to assess a company, product, brand, business idea, concept, the competition or, indeed, yourself. As such, a starting point to applying a SWOT is to clearly define what the subject of the SWOT is, and what its purpose is.

STRENGTH	**WEAKNESS**
OPPORTUNITY	**THREAT**

Figure 12.2 **The SWOT grid**

Figure 12.3 **The SWOT grid and action**

To make the SWOT analysis more useful, we can develop it to include a time period and potential actions. This is shown in Figure 12.3.

To operationalize the SWOT analysis, we follow three basic steps:

1 Profile the current situation. List all strengths and weaknesses that currently exist.
2 Profile the emerging situation. List all the opportunities and threats that could emerge.
3 Develop the plan of action. Determine how to address the various elements of the SWOT. In summary, we would normally:

- Build, maintain and exploit strengths
- Minimize or remove any weaknesses
- Prioritize and exploit opportunities
- Minimize and counteract any threats.

Table 12.1 provides an example of stages 1 and 2 of a SWOT analysis, in this case for the coffee chain Starbucks.

Table 12.1 **SWOT analysis for Starbucks**

Strengths	Weaknesses
• Very profitable organization • Global coffee brand built on a reputation for fine products and services • One of the Fortune 100 Best Companies to Work For in 2010 • A respected employer that values its workforce • Strong ethical values • Ethical mission statement	• Innovation may falter over time • Strong presence in the USA but needs to spread business risk • Dependent on the retail of coffee • Core product offering is easy to copy
Opportunities	**Threats**
• New products and services that can be retailed in its cafés, such as fair trade products • Expand global operations • New markets for coffee • Strategic alliances and co-branding	• If market for coffee shrinks • Supply of coffee beans in the future • Health risks associated with caffeine • Environmental risks associated with coffee production • Global exchange rates • Economic climate for disposable income • Rises in the cost of coffee and dairy products • Competitors and imitation brands entering the market

It is not a straightforward matter to determine what constitutes a strength, weakness, opportunity or threat. Clearly, the organizational context, subjective nature of the assessment and the often interconnected and complex relationships between factors can make identification and evaluation problematic.

Some features that could reduce this problem are:

- Be realistic in the scope of the analysis
- Clearly split actual evidence from potential changes
- Be specific
- Keep analysis focused and relevant
- Ensure strengths are relative and clearly defined.

12.3   Determining the strategic position

Completing a SWOT analysis allows us to better understand the strategic position of an organization. The strategic position is, in effect, where the organization is placed in competence terms (see Chapter 4) and competitive terms (Chapter 13) relative to the competitors in the market or industry. There is a range of additional frameworks that can be employed to explore this concept. One such framework is termed the SPACE matrix (Rowe et al., 1989).

The SPACE matrix (strategic position and action evaluation) helps to explain an organization's strategic position and the possible action that can be taken (Figure 12.4). The four quadrants of the matrix are created from the axes of two internal dimensions, namely financial strength (FS) and competitive advantage (CA) and two external dimensions, environmental stability (ES) and industry strength (IS). In the same way the SWOT analysis bridges internal and external environmental analysis, the SPACE analysis also provides such a bridge but with slightly different dimensions. Therefore, by applying both SPACE and SWOT analyses, a solid understanding of the organization and its strategic position can be gained.

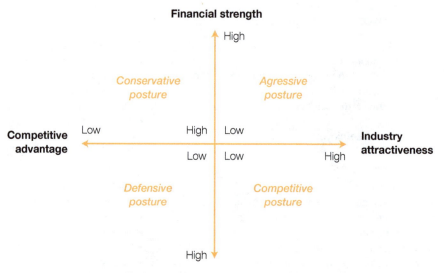

Figure 12.4 **SPACE analysis**

Using a SPACE analysis, four different strategic positions are highlighted. The organization will either be seen to be aggressive, conservative, defensive or competitive. This is useful for us to know as we move to Part 4 of the book and determine how to develop a business strategy.

STRATEGIC
PLANNING SOFTWARE

This is a helpful chapter to refer to when completing section 1.3 SWOT Analysis in Phase 1 of the **Strategic Planning Software** (www.planning-strategy.com).

For test questions, extra case studies, audio case studies, weblinks, videolinks and more to help you understand the topics covered in this chapter, visit our companion website at www.macmillanihe.com/companion/business/campbell.

3

VOCAB CHECKLIST FOR ESL STUDENTS

Arms trade (see 'arms' and 'trade')   Fair trade
Co-branding (see 'co-' and 'branding')   Faux pas
Effluent   Merchant banking

Definitions for these terms can be found in the 'Vocab Zone' of the companion website, which provides free access to the Macmillan English Dictionary online at www.macmillanihe.com/companion/business/campbell.

REVIEW QUESTIONS

1   Explain what we mean by an opportunity and a threat, and highlight the differences.
2   Explain how organizations can use a SWOT analysis to inform their strategic decision-making.
3   Explain what makes a 'good' SWOT analysis.
4   Explain why it is important to understand an organization's strategic position.

DISCUSSION TOPIC

The SWOT analysis is a pointless tool as it only captures one point in time and is a subjective review of what the managers of an organization may think, or want to think. Discuss.

HOT TOPICS – Research project areas to investigate

For your research project, why not investigate ...

■ ... how organizations use the SWOT analysis to inform their strategic decisions.
■ ... how organizations validate their interpretation of organizational strengths and weaknesses.
■ ... whether a recession leads to an inherently pessimistic view of organizational opportunities and threats.

Recommended reading

Hill, T. and Westbrook, R. (1997) 'SWOT analysis: it's time for a product recall', *Long Range Planning*, **30**(1): 46–52.

Panagiotou, G. (2003) 'Bringing SWOT into focus', *Business Strategy Review*, **14**(2): 8–10.

Piercy, N. and Giles, W. (1989) 'Making SWOT analysis work', *Journal of Marketing Intelligence & Planning*, **7**(5/6): 5–7.

Shinno, H., Yoshioka, S., Marpaung, S. and Hachiga, S. (2006) Qualitative SWOT analysis on the global competiveness of machine tool industry', *Journal of Engineering Design*, **17**(3): 251–8.

Valentin, E.K. (2001) 'SWOT analysis from a resource-based view', *Journal of Marketing Theory and Practice*, **9**(2): 54–68.

Weihrich, H. (1982) 'The Tows Matrix: a tool for situational analysis', *Long Range Planning*, **15**(2): 54–66.

Chapter reference

Rowe, A.J., Mason, R.O., Dickel, K.E. and Sayder, N.H. (1989) *Strategic Management: A Methodological Approach* (3rd edn), New York: Addison Wesley.

PART 4

THE BUSINESS STRATEGY

Having undertaken the internal and external environmental analysis in Parts 2 and 3, we can now start to explore the various strategic options available to an organization. To do this, we need to understand the nature of competitive advantage and the various sources of competitive advantage. We recognize that not all organizations seek to be 'competitive', but all organizations need to meet their potential or mission and vision. In this respect, competitive advantage relates to how an organization seeks to deliver what it needs to deliver in terms of efficiency or effectiveness (or both).

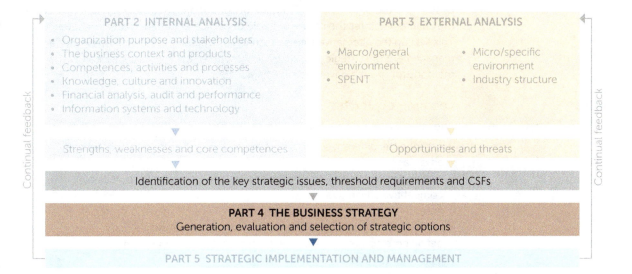

In developing the business strategy, we need to determine the sources of competitive advantage, and this is done is **Chapter 13**. **Chapter 14** explores how this advantage can be achieved, using various frameworks to generate strategic options and then evaluating and selecting strategies. **Chapter 15** examines how the various strategic options could be delivered and the different mechanisms and forms of strategic direction organizations can strive to achieve.

Chapter 13

Competitive advantage and strategy

Introduction and chapter overview

The key challenge for any organization is the ability to gain and sustain a competitive advantage in the market or industry. This advantage can be based on alignment to environmental and industry structures, or by the continual adaptation, creativity and innovative use of organizational resources and networks. This chapter explores the means by which organizations can gain and sustain a competitive advantage through the use of positioning or the creative use of resources. The schools of strategic thought are examined before focusing on the identification of generic strategies as building blocks for the overall strategic direction of the organization. Once the generic strategies have been determined, the chapter explores the nature and role of competences and core competences. This sets up the alternative forms of strategic direction, strategic frameworks, and management of strategic risk, which are discussed in Chapter 14, as well as the methods for growth developed in Chapter 15.

Learning objectives

After studying this chapter, you will be able to:

- describe the different schools of strategic thought relating to competitive advantage
- explain the concept of competitive advantage, and identify sources of competitive advantage
- describe and demonstrate the application of Porter's generic strategies
- explain low-cost, differentiation, focus and hybrid strategies
- define core competences and explain sources of competence

13.1 Sources of competitive advantage

The main goal of strategic management is to produce sustainable competitive advantage for a business. Competitive advantage can arise from deliberate, planned strategies and emergent strategies, which arise from opportunistic moves by the business. Competitive advantage is not easy to achieve and is even more difficult to sustain. Superior performance is built and sustained through continuous organizational learning and results in a constant process of new strategy development and improvement in the way in which business activities are carried out.

The rapid pace of technological, political, economic and social change, the increasing turbulence of the business environment, the growing sophistication of customer needs and the drastic shortening of product life cycles that typifies 'hypercompetition' all mean that competitive advantage is often contestable rather than sustainable. In other words, the search for strategies that produce and sustain superior performance over a long period of time has become increasingly difficult. Competitive advantage can only be developed and sustained through the creation of new business knowledge based on continuous organizational learning and the deployment of dynamic capabilities (Teece, 2009).

In Chapter 1, we learned that the different strands of theory in strategic management offer several explanations and potential methods by which competitive advantage can be achieved.

The 'competitive positioning' theory is based on the structure-conduct-performance paradigm and is typified by Porter's five forces, generic strategy and value chain frameworks (Porter, 1980, 1985), which have subsequently been augmented by the concept of a hybrid strategy. While dated and arguably inflexible, Porter's work still forms an excellent platform for understanding the positioning school. For Porter, the first question to be answered was: 'in which industry should the business compete?' Potential industry profitability, and hence industry attractiveness, was established through five forces analysis (Chapter 10). The factors that lead to industry attractiveness are:

> **Industry attractiveness** represents the potential to make a profit or gain strategic rent from a specific industry configuration.

- Industry's market size and growth potential
- The impact of environmental forces on the industry structure and dynamics
- Potential for entry and exit, and mobility in the industry
- Stability and dependability of demand
- Asset specificity, switching costs and capital costs
- Degree of risk and uncertainty in the industry's future
- Knowledge of the industry.

Once the choice of industry was made, the organization had to determine which generic strategy to pursue, and then decide the optimum configuration of its value-adding activities to support the chosen generic strategy. The approach is essentially 'outside-in', with choices initially being concerned with which industry was likely to prove the most profitable. As such, the competitive dynamics revolved around the degree to which perfect information or knowledge could be achieved and how barriers to entry and mobility could be exploited.

As an alternative, the resource-based school (Prahalad and Hamel, 1990; Barney, 1991; Grant, 1991) emerged on the basis that competitive advantage results from the development and exploitation of core competences by individual businesses, whatever industry they are in. This theory is built on the notion that certain firms outperform their competitors in the same industry. If this is the case, competitive advantage cannot be explained entirely by different industry conditions. The explanation for competitive advantage must rest, at least in part, within the firm itself. For this reason, the approach to strategy is best regarded as 'inside-out', and explains why firms in the same industry experience different levels of success and performance.

The third, knowledge-based school (Sveiby, 1997, 2001) suggests that competitive advantage arises from the creation, development and exploitation of new knowledge through a process of organizational learning. Interestingly, the competitive positioning, core competence and knowledge-based approaches need not be viewed as mutually exclusive. Knowledge can be viewed as the basis of an organization's core competences and generic strategy, leading to innovation, the ability to adapt and adopt. Equally, a generic strategy can be viewed as being dependent on a particular set of core competences underpinned by an appropriate configuration of value-adding activities or dynamic capabilities (Teece, 2009).

GURU GUIDE

Karl-Erik Sveiby is a professor of knowledge management at the Hanken Business School in Helsinki, Finland. He is a subject expert in knowledge management and is often regarded as one of the founding fathers of knowledge management. He has considerable management experience, having worked with several international firms and was the proprietor of one of Scandinavia's leading publishing houses. Dr Sveiby has also extensive consultancy experience, and is the founder of Sveiby Knowledge Associates (www.sveiby.com), a consultancy firm specializing in providing knowledge management solutions to global firms.

His work in measuring the value of intangible assets has been extensively adapted by Swedish companies and has become part of a international standard in this field.

The development of a strategy will inevitably draw on some analysis of the business, its objectives, its resources, competences, activities and its competitive environment. Even in the context of an emergent approach to strategy, managers still require an understanding of the business and the consequences of alternative courses of action.

This chapter provides tools that can be employed in developing our understanding of current strategy and future strategic alternatives. The frameworks are first explored separately and then the linkages between them are developed. It is important to note that there is no universal prescription for building competitive advantage. Competitive advantage is, however, more likely to result from doing things differently from competitors and doing them better rather than from trying to emulate them. Hamel and Prahalad (1985) made a strong case that organizations should develop a 'strategic intent' to stretch their resources and competences to the limits in order to achieve superior performance. Similarly, superior performance is more likely to result from an informed approach to management based on an understanding of the firm, the environment in which it operates and the strategic alternatives available to it. This chapter provides the basis of an informed approach to the development of corporate strategies.

Competitive and collaborative advantage

Competitive advantage will depend on the ability of a firm to outperform its competitors. Sustainable competitive advantage requires that the firm outperforms its rivals over a long period of time. While there is no recipe or formula that can guarantee sustained superior performance, there are certain organizational behaviours that have been shown to make success more likely:

- *strategic intent:* constantly stretching the organization to its limits

- *continuous improvement and innovation:* continually trying to improve products and services, relationships with customers and suppliers, and the way that activities are organized and carried out
- *doing things differently from competitors:* devising ways of doing business that are different from and better than the approaches adopted by competitors
- *being customer oriented:* always seeking to meet customer needs
- *building knowledge-based core competences and distinctive capabilities*
- *developing clear and consistent strategies* that are understood by managers and customers
- *awareness of factors in the business environment,* potential changes and their likely implications for the business
- *collaborating with other businesses and customers* to improve agility and flexibility.

Any strategy ought to take these factors into account, as by doing so, it is more likely that the strategy will be more difficult for competitors to emulate. Collaboration with suppliers, distributors and customers can be particularly important for building competitive advantage that is sustainable, as collaboration can be particularly difficult for competitors to replicate. For example, the association of Ferrari's Formula One team with Shell has led the team to win a number of world titles. Ferrari engines are powered by high performance race fuels developed by Shell, and their partnership has been a crucial factor in Ferrari's successful campaign in winning constructor and driver titles at Formula One world championships.

13.2   Michael Porter's generic strategies

Perhaps the oldest and best-known explanation of competitive advantage is given by Porter in his generic strategy framework. Although this framework has increasingly been called into question in recent years, it still provides useful insights into competitive behaviour. The framework and its limitations are considered in this section.

According to Porter (1985), competitive advantage arises from the selection of the generic strategy that best fits the organization's competitive environment and then organizing value-adding activities to support the chosen strategy.

There are three main alternatives:

- *cost leadership:* being the lowest cost producer of a product so that above-average profits are earned even though the price charged is not above average
- *differentiation:* creating a customer perception that a product is superior to that of competitors' products so that a premium price can be charged
- *focus:* utilizing either a differentiation or cost leadership strategy in a narrow profile of market segments (see Figure 13.1).

Porter argued that an organization must make two key decisions on its strategy:

1   Should the strategy be one of differentiation or cost leadership?
2   Should the scope of the strategy be broad or narrow?

In other words, the organization must decide whether to try to differentiate its products and sell them at a premium price, or whether to gain competitive

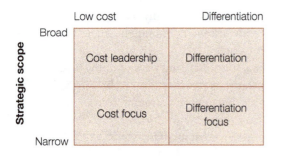

Figure 13.1 **The generic strategy framework**

Source: Adapted from Porter, 1998

advantage by producing at a lower cost than its competitors. Higher profits can be made by adopting either approach. Second, it must decide whether to target the whole market with its chosen strategy or whether to target a specific segment or niche of the market. Figure 13.1 shows cost focus and differentiation focus as two ends or extremes of a continuum. This is because actual strategies can exist at or anywhere in between the extremes. The same applies to the vertical direction. Broad and narrow are general extremes, where a broad strategy targets many markets and a disparate cross-section of customers, while a narrow or highly focused strategy may target a small number of segments (or possibly just one).

The point of Figure 13.1 is that it is best understood as a map. Companies in an industry can all be successful if they each choose different strategies. If, however, two or more competitors choose to compete in the same part of the map (that is, adopting the same or similar generic strategy), competition will become intensified among those pursuing the same strategy. By plotting competitors on the map, we can get an idea of where the most intense competition will occur. Sections containing only one competitor will experience the least competition.

Cost leadership strategy

A **cost leadership strategy** is based on a business organizing and managing its value-adding activities so as to be the lowest cost producer of a product (a good or service) within an industry.

There are several potential benefits of a cost leadership strategy:

- the business can earn higher profits by charging a price equal to, or even below, that of competitors because its unit costs are lower
- it allows the business the possibility to increase both sales and market share by reducing price below that charged by competitors (assuming that the product's demand is price elastic in nature)
- it allows the business the possibility of entering a new market by charging a lower price than competitors
- it can be particularly valuable in a market where consumers are price sensitive
- it creates an additional barrier to entry for organizations wishing to enter the industry.

A **cost leadership strategy** is based on a business organizing and managing its value-adding activities so as to be the lowest cost producer of a product (a good or service) within an industry.

A successful cost leadership strategy is likely to rest on a number of organizational features. Such features will relate to the means by which a cost advantage can be gained and maintained in the long run (although cost-based strategy tends to be difficult to sustain). As such, features such as lean supply chain, efficient production processes, aligned value systems, dedicated (tied in) supply, customer loyalty and price awareness of competitors are all critical.

Value chain analysis is central to identifying where cost savings can be made at various stages in the value chain and its internal and external linkages. Attainment of a position of cost leadership depends on the arrangement of value chain activities, so as to:

- reduce unit costs by copying rather than originating designs, using cheaper materials and other cheaper resources, producing products with 'no frills', reducing labour costs and increasing labour productivity

- achieving economies of scale by high-volume sales, perhaps based on advertising and promotion, allowing high fixed costs of investment in modern technology to be spread over a high volume of output
- using high-volume purchasing to obtain discounts for bulk buying of materials
- locating activities in areas where costs are low or government help, for example grant support, is available
- obtaining 'learning curve' economies.

A cost leadership strategy, coupled with low price, is best employed in a market or segment where **price elasticity of demand** exists, that is, where volume is relatively responsive to price. Under such circumstances, sales and market share are likely to increase significantly, thus increasing economies of scale, reducing unit costs further, so generating above-average profits. Alternatively, if a price similar to that of competitors is charged accompanied by advertising to boost sales, similar results will be obtained.

> The term **price elasticity of demand** describes the extent to which the volume of demand for a product is dependent upon its price.

Example   Price elasticity of demand

The coefficient of elasticity is expressed in a simple equation:

PED = percentage change in quantity/percentage change in price.

The value of PED (price elasticity) tells us the price responsiveness of the product's demand. If, for any given price change, PED is more than −1, it means that the change in price has brought about a higher proportionate change in volume sold. This relationship between price change and quantity is referred to as 'price elastic demand'.

Demand is said to be 'price inelastic' if the quantity change is proportionately smaller than the change in price (resulting in a PED of less than −1). The larger the value of PED, the more price elastic the demand, and the nearer PED is to 0, the more price inelastic the demand.

The price elasticity of demand (the value of PED) depends on the market's perception of a product. Products tend to be price elastic if the market sees a product as unnecessary but desirable. Products will have a price inelastic demand if the customer perceives a *need* for a product rather than a *want* (such as the demand for most medicines, or tobacco).

Companies whose activities include high-volume standardized products are often cost leaders. The no-frills airlines are good examples. A basic product is offered and costs per sale are minimized by online booking, faster aircraft turnaround between flights, and no on-board free food.

Example   Ryanair: a cost leader

Ryanair has proved to be one of the most, if not the most, successful low-cost airlines. Despite the economic downturn of 2009, Ryanair maintained its performance and profitability. How it achieved this is well articulated in an interview by Tom Chesshyre (2002) of Michael O'Leary, chief executive of the Irish-based, low-cost airline Ryanair, which appeared in *The Times*.

In the article, Tom Chesshyre explains that *The Times* travel desk receives more complaints about Ryanair than any other airline and that complaints about delays, poor in-flight service, damaged luggage and lengthy check-in queues are common. Yet, O'Leary is quick to recognize that Ryanair rarely apologizes or offers compensation for these complaints.

When the interviewer questions this

4

attitude, O'Leary responds: 'Our customer service is about the most well-defined in the world. We guarantee to give you the lowest airfare. You get a safe flight. You get a normally on-time flight. That's the package. We don't and won't give you anything more on top of that.' He adds: 'Listen, we care for our customers in the most fundamental way possible: we don't screw them every time we fly them. We care for our customers by giving them the cheapest airfares. I have no time for certain large airlines which say they care and then screw you for six or seven hundred quid almost every time you fly.'

However, the article states that many people are now tiring of this attitude and the Air Transport Users Council, which monitors airline complaints, testifies that Ryanair is one of the worst offenders. It explains that several of Ryanair's customers have complained about how difficult it is to talk to anyone when they have a problem, as they have to ring several times before eventually being put through to an operator. In response to this, O'Leary states that: 'Generally speaking, we won't take any phone calls ... because they keep you on the bloody phone all day. We employ four people in our customer care department. Every complaint must be put in writing and we undertake to respond to that complaint within 24 hours. Anyway, do you know what 70 per cent of our complaints are about? They're about people who want to make changes to what are clearly stated as being "non-changeable, non-transferable and non-refundable" tickets.'

Asked if he thinks people should be able to get refunds for his airline tickets, he replies: 'No ... because even if you can't change your ticket and you've got to buy a second one, you're still going to save money compared with buying a single ticket from the major airlines. Anyway, with our new system you can make some changes. If you pay 20 euros (at that time £12.30), you can change the time of your flight, but not the name on the ticket.'

Which, as the article correctly states, is a start.

Differentiation strategy

A **differentiation strategy** is based on persuading customers that a product is superior to that offered by competitors.

A **differentiation strategy** is based on persuading customers that a product is superior to that offered by competitors. This relies on creating added value for the consumer, be it real value or perceived. Value can be in terms of social, economic, political, belonging, emotional or situational, and is at the heart of understanding consumers reserved price for goods and services, or their willingness to pay a premium.

Differentiation can be based on premium product features or simply by creating consumer perceptions that a product is superior. The major benefits to a business of a successful differentiation strategy are:

- its products will command a premium price
- demand for its product will be less price elastic than that for competitors' products
- above-average profits can be earned
- it creates an additional barrier to entry to new businesses wishing to enter the industry.

A business seeking to differentiate itself will organize its value chain activities to help create differentiated products and to create a perception among customers that these offerings are worth a higher price.

Differentiation can be achieved in several ways:

- by creating products that are superior to competitors by virtue of design, technology, performance and so on
- by offering superior after-sales service
- by superior distribution channels, perhaps in prime locations, especially important in the retail sector
- by creating a strong brand name through design, innovation or advertising
- by distinctive or superior product packaging.

A differentiation strategy is likely to necessitate emphasis on innovation, design, R&D, awareness of particular customer needs and marketing. To say that differentiation is in the eyes of the customer is no exaggeration. It could be argued that it is often the brand name or logo that distinguishes a product rather than real product superiority. For example, men's shirts bearing the logo of Ralph Lauren, Calvin Klein or Yves St Laurent command a price well above that of arguably similar shirts that bear no logo. There is little empirical evidence of objectively better design or better quality materials. Differentiation appears merely to be based on the fact that the designer's name is fashionable and that their products bear the logo.

This strategy is employed in order to reduce price elasticity of demand for the product so that its price can be raised above that of competitors without reducing sales volume. This will, in turn, generate above-average profits when measured against sales (return on sales).

Figure 13.2 provides a simplified understanding of cost and differentiation strategies.

4

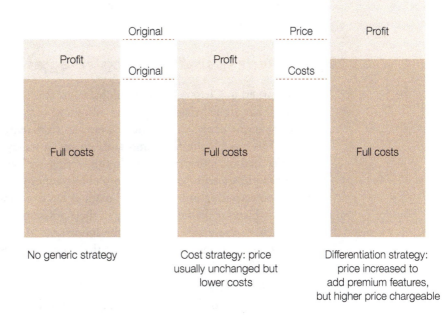

Figure 13.2 **A simplified understanding of cost and differentiation strategies**

Note: price = full costs plus profits

Focus strategy

A focus strategy is aimed at a segment of the market for a product rather than at the whole market or many markets. A particular group of customers is identified on the basis of age, income, lifestyle, sex, geographic location, some other distinguishing segmental characteristic or a combination of these. Within the segment, a business then employs either a cost leadership or a differentiation strategy.

The major benefits of a focus strategy are:

- it requires a lower investment in resources compared to a strategy aimed at an entire market or many markets
- it allows specialization and greater knowledge of the segment being served
- it makes entry to a new market less costly and simpler.

A focus strategy will require:

- identification of a suitable target customer group, which forms a distinct market segment
- identification of the specific needs of that group
- establishing that the segment is sufficiently large to sustain the business
- establishing the extent of competition within the segment
- production of products to meet the specific needs of that group
- deciding whether to operate a differentiation or cost leadership strategy within the market segment.

An example of a business that pursues a focus strategy is Ferrari, which targets the market for high performance sports cars (a relatively small number of customers in relation to the total market for cars). Ferrari, unlike Toyota or Fiat, does not produce family saloons, minis, off-road vehicles or people carriers. It only produces high performance cars. Its strategy is clearly one of differentiation based on design, superior performance and its Grand Prix record, which allows it to charge a price well above that of its competitors.

Many businesses use a focus strategy to enter a market before broadening their activities into other related segments.

13.3   Porter's global generic strategies

We learned in Chapter 11 that a global context is important. In parallel, Porter (1980) has argued that competitive advantage rests on a business selecting and adopting one of the three generic strategies (differentiation, cost leadership or focus) to modify the five competitive forces in its favour so as to earn higher profits than the industry average. In this section, we look at how Porter extended the generic strategy framework to global business. The model suggests that a business operating in international markets has five strategy alternatives (Figure 13.3), which are defined according to their position in respect to two intersecting factors; the extent to which the industry is globalized or country-centred (horizontal axis) and the breadth of the segments served by competitors in an industry (vertical axis).

The five strategic positions are:

1   *Global cost leadership:* the business seeks to be the lowest cost producer of a product globally. Globalization provides the opportunity for high-volume sales and greater economies of scale and scope than domestic competitors.

CASE STUDY   Mattel

If you are to stand the best possible chance of making and delivering products and services that your customers need and want from you, then you need to know what customers' needs and wants are.

However, knowing what your customers genuinely need and want from you, how much they are prepared to pay for this, and how often they are prepared to do business with you are the foundations of success, and, as such, distinguish the successful from the less so and the failures.

The Barbie organization was one of the first to recognize the importance of this, and, crucially, to take the next step and integrate the management of market and customer information into its product and brand development strategy. The Barbie organization was founded by Ruth Handler, who came across a German toy doll called Bild Lilli and reworked the design of the doll and named it after her own small daughter Barbara's family nickname – Barbie. The doll went into production and the company started operations in 1956.

The company set out to know everything that it possibly could about its customers – their buying habits, frequency of purchases, attitudes and values. They sought to understand the kinds of products that customers would and would not buy, and the life span of the dolls and their accessories. The result was akin to military intelligence gathering in its coverage and comprehensiveness, and both Ruth Handler and the Mattel organization (which took over the Barbie range of products in 1961) subsequently always boasted that they knew more about their customers than anyone else in the world.

The result was that when the first dolls arrived on the shelves of the world's toy shops in 1959, everyone was eagerly anticipating what they would look like and how the venture would go from a business point of view – quite literally: 'how it would play'. It became clear that there was a huge demand, not just for the dolls as they were, but also for products that would go with them – clothes, accessories and other add-ons.

From all of this grew what has come to be known as 'the eleven-inch doll market'. There was (and remains) a clear structure to this market:

- the products are bought by mothers and aunts for girls aged two and over
- the products are of value to girls aged two and over, as well as being acceptable and of value to those who buy them
- the products are played with and enjoyed by girls, and they also have to be acceptable to her friends and others whose opinions they value and respond to
- the products have a limited useful life, and the clothes, accessories and add-ons are a fundamental part of product effectiveness and value and brand development.

To remain successful, the company needed a regular flow of new products coming on stream all the time. It therefore needed to know and understand the kinds of products that would keep the customers coming back again and again. Part of the problem that had to be overcome was the availability of choices, both within the eleven-inch doll market, and also outside it (nobody likes to be limited to any one thing, and the buyers and consumers of Barbie dolls are no different). So the brand logo and distinctive colour scheme (a bright pink) were developed so as to be capable of being attached to every product that came out. Also, the core range of products had to be universally available, and at prices that would allow for unconsidered, whim and largely cash purchases to be made. So the products were made available at all possible outlets, including supermarkets, department stores and independent corner shops. In the UK and many parts of the USA and the EU, the decline of independent toy shops made this range of outlets essential.

As the result, the product range now covers themed toys (castles, stables, cars, accessories for dolls' houses), films and video productions, cards and books, and other dolls (Barbie now has a large circle of

4

friends and acquaintances, and a boyfriend Ken, who she separated from in 2004, but in 2006 they were hoping to rekindle their relationship, after Ken had a makeover). There is also a large range of accessories and add-ons for girls to use, including shoes, bracelets, bags, and hair and cosmetic products, which all carry the Barbie brand. There are limited editions, Christmas and seasonal specials, collectors' items and other exclusives. Barbie has had many careers, including surgeon, nanny, show jumper and schoolteacher, and each career has carried its own range of clothes and accessories. She has had over 40 pets and owned a wide range of vehicles. The first Barbie department store opened in Shanghai in 2009, and more are expected to follow.

The company carefully evaluates everything that carries the Barbie brand for compatibility as well as acceptability, and this remains a core priority of the market intelligence operation as well as product design. The fundamental wholesomeness of the products,

and especially the images of girls and women that are portrayed, continues to be debated. Nevertheless, it is estimated that over a billion Barbie dolls have been sold worldwide in over 150 countries and the company states that it sells one Barbie product every seven seconds somewhere in the world. The overall strategic approach is structured so as to produce an income per customer in the UK of £80 per annum.

Case study questions

1 Where does the source of competitive advantage lie for products such as these?
2 Identify in detail the elements of strategy necessary to ensure that the product remains viable for the next two, five and ten years.
3 What are the main lessons for leaders and managers in all organizations to be learned from the experience and success of the Barbie product and the Mattel organization?

2 *Global differentiation:* the business seeks to differentiate products and services globally, often on the basis of a global brand name.
3 *Global segmentation:* this is the global variant of a focus strategy, when a single market segment is targeted on a worldwide basis employing either cost leadership or differentiation.
4 *Protected markets:* a business that identifies national markets where its particular business is favoured or protected by the host government.
5 *National responsiveness:* the business adapts its strategy to meet the distinctive needs of local markets, that is, not a global strategy. Suitable for purely domestic businesses.

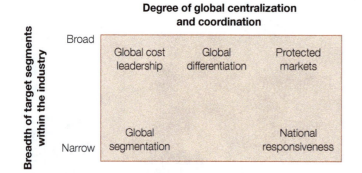

Figure 13.3 Porter's global strategy framework
Source: Adapted from Porter, 1986

The model suffers from some flaws, in that a hybrid can be adopted rather than falling neatly into one of the areas. As in the case of the conventional understanding of generic strategy, it is possible for a business to pursue a hybrid international strategy. Nissan, for example, concentrates on cost control but also ensures that it differentiates its products on the basis of their reliability.

Configuration and coordination of internal activities

One of Porter's most important contributions to understanding global strategy is his work on the global value chain (1986, 1990). Porter makes the case that global competitive advantage depends on configuring and coordinating the activities of a business in a unique way on a worldwide basis. To put it another way, competitive advantage results from the global scope of an organization's activities and the effectiveness with which it coordinates them. Porter (1986, 1990) argues that global competitive advantage depends on two sets of decisions:

1 *Configuration of value-adding activities:* managers must decide in which nations they will carry out each of the activities in the value chain of their business. Configuration can be broad (involving many countries) or narrow (one country or just a few).

2 *Coordination of value-adding activities:* managers must decide the most effective way of coordinating the value-adding activities that are carried out in different parts of the world.

Configuration of activities

	Geographically dispersed	Geographically concentrated
High	High degree of dispersal of activities with a high degree of coordination among subsidiaries	Purest global strategy (high degree of concentration of activities and coordination)
Low	Country-centred strategy for company with several national subsidiaries, each operating in only one country. Activity dispersed and little cooperation	Strategy based upon exporting of product with decentralised marketing in each host country – activities concentrated but not coordinated

(Vertical axis label: Coordination of activities)

Figure 13.4 Configuration and coordination for international strategy

Source: Adapted from Porter, 1986

Configuration and coordination present four broad alternatives, as illustrated in Figure 13.4. In the case of configuration, an organization can choose to disperse its activities to a range of locations around the world or it may choose to concentrate key activities in locations that present certain advantages. Many businesses concentrate the manufacture of their products in countries where costs are low but skill levels are good. Many clothing manufacturers manufacture their products in East Asia where labour costs are low but tailoring standards

Coordination of value-adding activities: garment manufacturing abroad

are high. An organization can decide to coordinate its worldwide activities or to mange them locally in each part of the world. The latter approach misses the opportunity for global management economies of scale. For Porter, the 'purest global strategy' is when an organization concentrates its key activities in locations giving competitive advantages and coordinates activities on a global basis. In the long term, according to Porter, organizations should move towards the 'purest global strategy' as far as is practicable.

Hybrid strategies

There is a body of evidence that suggests that successful strategy can be based on a hybrid (mixture) of differentiation, price and cost control. The hybrid strategy framework developed here is based on the following assumptions:

- strategy can employ a combination of differentiation, price and cost control
- differentiation can be used as the basis for charging a premium price or to increase sales and/or market share
- there are clear linkages between core competences, strategy and value-adding activities
- the framework is not intended as a recipe for competitive advantage, but rather as way of grouping different strategies.

Figure 13.5 Hybrid strategy

The extent of differentiation, price and cost control will depend on the nature of the market in which the business is operating. In markets where consumers show a preference for quality, the emphasis will be less on price and costs, while in markets where demand is price sensitive, the emphasis will be on keeping both prices and costs as low as possible (Figure 13.5). Of course, organizations may also seek to shape customer attitudes by advertising and promotion so as to modify market conditions. Supermarkets like Tesco and Sainsbury's operate with a hybrid strategy; their product price range varies with quality and consumer choice. For example, Tesco has four cola varieties ranging from normal to diet to sugar-free versions. Each of them is priced differently, so Tesco fulfils the needs of both cost- and quality-conscious consumers.

13.4   Competence-based competitive strategy

The generic strategy model is not the only one that seeks to provide an explanation of the sources of competitive advantage. The competence or resource-based model emphasizes that competitive edge stems from the competences of an organization, which distinguish it from its competitors, allowing it to outperform them (see Chapter 4).

Part 2 of this book explained the ways in which internal analysis makes it possible to better understand core competences by a process of deconstructing them into the component resources and competences that act as their foundation. Here we build on this analysis to explore the ways in which existing competences can be extended and new ones cultivated, and examine how and where these core competences can be exploited so as to acquire and sustain competitive advantage. Much of the recent attention to the concept of core competence is based on the work of Prahalad and Hamel (1989, 1990) and Stalk et al. (1992), who advocated the idea of competing on the basis of capabilities. Similarly, Kay (1993) advanced the idea that competitive advantage is based on distinctive capability.

Perhaps the best-known explanation of core competence is that provided by Prahalad and Hamel (1990, p. 79):

> Core competencies are the collective learning of the organization, especially how to co-ordinate diverse production skills and integrate multiple streams of technologies.

Prahalad and Hamel specified three tests to be applied in the identification and development of core competence. A core competence should:

- equip a business with the ability to enter and successfully compete in several markets
- add greater perceived customer value to the business's products than that perceived in competitor's products
- be difficult for competitors to imitate.

According to Prahalad and Hamel, there are many examples of core competence resulting in competitive advantage. Philips' development of optical media, including the laser disc, has led to a whole range of new hi-fi and IT products. Honda's engine technology has led to advantages in the car, motorcycle, lawn mower and generator businesses. Canon's expertise in optics, imaging and microprocessor controls has given it access to diverse markets including those for copiers, laser printers, cameras and image scanners.

Prahalad and Hamel argued that, in practice, competitive advantage is likely to be based on no more than five or six competences. These competences will allow management to produce new and unanticipated products, and to be responsive to changing opportunities because of production skills and the harnessing of technology. Given the turbulent business environment in many industries, this adaptability is essential if competitive advantage is to be built and sustained.

Kay (1993) took the concept of capability, initially identified by Stalk et al. (1992), to develop a framework that explains competitive advantage in terms of what he defines as 'distinctive capability'. This idea of distinctive capability has much in common with that of core competence, in that it views competitive advantage as being dependent on the unique attributes of a particular business and its products.

According to Kay (1993), distinctive capability results from one or more of the following sources:

- *Architecture:* the unique network of internal and external relationships of a business that produces superior performance. These can be unique relationships with suppliers, distributors or customers that competitors do not possess. Equally, the unique relationships may be internal to the business and based on the way that it organizes its activities in the value chain.
- *Reputation:* this stems from several sources, including superior product quality, characteristics, design, service and so on.
- *Innovation:* the ability of the business to get ahead and stay ahead of competitors depends on its success in researching, designing, developing and

marketing new products. Equally, it depends on the ability of the business to improve the design and organization of its value-adding activities.

- *Strategic assets:* businesses can also obtain competitive advantage from assets such as natural monopoly, patents and copyrights, which restrict competition.

So what do the concepts of core competence and distinctive capability add to our understanding of competitive advantage? First, they provide us with insight into how a business can build attributes that can deliver superior performance. Second, they inform the process of determining where such competences and capabilities can be exploited.

The process of building new core competences or extending existing ones must take into account the following considerations:

- *Customer perceptions:* competences, capabilities and products must be perceived by customers as being better value for money than those of competitors. The business's reputation can be particularly important in this regard.
- *Uniqueness:* core competences must be unique to the business and must be difficult for competitors to emulate. Similarly, there must be no close substitutes for these competences.
- *Continuous improvement:* core competences, goods and services must be continuously upgraded to stay ahead of competitors. Product and process innovation are particularly important.
- *Collaboration:* competitive advantage can result from the business's unique network of relationships with suppliers, distributors, customers and even competitors. There is the potential for 'multiplier effects' resulting from the complementary core competences of separate businesses being combined.
- *Organizational knowledge:* competences must be based on organizational knowledge and learning. Managers must improve the processes by which the organization learns, builds and manages its knowledge. Today, knowledge is potentially the greatest source of added value.

Core competence, generic strategy and the value chain: a synthesis

It has been argued (see for example Heene and Sanchez, 1997) that the resource or competence-based approach is largely incompatible with the competitive positioning or generic strategy approach advocated by Porter (1980, 1985). Mintzberg et al. (1995), however, make the case that the two approaches are in many respects complementary rather than mutually contradictory. Perhaps the best way of illustrating the linkages between the approaches is through the value chain of the organization.

As competitive advantage is based on the unique approach of the individual business to its environment, it is not possible to identify a one-for-all prescription that will guarantee superior performance in all situations. Both the competitive positioning and the resource-based approach, however, provide frameworks that allow broad sources of competitive advantage to be categorized for the purposes of analysis and development of future strategy. A differentiation strategy, for example, will be likely to be dependent on core competences in areas of the value chain like design, marketing and service. Similarly, a cost or price-based strategy may well require core competences in value chain activities like operations (production), procurement and perhaps marketing. It is much less likely that a cost leader will have core competences based on design and service. The possible relationships between core competences, generic strategies and the value chain are shown in Table 13.1.

Table 13.1 Core competences, generic strategies and the value chain

Value chain activity	Areas of competence associated with differentiation strategies	Areas of competence associated with cost/price-based strategies
Primary activities		
Inbound logistics	Control of quality of materials	Strict control of the cost of materials. Tendency to buy larger volumes of standard inputs
Operations	Control of quality of output, raising standards	Lowering production costs and achieving high-volume production
Marketing and sales	Sales (and customer relations) on the basis of quality technology, performance, reputation, outlets and so on	Achieving high-volume sales through advertising and promotion
Outbound logistics	Ensuring efficient distribution	Maintaining low distribution costs
Service	Adding to product value by high-quality and differentiated service	Minimal service to keep costs low
Support activities		
The business's infrastructure	Emphasis on quality	Emphasis on efficiency and cost reduction
Human resource development	Training to create a skills culture, which emphasizes quality, customer service, product development	Training to reduce costs
Technology development	Developing new products, improving product quality, product performance and customer service	Reducing production costs and increasing efficiency
Procurement	Obtaining high-quality resources and materials	Obtaining low-cost resources and materials

4

GURU GUIDE

James Brian Quinn received a BSc from Yale University in 1949. Professor Quinn is currently the Emeritus Professor of Management at Amos Tuck School of Management at Dartmouth College, Hanover, New Hampshire. During his distinguished academic career, Professor Quinn has taught courses in technology management, entrepreneurship and business policy. He is a well-known authority in the fields of management of technological change, outsourcing and strategic planning. He is a respected lecturer and has acted as consultant for numerous leading US and foreign corporations, the US and foreign governments, and small enterprises. His work has been widely appreciated and has won several prizes, including the McKinsey prize for the most outstanding articles appearing in *Harvard Business Review* and the American Academy of Management's Book of the Year Award for Outstanding Contribution to Advancing Management Knowledge. In 1989, Professor Quinn was awarded the Outstanding Educator award by the Academy of Management, and in a rare gesture, his former students created the James Brian Quinn Chair in Technology and Strategy at Dartmouth College in 1999.

Professor Quinn has been a member of the board on Science and Technology for International Development for the National Academy of Sciences and served as the chairman of National Academy of Engineering committees on the Productivity of Information Technology in Services, Technology in the Services Sector, and Environmental Impacts of Services. He is also a visiting professor at various universities, including Monash University, Dalien University, University of Western Australia and the International University of Japan.

Where to exploit core competences and strategies

As core competences and business strategies are developed, it is necessary to decide where they should be exploited. Core competences and strategies can be targeted on existing customers in existing markets or it may be possible to target new customers in existing markets. Alternatively, it may be possible to target new customers in new markets. These markets may be related to markets currently served by the organization or they may be unrelated markets. The organization may also consider employing its competences in a new industry. These decisions are concerned with determining the 'strategic direction' of the business. Once this decision has been made, decisions must be made on the methods to be employed in following the chosen strategic direction.

The process of exploiting existing core competences in new markets is known as 'competence leveraging'. In order to enter new markets, it is often necessary for the organization to build new core competences, alongside the existing core competences that are being leveraged, so as to satisfy new customer needs. The identification of customer needs to be served by core competences is based on analysis of the organization's competitive environment using the resource-based framework. Chapter 14 considers the alternative strategic directions an organization can pursue and the methods that can be employed in following these strategic directions.

STRATEGIC
PLANNING SOFTWARE

This is a helpful chapter to refer to when completing 1.1.3 Industry Life Cycle and 1.1.4 Porter's Five Forces within the External Analysis section and 1.2.2 Value Chain within the Internal Analysis section in Phase 1 of the **Strategic Planning Software** (www.planning-strategy.com). It would also be useful to recap the chapter before attempting to complete section 2.2 Competitive Strategy in Phase 2 of the **Strategic Planning Software** (www.planning-strategy.com).

For test questions, extra case studies, audio case studies, weblinks, videolinks and more to help you understand the topics covered in this chapter, visit our companion website at www.macmillanihe.com/companion/business/campbell.

VOCAB CHECKLIST FOR ESL STUDENTS

Coefficient	Logistics	Outsourcing
Distribution channel	'No frills'	Procurement
Hypercompetition (see	Opportunistic	Synthesis
'hypercompetitive')	Optical media (see 'optical' and	Unit cost
Infrastructure	'media')	Whim

Definitions for these terms can be found in the 'Vocab Zone' of the companion website, which provides free access to the Macmillan English Dictionary online at www.macmillanihe.com/companion/business/campbell.

REVIEW QUESTIONS

1 Explain what is meant by competitive advantage and where it comes from.
2 Describe how Porter's generic strategies can be used by an organization.
3 Explain what is meant by low-cost, differentiation, focus and hybrid strategies.
4 Define what a core competence is and how it can be used to gain competitive advantage.

DISCUSSION TOPIC

Porter's generic strategies related to the 1970s and 80s, and they are simply not applicable to 21st-century organizations. Discuss.

HOT TOPICS – Research project areas to investigate

For your research project, why not investigate ...

- ... which generic strategies are adopted by airlines operating in Continental Europe.
- ... which core competences lead to the greatest cost focus advantage.
- ... managers' attitudes to the applicability of hybrid strategies in music retail companies in your region.

Recommended reading

Grant, R.M. (1996) 'Prospering in dynamically-competitive environments: organizational capability as knowledge integration', *Organization Science*, **7**(4): 375–87.

Kay, J. (1995) 'Learning to define the core business', *Financial Times*, 1 December.

McKiernan, P. (1997) 'Strategy past; strategy futures', *Long Range Planning*, **30**(5): 790–8.

Newbert, S. (2005) 'New firm formation: a dynamic capability perspective', *Journal of Small Business Management*, **43**(1): 55–77.

Rumelt, R. (1991) 'How much does industry matter?', *Strategic Management Journal*, **12**(3): 167–85.

Teece, D.J., Pisano, G. and Shuen, A. (1998) 'Dynamic capabilities and strategic management', *Strategic Management Journal*, **18**(7): 509–33.

Chapter references

Barney, J.B. (1991) 'Firm resources and sustained competitive advantage', *Journal of Management*, **17**(1): 99–120.

Chesshyre, T. (2002) 'It's cheap but why not more cheerful?', *The Times*, 5 January.

Grant, R. (1991) 'The resource based theory of competitive advantage: implications for strategy formulation', *California Management Review*, **33**(3): 114–35.

Hamel, G. and Prahalad, C.K. (1985) 'Do you really have a global strategy?', *Harvard Business Review*, **63**(4): 139–48.

Heene, A. and Sanchez, R. (eds) (1997) *Competence-based Strategic Management*, London: John Wiley.

Kay, J. (1993) *Foundations of Corporate Success*, Oxford: Oxford University Press.

Mintzberg, H., Quinn, J.B. and Ghoshal, S. (1995) *The Strategy Process: Concepts, Contexts and Cases*, Englewood Cliffs, NJ: Prentice Hall.

Porter, M.E. (1980) *Competitive Strategy: Techniques for Analysing Industries and Competitors*, New York: Free Press.

Porter, M.E. (1985) *Competitive Advantage*, New York: Free Press.

Porter, M.E. (1986) 'What is strategy?', *Harvard Business Review*, **74**(6): 61–78.

Prahalad, C.K. and Hamel, G. (1990) 'The core competence of the corporation', *Harvard Business Review*, **68**(3): 79–91.

Stalk, G., Evans, P. and Shulmann, L.E. (1992) 'Competing on capabilities: the new rules of corporate strategy', *Harvard Business Review*, **70**(3): 57–69.

Sveiby, K.E. (1997) *The New Organizational Wealth: Managing and Measuring Knowledge-based Assets*, San Francisco, CA: Berrett-Koehler.

Sveiby, K.E. (2001) *What is Knowledge Management?*, www.sveiby.com.au/KnowledgeManagement.html.

Teece, D. (2009) *Dynamic Capabilities and Strategic Management: Organizing for Innovation and Growth*, Oxford: Oxford University Press.

4

Chapter 14
Strategic options, evaluation and selection of strategies

Introduction and chapter overview

Previous chapters have guided us through the process of understanding the nature of the organization, its purpose and the environment it operates in. We have explored the need for competitive advantage, examined the sources of advantage, and highlighted the importance of sustainability of such advantage. Now we can start to determine what strategic options are open to organizations, that is, what can they do? Once we understand this, we can establish a framework to evaluate the strategic options and select the 'best' (if there is such a thing as a 'best') option.

This chapter guides us through this journey from generating the various strategic directions or options, through to the criteria for evaluating these options and then the selection. Chapter 15 then explores the methods by which the options can be implemented.

Learning objectives

After studying this chapter, you should be able to:

- determine between the different strategic options available to organizations
- apply Ansoff's product/market matrix
- evaluate the criteria for evaluating and selecting strategic direction
- profile a range of tools for strategy evaluation
- explain how Ansoff's matrix can be used to understand strategic risks

14.1 Identifying the strategic options

At the start of this chapter, we must remind ourselves of what makes a decision 'strategic' in nature as opposed to one that is 'operational'. We encountered these terms in Chapters 1 and 2 in the context of the nature of strategic objectives.

Strategic decisions are those that are concerned with how the whole organization will be positioned in respect of its product and resource markets, its competitors and its macro-influences. They are often taken at the highest level of an organization. Accordingly, the options at the strategic level are those that offer solutions to the 'big questions' in this regard.

Strategic decisions are those that are concerned with how the whole organization will be positioned in respect of its product and resource markets, its competitors and its macro-influences.

Operational decisions are those that are concerned with how the internal parts of the organization should be configured and managed so that they best achieve the strategic objectives.

Operational decisions are those that are concerned with how the internal parts of the organization should be configured and managed so that they best achieve the strategic objectives.

The 'big questions' that are considered in strategic selection usually concern three major areas:

- decisions on products and markets
- decisions on generic strategy and scope
- decisions on growth and development options.

In most cases, a business will need to make continual decision on all these matters. We should not lose sight of the fact that the strategic process is just that, a process. Strategic selection is no more of a 'once and for all' activity than either strategic analysis or strategic implementation and management. For organizations that exist in rapidly changing environments, decisions on strategic options will be required on a continual basis, hence the importance of ensuring we have a good grasp of the issues that are discussed in this chapter.

Product and market decisions

The questions over which products and which markets are extremely important because they can determine not only the levels of profitability, but also the survival of the business itself.

There are a number of product and market decisions to be made.

Product and market categories

First, decisions must be made about the categories of products that the business will offer. We encountered the major product classifications when we examined market and product segmentation, particularly those distinctions between:

- goods and/or services
- consumer and/or industrial products
- convenience, shopping and specialty products (Copeland, 1923).

For markets, the business will have to reach decisions on geographic coverage, international exposure and the benefits and risks that attend such options.

Product features

Second, decisions must be made on the features that the product will possess. The mix of product benefits that a product will possess will not only strongly affect costs, but also the position that the product will assume in the market. We encountered Kotler's (1997) five 'levels' of product features (or 'benefits') in Chapter 3 and the inclusion or exclusion of any of these will have a strong bearing on any proposed strategy.

Product and market portfolios

Third, product and market decisions must include a consideration of portfolio. The extent to which the products and markets are focused or spread can be important. A broad portfolio (presence in many product market sectors) offers the advantages of the ability to withstand a downturn in one sector and to exploit opportunities that arise in any of the areas in which the business operates. For example, car manufacturer Tata Motors acquired the premier marque Jaguar to broaden its product portfolio. The impetus for such a move stemmed from the need to supply a broad product range to the Indian market. Currently, its product range encompasses the world cheapest car, the 'Nano', and luxury Jaguar XF cars. Conversely, a narrow portfolio enables an organization's management to be more focused and to develop expertise in its narrower field of operation.

Life cycle considerations

The final consideration to be made for products and markets concerns their life cycle positions. It is perhaps intuitively obvious to say that products or markets that are approaching late maturity or are in decline should be of particular concern, but there is also a need to produce new products or develop new markets on an ongoing basis.

Generic strategy decisions

Decisions over the organization's generic strategy are important not only because they define the organization's competitive position, but also because they will determine the way that the internal value chain activities are configured (see Chapter 13).

If the company elects to pursue a differentiation strategy, for example, the implications of this will be felt in all parts of the organization. The culture and structure will need to be configured in a way that supports the generic strategy and the product features and quality will also reflect it. Similarly, the way that the organization configures its resource base will need to support the strategy.

The same issues will be considered if a cost-driven strategy is chosen, although the way in which the internal activities are configured will be somewhat different.

Therefore, the generic strategy will reflect the mission of the organization and 'drive' the strategic direction and the growth and development decisions made.

Growth and development decisions

Unless the strategy choices include a 'no change' option, it is likely that strategy will involve a change in the company's size. This may be a 'grow smaller' element, such as when the company has a presence in a declining market, but most growth strategies are 'grow bigger' in nature.

Two types of decisions are taken in this regard. The first decisions concern the generic growth direction that the organization will pursue. These strategies arise from Igor Ansoff's (1988) framework and should not be confused with Porter's generic strategies (Porter, 1985). The second set of decisions concern the mechanism that the company will employ to pursue its generic growth strategy (see Chapter 15).

Ansoff's generic growth strategies concern whether growth will involve new or existing markets and products. The growth mechanisms can be either internal (organic) or external. Each growth option has its own benefits and risks and the strategy evaluation and selection stage will usually involve a full analysis of these.

14.2   Ansoff's product/market framework

The most commonly used model for analysing the possible strategic directions that an organization can follow is the Ansoff matrix, shown in Figure 14.1. This matrix shows potential areas where core competences and generic strategies can be deployed. There are four broad alternatives:

- *market penetration:* increase market share of existing products in existing markets
- *market development:* enter new markets and segments using existing products
- *product development:* develop new products to serve existing markets
- *diversification:* develop new products to serve new markets.

Market penetration

Market penetration aims to increase market share using existing products within existing markets.

Market penetration aims to increase market share using existing products within existing markets. This may involve taking steps to enhance existing core competences or building new ones. Such competence development may be intended to improve service or quality so as to enhance the reputation of the organization and differentiate it from its competitors. Equally, competence development may be centred on improving efficiency so as to reduce costs below those of competitors.

Mature or declining markets are more difficult to penetrate than those which are still in the growth phase. In the case of a declining market, the organization may also consider the possibility of withdrawal so as to redeploy resources to more lucrative markets. For example, CD manufacturers have found it difficult to maintain profitability due to the continued onslaught from ever expanding (in terms of capacity) pen drives and portable hard drives. Many manufacturers have withdrawn from CD manufacturing and have invested their resources elsewhere.

When a business's current market shows signs of saturation, it may wish to consider alternative directions for development.

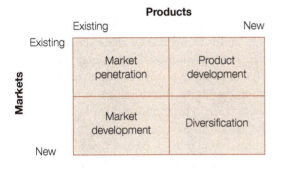

Figure 14.1 **The Ansoff matrix (growth vector components)**

Source: Adapted from Ansoff, 1988

4

A good example of market penetration is the acquisition of Safeway by Morrisons. The family-run supermarket group Morrisons acquired Safeway, a quality British supermarket chain, in 2004, in a deal worth nearly £3bn. Before acquisition, Morrisons, who were largely based in the north of England, had a market share of 6% and a store strength of 112 stores. In a toughly contested UK supermarket scene dominated by leading players Tesco, Asda and Sainsbury's, the acquisition gave Morrisons access to markets in southern England and Scotland and has propelled the group to fourth largest supermarket chain in UK. The enlarged group now has 420 stores and accounts for nearly 11% of total market share (2009). The acquisition was largely based on Morrisons decision to increase its market presence and when the opportunity arose to acquire Safeway, Morrisons board decided in the favour of the proposal and won the battle against some fierce opposition from larger rivals and private equity players.

Market development

Market development is based on entry into new markets or new segments of existing markets while employing existing products. Entering new markets is likely to be based on leveraging existing competences but may also require the development of new competences. Entering new segments of existing markets may require the development of new competences that serve the particular needs of customers in these segments.

Internationalization and globalization are commonly used examples of market development. It is likely that an organization will need to build new competences when entering international markets to deal with linguistic, cultural, logistical and other potential problems.

The major risk of market development is that it centres on entry into markets in which the business may have only limited experience.

Product development

Product development centres on the development of new products for existing markets. As with the previous two growth directions, the intention is to attract new customers, retain existing ones and increase market share. Providing new products will be based on exploiting existing competences but may also require that new competences are built (as in product research). For example, Apple has a ritual of periodically launching cutting-edge technology products (iPod, iPhone, iPad and MacBook Air), and does so by continually exploiting its core competency in technology and innovative design.

Product development offers the advantage to a business of dealing with customer needs of which it has some experience because they are within its existing market. In a world of shortening product life cycles, product development has become an essential form of strategic development for many organizations.

Diversification

Diversification is business growth through new products and new markets. It is an appropriate option when current markets are saturated or when products are reaching the end of their life cycle. It can produce important synergies and can also help to spread risk by broadening the product and market portfolio. Diversification can take two main forms depending on just how different the products and markets are to existing ones:

- *Related diversification* is said to have occurred when the products and/or markets share some degree of commonality with existing ones. This 'closeness' can reduce the risk of diversification. In practice, related diversification usually means growth into similar industries or forward or backward in a business's existing supply chain. For example, the Walt Disney Company has concentrated its growth around entertainment and has diversified into theme parks, toys, movie production, games and broadcasting.
- *Unrelated diversification* is growth into product and market areas that are completely new and with which the business shares no commonality at all. It is sometimes referred to as *conglomerate* diversification. Virgin Group Ltd is a prime example of conglomerate diversification; it has interests in space tourism, travel (air and train), hospitality, finance and entertainment, to name but a few.

GURU GUIDE

Igor Ansoff was born in Vladivostok in 1918. He began his career as an instructor at the US Naval Academy and worked as an applied mathematician with Rand Corporation. He further worked with Lockheed Aircraft Corporation and later on rose to become the vice president of planning and director of diversification. His academic career includes stints at UCLA and Carnegie Mellon University. He was the founding dean and professor of management at Vanderbilt University and was a professor at Stockholm School of Economics and at United States International University. During his career, he served as a consultant for several high-profile firms including IBM, Philips and General Electric.

He is regarded as the father of strategic management and is one of the most influential and distinguished figures in the study of management. His is known worldwide for his research in three specific areas: the concept of environmental turbulence; the contingent strategic success paradigm; and real-time strategic management. Professor Ansoff died in 2002 and in his honour, the Japanese Strategic Management Society established an annual award in his name, while Vanderbilt University has established an annual Ansoff MBA scholarship.

14.3 Strategic development and risk

There are risks associated with all forms of strategic development. The risks are smallest when development is largely based on existing core competences and when it takes place in existing markets. The risks are greatest when development requires entry to unrelated markets. Whether or not the risks are worth taking will depend on the current position of the business and the state of its markets and products. Entry to new markets, whether related or unrelated, will depend on the business's assessment of the opportunities in new markets compared to opportunities in its existing markets.

New product development

Changes in society, markets and economies have led to a shortening of life cycles, and this has intensified the need for most organizations to innovate in terms of the products they offer. New products can provide the mechanism whereby further growth can take place. Increasing competition, often itself coming from new or modified products, means that innovation is frequently not an option but a necessity.

'Newness' can vary from restyling or minor modification to producing products that are 'new to the world', which then lead to new markets. The higher the degree of newness, the more likely it is that major gains in sales and profits may be made, but at the same time, the risks of incurring high costs and market failure are also increased. A single new product failure, if big enough, could bankrupt an organization. It is generally accepted that a large proportion of new products fail, although precise quantification is impossible, as many new products may be kept on the market despite not meeting their original objectives.

Organizations are faced with a dilemma in the management of new product development: new product development is essential, but is also fraught with risks. The successful management of this dilemma is often to produce a large number of new product ideas, most of which will never reach the market because they have been weeded out by an appropriate screening process.

New product idea generation

Ideas for new products can come from many sources. The greater the range of sources used, the more likely it is that a wide range and large number of new ideas will be produced (Sowrey, 1990).

Ideas from customers

For most organizations, the most important source of new ideas will be customers. Obtaining ideas from customers is a good way of ensuring that ideas are generated that will produce products as a result of 'market pull'. This means that there will be a market for the products that result because they are specifically requested by customers. Customer feedback can act as a focal point in idea generation, as, for example, when Starbucks introduced soya milk as an alternate to cow's milk to meet the demands of vegan and lactose-intolerant customers. Surveys and focus groups can help to produce ideas. The more straightforward approaches may give ideas for improvements, but more subtle approaches may reveal new needs.

Eric von Hippel (1978) showed that a successful approach for new ideas in industrial markets was to work with lead customers (respected, technically advanced buyers) to overcome their particular problems, and then to use the resulting new products to sell to other customers. Sometimes the products may require modification at some cost for the other customers, but the products then have unique value for these customers and thus price inelasticity of demand (Coates and Robinson, 1995).

Ideas from research and development

R&D departments are useful at idea generation when a market opportunity has been identified but a solution has not yet been found. In this respect, R&D can lead to competitive advantage, as developments in the pharmaceuticals industry have proved on several occasions, for example the introduction of the anti-impotence drug Viagra by Pfizer.

In some organizations, ideas emerge from R&D without a trigger from marketing intelligence. This is called 'technological push' and can sometimes lead to overspecified and high-cost products. At other times, technological push can result in a genuine breakthrough that marketing people can then 'run with'. For example, Dyson's research team of 250 engineers have come up with breakthrough products that have altered market preferences. The famous cyclone vacuum cleaners and blade hand dryers were results of 'technological push' and found acceptance among consumers.

Other sources of ideas

It is difficult to construct a comprehensive list of sources of new products but the following have proved themselves to be useful in the past:

- advertising agencies, who sometimes have their 'finger on the pulse' of market requirements
- consultants, who may carry out market research on a company's behalf
- universities and other academic institutions
- competitors, where an organization copies a competitive product
- suppliers, who may have devised a way to use a component or material
- employees, sometimes through 'employee idea' schemes
- distributors and agents.

Screening

Once an idea for a new product has been generated, a company must then sift through them to develop only those with genuine potential – a process known as 'screening'. As far as possible, the screening process has to attempt to avoid two potential types of errors – 'go errors', where products are developed that ultimately fail, or do not meet objectives, and 'drop errors', where ideas are abandoned that would ultimately have succeeded. Go errors are recognizable, at least by the organization that makes them, but most drop errors are unrecognized because the project has not gone ahead, unless of course a competitor makes a success of an idea that has been abandoned. Dyson came up with a revolutionary two-drum washing machine that simulated the flexibility of traditional hand washing, but the product was dropped because it was too expensive to manufacture and market.

In practice, the screening process is normally multi-stage, with at least some kind of review at several points in the process. Since risks may be high, and organizational politics may play a part, it is usually recommended that in at least one of the stages, a formal process is undergone where the idea is evaluated against predetermined objective criteria.

Development stages

The stages in development will vary according to the nature of the product and the work required to develop a new version, but it is important to include stages of the screening process before activities that involve the commitment of large amounts of finance, and it would not make sense to spend large amounts of money developing a new product without producing evidence that there would be some demand for it.

Stages in the process are typically:

1   initial appraisal
2   detailed business analysis and investment appraisal
3   technical development
4   market testing
5   launch.

A traditional view of the development process is that one stage should precede another. With increasing competition, reducing time to market has become important in many industries. To reduce the time to market, some of the activities may go on at the same time, sometimes known as 'parallel processing'. This puts a premium on good communications in the company between functions such as technical R&D and marketing. To avoid the delays and complications that might be involved in handing a project from one function in the organization to another, multidisciplinary teams known as 'venture teams' may be created, and in some circumstances the team may be given the new product to manage when it is on the market. If such a team is created, it is likely that higher management will make the go or drop decisions to avoid the risk of the bias of an enthusiastic but optimistic team taking over.

14.4   The Ansoff matrix and strategic risks

As one of the most important frameworks for understanding strategic directions, the Ansoff matrix can be adapted to model the risks that are inherent with any new business direction. Whenever a business engages with a new product or a new market, there is a chance that things will not work out as well as hoped and anticipated. These product and market risks can be modelled on the Ansoff matrix using the idea of risk contours.

Before discussing risk contours, however, it is necessary to explain the key terms. Risk is usually considered to be an unrealized loss or liability – a loss may occur but it hasn't happened yet. Crucially, there are two aspects to this: what the probability or likelihood is of that loss occurring, and what the impact would be if that loss did occur. For example, the risk of getting a puncture on a bicycle if ridden for a period of several months is a high probability but low impact event. There is a good chance of getting a puncture every few months, but it is likely to be a source of inconvenience at most. Conversely, a meteorite crash on a major city is a low probability but high impact event.

These characteristics apply to all risks, including those associated with strategic expansion. The Ansoff matrix considers two of these: market risk and product risk:

Market risk is incurred whenever a business attempts to develop markets or differentiate using customer groups it has hitherto not served.

Product risk is incurred whenever a business introduces a new product.

- **Market risk** is incurred whenever a business attempts to develop markets or differentiate using customer groups it has hitherto not served. The risk is incurred because of the chance that the new markets will not accept the products which, to them, are new. The point with the Ansoff matrix is that expansion is sought using the two variables of market and product. Market risk is therefore the probability that the new markets will resist development and the impact that that failure would have on the expanding business.
- **Product risk** is incurred whenever a business introduces a new product. There is a chance of failure because the new or amended product may not work as expected or have the benefits hoped for. Again, this can be considered in terms of probability of failure and the impact of failure if it were to occur.

Having defined the terms, we can now return to the Ansoff matrix to see how it can be used for risk modelling. The key to its usefulness is to understand the Ansoff matrix as a map and not a static 'two-by-two' box. Figure 14.2 shows the Ansoff matrix when the 'boxes' are stripped out and the axes are left. The nature of the continua that make up the matrix can now be seen. Both axes (the two continua) describe a scale of 'newness', from 'only just different to existing' to 'totally new and with no connection to existing'. Figure 14.2 shows how contours can be overlaid onto the matrix. As with height contours or isobars of a geographic map, these contours show areas of common risk exposure (this is a notional construct – not a measureable one as on a geographic map). The top-left corner, nearest the origin, contains the lowest risk strategies because that area has the least 'newness' from the existing products and markets. Conversely, the bottom-right corner describes strategies with newness of both products and markets and hence the highest risk (containing high levels of both product and market risk).

Figure 14.3 shows four strategies plotted on the matrix. Strategy C is clearly the lowest risk because it is nearest the origin, and strategy D is the highest risk,

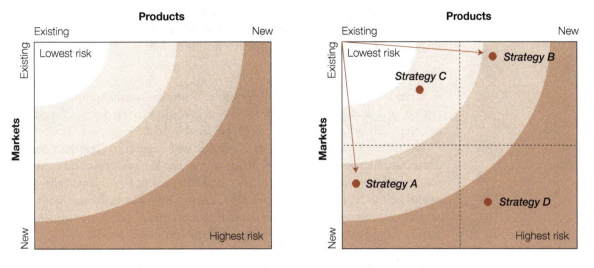

| Figure 14.2 **Ansoff matrix showing risk contours** | Figure 14.3 **Map showing different risk profile strategies** |

being furthest from the origin. Strategies A and B have similar overall risks despite being completely different strategies. Strategy A is a market development strategy so its risk arises from the probability of failure with a new market segment for relatively unchanged products. Conversely, strategy B is a product development strategy, with the risk arising from the failure of a new product. In both cases, however, the vector leading to A and B is the same length, meaning that the same overall level of risk is associated with each.

14.5   Applying evaluation criteria

The strategic option phase can often result in the generation of a range of strategic options. Clearly, an organization cannot commit time and resources to adopting every option and often options may have conflicting or opposing underlying influences. As such, choices need to be made. This requires options to be evaluated. When considering which course of action to pursue, it is normally the case that a number of options present themselves to an organization's top management. In order to ensure that each option is fairly and equally assessed, a number of criteria are applied.

For each option, four criteria are applied – questions to ask of each option. In order to 'pass', the option must usually receive an affirmative answer to each question:

1   Is the strategic option *suitable*?
2   Is the strategic option *feasible*?
3   Is the strategic option *acceptable*?
4   Will the strategic option enable the organization to *achieve competitive advantage*?

Suitability criteria

A strategic option is suitable if it will enable the organization to actually achieve its strategic objectives. If it will in any way fall short of achieving these objectives, there is no point in pursuing it and the option should be discarded.

Thus, if an organization's objective is to spread market portfolio by gaining a presence in foreign markets, then the option of increasing the company's investment in its domestic home would clearly be unsuitable.

Feasibility criteria

A strategic option is feasible if it is possible. When evaluating options using this criteria, it is likely that the options will be feasible to varying degrees. Some will be completely unfeasible, others 'might be' feasible, while others are definitely so.

The extent to which an option is suitable will depend in large part on the organization's resource base. A deficit in any of the key resource areas (physical resources, financial, human and intellectual) will present a problem at this stage of evaluation. If an option requires capital that is unavailable, human skills that are difficult to buy in, land or equipment that is equally difficult to obtain or a scarce intellectual resource, it is likely to fail the feasibility criteria.

Acceptability criteria

A strategic option is acceptable if those who must agree to the strategy accept the option. This raises an obvious question – who are those who agree that the option is acceptable? These are the stakeholders. The extent that stakeholders can exert influence on an organization's strategic decision-making rests on two variables, power and interest. Stakeholders with the highest combination of both the ability to influence (power) and the willingness to influence (interest) will have the most *effective* influence. Where two or more stakeholder groups have comparable influence, the possibility of conflict over acceptability will be heightened. In most cases, the board of directors will be the most influential stakeholder.

Competitive advantage criteria

In Chapter 1, we learned that one of the key objectives in strategy is to create competitive advantage. This criteria asks a simple question of any strategic option – what is the point of pursuing an option if it isn't going to result in superior performance (compared to competitors) or above-average profitability? In other words, a strategic option would fail this test if it was likely to only result in the business being 'ordinary' or average with regard to the industry norm.

This is particularly important when considering product options. For example, if a new product option is forecast to receive an uncertain reception from the market, we might well ask what is the point of the launch at all. It would be unlikely to result in competitive advantage for the business.

14.6 Financial tools for evaluation

In the evaluation and selection stage, a number of 'tools' are available to managers that may assist in deciding the most appropriate option. Not all of them will be appropriate in every circumstance and some are more widely used than others. They are used to explore the implications of the options so that the decisions made are based on the best possible information.

Accountants are usually involved in strategic evaluation and selection because of their expertise in understanding the financial implications of the possible courses of action. There are two major areas of financial analysis:

CASE STUDY   CoffeeShops UK Ltd

CoffeeShops UK Ltd (CSUK) is a nationwide chain of cafés and restaurants. It has 200 outlets, of which 120 are coffee shops and bars, 40 are ice cream parlours, and 40 are franchise outlets at railway stations across the country.

Eleanor Young and Julia Richards founded CSUK 10 years ago. As an alternative to Starbucks, CSUK immediately took off. People liked the fact that it was a domestic UK company and that Eleanor and Julia were 'new entrepreneurs'. They opened their first coffee shop in Northampton, which gained them an immediate presence and recognition, not least because it was not a London venture. Six other coffee shops followed soon afterwards, all in the Midlands, and soon everyone knew who they were.

Then, in the early part of the 21st century, Young and Richards secured additional backing through an appearance on *Dragon's Den*, the UK business venture TV series, which gave them the opportunity to buy up premises in 40 towns, including central London. Young and Richards chose to use the opportunity to pursue the twin strategies of consolidation and diversification. A substantial strategic and well-ordered marketing, promotional and PR campaign centred on the coffee shops supported the consolidation. Richards used some of the money secured from the *Dragon's Den* appearance to research diversification opportunities, such as in railway station catering and ice cream parlours.

The initial findings of the diversification inquiries were disquieting. After all, railway station catering had a dreadful reputation for serving overpriced bad food and drinks in dingy, dirty and often downright dangerous surroundings. This, stated Richards, was what would give CSUK its entry and its advantage. The stations would be carefully selected, and if they concentrated on network meeting points, junctions and crossovers, they could build a substantial and valuable – and profitable – niche.

And so it had proved. The railway station franchises now brought in over 40% of turnover and 70% of profit (see table).

Committing to the ice cream venture had been less certain. The data gathered had shown that there was indeed a substantial and underserved market for good quality ice cream and other summer products (cold drinks, iced coffees) at medium prices. Ice cream products at existing outlets were either very good but expensive, or else the products were poor and overpriced, especially in central London and other main tourist traps.

Moreover, CSUK's *Dragon's Den* backer had questioned the line of approach or the need to open a chain of ice cream parlours. Even if there was a market,

the backer reasoned that this could be served by expanding the product range at the coffee shop outlets; or, if they were to open new outlets, why not open them as CSUK outlets with the full range of products, and so be able to sell everything under the one roof. If the ice cream and cold products were indeed good value and in demand, people would in any case come and buy them. There would also be the problem that if people wanting the ice cream and cold products could not get them from the main CSUK stores, then they may actually gain an adverse or negative reputation – a reputation for not having what people wanted.

Young and Richards debated the ice cream venture long and hard. Eventually, they decided to go ahead, and they opened their first ice cream parlours in central London, Edinburgh, Cardiff and Stratford-upon-Avon. They were immediately very popular and successful, doing exactly what they promised, which was to provide good quality ice cream and cold products at reasonable prices. Surveys showed that they were regarded as the best value of any of the equivalent companies, products and services, and better value than iced coffee and other cold products from Starbucks and Coffee Republic. Accordingly, a total of 36 further ice cream parlours were opened, in popular tourist and seaside towns.

CSUK: key financial data		
Activity (£ million)	Last year	This year
Coffee shops and bars		
Turnover	27	29
Profit	4	4.2
Railway franchises		
Turnover	14	20
Profit	4	11
Ice cream parlours		
Turnover	0.6	0.9
Profit	0.09	0.4

As shown in the table above, the ice cream venture was immediately successful in its own terms, at least as a niche range of products and services. It demonstrably operated as a marginal service and range of outlets, generating operating profits of 45% of turnover by last year.

Having established successful ventures in each of the three areas of business, Young and Richards now sat down with their *Dragon's Den* backer to evaluate progress to date, and to determine how to develop the next phase of the business life of CSUK.

Case study questions

1   How would you evaluate CoffeeShops UK Ltd's progress to date? What financial tools, market and environmental analyses are appropriate in this case and why?
2   How would you choose and select future strategies for this company and assess them for acceptability, feasibility and suitability?

- *Cash flow forecasting:* One of the most straightforward financial tools is cash flow analysis – sometimes called 'funds flow analysis'. Essentially, it involves a forecast of the expected income from an option, the costs that will be incurred and, from this, the forecast net cash inflows or outflows. For most options, the forecast will be broken down into monthly 'chunks' and a profit and loss statement will be constructed for each month. If the same procedure is carried out for each option, the most favourable can be identified.
- *Investment appraisal:* An investment, at its simplest, is some money put up for a project in the expectation that it will enable more money to be made in the future. The questions surrounding investment appraisal concern how much the organization will make against each investment option. There is a strong time element to investment appraisal techniques because the returns on the investment may remain for several years or even decades. It is for this reason that a factor is often built in to the calculation to account for inflation.

The first and most obvious thing that accountants want to know about any investment is the 'payback period'. This is the time taken to repay the investment – the shorter the better. If, for example, an investment of £1,000 is expected to increase profits by £100 a month, the payback period will be 10 months. In practice, payback periods are rarely this short and it is this fact that makes investment appraisal calculations more complicated. When the effects of inflation are taken into account, the returns on an investment can be eroded over time. So accountants include a factor to account for the effects of inflation, usually on a 'best-guess' basis.

Limitations of financial tools

The limitations of financial tools rest on the problem of the unpredictability of the future. We learned in Chapters 9, 10 and 11 that environments can change, often rapidly. Accordingly, the actual returns that an organization make on an investment may not always be what was expected.

A similar limitation applies to forecasting the level of inflation for net present value calculations. In major developed economies, such as those in Western Europe, North America, Japan and Australia, the level of inflation has historically been relatively stable at between 2 and 10%, with an occasional 'shock' such as in the mid-1970s when, in the UK, it reached 24%. In other parts of the world, however, problems with the supply of goods and the value of currency can lead to much higher inflation levels – sometimes exceeding 1000% a year. A presumption of low and stable inflation will therefore tend to encourage investment rather than high and unpredictable inflation.

14.7　Other tools for evaluation

The financial evaluation of strategic options is important, but for most organizations, other tools can also provide useful information. These may require financial information as an input and so they should be seen not as 'instead of' financial analyses, but 'as well as'. They enrich the information, enabling management to select the best strategic option.

Cost–benefit analysis

Cost–benefit analysis applies to almost every area of life, not just strategic evaluation and selection. Each option will have a cost associated with it and will be expected to return certain benefits. If both of these can be quantified in financial terms, the cost–benefit calculation will be relatively straightforward. The problem is that this is rarely the case.

The costs of pursuing one particular option will have a number of elements. Any financial investment costs will be easily quantifiable. Against this, the cost of not pursuing the next best option needs to be taken into account – the opportunity cost. There may also be a number of social and environmental costs that are much harder to attach a value to.

The same problems apply to the benefits. In addition to financial benefits, an organization may also take into account social benefits and other benefits such as improved reputation or improved service. All organizations have an impact on the society in which they operate, and their activities and/or products have an effect on the condition of employment, social wellbeing, health, chemical emissions, pollution, aesthetic appearance, for example 'eyesores', and so on. A strategic option will have an element of social cost and social benefit.

For the purposes of a cost–benefit analysis, intangible benefits are difficult to attach a value to, as they can take a long time to work through in increased financial performance.

4

> **KEY CONCEPTS**
>
> A **social cost** is a deterioration in the condition of society, for example an increase in unemployment, higher levels of emissions and pollution, declining salaries and so on.
> A **social benefit** will result in an improvement in the condition of society, for example increasing employment, cleaner industry, better working conditions and so on.

Impact analysis

When a strategic option may be reasonably expected to have far-reaching consequences in either social or financial terms, an impact study may be appropriate. Essentially, this involves asking the question, 'If this option goes ahead, what will its impact be on ...?'

The thing that might be impacted on will depend on the particular circumstances of the option. For a proposed development of a new nuclear power station, for example, the impact study would typically take into account the development's implications for local employment, local tourism, health risk to employees and local residents, the reputation and appearance of the town or region, local flora and fauna and so on.

In many cases, an impact study will be an intrinsic part of the cost–benefit calculation, and it suffers from the same limitations – that of evaluating the true value of each thing that may be impacted.

'What if?' and sensitivity analysis

The uncertainties of the future, as we have seen, make any prediction inexact. While an organization can never be certain of any sequence of future events, 'what if?' analysis and sensitivity analysis can give an idea of how the outcome would be affected by a number of possible disruptions.

The development of computerized applications such as spreadsheets has made this activity easier than it used to be. A financial model on a spreadsheet, which makes a number of assumptions such as revenue projections, cost forecasts, inflation rate and so on, can be modified to instantly show the effect of, say, a 10% increase in costs or a higher-than-expected rate of inflation. This is designed to show how sensitive the cash flow is to its assumptions – hence the name.

Qualitative variables can also be analysed. If an option has a high dependency on the availability of a key raw material or the oversight of a key manager, a 'what if?' study will show the effect that the loss or reduction in the key input would have.

STRATEGIC
PLANNING SOFTWARE

This is a helpful chapter to refer to when completing section 2.3 Development Strategy within Phase 2 of the **Strategic Planning Software** (www.planning-software.com). Chapter 15 is also useful here (see the section on growth and diversification, mergers and acquisitions, and market development), as is Chapter 11's section on market development.

Companion Website

For test questions, extra case studies, audio case studies, weblinks, videolinks and more to help you understand the topics covered in this chapter, visit our companion website at www.macmillanihe.com/companion/business/campbell.

VOCAB CHECKLIST FOR ESL STUDENTS

'Best guess'	Nebulous
Continua (see 'continuum')	Private equity
'Eyesores'	Saturation
Isobars	Screening
Lucrative	Vector

Definitions for these terms can be found in the 'Vocab Zone' of the companion website, which provides free access to the Macmillan English Dictionary online at www.macmillanihe.com/companion/business/campbell.

REVIEW QUESTIONS

1   Explain how Ansoff's product/market matrix can be used to generate strategic direction options.
2   Describe the different approaches to evaluating strategic options.
3   Explain the difference between suitable, acceptable and feasible when selecting strategic options.
4   Explain how Ansoff's matrix can be used to understand strategic risks.

DISCUSSION TOPIC

Unrelated diversification is always the most risky strategic option. Discuss.

HOT TOPICS – Research project areas to investigate

For your research project, why not investigate ...

- ... how organizations choose to develop in emerging international markets.
- ... whether product development is favoured over market development in the mobile phone industry.
- ... managers' attitudes to the applicability of Ansoff's matrix in public service organizations.

Recommended reading

Abraham, S. (2005) 'Stretching strategic thinking', *Strategy & Leadership*, **33**(5): 5–12.

Ambrosini, V. and Bowman, C. (2009) 'What are dynamic capabilities and are they a useful construct in strategic management?', *International Journal of Management Reviews*, **11**(1): 29–49.

Barney, J.B. (1991) 'Firm resources and sustained competitive advantage', *Journal of Management,* **17**(1): 92–120.

Campbell-Hunt, C. (2000) 'What have we learned about generic strategy? A meta-analysis', *Strategic Management Journal*, **21**(2): 127–54.

Easterby-Smith, M., Lyles, M.A. and Peteraf, M.A. (2009)

'Dynamic capabilities: current debates and future directions', *British Journal of Management*, **20**(1): S1–8.

Kim, W.C. and Mauborgne, R. (2005) *Blue Ocean Strategy*, Boston, MA: Harvard Business School Press.

McKiernan, P. (1997) 'Strategy past; strategy futures', *Long Range Planning*, **30**(5): 790–8.

Newbert, S. (2005) 'New firm formation: a dynamic capability perspective', *Journal of Small Business Management*, **43**(1): 55–77.

Teece, D.J., Pisano, G. and Shuen, A. (1998) 'Dynamic capabilities and strategic management', *Strategic Management Journal*, **18**(7): 509–33.

Chapter references

Ansoff, H.I. (1988) *New Corporate Strategy*, New York: John Wiley & Sons.

Coates, N. and Robinson, H. (1995) 'Making industrial new product development market led', *Marketing Intelligence and Planning*, **13**(6): 12–15.

Copeland, M.T. (1923) 'Relation of consumers' buying habits to marketing methods', *Harvard Business Review*, 1: 282–9.

Kotler, P. (1997) *Marketing Management Analysis, Planning,*

Implementation, and Control (9th edn), Englewood Cliffs, NJ: Prentice Hall.

Porter, M.E. (1985) *Competitive Advantage*, New York: Free Press.

Sowrey, T. (1990) 'Idea generation: identifying the most useful techniques', *European Journal of Marketing*, **42**(5): 20–9.

Von Hippel, E. (1978) 'Successful industrial products from customer ideas', *Journal of Marketing*, **42**(1): 39–49.

4

Chapter 15

Strategic development: directions and mechanisms

Introduction and chapter overview

Once the strategic capabilities of the organization are understood and the relative strengths and strategic position determined, the next challenge for management is to determine the most appropriate and feasible strategic direction. We explored strategic choice in Chapter 14, along with how options are evaluated and appropriate selections made. Now, in this chapter, we explore how the strategic direction can be developed, that is, the methods that exist for organizations to realize the chosen strategic direction and exploit its benefits.

Learning objectives

After studying this chapter, you should be able to:

- differentiate between organic and non-organic growth
- determine different directions for growth
- evaluate external mechanisms for growth
- highlight the nature and issues associated with mergers and acquisitions
- evaluate the potential and characteristics of strategic alliances
- understand issues associated with disposals
- recognize the regulatory frameworks associated with external growth

15.1 Directions of growth

Before we review the mechanisms of business growth, it is worth taking a moment to examine the directions that growth can take. In Chapter 14, we encountered the Ansoff matrix. This is useful for examining the generic direction of growth (not to be confused with Porter's generic strategies), or the extent to which the strategy relies on new and existing products and markets. However, it is possible to pursue each of Ansoff's directions in a number of ways.

Growth can be within the same industry or in a different industry. The former is typically referred to as 'related', while the latter is 'unrelated', but these characterizations are often less than useful because the division of growth directions into only two types is an oversimplification. When it comes to risk and the chances of success of a given growth strategy, the most important element is often the extent to which the competences that exist within the business can be leveraged in the new setting, whether it is in a new industry or the same one.

Unrelated development

With this reservation in mind, it is nevertheless possible to classify directions into types for ease of understanding. Unrelated developments (which are usually classified as 'diversification' in the Ansoff matrix) – those in which a different industry is entered – can be classified according to how different the 'new' industry's activities are compared to the existing one. If it is possible to exploit existing competences in the new industry, for example similarities in technology, marketing or design concept, the chances of success are increased. We refer to this type of unrelated development as 'concentric'. If, however, the new industry entered does not enable any existing competences to be leveraged and/or there are no common links between new and existing, the risk is higher. This is referred to as a 'conglomerate' development. Conglomerated companies are those containing a broad range of business interests, many of which have no apparent link to each other.

Related development

Most growth and development, however, occurs within the areas in which a business is most acquainted – its microenvironment. Within this setting, growth can occur in two ways – vertically or horizontally:

- **Vertical development** allows for growth based on moving backwards (backward integration) or forwards (forward integration) along the supply chain of which it is a part.
- **Horizontal development** is a move resulting in higher market share within the same industry. The acquisition of or merger with a competitor would be one way of achieving this. The strategic logic behind horizontal development is typically to gain leverage or market power over suppliers or buyers. Higher volume generally confers greater scale economies in purchasing, while larger product market share confers greater pricing power over customers.

Vertical development allows for growth based on moving backwards (backward integration) or forwards (forward integration) along the supply chain of which it is a part.

Horizontal development is a move resulting in higher market share within the same industry.

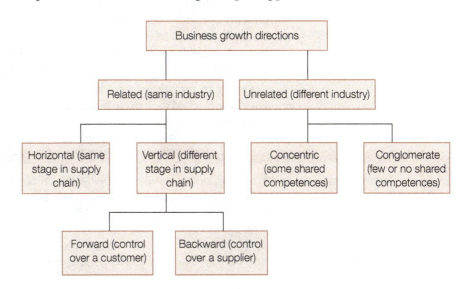

Figure 15.1 Strategic growth directions

Vertical development can be further broken down:

Backward vertical development or backward integration represents a move backwards in the supply chain, towards the supplier or raw materials.

Forward vertical development is growth towards the next stage in the supply chain by gaining an interest in a buyer of the company's outputs.

- **Backward vertical development** or backward integration represents a move backwards in the supply chain, towards the supplier or raw materials; in effect, purchasing or gaining control over the raw materials or supplier of the components of your product or service.
- **Forward vertical development** is growth towards the next stage in the supply chain by gaining an interest in a buyer of the company's outputs. In both cases, the strategic logic is to secure a foothold in the same supply chain to guarantee supply or distribution.

These four directions can be seen in Figure 15.1. In the remainder of this chapter, we will examine the mechanisms of how these directions can be pursued.

15.2 Organic (internal) growth

Organic growth is the most straightforward mechanism of business growth. Most companies have used internal growth as their main method of growth at some time, and so its popularity is obvious. The essential feature of organic growth is the reinvestment of the previous years' profits in the same business that generated the profit. By increasing capacity, by, say, the purchase of enlarged premises or more machines, the business takes on more employees to cope with the extra demand. In so doing, turnover increases and so does the capital (balance sheet) value of the business.

Organic growth is common during the early stages of corporate development as companies build markets and develop new products. However, large companies may use it alongside external growth to consolidate market position. The development of a new supermarket outlet is an example of internal growth. Profits from earlier years are channelled into the development and the company benefits from the increased market share and increased turnover.

Organic growth offers the advantage that is it usually a lower risk option than external growth. The fact that the increase in capacity remains fully under the control of the existing management means that the risks of dealing with other companies are avoided. Core competences can usually be exploited and existing expertise can be capitalized upon.

On the other hand, organic growth is usually a slower mechanism compared to external growth. The 'bolting on' of a new company by external growth is a faster route to growth than gradual growth by internal means. Some large companies have reached their present size largely through successful year-on-year organic growth.

KEY CONCEPT

Internal (organic) growth is expansion by means of the reinvestment of the previous year's profits and loan capital in the same business that generated the profits. This results in increased capacity, increased employment and, ultimately, increased turnover. Its advantages are: lower risk, is within existing area of expertise, and avoids high exposure to costs of alternative growth mechanisms, for example by debt servicing. Its disadvantages are: slower than external growth, little scope for diversification, and relies on existing management skills in the business.

15.3 External mechanisms of growth: mergers and acquisitions

At certain times, it is common to open the business press and encounter details of a proposed or progressing merger or acquisition. The term 'merger' is, however, sometimes replaced in such text with the word 'takeover' or 'acquisition'. The same news story may use all three terms as though the words meant the same thing. For the purposes of a strategy text such as this, it is important to clarify the main terms generally used in connection with this process:

In a **merger**, the organization's shareholders come together, normally willingly, to share the resources of the enlarged (merged) organization.

An **acquisition** is a joining of unequal partners, with one organization buying and subsuming the other party.

A **takeover** is technically the same as an acquisition.

A **hostile takeover** describes an offer for the shares of a target public limited company which the target's directors reject.

- In a merger, the organization's shareholders come together, normally willingly, to share the resources of the enlarged (merged) organization, with shareholders from both sides of the merger becoming shareholders in the new organization.
- An acquisition is a joining of unequal partners, with one organization buying and subsuming the other party. In such a transaction, the shareholders of the target organization (the smaller one) cease to be owners of the enlarged organization unless payment to the shareholders is paid partly in shares in the acquiring company. The shares in the smaller company are bought by the larger.
- A takeover is technically the same as an acquisition, but the term is often taken to mean that the approach of the larger acquiring company is unwelcome from the point of view of the smaller target company.
- A hostile takeover describes an offer for the shares of a target public limited company which the target's directors reject. If the shareholders then accept the offer (despite the recommendation of the directors), the hostile takeover goes ahead.

Whichever of these routes is taken, the result is a larger and more financially powerful company. 'Integration' is the collective term used to describe these growth mechanisms.

A brief history of mergers and acquisitions

The popularity of mergers and acquisitions (M&A) has changed over time. The early 1970s, late 1980s and mid to late 1990s were all periods of high levels of M&A activity. In addition to the general state of the macroeconomy as an explanation for such periods of increased M&A activity, it is also probably true that increased business internationalization has contributed to a general increase over time. The reconfiguration of some new technology based industries and more laissez-faire government attitudes towards industry structure are also strong influences.

4

KEY CONCEPTS

The **market value** of public limited companies equals the number of shares on the stock market (the share volume) multiplied by the share price. It is taken to be a good indicator of the value of a company because it accounts for the company's asset value plus the 'goodwill' that the market attaches to the share.

The **combined market value** of a merger or acquisition is the two company's values added together. It is an indication of what the company will be valued at after the integration goes ahead.

While the M&A process is a well-used mechanism in strategic development, recent history has shown that UK-based companies have used it rather more than those based in Continental Europe. Only in the USA have companies used the mechanism to a similar extent. However, recent figures show increased M&A activity in the global economy generally as companies feel the need to increase in size to become more internationally competitive.

One of the consequences of M&A activity is that many of the well-known 'names' of yesteryear have disappeared, while some of today's best-known companies are relatively young in their current form. GlaxoSmithKline plc, one of the world's leading research-based pharmaceutical companies, came about through the merger of Glaxo Wellcome and SmithKline Beecham in the late 1990s. Similarly, Diageo, the giant food and drinks company, was formed by the merger between Guinness and Grand Metropolitan (hence becoming the 'beer and Burger King' company).

A common misunderstanding surrounding the integration process is that two organizations always come together in their entirety. In practice, many integrations are the result of one organization joining with a divested part of another. In other words, one company has made a strategic decision to withdraw from an industry or market and in an attempt to maximize the value of the resources it no longer wants (an unwanted part of the previous company structure), it sells them to another company. The reasons why companies demerge and sell subsidiaries in non-core elements is addressed later in this chapter.

Diageo now owns Guinness

Explanations and motivations for M&A

There are a number of potential reasons for pursuing an external growth strategy. We have already encountered the overall objective of growth, but growth is seldom a stand-alone objective. The question is: Why is growth a desired objective? The following is a summary of these motivations:

- To *increase market share* in order to increase pricing power in an industry
- To *enter a new market*, possibly to offset the effects of decline in current markets or to broaden market portfolio
- To *reduce competition*, possibly by purchasing a competitor
- To *gain control of valuable brand names* or pieces of intellectual property like patents
- To *gain preferential access to distribution channels* (to gain factor inputs on preferential terms or to secure important supplies) by purchasing a supplier
- To *broaden product range* in order to exploit more market opportunities and spread risk
- To *develop new products* for the market faster than internal R&D could do
- To *gain access to new production or information technologies* in order to reduce costs, increase quality or increase product differentiation
- To *gain economies of scale*, such as by increasing purchasing power so that inputs can be purchased at lower unit cost
- To *make productive use of spare or underused resources*, such as finance that is sitting on deposit in a bank
- To *asset strip* – the practice of breaking up an acquired company and recovering more than the price paid by selling the parts separately
- To *enhance corporate reputation* – appropriate if the existing company name has been associated with an alleged misdemeanour.

The precise nature of the integration selected will depend on the specific objectives being pursued. If, for example, market share is the most important objective, it is likely that a company will seek a suitable horizontal integration. On the other hand, a vertical integration would be more appropriate if supply or distribution concerns are uppermost among a company's threats. An example of horizontal integration is Yahoo!'s acquisition of Flickr, the image and video hosting website. Yahoo! lacked a comprehensive photo and video hosting portal to take on the competition from Google and Microsoft. It acquired Flickr to reduce risk, increase market share and diversify its portfolio. Similarly, Tata Steel's acquisition of Corus not only helped in gaining entry to newer supply chains but also gave it access and opportunity to integrate existing supply chains.

External growth is usually expensive and therefore has significant financial resource implications, not to mention a sizeable legal bill. Accordingly, it is entered into for specific strategic purposes that cannot be served through the normal progression of organic development.

Synergy: the main objective of M&A

Overriding all other purposes served by integration is that of synergy. Synergy refers to the benefits that can be gained when organizations join forces rather than work apart. An integration can be said to be synergistic when the whole is greater than the sum of the parts. More popularly, synergy can be expressed as 2 + 2 = 5. If the integration is to achieve synergy, the 'new' company must perform more efficiently than either of the two parties would, had they remained separate.

Synergy refers to the benefits that can be gained when organizations join forces rather than work apart. An integration can be said to be synergistic when the whole is greater than the sum of the parts.

On a simple level, we can conceptualize synergy using a human example. When two people work together performing a task like lifting heavy logs onto a lorry, they can achieve far more work than two people lifting logs separately. A rally team of two enables the team to win a race if they work together, with one driving and one navigating. If the two were to work separately, each person would have to drive and navigate at the same time.

Synergy is measured in terms of increased added value. Kay (1993, p. 149) makes the point that:

> Value is added, and only added [in an integration], if distinctive capabilities or strategic assets are exploited more effectively. A merger adds no value if all that is acquired is a distinctive capability which is already fully exploited, as the price paid will reflect the competitive advantage held.

Thus integrations that do not enable the 'new' organization to produce higher profits or consolidate a stronger market position are usually deemed to have been relatively unsuccessful. The next section describes why failures sometimes occur.

Potential problems with M&A

The fact that M&A are undoubtedly popular as methods of business growth may lead us to conclude that they are always successful. In practice, this is not always true. A number of studies have analysed the performance of companies after integrations and the findings are not very encouraging (see for example Porter, 1985; Ravenscraft and Scherer, 1987; Kay, 1993). These studies found that many corporate 'marriages' failed to work and ended in divorce. Of those that did survive, Kay (1993) found that when profitability before and after the integration was compared, a 'nil to negative effect' was achieved.

There are a number of reasons why integrations do not work. We can summarize these 'failure factors' under six headings:

- *lack of research* into the circumstances of the target company, and hence incomplete knowledge. Failure in this regard can result in some nasty surprises after the integration
- *cultural incompatibility* between the two parties
- *lack of communication* within and between the two parties
- *loss of key personnel* in the target company after the integration
- *paying too much for the acquired company* and hence overexposing the acquiring company to financial risk
- *assuming that growth in a target company's market will continue indefinitely.* Market trends can fall as well as rise.

Government policy on mergers may have contributed to some integration failures. Corporate growth can be restricted by government, which in the UK is represented by the Competition Commission, as companies are only allowed to establish a certain market share. In the UK, an integration that would result in the new organization controlling over 25% of the market is generally subject to scrutiny by the Competition Commission, which often results in such a merger being blocked. Being prevented from expanding in a related area may force some companies to take the more risky route of diversification – acquiring a company making different products in different markets.

Success factors for M&A

History has shown that mergers and acquisitions work best when the initiator company follows a number of intuitively obvious 'rules'. They are designed to offset the failure factors identified above. These success factors are:

- Success depends on the *identification of a suitable 'target' candidate* with whom to merge or acquire.
- Preparation for an approach should involve a *detailed evaluation of the target company's competitive position*. This would typically comprise a survey of its profitability, its market share, its product portfolio, its competitiveness in resource markets and so on.
- Consideration should be given to the *compatibility of the two companies' management styles and culture*. Because integrations often involve the merging of the two boards of directors, it is usually important that the directors from the two companies are able to work together. In addition, the cultures, if not identical in character, should be able to be brought together successfully.
- There should be the *possibility of a successful marriage between the two corporate structures*. If one is, for example, very tall and centralized and the other is shorter and decentralized, problems may occur in attempting to bring the two together.
- If the target company has key personnel, say a key manager or a distinctive research capability resident within a number of uniquely qualified scientists, measures should be taken to ensure that these *key people are retained after the integration*. This can often be achieved by holding contractual talks with these people before the integration goes ahead.
- The initiating company should ensure that the *price paid for the target* (the valuation of its shares) *is realistic*. A key calculation of any investment is the

return made on it and this is usually measured as the profit before interest and tax divided by the price paid for it. It follows that the return on investment (as a percentage) will depend on the price paid for the target company. The valuation of a company is a complex accounting calculation, which depends the balance sheet value, the prospects and performance of the company, and the value of its intangible assets, such as its brands and patents.

Porter (1987) identified three criteria for success in M&A:

1. *Attractiveness* describes the likelihood of making above-average profits in the target company's industry or industry segment. This can be seen as an objective test of the industry's future prospects.

2. *Cost of entry* describes the overall cost of the merger or acquisition and includes the major capital sum (for the target's shares) plus additional and sometimes hidden costs such as payments to advisers (such as merchant banks and legal people) and the indirect or invisible costs such as management time and integration costs.

3. *Competitive advantage* asks whether synergistic gains actually exist between the two companies.

15.4 External growth: strategic networks and alliances

A **strategic alliance** describes a range of collaborative arrangements between two or more organizations that agree to act in a particular way for the achievement of a common goal or aim.

A **strategic alliance** describes a range of collaborative arrangements between two or more organizations that agree to act in a particular way for the achievement of a common goal or aim. These agreements can vary from a formalized, long-term agreement, which could see the creation of a new jointly owned limited company, to an informal arrangement for a short-term project.

The legal structure of the organization is not a barrier to cooperation. In recent years, for example, many government departments and quangos have entered into partnerships with public companies through the UK government's private finance initiative. In the private sector, public limited companies have also employed this approach to further their particular strategic objectives, as when BT and Securicor got together in a highly formalized agreement to form Cellnet, the mobile phone company.

Strategic alliances can therefore assume a number of different forms depending on the structure, the mechanism of decision-making, the nature of the capital commitment and apportionment of profit. Some exist for a particular project only and have a short timescale, while others are more permanent. The choice of arrangement will depend on the specific objectives that the participants have at the time.

Types of strategic alliance

Joint ventures represent contractually legal binding agreements between two or more companies with shared benefit and risk (as per the contract).

Joint ventures represent contractually legal binding agreements between two or more companies with shared benefit and risk (as per the contract). The degree of involvement between the joint venture partners can range between the focused and the complex. Focused alliances tend to focus on collaboration at one or possibly two stages of the value chain. They may, for example, purchase as one in order to exert greater buying power on a supplier. Others may collaborate on product distribution or technology. More complex alliances are those that involve cooperation over a wide range of activities on the value chain. The relationship that existed between 1979 and 1994 between Honda from Japan and the British Rover Group was a complex alliance. Although the two companies remained legally separate, they cooperated in all the primary value-adding activities, including product design.

The term 'consortium' is often used when referring to an alliance that involves more than two organizations. A consortium is a group of companies that combine to exploit each others' resources and competences to the benefit of the group and to provide a critical mass beyond their own means directed towards a particular task. Consortiums are often created for time-limited projects such as civil engineering or construction developments. The Channel Tunnel, in common with other large construction projects, was built by a number of construction companies working together for the duration of the project. The British/French consortium was called TransManche Link and it was dissolved on completion of the project. Camelot, the UK national lottery operator, is another example of a consortium.

The complexity of the alliance will depend on the objectives that the two parties are pursuing. Alliance partners tend to seek cooperation on the minimum number of areas that are needed in order to avoid overexposure to the risk of one of the parties leaving abruptly or 'finding out too much'. The selection of partners for a consortium will depend on matching the resource and skill requirements of the project with those organizations that are willing to contribute to the effort. Organizations with previous experience of projects of the type proposed will obviously be most in demand as consortium participants.

> A **consortium** is a group of companies that combine to exploit each others' resources and competences to the benefit of the group and to provide a critical mass beyond their own means directed towards a particular task.

Motivations for forming strategic alliances

Two motivations for forming strategic alliances are noteworthy.

International competitive pressures

One of the major drivers towards the use of strategic alliances in corporate development is the growth in international market development. As organizations seek out new markets for their products, many recognize that they have skills or knowledge deficiencies where an in-depth knowledge of a foreign market is required. The need to develop local knowledge is increased if overseas production (with an overseas alliance partner) is being considered to meet market demands. While local knowledge can be hired (say, through a local importing agent), it is often quicker and more reliable to seek assistance from an already established producing organization of the host country. It should also be noted that a legal requirement of many countries is that foreign organizations must have host partners before they can trade, making a joint venture an essential method of development.

Capital pooling

While the globalization of markets may have encouraged some organizations to consider the use of alliances, there are other factors that have encouraged companies to develop them further within national boundaries. The high capital requirements of many projects, in terms of set-up costs, ongoing running costs and delays in profit generation, together with high levels of risk generally generated by such delays, are reasons for considering the use of alliances. The desire to gain economies of scale in areas such as R&D and the desire to secure access to markets are other reasons why companies choose alliances.

Successful alliances

The success of an alliance is attributed to a number of factors, some of which are similar to the factors present in a successful integration. Faulkner (1995) suggested the following critical success factors:

- complementary skills and capabilities of the partners
- the degree of overlap between the parties' markets be kept to a minimum
- a high level of autonomy, with strong leadership and commitment from the parent organizations (if appropriate)
- the need to build up trust and not to depend solely on the contractual framework of the relationship
- recognizing that the two partners may have different cultures.

Researchers in this area have noted that alliances seem to work best when the partners are from related industries or the same industry, or when the objective of the alliance is the development of a new geographical region. Success is further enhanced when the parties are of a similar size and are equally committed (in resource terms) to the alliance. Strict adherence to the initial objectives of the alliance can often limit its success, as modification of the original purpose may become necessary if the business environment changes. Thus there is a need to continually reappraise the parameters of the agreement.

Brouthers et al. (1995) advanced a more succinct version of Faulkner's success factors in the '3 Cs' of successful alliances. The two parties should have:

- complementary skills
- compatible goals
- cooperative cultures.

Example   The Wintel alliance

In the early 1990s, Microsoft and Intel entered into a partnership that has revolutionized the PC industry, commonly known as the Wintel alliance. Microsoft, the software giant, and Intel, a pioneer in microprocessor manufacturing, entered into an alliance aimed at developing a PC architecture that would allow greater integration of Microsoft's popular Windows-based operating systems with chipsets developed by Intel. Their collaboration resulted in the development of a PC architecture that has not only become the de facto model but has also captured more that 90% of the world market. Their partnership has redefined computing and has resulted in the introduction of well-known operating systems (Windows XP, Windows ME, Windows 3.x, Windows Vista, and Windows 7) as well as powerful chipsets (Intel Centrino, Intel Pentium II, III, Xeon and so on). The alliance is immensely successful because both companies have the shared goal of market leadership and complementary skill sets. Microsoft concentrates on the development of software products, while Intel sides with the development of hardware components. They piggyback on the strength of each other's products; Microsoft needs a powerful chipset to work its operating systems, while Intel needs a platform to showcase its microprocessor's true capabilities. These complementary needs work in the partnership's favour and a conducive corporate culture plays a huge part in their success. Their latest effort can be seen in the development and introduction of the Windows 7 operating system. Both Microsoft and Intel contributed hundreds of engineers to develop this latest operating system and are beta testing the mobile version of the system. The decision to invest in the alliance has paid rich dividends and has led to both becoming market leaders in their respective industries.

4

15.5   Disposals

We should not assume that business strategies are always designed to cause business growth. There are times when organizations may wish to become smaller. As with growth strategy, size reduction can be achieved by organic reduction (by winding down production of a product area), by divestment, the opposite of acquisition, or by demerger, the opposite of merger.

Disposals (demergers and divestments) involve taking a part of a company and selling it off as a 'self-contained' unit, with its own management, structure and employees in place. The unit may be sold to a single buyer, for whom it will be an acquisition, or it may be floated on the stock market as a public limited company.

> **Disposals** (demergers and divestments) involve taking a part of a company and selling it off as a 'self-contained' unit, with its own management, structure and employees in place.

Reasons for disposal

There are a number of reasons why a company may elect to dispose of a part of its structure. The most prominent reasons include:

- underperformance of the part in question, for example poor profitability, possibly due to negative synergy
- a change in the strategic focus of the organization, in which the candidate for disposal is no longer required
- the medium- to long-term prospects for the disposal candidate are poor
- the disposal candidate is an unwanted acquisition, or an unwanted subsidiary of an acquired company that is otherwise wanted
- the need to raise capital from the disposal to reinvest in core areas or to increase liquidity in the selling company
- the belief that the disposal candidate would be more productive if it were removed from the seller's structure
- in some circumstances, disposal may be used a tactic to deflect a hostile takeover bid, particularly if the predatory company is primarily interested in acquiring the company to gain control over the disposal candidate
- as part of a programme of 'asset stripping' – the process of breaking up a company into its parts and selling them off for a sum greater than that paid for the whole.

Shareholders and disposals

The most common method of corporate disposal is a 'private' transaction between two companies, which is intended to be of benefit to both parties. The seller gains the funds from the transaction and is able to focus on its core areas. The buyer gains the product and market presence of the disposal, which, in turn, will be to its strategic advantage.

Disposals are designed to create synergy to the shareholders in the same way as integrations. We should not lose sight of the fact that business organizations are owned by shareholders and it is the role of company directors (as the shareholders' agents) to act in such a way that shareholder wealth is maximized. If this can be achieved by breaking off a part of the company, this option will be pursued.

The value of disposals to shareholders can be illustrated by an example where a demerger was successful. As part of a strategic review in ICI plc (the British chemical multinational) in the early 1990s, the main board made the decision to focus on its core areas of specialty chemicals. This necessarily meant that parts of the company that did not fit into the realigned structure would be disposed of. Some parts, especially the bulk chemicals plants, were divested to competitors for whom the bulk business was within their core. What was previously ICI's pharmaceutical division was not divested – the board decided that it should be demerged. The division was made into a stand-alone company called Zeneca plc, and it was then floated on the stock exchange, with the proceeds from the flotation going to benefit ICI's shareholders. The stock market welcomed the flotation of Zeneca, as it believed it could now compete in the competitive pharmaceutical industry without the encumbrance of being a part of a widely diversified chemical group (ICI). In the months following the demerger, the value of ICI shares increased by over 75% and Zeneca's share price increased by some 400%.

Other methods of disposal

In addition to divestments and demergers, two other disposal methods are noteworthy.

Equity carve-outs

Equity carve-outs are similar to demergers, insofar as the spin-off company is floated on the stock exchange. However, in an equity carve-out, the selling company retains a shareholding in the disposal, with the balance of shares being offered to the stock market. In this respect, equity carve-outs can be seen as a semi-disposal – part of the disposal is kept, but not as a wholly owned subsidiary. The decision of the Thomson Corporation of Canada to float the Thomson Travel Group in 1998 is an example of such a policy. In this case, the Thomson family retained 20% of the new company's equity in order to gain an ongoing return on the stock, albeit without strategic control over the company.

> In an **equity carve-out**, the selling company retains a shareholding in the disposal, with the balance of shares being offered to the stock market.

Management buyouts

A management buyout (MBO) is when a company that a parent company wishes to dispose of is sold to its current management. MBOs are often a mutually satisfactory outcome when the disposal candidate is unwanted by its parent but when it has the possibility of being run successfully when the existing management have the requisite commitment and skills. Virgin Comics and Virgin Radio underwent management buyouts and have rebranded themselves as Liquid Comics and Absolute Radio.

> A **management buyout** (MBO) is when a company that a parent company wishes to dispose of is sold to its current management.

The advantages of MBOs are:

1 The selling parent successfully disposes of its non-core business and receives a suitable price for it which it can then reinvest in its main areas of activity.

2 The divested organization benefits from committed managers, who become its owners. When the management team finds itself personally in debt as a result of the buyout, having had to find the money for the purchase, their motivation and commitment tends to be maximized. In some MBOs, some of the capital for the purchase is provided by venture capital companies.

3 If part of the MBO capital is met by the company's existing employees, the organization benefits from the commitment of people who have part-ownership, and who therefore share in the company's success through dividends on shares and growth in the share price.

CASE STUDY   British Airways

In October 2008, British Airways (BA) announced a major company restructuring. In common with all sectors, BA was experiencing a business downturn brought on by the worldwide recession, which, in its particular case, had resulted in reduced demand for air travel.

Working in conjunction with McKinsey, the top management consultancy, BA set the scene for the restructuring by stating that it was responding to the adverse trading conditions of the time, based on the twin criteria of falling sales and revenues and increasing costs and future uncertainties over some of the critical charges that the airline and the sector would inevitably have to pay. BA also needed to rebuild the company so that it would be able to operate in the commercial environment of the future. Of particular concern to BA were the following:

■ uncertainties over fuel prices, and the knowledge that these prices would rise steeply once the world came out of recession
■ steady or falling passenger numbers, together with downward pressures on fares
■ reductions in the numbers of people wanting to fly in the premium classes, especially first class and business/club class
■ increased competition and availability of alternatives, especially on short-haul routes.

The company also had enduring concerns and obligations that it had to be able to continue to meet. High on this list was the range of fixed costs and charges that had to be paid on the large, complex and state-of-the-art head office facilities at Waterside on the western outskirts of London near the company's main operational base at Heathrow Airport.

There was also the bedding in and integration of activities around Terminal 5 (T5) at London's Heathrow Airport. At an early stage, BA had decided that it would try to concentrate as many of its flights as possible from T5. In the pursuit of this, BA was also looking to reduce its use of Gatwick Airport, by moving many of its short-haul flights from Gatwick to Heathrow and T5. There were also concerns with the overall size, structure and uncertainty of all the company's markets for the foreseeable future, bearing in mind the credit crunch and rising fuel and energy charges.

In conjunction with McKinsey, BA completed the review of its activities and position. The developmental approach decided on was couched in terms that required the company and its staff to 'embrace ambiguity'. This was

endorsed by top and senior management, and became the policy standpoint for the company reorganization that would now take place. The company followed up the policy position by starting on the restructuring effort. First, the company carried out a mailshot to 4,000 technology, management and administrative staff, in which the following were offered:

■ voluntary redundancy on enhanced terms, in which those who accepted would receive three weeks' pay for every year of service, plus a stated and assured pension at the age of 60
■ a repositioning of departments, divisions and functions under generic headings and titles, in which the present, emerging and future functions would 'begin to emerge'
■ the opportunity to apply for any job (but with no guarantee of acceptance) within the organization, regardless of previous experience, because this was to be a major strategic restructuring and BA would look very different in the future compared to the present.

This resulted in 450 staff taking up the offer and leaving the company, with the rest duly employed in the new organization, which now began to take shape.

The stated position of 'embracing and coping with ambiguity' meant that the new departments and divisions started to create and develop their own roles and functions. This was (and remains) defined in accordance with broader goals and a stated strategic outlook requiring 'repositioning' to 'embrace the future and all of its challenges'.

However, results continued to be disappointing, with losses incurred in each of the three quarters following the publication of the McKinsey review and the stated determination to 'embrace ambiguity'. This led to a high-profile, in-company drive for cost cutting at every turn. This was led by the CEO Willie Walsh, who declared that he would work one month for no pay; this lead was followed by all the top managers and also 1,500 staff. BA then stated its intention to stop serving meals on all flights of less than two hours' duration.

Following this, BA did indeed return to operational profitability for the next quarter. However, the enduring concerns of sales volumes and values continued to be a problem and a priority to be resolved. It now became

clear that the projections and forecasts on which the company had based its assessment of the future would have to be rethought.

Case study questions

1   Comment on British Airways' stated policy position of 'embracing ambiguity'. What else do the top and senior managers of organizations need to do when setting out such a position?

2   To what extent has the reorganization addressed the key problems of falling sales revenues and passenger numbers, and uncertainties over fuel costs and charges?

3   What value does the use of consultants have in cases such as this, and how are their limitations best addressed and managed?

4   What additional problems might be foreseen for the immediate and medium-term future?

15.6   The regulatory framework for external growth

Most governments have taken the view that there is some need to put in place a regulatory framework for external business growth because of the implications for competition in markets. There is a careful balance to be struck in this regard. Governments are usually keen to encourage business activity in their countries because of their beneficial effects on employment, tax revenues, exports and standard of living. At the same time, it is generally true that the larger organizations become, the more difficult it is for smaller competitors to make headway against them in terms of pricing and market share. Regulation is therefore a matter of some discretion.

In the UK, regulation arises from two sources – the national level and the European level. They have two areas of concern in common – company size and, more specifically, market share.

European Union regulation

Since Britain joined the European Community in 1973, it has been subject to EU regulations and directives. European competition regulations are provided for in the 1957 Treaty of Rome (the primary legislation of the EU), in the form of two articles that regulate integration between companies resident within two or more EU states. Articles 85 and 86 are designed to stimulate competition between companies in member states. They can be used by authorities within the EU to influence the behaviour of business that may seek to enter into integrations that may reduce competition in a market. Article 86 refers particularly to mergers and acquisitions.

Article 86 is designed to prohibit the abuse of a dominant market position, that is, a high market share. It does not prohibit monopoly as such, but seeks to ensure that large businesses do not use their power against consumer and competitor interests. This indirectly acts against large companies seeking to acquire a high market share by integration.

The administrative part of the EU – the European Commission – has the responsibility of implementing Article 86. It can prohibit mergers or acquisitions resulting in a combined national market share of 25% or when the combined turnover in EU markets exceeds a certain financial figure (€250m). On a more operational level, the way that integrations are conducted is also regulated. There are rules regarding the transparency of approach, that is, how it should be announced, and how shareholders should be informed of proposed integrations.

UK regulation

Integrations between companies based in the UK are subject to possible scrutiny by the Office of Fair Trading (OFT) and the Competition Commission (CC). Their activity is governed by two major pieces of British legislation: the Fair Trading Act 1973 and, to a lesser extent, the Competition Act 1998. The OFT and the CCC act independently of the government under the instruction of the secretary of state for trade and industry and exist in the legal form of quangos.

The Fair Trading Act 1973 targets three areas in pursuit of maintaining healthy levels of competition in markets:

1   monopoly practices
2   restrictive practices
3   mergers and acquisitions.

Under its provisions to review mergers and acquisitions, this Act allows the government's regulatory bodies to review an integration if the combined market share exceeds 25%. In this regard, it is in agreement with Article 86.

The Office of Fair Trading

The OFT was established in 1973 and is headed by the director general of fair trading (DGFT), who is charged with, among other things, the enforcement of the terms of the Fair Trading Act. The OFT is also required to act as a central bureau that collects and publishes information on competition and anti-competitive practices in the UK.

The DGFT has six broad areas of responsibility: the first and most important of these is to collect information on business activities that are potentially harmful to competition or the public interest including mergers and acquisitions (the DGFT has the power to refer cases to other authorities for review).

In this regard, the OFT is able to review an integration when:

- two or more enterprises cease to be distinct
- at least one of them is a UK or UK-controlled company
- there is a combined market share of 25% or assets to the value of £70m.

In applying the above criteria, the following factors need to be taken into account by the DGFT:

- the extent of competition within the UK in respect of the market in question
- the level of efficiency of the companies intending to integrate
- the impact the proposed integration will have on employment in a national and regional context
- the competitive position of UK companies on an international basis
- the national strategic interest (rarely an important factor)
- the implications of the method of financing used to fund the merger, particularly with respect to the welfare of shareholders or the banking sector
- the probability that a weak partner will be turned round by the acquirer.

The Competition Commission

The role of the CC (formerly known as the Monopolies and Mergers Commission – MMC) is to look into proposed mergers and acquisitions when instructed to do so by the OFT or the secretary of state for trade and industry. It is headed by a full-time chairman to whom three part-time deputy chairmen report. This team then draws on the expertise of specialist members from a range of backgrounds including business, finance, academia and trade unions. All the members, including the chairman, are appointed by the secretary of state.

The CC is unable to act on its own initiative, and its recommendations after an investigation are advisory, and only the secretary of state may elect to adopt of reject its findings.

The CC describes itself having two distinct functions. On its reporting side, the CC has taken on the former MMC role of carrying out enquiries into matters referred to it by the other UK competition authorities concerning monopolies, mergers and the economic regulation of utility companies. Second, the Competition Appeal Tribunal hears appeals against decisions of the DGFT and the regulators of utilities in respect of infringements of the prohibitions contained in the Act concerning anti-competitive agreements and abuse of a dominant position.

Example   **EU Commission investigates Microsoft**

In early 2009, the EU Commission announced that it would investigate Microsoft's practice of bundling its popular Internet Explorer with its operating systems. The EU Commission found that Microsoft had abused its monopoly position and forced consumers to choose Internet Explorer ahead of other available browsers. The EU Commission found Microsoft guilty of restrictive practices, undermining product innovation, and reducing consumer choice. Microsoft was eventually allowed to release its operating system with a 'ballot box' screen allowing consumers to choose from the 12 most popular browsers available in the market.

This is a helpful chapter to refer to when completing section 2.3 Development Strategy within Phase 2 of the **Strategic Planning Software** (www.planning-software.com).

4

For test questions, extra case studies, audio case studies, weblinks, videolinks and more to help you understand the topics covered in this chapter, visit our companion website at www.macmillanihe.com/companion/business/campbell.

 VOCAB CHECKLIST FOR ESL STUDENTS

Balance sheet	Divested	Quangos
Beta testing (see 'beta test')	Encumbrance	Telecoms (see
Concentric	Intangible assets	'telecommunications')
Conglomerate	Organic growth (see 'organic'	Turnover
De facto	and 'growth')	Yesteryear
Disposals		

Definitions for these terms can be found in the 'Vocab Zone' of the companion website, which provides free access to the Macmillan English Dictionary online at www.macmillanihe.com/companion/business/campbell.

Recommended reading

Abraham, S. (2005) 'Stretching strategic thinking', *Strategy & Leadership*, **33**(5): 5–12.

Ansoff, H. (1987) *Corporate Strategy*, London: Penguin.

Bishop, M. and Kay, J. (1993) *European Mergers and Merger Policy*, Oxford: Oxford University Press.

Cartwright, S. and Schoenberg, R. (2006) 'Thirty years of mergers and acquisitions research: recent advances and future opportunities', *British Journal of Management*, **17**(1): 1–5.

DePamphilis, D. (2008) *Mergers, Acquisitions, and Other Restructuring Activities*. New York: Elsevier/Academic Press.

Firth, M. (1991) 'Corporate takeovers, stockholder returns and executive rewards', *Managerial and Decision Economics*, **12**(6): 421–8.

Franks, J. and Harris, R. (1989) 'Shareholders wealth effects of corporate takeover: the UK experience 1955–85', *Journal of Financial Economics*, 23: 225–49.

Geroski, P.A. and Vlassopoulos, A. (1990) 'Recent patterns of European merger activity', *Business Strategy Review*, **1**(2): 17–27.

Glaister, K.W. and Buckley, P. (1994) 'UK international joint ventures: an analysis of patterns of activity and distribution', *British Journal of Management*, **5**(1): 35–51.

Grundy, T. (1996) 'Strategy, acquisition & value', *European Management Journal*, **14**(2): 181–8.

Harwood, I.A. (2006) 'Confidentiality constraints within mergers and acquisitions: gaining insights through a "bubble" metaphor', *British Journal of Management*, **17**(4): 347–59.

Haspeslagh, P. and Jemison, D. (1991) *Managing Acquisitions: Creating Value through Corporate Renewal*, New York: Free Press.

Kitching, J. (1974) 'Why acquisitions are abortive', *Management Today*, November: 82–7.

Meeks, G. (1977) *Disappointing Marriage: A Study of the Gains from Mergers*, Cambridge: Cambridge University Press.

Porter, M.E. (1980) *Competitive Strategy*, New York: Free Press.

Rosenbaum, J. and Joshua, P. (2009) *Investment Banking: Valuation, Leveraged Buyouts, and Mergers & Acquisitions*, Hoboken, NJ: John Wiley & Sons.

Straub, T. (2007) *Reasons for Frequent Failure in Mergers and Acquisitions: A Comprehensive Analysis*, Wiesbaden: Deutscher Universitätsverlag.

Chapter references

Brouthers, K.D., Brouthers, L.E. and Wilkinson, T.J. (1995) 'Strategic alliances: choose your partners', *Long Range Planning*, **28**(3): 18–25.

Faulkner, D. (1995) *Strategic Alliances: Cooperating to Compete*, New York: McGraw-Hill.

Kay, J. (1993) *Foundations of Corporate Success*, Oxford: Oxford University Press.

Porter, M.E. (1985) *Competitive Advantage*, New York: Free Press.

Porter, M.E. (1987) 'From competitive advantage to corporate strategy', *Harvard Business Review*, **65**(3): 43–59.

Ravenscraft, D.J. and Scherer, F.M. (1987) *Mergers, Sell-offs and Economic Efficiency*, Washington, DC: Brooking Institution.

4

PART 5

STRATEGIC IMPLEMENTATION AND MANAGEMENT

Part 5 explores the final stage in the business strategy process, strategic implementation and management. **Chapter 16** examines where implementation fits into the overall business strategy process and how we develop a resource audit to understand what and where resources are required. It also discusses how culture influences implementation and what role technology and organizational structures play in the overall process.

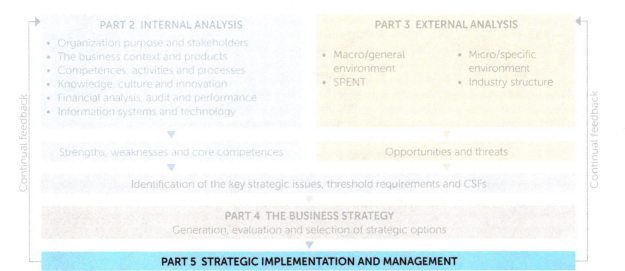

Chapter 17 explains the nature of change and how change can be managed as well as focusing on a key component of implementation – leadership. Various leadership styles are examined.

Chapters 16 and 17 allow for an understanding of how you can make strategy actually happen, arguably the most difficult practical element of any business strategy.

Chapter 16
Strategic implementation

Introduction and chapter overview

Previous chapters have examined the processes of developing and choosing strategy. This chapter now explores the issues and elements associated with implementing the chosen strategy. It starts by examining the linear and prescribed process before focusing on issues to do with resources, culture and structure. The chapter concludes with the role of technology and planning technology and the use of models and frameworks for evaluation and strategic reviews.

Learning objectives

After studying this chapter, you should be able to:

- explain where implementation fits into the strategy process
- identify the core components of a resource audit
- determine how resources can be controlled and the various planning activities associated with controlling resources
- define what is meant by culture and the different typologies and cultural postures
- explain what different structures are and how they influence the operation of a business
- determine the role of technology in implementation and the stages of technology planning
- evaluate how the various strategic management tools and techniques can be applied to undertake a strategic evaluation and strategic review

16.1   Implementation and the strategic process

Most people intuitively understand that a lot of information is required before any big decision is made. We wouldn't buy a house without a thorough survey and we would normally find out something about a company before we accepted a job with it. In the same way, a business would be risking a great deal if it were to pursue a strategic option without first carrying out a detailed analysis of its internal and external environments.

Successful strategy selection and implementation relies on the information obtained in the strategic analysis (Parts 2 and 3). It is important that the company is aware of its internal strengths and weaknesses and its external opportunities and threats. Without this information, a company cannot have any degree of confidence in its chosen strategy. The process leading to implementation is shown below in Figure 16.1.

In order to successfully carry out (implement) a strategy, an organization will need to work out how to resource it, that is, how it will obtain the requisite finance, human resources (usually in the form of appropriately skilled employees) and the plant, equipment and buildings. It should also reconfigure its culture and structure to 'fit' the proposed strategy. Finally, strategic implementation often means change inside the organization in order to achieve the required objectives. Change management is thus the third area to be considered in strategic implementation. This chapter will briefly consider each of these issues, with change management explained more fully in Chapter 17.

In Chapter 2, we reviewed Mintzberg and Waters' (1985) division of strategy into deliberate and emergent. This is relevant to implementation, as some strategies are implemented in intentional and sequential ways, whereas others (emergent strategies) tend to be implemented in an incremental way. While deliberate strategies are often planned in detail, emergent strategies may be implemented on a more ad hoc basis, typically with much shorter timescales and a more flexible approach.

The implementation stage in the process often sees a shift in responsibility, from the strategic level down to divisional or functional managers. This transfer may also act as a barrier to the implementation of the desired strategy as responsibility is shifted from the few to the many. Each new implementer may have slightly different interpretations of what is required of them, thus creating an uneven application of the strategy and strategic 'drift'. These distortions are further exaggerated if the implementers are working in different units of an organization and in different locations.

Alexander (1985) identified inadequate planning and communication as two major obstacles to the successful implementation of strategies. The lack of support at the implementation stage from those responsible for developing the strategy was also identified as a major problem. Other writers in the field have found similar problems. Many strategies do not succeed because of a failure to take account of internal issues such as information systems, organizational structure and the ability of the company's culture to adapt.

Strategic analysis
- Internal and external analyses
- Identification of internal strengths and weaknesses
- Identification of external opportunities and threats

Strategic selection
- Identification of key issues arising from the strategic analyses
- Generation of strategic options
- Evaluation of each option
- Selection of the most appropriate strategic option

Strategic implementation
- Putting the chosen strategy into practice
- Resourcing the strategy
- Configuring the organization's culture and structure to fit the strategy
- Managing the change

Figure 16.1 The linear-rational (prescriptive) strategic process

16.2   Resources and implementation

In the same way that people and animals need the inputs of air, food or warmth, so organizations also need inputs in order to function normally. Economics textbooks refer to these inputs as the 'factors of production'. These factors fall into four broad categories:

1 *physical resources:* land, buildings, plant or equipment
2 *financial resources:* investment capital – shares, loans, debentures or bond capital required for development and expansion
3 *human resources:* having the requisite number of appropriately skilled employees, agents or contractors
4 *intellectual or 'intangible' resources:* non-physical inputs that may be necessary in some industries, such as databases, legal permissions, brand or design registration, or contacts (see Hall, 1992).

In most industries, competitors must obtain resource inputs in competitive markets. This means that they must compete with other businesses for the best people, the cheapest and most adequate finance, or the best locations for development. All these inputs have a cost attached to them and so careful planning for resource requirements is usually a key calculation in strategic implementation.

Matching strategy with resources

Once a strategic option has been settled on (in the strategic selection stage), management attention turns to evaluating the resource implications of the strategy. The extent to which the resource base needs to be adjusted will, of course, depend on the degree of change that the proposed strategy entails.

Broadly speaking, resource planning falls into three categories (Johnson and Scholes, 1998):

GURU GUIDE

Gerry Johnson started his academic career as a senior lecturer with Hull College of Higher Education and is currently the Emeritus Professor of Strategic Management at Lancaster University. His earlier research interests focused on the practices and processes associated with strategy development, organizational change and culture. This research gave rise to a book which is now widely cited in the academic community as well as frameworks used in teaching and by consultants. He has worked on collaborative projects concerning managers' understanding of competitive structures of markets, and also examining the institutionalization processes of operating companies during British Rail's privatization.

Johnson has extensive consulting experience and is a recipient of several research grants from the UK Economic and Social Research Council. He is also a senior fellow at the Advanced Institute of Management Research and his current research focuses on studying strategy as practice and the phenomenon of strategy workshops and awaydays.

Kevan Scholes was formerly the director of Sheffield Business School and is currently the principal partner in Scholes Associates, a management consultancy firm. He is well known for his expertise in strategic management. He is a visiting professor of strategic management at Sheffield Hallam University and has been an adviser to several national bodies. He is also a companion of the Charted Institute of Management and a past president of the Sheffield and Chesterfield branch of the Institute.

1   Some strategies, particularly those that are not particularly ambitious, require *few changes* in the resource base. They may require, for example, a slight increase in financing to fund modest expansion or the recruitment or retraining of a small number of new employees to meet a skill shortage in one or two areas. Conversely of course, they may require the disposal of some assets or a slight reduction in the HR base.

2   Some strategies require an *increase* in the resource base in order to facilitate a more substantial programme of growth. This usually entails two things: an internal reallocation of resources and the purchasing of fresh resource inputs from external suppliers. Internal reallocation entails reducing resource employment in one area of the business and moving it across to where it is needed, say, by redeploying HR or by selling some equipment to reinvest the money in the area of growth. New resources (from outside the organization) are obtained through the usual channels –the job market, the property market, the financial markets and so on.

3   Some strategies involve a *reduction* in the resource base in order to successfully manage decline in one or more areas of the business. If an organization finds, after a resource audit, that it has too many resources (say, too many employees or too much land), then measures are put in place to carry out some reduction. Excess capital or physical resources can often be successfully reinvested in business areas in more buoyant markets, while excess HR must usually be made redundant.

A resource audit is the purposeful checking or testing of resources for:

■ *sufficiency:* is there enough for the purpose?
■ *adequacy:* is the condition, location, state, or quality of the resource adequate for the purpose?
■ *availability:* are the required resources available at the time and in the quantities required?

An audit of an organization's physical resources might take the form of assessing whether the floor area is *sufficient* for current needs and any planned expansion. This might be followed by an evaluation of its *adequacy* – its location relative to customers, its condition and so on. Finally, if more is required or if development of the land or buildings is needed, *availability* is examined, either of additional property or of permissions for development.

> A **resource audit** is the purposeful checking or testing of resources for sufficiency, adequacy and availability.

Developing and controlling resources

In order to meet the resource requirements of a proposed strategy, resources are developed and then controlled to ensure they meet the needs of the strategy.

Financial planning

Financial planning takes the form of financing the proposed strategy. Capital budgeting concerns projecting the capital needs of a strategy. This is usually a relatively straightforward operation as costs can normally be forecast with some accuracy. Once the capital requirements are known, a plan is put in place to finance any shortfall. While some strategies can be financed from retained profits, depending on how much retained profit the company has on its balance sheet, others are financed from external sources, such as share (rights) issues, debt capital or the issuing of corporate bonds or debentures.

5

Human resource planning

HR planning involves projecting the human capital required for the successful execution of the proposed strategy. It would typically take the form of forecasts of both the numbers of people required and the types of skills and abilities that will be in demand. If a shortfall in either of these is identified, the 'skills gap' will be filled by either training existing staff or appointing new people. Training, retraining and staff development are designed to close the skills gap by developing existing employees, while appointing new employees is appropriate where HR needs cannot be met internally.

HR planning: training staff

Physical resource planning

Physical resource planning is slightly more complex that financial and HR planning, because so many inputs fall into this category. Physical resources include land, buildings, location, plant, equipment and raw material stock.

Some physical resources are more easily obtained than others. Most stock, plant and equipment is relatively easily obtained, unless the requirement is highly specialized. More problematic is obtaining location, land and buildings. Businesses that have requirements for key locations and buildings of particular specificity expose themselves to the possibility of having to settle for second best if they are unable to effectively compete in these particular resource markets.

One industry that exemplifies competition for physical resources is retailing. The location of a retail outlet will often be a key determinant in the success of the business. Successfully competing with other retailers for prime locations and the best buildings will be of paramount importance, especially when these locations are in short supply, which they are in the best parts of most high streets.

Intellectual resource planning

Intellectual resources – inputs that cannot be seen and touched – can be the most important resource inputs of all. Some proposed strategies have a requirement for a legal permission, a database, say, of key customers in a certain market segment, a patent registration and so on.

It is the possession (or not) of key intellectual resources that often determines the success of strategy. Some business operations require a legal licence or permission, examples of these being energy production, defence equipment, pharmaceuticals and construction. Others rely on a particular information input such as a database, superior market knowledge or superior technical knowledge.

CASE STUDY Ryanair

When Michael O'Leary became chief executive of Ryanair, the company was on the point of bankruptcy. The Ryan family, one of Ireland's oldest and most respected families, had founded Ryanair in 1975 as a exclusive, luxury alternative to Aer Lingus, offering air travel between Dublin and London and other cities in Continental Europe.

There were many problems at Aer Lingus. Above all, the quality of service was poor. There were regular complaints from large numbers of the travelling public about the unreliability of the service. There seemed to be an institutional inability to provide good information, and people had difficulty confirming bookings and flights. Baggage losses and lack of security were also serious problems.

So the Ryan family started an airline that offered an excellent service for passengers; underpinned by a commitment to punctuality, reliability and security of baggage and service. The fares charged were much higher than Aer Lingus, which gave people a choice – they could either travel with the unreliable provider for a lower fare, or they could travel in full security and confidence for the premium charge.

The plan did not work. The Ryans found that people continued to travel with Aer Lingus, or else made arrangements to fly with other airlines, but not Ryanair. In desperation, and with the company dependent on subsidies from the family fortune for its very existence, they turned to their company auditor and asked his advice.

That auditor was Michael O'Leary. In return for a free hand in the development and implementation of company strategy, and in the running of the company, he said that he would give it a try. He started by taking the company to the other end of the market, making the fares so cheap that people would be forced to sit up and pay attention. This changed the whole perception of air travel and the culture of the airline and air travel industry. From a previously well-understood position of exclusivity delivered by branded national airlines, anyone could now travel where they liked, when they liked, across a large route network.

In the selection and implementation of strategy, Ryanair adopted a position of cost leadership and advantage. Everything was then structured in order to maintain this position. The airliner fleet was to be all the same, because this would streamline all aspects of operations, including fuelling and maintenance, on-board service (which would make staff training easier), baggage management and docking. For the airliner fleet, Ryanair offered the contract to Boeing (for the 737) and Airbus (for the A319). The Boeing fleet was chosen purely on the basis of cost when Airbus would

not reduce its prices any further. Additionally, Ryanair took a huge step in cost structuring and cost base management by taking full advantage of the advancing web technology to turn the internet into the main (and subsequently only) point of sale for its tickets.

Ryanair opened bases at Stansted, Gatwick and Luton, and Stansted quickly became the main focus of UK operations. The strength of a UK base was vital, as it was a crossroads for so many of the world's other travelling networks. Other hubs were subsequently opened at Barcelona (Reus), Krakow, Milan and Madrid. This meant that the route network could be opened up still further, and so Ryanair came to have destinations in North Africa and the further reaches of Central and Eastern Europe.

The destinations themselves became a point of colour and, in some cases, controversy. In the pursuit of cost advantage, Ryanair sought not to use regular airports, but alternatives close by. In many cases, 'close by' turned out to be a very broad term indeed. For example, Skavsta Airport, described by Ryanair as 'Stockholm', is 80 miles away from the Swedish capital, and Torp Airport, which Ryanair describes as Oslo, is nearly 80 miles away from the Norwegian capital.

Ryanair turned all this to its advantage. It was all low-cost, word-of-mouth marketing, and this in turn reinforced the cheap, yet distinctive advertising and promotional campaigns that the company had mounted ever since O'Leary first took charge. O'Leary himself became something of an iconic figure, and people now started to swap stories (not always good) about their travelling experiences with Ryanair.

However, a major bugbear remained – the passenger handling charges that continued to be levied by airports, especially in the UK. Together with the recession and rising fuel charges, the low-cost model was becoming ever more difficult to maintain. So Ryanair announced that it would be closing or reducing some routes out of Stansted, and seeking other airport facilities in the UK. After detailed research and evaluation, the place chosen was Manchester. Ryanair already flew to 10 destinations from Manchester, and now a route network to 30 further destinations was agreed in principle. The only sticking point was the passenger handling charges, and these were not expected to be a problem once negotiations were begun.

Suddenly, the whole idea was cancelled, and Ryanair announced that it would be closing all its routes from Manchester and relocating them to Leeds Bradford, 30 miles away. Further, it would now be extending the route network from Leeds Bradford to include all the destinations that it had had in mind when choosing Manchester. When asked for the reasons for this

5

sudden change of heart (and mind), Ryanair stated that Manchester was unwilling to reduce its passenger handling charges.

Case study questions

1 Where does the source of competitive advantage lie for Ryanair, and what obligations does this bring with it?

2 Why did the culture of the airline and air travel industry change so radically?

3 Where do the priorities lie in resource management in the implementation of this form of strategy?

4 In the case of the relocation to Leeds Bradford, what else has to be taken into account at the implementation phase?

16.3 Culture and implementation

We encountered the concept of culture in Chapter 5. Strategic implementation usually involves making an assessment of the suitability of a culture to undertake the strategy. In the same way that human personalities differ in their readiness to undertake certain courses of action, so also some organizational 'personalities' differ.

In the context of implementation, culture is usually analysed for its suitability. If we consider human personalities, we can readily appreciate that they are not equally suitable for all jobs or tasks. Some people, for example, have a personality that is ready to embrace a new challenge and who take to change with vigour and excitement. Other people prefer things not to change and have a more conservative nature. These two personality types highlight the suitability contrasts that can exist.

In Chapter 5 we encountered two typologies of corporate culture. Handy (1993) identified four types of culture – power, role, task and person. Miles and Snow (1978) also identified four culture types by their reaction tendency, and this is probably the more useful typology in this context.

Miles and Snow's typology and cultural postures

Miles and Snow's (1978) typology divided culture types according to how they approach strategy. These distinctions are important as they tell us how each culture type will react to different strategic options. The four cultures are:

1 *Defender cultures* are suitable for organizations that exist in relatively well-defined market areas and where improving the position in existing markets is the most appropriate strategic option (market penetration). The culture would feel uncomfortable with having to develop new markets or diversification. The values resident within defender cultures work well if markets are stable and relatively mature.

2 *Prospector cultures* are continually seeking out new product and market opportunities. Accordingly, they often create change and uncertainty. The cultural norms within such organizations are more able to develop new markets and products.

3 *Analyser cultures* exhibit features of both defenders and prospectors. They have developed a culture that is able to accommodate both stability (which defenders like) and instability (which prospectors have learned to adjust to). The culture can be formal in some circumstances and flexible and 'organic' in others.

4   *Reactor cultures* can sometimes lack strategic focus and are sometimes accused of being 'blown around' by changes in their environments. They do not innovate and tend to emulate the successes of competitors.

It is evident that the ability of cultures to undertake different strategic courses of action varies. It is likely, for example, that defender cultures and those like them would be less able to undertake a programme of radical change than, say, those which exhibit prospector characteristics.

The difference between *what is* and *what is required* for a strategy is one of the most important aspects of strategic implementation. The gap between the two presents a challenge to management in respect of either changing the culture or compromising on strategic objectives such that cultural change is required to a lesser extent. We will return to the nature of change and cultural change in Chapter 17.

16.4   Structure and implementation

Organizational structure refers to the 'shape' of the business, in terms of its 'height', 'width' and complexity.

Organizational structure refers to the 'shape' of the business. The importance of structure to strategic success is intuitively easy to grasp by using the structure of a human body as a metaphor. Some people are naturally large and may be a tad overweight, while others are smaller, lithe and fit. The skeletal and muscle structure of people is a major determinant of their suitability for certain activities. People who are large and overweight are less suitable for ballet dancing but are more suitable as sumo wrestlers. Conversely, smaller and fitter people are better at running, rowing and horse racing.

Organizational structure tends to be described in terms of 'height', 'width' and complexity. A fourth, related way of describing organizational structures is according to their method of division. These four features are now described.

The 'height' of structures

Height refers to the number of layers that exist within the structure. It is perhaps intuitively obvious that larger organizations are higher than smaller ones. The guide to how high an organizational structure should be depends on the complexity of the tasks that a proposed strategy entails. A small, single site manufacturer will typically be involved in competing in one industry, sometimes with a single product type. This scenario is much less complex than a multinational chemical company that competes in many national markets, in several product types and with a high dependence on research and legal compliance.

Essentially, height facilitates the engagement of specialist managers in the middle of an organization who can oversee and direct the many activities that some large organizations are involved in. Not all organizations have this requirement and it would be more appropriate for such organizations to have a flatter structure (see Figure 16.2).

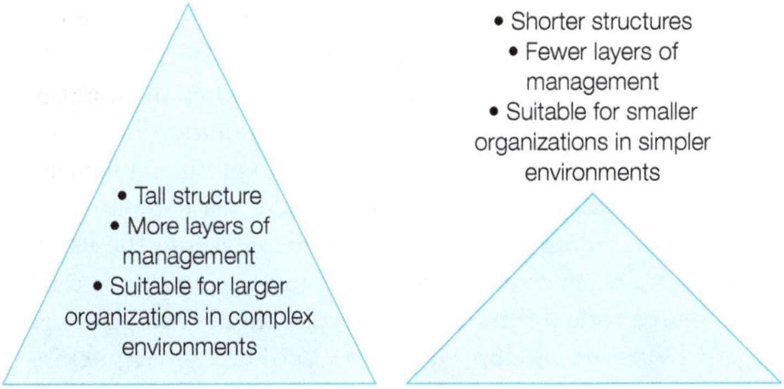

- Tall structure
- More layers of management
- Suitable for larger organizations in complex environments

- Shorter structures
- Fewer layers of management
- Suitable for smaller organizations in simpler environments

Figure 16.2 **The height of organizations**

The 'width' of structures

The 'width' of an organizational structure refers to the extent to which the organization is centralized or decentralized. A decentralized organizational structure is one in which the centre elects to devolve some degree of decision-making power to other parts of the organization. A centralized organization is one in which little or no power is devolved from the centre. In practice, a continuum exists between the two extremes along which the varying extents of decentralization can be visualized (see Figure 16.3).

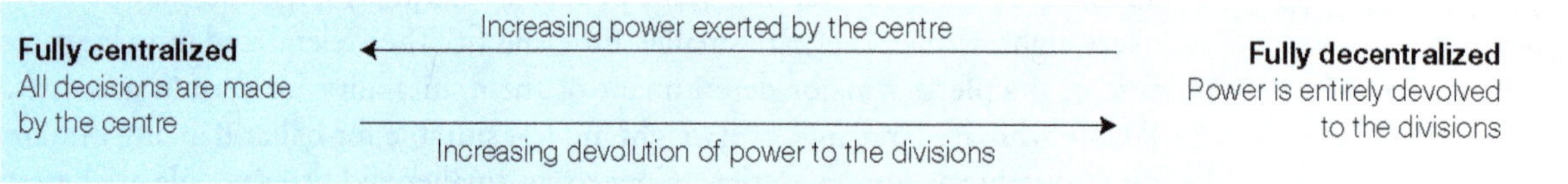

Fully centralized
All decisions are made
by the centre

Increasing power exerted by the centre

Increasing devolution of power to the divisions

Fully decentralized
Power is entirely devolved
to the divisions

Figure 16.3 **The centralization–decentralization continuum**

As with the height of structures, there is a trade-off between the costs and benefits of width. The advantages of centralization are mainly concerned with the ability of the centre to maintain tighter direct control over the activities of the organization. This is usually more appropriate when the organization is smaller and engages in few product or market segments. Some degree of decentralization is advantageous when the organization operates in a number of markets and specialized local knowledge is an important determinant of overall success.

Complexity of structure

The complexity of structure is usually taken to mean the extent to which the organization observes a formal hierarchy in its reporting relationships. A strict hierarchy is not always an appropriate form of organization, especially when it cannot be automatically assumed that seniority guarantees superior management skill.

In some contexts, a formal hierarchy is entirely appropriate in implementing strategy. In others, however, allowing employees to act with some degree of independence can enable the organization to be more efficient. The use of matrix structures, for example, can result in the organization being able to carry out many more tasks than a formal hierarchical structure. Many companies go 'halfway' in this regard, by seconding employees into special task forces or cross-functional teams that are not part of the hierarchical structure and which act semi-independently.

Methods of divisionalization

The fourth and final way of understanding how structure fits into strategic implementation is by considering how the parts of the organization are to be divided. As with all the other matters to be considered in structure, the method of division is entirely dependent on the context of the company and its strategic position. It is a case of establishing the most appropriate divisional structure to meet the objectives of the proposed strategy.

Divisions are based on the grouping together of people with a shared specialism. By acting together within their specialism, it is argued that synergies can be obtained both within and between divisions. There are four common methods of divisionalization:

- *functional specialism:* typically operations, HR management, marketing, finance, R&D
- *geographic concentration:* where divisions are regionally located and have specialized knowledge of local market conditions
- *product specialism:* where divisions, usually within multi-product companies, have detailed knowledge of their particular product area
- *customer focus:* where the company orients itself by divisions dedicated to serving particular customer types, for example retail customers or industrial customers.

16.5   Technology and implementation

In Chapter 7, we explored the role of information systems and technology in delivering the strategic goals of the organization and seeking to add value to processes and customer perceptions. Implementing technology is core to the future of organizations and so consideration needs to be given to the technological fit, in terms of technology planning and alignment to the business, and the take-up of technology by customers and staff.

In terms of technological fit, the technology plan is the single most important element to effectively using technology in the organization. The planning process helps reduce technology-related crises, future proofing (or at least ensure business continuity), use staff time efficiently, and gain maximum value from sunk costs and resources. Podolsky (2003) highlights the technology planning cycle and identifies six stages. For the purpose of our book, we highlight these six stages. For more details on technology planning, we refer you to Podolsky's (2003) work.

Implementing technology in the workplace

The six stages of technology planning are:

1. Select the issues and processes to be addressed
2. Describe the improvement opportunities
3. Document current processes surrounding improvement opportunities
4. Determine possible causes of problems in current processes
5. Develop solutions and create effective and workable action plans
6. Determine targets for improvement and measure success.

These stages are about aligning the technology to the business and its aspirations, not about selecting the technology itself. In effect, detaching the technology options from 'what you want the technology to do' allows for more effective planning and the creation of a specification that can be used for technology vendors to tender against, that is, a needs analysis.

In terms of take-up by customers and staff, a common framework to allow an understanding of this is the technology acceptance model (TAM). The TAM is widely used by researchers and practitioners to help to predict and make sense of user acceptance of IT (see Venkatesh et al., 2003). The main value proposition of using TAM is the ability to describe how individual customer beliefs and attitudes relate towards using 'something', in this case the technology being proposed by the business, and whether or not the system will be used as intended.

This information helps managers and developers to predict the behavioural intentions of users and can lead to actual changes and modifications in people's behaviour. For an example of an application in internet banking, see Yiu et al. (2007).

At this stage, it is worth noting that the strategy process as we have developed it can be used in a range of ways. Two key ways are to use the tools and techniques as vehicles for reflecting on what is happening in an organization, in essence from the outside in (an evaluation or review), and as tools and techniques to build a strategy for the future.

Strategic evaluation and review have become increasingly important to public sector organizations in the pursuit of best value, lean sigma, and the configuration of the organization. In essence, the process is used to scrutinize, test and refine each element of the strategy and business model and score the appropriateness and effectiveness of the strategy and strategic architecture.

STRATEGIC
PLANNING SOFTWARE

This is a helpful chapter to refer to when completing 1.2.1 Resource Audit within the Internal Analysis section in Phase 1 of the **Strategic Planning Software** (www.planning-strategy.com).

Companion Website

For test questions, extra case studies, audio case studies, weblinks, videolinks and more to help you understand the topics covered in this chapter, visit our companion website at www.macmillanihe.com/companion/business/campbell.

VOCAB CHECKLIST FOR ESL STUDENTS		
Ad hoc	Future proofing	Seconding
Auditor	Linear	Sequential
Buoyant	Resource audit (see 'resource'	Typologies
Debenture	and 'audit')	
Devolve	Retailers	

Definitions for these terms can be found in the 'Vocab Zone' of the companion website, which provides free access to the Macmillan English Dictionary online at www.macmillanihe.com/companion/business/campbell.

1   Explain the core elements of a resource audit.

2   Describe the different cultural typologies and cultural postures.

3   Explain the role of technology in the implementation process and how to undertake technology planning.

DISCUSSION TOPIC

For business strategy to be effective, the strategy implementation process must occur at the same time as the strategy formulation process. Discuss.

HOT TOPICS – Research project areas to investigate

For your research project, why not investigate …

■ … how organizations maintain control over resources during strategy implementation.

■ … what role culture plays in the implementation process.

■ … what the critical success factors are for ensuring the intended strategy is realized.

Recommended reading

Chan, Y.E. (2002) 'Why haven't we mastered alignment?: The importance of the informal organization structure', *MIS Quarterly Executive*, **1**(2): 97–112.

Grant, K., Hackney, R. and Edgar, D. (2010) *Strategic Information Systems Management*, Andover: Cengage Learning.

Henderson, J.C. and Venkatraman, H. (1993) 'Strategic alignment: leveraging information technology for transforming organizations', *IBM Systems Journal*, **32**(1): 472–84.

Iansiti, M. and Levien, R. (2004) 'Strategy as ecology', *Harvard Business Review*, **82**(3): 68–78.

Luftman, J. and Brier, T. (1999) 'Achieving and sustaining business-IT alignment', *California Management Review*, **42**(1): 109–22.

Chapter references

Alexander, L.D. (1985) 'Successfully implementing strategic decisions', *Long Range Planning*, **18**(3): 91–7.

Hall, R. (1992) 'The strategic analysis of intangible resources', *Strategic Management Journal*, **13**(2): 135–44.

Handy, C.B. (1993) *Understanding Organisations* (4th edn), London: Penguin.

Johnson, G. and Scholes, K. (1998) *Exploring Corporate Strategy* (5th edn), Hemel Hempstead: Prentice Hall.

Miles, R.E. and Snow, C.C. (1978) *Organisational Strategy, Structure and Process*, New York: McGraw-Hill.

Mintzberg, H. and Waters, J.A. (1985) 'Of strategies, deliberate and emergent', *Strategic Management Journal*, **6**(3): 257–72.

Podolsky, J. (2003) *Wired for Good: Strategic Technology Planning for Nonprofits*, San Francisco, CA: Jossey-Bass.

Venkatesh, V., Morris, M.G., Davis, G.B. and Davis, F.D. (2003) 'User acceptance of information technology: toward a unified view', *MIS Quarterly*, **27**(3): 425–78.

Yiu, C.S., Grant, K. and Edgar, D. (2007) 'Factors affecting the adoption of internet banking in Hong Kong: implications for the banking sector', *International Journal of Information Management*, **27**(5): 336–51.

5

Chapter 17

Change management and leadership

Introduction and chapter overview

This chapter deals with two critical elements of implementing strategy. The first is change and how change can be managed, and the second is leadership. In this chapter we explore what change is and what the change management process involves. In doing so, we examine different models for managing change and highlight the issues associated with change management. In terms of leadership, we consider the different schools of leadership theory and highlight key theories for further study.

Learning objectives

After studying this chapter, you should be able to:

- explain the nature of change and what models exist for managing the change process
- identify issues associated with managing change
- recognize the role of leadership in the change management process
- identify the different schools of leadership theory
- determine different leadership theories and the nature of leadership styles and approaches
- recognize the importance of leadership and change in the strategy process

17.1 The nature of change

In Chapters 9 and 10, we discussed the nature of the environment and how changes in the environment can change the industry structure, operating environments and overall dynamics of the markets. In Chapter 2, we learned about planned and emergent change. As such, change shapes the environment (both external and internal) and impacts on the nature of, as well as shaping, strategic decisions. However, we are interested in change that is managed and deliberate, in effect, changes being imposed on the organization, by the organization.

Change can be cyclical or structural in impact:

- *Cyclical changes* are reoccurring changes that can often be predicted and require temporary reactions or measures

- *Structural change* is permanent in nature and requires responses to deal with the permanent reconfiguration of the industry, company or technology base.

Change can relate to various organizational dimensions, systems/procedures, processes, and organizational configuration or structure:

- Changes to systems or procedures usually represent a refinement of procedures and are geared towards streamlining bureaucracy or layering bureaucracy to tighten control over resources or 'quality'.
- Changes to processes are often exemplified by business process redesign or restructuring, lean, value management and various quality regimes. The change relates to how the organization operates and how it configures its activities through the value and supply chain.
- Organizational configuration/structure refers to how the administration of the organization is put together and is often called the organizational chart or structure. It relates to the formal and informal relationships, power and authority lines.

Types of change can also relate to the pace of change and magnitude of such change. This is captured well by the work of Ansoff, Andrews, Mintzberg and others. In essence, there are different forms of change, ranging from continuity (no change), to incremental change (Ansoff's science of muddling through, or Quinn's logical incrementalism), to flux (oscillating changes back and forth) to transformational or fundamental change, which is usually a major event for an organization and involves a shift in mindset or resource base beyond the comfort zone.

17.2   Managing the change process

At its simplest, strategy is all about change. In this book, we have encountered the importance of an organization's resource base, its culture and its structure. In order to bring about strategic repositioning, say, in respect of products and markets, all these may need to be changed.

Different organizations exhibit differing attitudes to change. We can draw a parallel here with different types of people. Some people are very conservative and fear change and resist it. They configure their lives so as to minimize change. Other people seem to get bored easily and are always looking for new challenges, new jobs and so on. Organizations reflect this spectrum of attitudes. It is here that we encounter the concept of 'inertia'.

Inertia: identifying barriers to change

Inertia refers to the force that needs to be exerted on a body to overcome its state in relation to its motion.

Inertia is a term borrowed from physics. Inertia refers to the force that needs to be exerted on a body to overcome its state in relation to its motion. If a body is stationary (at rest), then we would need to exert a force on it to make it move. The size and shape of the body will have a large bearing on its ability to be moved – compare the inertia of a football to that of a train. In the same way, different organizations present management with varying degrees of inertia. Some are easy to change and others are much more reluctant. The willingness to change may depend on the culture of the organization, its size, its existing structure, its product and/or market positioning and even its age – how long it has existed in its present form.

5

For most purposes, we can say that resistance to change on the part of employees can be caused by one or more of the following attitudes:

- *lack an understanding:* they may not have had the reasons for the change explained to them or they may not be aware of how they will personally be affected. This can normally be overcome relatively easily by management taking the requisite measures to close the information gap
- *lack of trust:* on the part of employees in respect of management
- *fear:* particularly in respect of their personal position or their social relationships. Those affected by the change may fear that the proposed changes will adversely affect their place in the structure or the relationships they enjoy in the organization
- *uncertainty:* some inertia is driven by uncertainty about the future. Attitudes to uncertainty vary significantly between people, with some showing a much more adverse reaction to it than others.

Lewin's three-step change model

Lewin (1947) suggested that organizational change could be understood in terms of three consecutive processes: unfreezing, changing and refreezing:

- *Unfreezing:* This involves introducing measures that will enable employees to abandon their current practices or cultural norms in preparation for the change. In many organizations, nothing has changed for many years and unfreezing is necessary as a 'shaking-up' phase. The impetus for unfreezing can come from inside or outside the organization. Changing market conditions, for example, sometimes give employees warning that change will be imminent. A particular market crisis may precipitate the expectation among employees that change must happen as a result. Internally, a management shake-up, a profit warning or talk of restructuring may bring about similar expectations.
- *Changing:* This transition phase involves bringing about the requisite change itself. The time period for this phase varies widely. Structural change can usually be brought about relatively quickly. Changes in internal systems sometimes take longer, such as the introduction of new quality or information systems, while changing culture can take years.
- *Refreezing:* This is necessary to 'lock in' the changes and prevent the organization from going back to its old ways. Again, we would usually take cultural changes to require more 'cementing in' than some other changes and some resolve might be required on the part of senior management.

Step and incremental change

The pace at which change happens can usually be divided into one of two categories – step and incremental (see Figure 17.1). There are two factors that determine which is the most appropriate (Quinn and Voyer, 1998):

1 How urgent the need for change is. A market crisis will typically bring about an urgent need for rapid change, whereas preparing for the introduction of a new legal regulation in five years' time will usually allow change to be brought about more slowly and perhaps more painlessly.
2 How much inertia is resident within the organization's culture. The time taken to unfreeze the inertia will necessarily take longer in some organizations than in others.

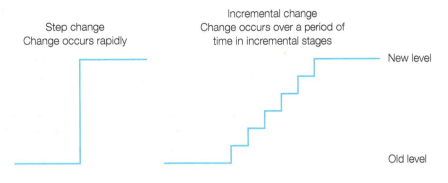

Figure 17.1 **Step and incremental change**

Step change offers the advantage of 'getting it over with'. It enables the organization to respond quickly to changes in its environment and thus conform to new conditions without lagging behind. Its disadvantages include the 'pain' factor – it may require some coercion or force on the part of management, which in turn may damage employee–management relationships.

Incremental change offers the advantage of a step-by-step approach to change. For organizations with high inertia, incremental change enables management to gain acceptance before and during the change process, so it tends to be more inclusive. The process is divided into a number of distinct phases and there may be periods of 'rest' between the phases. It would be an inappropriate technique to use in situations of rapid environmental change.

17.3 Models for managing change

The process of actually managing strategic change brings us to consider a number of managerial approaches and their appropriateness in various contexts. Writers in this area have tended towards two complementary approaches, managerialist and change agent.

Managerialist approaches

Some writers have suggested that change can be successfully managed by employing a range of managerial practices. We can conceive of this approach as an 'if this doesn't work, try this' mechanism.

Most academics and managers have agreed that the process should begin with *education* and *communication*. The purpose of this is to inform those (usually internal) stakeholders who will be affected by the change. The message communicated will usually contain an explanation of the reasons for the change and an overview of its timescale and extent. In some organizational contexts, this procedure alone will be sufficient to overcome inertia and get the change process underway. In others, this will not be enough.

The next step will be to progress to *negotiation* and *participation*. Affected stakeholders will be invited to contribute to the process and participate in its execution. It is hoped that this process will bring employees 'on board' – they will feel some sense of ownership of the change. Some managers may introduce some degree of manipulation of employees in this stage, possibly by appealing to

Step change offers the advantage of 'getting it over with', and enables the organization to respond quickly to changes in its environment.

Incremental change offers the advantage of a step-by-step approach to change, and enables management to gain acceptance before and during the change process.

5

the emotional responses of employees or by over- or understating the reality of the changes in the environment.

Finally, if all else has failed to bring about the willing participation of employees, management may be able to introduce some degree of *coercion*. This tactic is far from being appropriate in all contexts, but where it is possible, it can be used to significant effect. Coercion is the practice of forcing through change by exploiting the power asymmetry between executive management and 'rank-and-file' employees. It is usually only used as a last resort – it can have a negative effect on management–employee relationships after the change.

The change agent approach

Some texts refer to the change agent approach as the 'champion of change' model. Here, the change process is managed from start to finish by a single individual (change agent), who could be a key manager within the organization or someone who is brought in as a consultant for the duration of the process.

The change agent approach offers a number of advantages:

1   It provides a focus for the change in the form of a tangible person who becomes the personification of the process. A 'walking symbol' of change can act as a stimulus to change and can ensure that complacency is avoided.
2   In many cases, the change agent will be engaged because they are an expert in their field. They may have overseen the same change process in many other organizations and so are well acquainted with the usual problems and how to solve them.
3   The appointment of a change agent sometimes means that senior management time need not be fully occupied with the change process. The responsibility for the change is delegated to the change agent and management gain the normal advantages of delegation. Thus senior management are freed up to concentrate on developing future strategy.

17.4   Issues in managing change

Issues in managing change are usually associated with 'people' issues. Work by Andrews (1987) highlighted the importance of communication in attempting to implement any strategy and enforce any change. In a similar way, barriers to change can be seen to revolve around 'soft' factors such as staff (and management) perceptions and emotions, or cultural barriers, and 'hard' issues such as the business environment and resources.

Soft factors

Perception and emotion problems are often embedded in the emergent and cyclical approaches to strategy where, it could be argued, implementation issues are actually part of the strategy formulation process. As such, the perceptions of a strategic situation will impact on the ability to manage the change. These perceptions and emotions may lead to poor proposed solutions that do not address the heart of the problem, as they are too sensitive to company history, staff or sentiment. The issues relating to perceptions can be seen to be:

■   We do not seek real change, we merely tinker around the edges of the problem and avoid elements close to us or deemed as embedded in our belief system or culture

- We only see what we want to see and so do not identify the core of the problem, resulting in too narrow a focus
- A narrow focus often results in scapegoating or protection of a particular area of the business
- On occasion, too much information and data are sought to justify and defend decisions. This can result in information overload and, ultimately, change fatigue.

As we saw in Chapter 5, culture drives the way an organization thinks, acts and behaves. Thus, the culture of the organization will impact on the ability to change and so poses an issue for managing change. This may involve the accepted norms of the organization, rituals, beliefs, attitudes and personalities. Often, change management involves changing ways of thinking and doing and, in essence, changing culture. However, as the phrase often attributed to Peter Drucker claims: 'Culture eats strategy for breakfast.'

Hard factors

Hard factors are typified by an organization's structure, systems, resources and general support for the change process. Problems may include a lack of support from all levels in the organization, where staff and management perceive changes as a threat to them and their personal status. This results in a lack of cooperation and the creation of barriers to prevent the process occurring, or perhaps questioning the legality and governance of the process. As mentioned earlier, changes move the whole organization, individuals included, out of their comfort zone, the result being that some staff will not comply or engage but seek to actively or passively resist change.

The most obvious hard factors include a lack of physical resources to support the change process, a lack of senior management support, and the impact of rushed and unplanned change on customers, staff and suppliers.

17.5   Leadership styles and approaches

Leaders play a critical role when any change is imposed. Theory and experience highlight that the change is secondary in importance to subordinates' views and perceptions of the leader, and confidence in them. Many studies highlight the critical role played by senior management in implementing strategy and leading change programmes. As organizations flatten and responsibility is driven to all levels of the organization, knowledge of leadership styles, traits and theories is useful in understanding the position of leadership in the overall process.

To understand leadership styles and approaches, it is useful to look at the various theories of leadership. Leadership theory has evolved significantly since 1947 and the formalization of the great man theory, through trait theory and to current thinking around service leadership, strategic leadership, authentic leadership and spiritual leadership. This section examines the key theories that have led to current thinking. We provide an overview to understanding, but it is important to note that the various theories can be viewed as a continuum and

5

that there is no smooth transition from one to the other. Scholars and managers believe in their own stance and often such a stance can be a combination of schools. The subject of leadership is rich and deep in details. It is worth taking time to read some of the source materials for a more specialist understanding of the field.

Table 17.1 shows the key schools of thinking, and is presented in roughly chronological order of how each school evolved. Each theory is then explored below.

Table 17.1 Theories of leadership and key authors

Theory	Key authors
Great man theory	Popularized in the 1840s by Thomas Carlyle
Trait theory	Stogdill 1974 McCall and Lombardo 1983 Bennis and Biederman 1998
Behaviourist theories	Merton 1957 McGregor 1960 Blake and Mouton 1961, 1964 Pfeffer and Salancik 1975
Situational leadership	Lewin et al. 1939 Maier 1963 Likert 1967 Hersey and Blanchard 1969 Adair 1973 Vroom and Yetton 1973 House and Mitchell 1974 Yukl 1989
Contingency theory	Tannenbaum and Schmitt 1958 Fiedler 1967 Hickson et al. 1971 Adair 1973 Fiedler and Garcia 1987
Transactional theory	Dansereau et al. 1975 Graen and Cashman 1975
Transformational theory	Burns 1978 Bass 1985, 1990 Tichy and Devanna 1986 Covey 1992 Bass and Avolio 1994 Hooper and Potter 1997 Bass and Steidlmeier 1998 Adair 2002 Kouzes and Posner 2003

Robert Tannenbaum

Great man theory

The great man theory is based on the premise that leaders are born and not made. This probably stems from the fact that most studies conducted into leadership focused on existing great leaders. These existing leaders tended to emerge from the nobility or aristocracy and led to the misconception that breeding influenced leadership ability.

The **great man theory** of leadership is based on the premise that leaders are born and not made.

Trait theory

Trait theory extended the great man theory by recognizing that perhaps natural leaders exhibited inherent skills and abilities, which did not necessarily stem from breeding and bloodline. Again, trait theory is based on the premise that leaders are born rather than made but shifted the focus of research to identifying and examining the traits. A key study in this area was carried out by Stogdill (1974), who identified the skills and traits described in Table 17.2.

Trait theory is based on the premise that leaders are born rather than made and focuses on identifying the traits.

Table 17.2 **Skills and traits critical to leaders**

Traits	Skills
Energetic	Intelligent
Alert and sensitive to the social environment	Organized
Cooperative	Knowledgeable about group task
Adaptability to different context and situations	Technically and conceptually skilled
Dependable	Creative and innovative
Achievement oriented	Persuasive and convincing
Persistent	Diplomatic, politic and tactful
Dominant	Excellent intercommunication
Self-confident	
Able to tolerate stress	
Decisive and willing to assume responsibility	
Assertive	

Source: Adapted from Stogdill, 1974

GURU GUIDE

Warren G. Bennis was born in 1925. He graduated with a BA in psychology from Antioch College in 1951 and obtained his PhD in social sciences and economics from MIT in 1955. He is currently the Distinguished Professor of Business Administration at the University of Southern California. Professor Bennis has served on the faculties of Harvard Business School, Indian Institute of Management Calcutta, Boston University, INSEAD and Sloan School of Management at MIT. He was also an adviser to four US presidents and was the founding chairman of the Leadership Institute at the University of Southern California. He has acted as a consultant for several multinational firms and is the chairman of the Centre for Public Leadership at Harvard University's Kennedy School.

Professor Bennis has honorary doctorates from the LSE, the University of Cincinnati and the University of Buffalo. He is also the recipient of the International Leadership Association's Distinguished Leadership Award and the Marion Gislason Award for Leadership in Executive Development from Boston University School of Management. He is a senior fellow at UCLA and a visiting professor of leadership at the University of Exeter, UK.

Professor Bennis is regarded as an influential authority in the field of leadership studies. His work was pioneering in thinking in terms of the need for 'adhocracy', that is, free-moving project team approaches to work ideas, later developed by Toffler and Mintzberg, and in considering the leader as a 'social architect', a transformer of organizations.

5

Stogdill's study was followed up by other researchers such as McCall and Lombardo (1983) and Bennis and Biederman (1998). McCall and Lombardo (1983) identified four primary traits of leaders. These were:

- emotional stability and composure (confidence, consistency)
- admitting error

- good interpersonal skills (empathy)
- intellectual breadth (knowledgeable about a wide range of areas).

Bennis and Biederman (1998) see the leader as the person who transforms an organization through their ability to bring about change by positive motivation and the four key abilities of the management of attention, meaning, trust and self.

Behaviourist theories

The **behavioural theory** of leadership believes that leaders can be made rather than born, so leadership can be learned if the behaviours can be isolated and taught.

The behavioural theory represents a shift in thinking, away from leaders being born and already having leadership ability, traits and skills, to a perspective that believes that leaders can be made rather than born. As such, leadership could be learned if the behaviours could be isolated and taught. The focus of research in this area therefore became more about what leaders do rather than what they are. The result of this stage in leadership theory was the development of profiles of leadership styles. This is evident by the emergence of theories such as McGregor's theory X and theory Y, Blake and Mouton's managerial grid, and role theory.

McGregor's theory X and theory Y (1960) summarized two contrasting sets of assumptions made by managers in industry (Table 17.3).

Table 17.3 **McGregor's theory X and theory Y manager**

Theory X managers' beliefs	Theory Y managers' beliefs
The average human being has an inherent dislike of work and will avoid it if possible	The expenditure of physical and mental effort in work is as natural as play or rest, and the average human being, under proper conditions, learns not only to accept but to seek responsibility
Most people must be coerced, controlled, directed or threatened with punishment to get them to work to achieve organizational objectives	People will exercise self-direction and self-control to achieve objectives to which they are committed
Workers prefer to be directed, avoid responsibility, have little ambition, and want security above all else	The capacity to exercise a relatively high level of imagination, ingenuity and creativity in the solution of organizational problems is widely, not narrowly, distributed in the population, and the intellectual potentialities of the average human being are only partially utilized under the conditions of modern industrial life

Source: Adapted from McGregor, 1960

GURU GUIDE

Douglas Murray McGregor was born in 1906 in Detroit. He was involved with the family-run McGregor Institute in a part-time capacity but his early career was with a regional gas station, where he started as an attendant before rising to the position of manager.

In 1937, he joined MIT and was instrumental in setting up the university's industrial relations section. In 1953, he rejoined MIT as a faculty member and went to write several influential articles and books on leadership, leadership styles and human relations. In addition to his teaching work at MIT, McGregor took on increasing amounts of industrial relations consultancy work, particularly at Dewey Almy, a local rubber and sealants company.

He was a pioneer in industrial relations and his consultancy work helped him to develop the well-known theory X and theory Y of leadership styles. These theories are expounded in his 1960 bestseller *The Human Side of Enterprise* which gave him instant global fame. In the 1970s, the McGregor School, a graduate level business school, was founded by Antioch College in his honour. He died in 1964.

The managerial grid developed by Blake and Mouton (1961) focuses on task (production) and employee (people) orientations of managers. The theory is represented by a grid, with concern for production on the horizontal axis, and concern for people on the vertical axis. Five basic leadership styles are plotted on the grid depending on the manager's emphasis or perspectives. The grid results in five positions:

- *country club management:* high concern for people, low concern for production
- *team management:* high for both
- *organization man management:* moderate for both
- *impoverished management:* low stance for both
- *authority obedience:* low concern for people, high concern for production.

Blake and Mouton propose that team management is the most effective type of leadership behaviour.

The final element in this area is role theory, explored by Merton (1957) and Pfeffer and Salancik (1975). In organizations, actors (management or staff) will form roles for themselves and expectations of these roles. The leadership behaviour is expected to reflect the role held and is guided by the signals received from staff looking for support and guidance from various roles. This can be a subtle process or may be highly formalized. The shaping of expectations and behaviours becomes a key driver.

Situational and participative theories

The situational and participative theories view leadership as relating to context and the involvement of others, rather than taking autocratic decisions. This collection of theories seeks to involve other people in the process at various levels inside and outside the organization.

There are a number of theories to be considered, some blurring the lines between situational and participative. Here we touch on four sets of writers, Hersey and Blanchard (1969), Lewin et al. (1939), Likert (1967) and Yukl (1989).

The Hersey-Blanchard (1969) leadership model takes a situational perspective of leadership. Their model proposes that the readiness and developmental levels of a leader's subordinates play the greatest role in determining which leadership styles (behaviours) are most appropriate. The model is based on the direction (task behaviour) and socio-emotional support (relationship behaviour) needed by followers, where 'task behaviour' is the degree of instruction required for a particular set of duties and 'relationship behaviour' is the extent to which the leader engages in communications. The resulting 'maturity' is the willingness and ability of a person to take responsibility for directing their own behaviour.

Four leadership styles result:

1 *Directing:* The leader provides clear instructions and specific direction. This is for low follower readiness levels.
2 *Coaching:* The leader encourages two-way communication and helps build confidence and motivation. This is best matched with a moderate follower readiness level.
3 *Supporting:* The leader and followers share decision-making. This is best matched with a moderate follower readiness level.
4 *Delegating:* This style is appropriate for leaders whose followers are ready to accomplish a particular task and are both competent and motivated. This is best matched with a high follower readiness level.

On the other hand, Lewin et al. (1939) identified three styles of leader:

The **situational and participative theories** of leadership view leadership as relating to context and the involvement of others.

5

- *autocratic:* leader takes decision without consultation
- *democratic:* leader involves others in the decision-making process
- *laissez-faire:* minimal involvement of leader in decision-making.

Meanwhile, Likert (1967) identified four leadership styles:

- *Exploitive authoritative:* the leader has a low concern for people and uses threats and other fear-based methods to achieve conformance
- *Benevolent authoritative:* the leader adds concern for people to an authoritative position
- *Consultative:* upward flow of information is cautious, although the leader makes genuine efforts to listen carefully to ideas
- *Participative:* the leader makes maximum use of participative methods, engaging people lower down the organization in decision-making.

A leader's behaviour is dependent upon the perception of themselves and other factors such as stress. Yukl (1989) identifies six other variables:

- *Subordinate effort:* the motivation and actual effort expended
- *Subordinate ability and role clarity:* followers knowing what to do and how to do it
- *Organization of the work:* the structure of the work and utilization of resources
- *Cooperation and cohesiveness:* of the group in working together
- *Resources and support:* the availability of tools, materials, people and so on
- *External coordination:* the need to collaborate with other groups.

Leaders here work on such factors as external relationships, acquisition of resources, managing demands on the group and managing the structures and culture of the group.

Contingency theory

The **contingency theory** of leadership states that a leader's ability to lead is contingent on a variety of situational and behavioural factors.

The contingency theory of leadership states that a leader's ability to lead is contingent on a variety of situational and behavioural factors. Thus leaders may be very successful in one context, but if they move to a different context or situation, they may not be able to replicate such success.

Fiedler's work makes a considerable contribution to this field, along with the work of Fiedler and Garcia (1987). Fiedler's (1967) contingency theory argues that there is no single best way for managers to lead. Situations will create different leadership style requirements for a manager.

Fiedler (1967) examined three situations defining the leadership condition:

- *Leader–member relations:* loyalty, support and commitment
- *Task structure:* how highly structured the task is
- *Position power:* the manager's level of authority.

These factors determine the degree of contextual or situational control. In a favourable relationship, the manager has a high task structure and is able to reward and or punish employees without any problems. In an unfavourable relationship, the task is usually unstructured and the leader possesses limited authority.

Building on contingency theory, Tannenbaum and Schmidt (1958) suggested that leadership behaviour varies along a continuum of autocratic behaviour to a more devolved mode of leadership (democratic). Seven leadership styles occur across the continuum: tells, sells, suggests, consults, joins, delegates and abdicates:

- *Tells:* The leader takes the decisions and announces them. Subordinates carry them out without question
- *Sells:* The leader takes all the decisions without discussion or consultation. On this occasion, however, subordinates will be better motivated if they are persuaded that the decisions are good ones
- *Suggests:* The leader presents ideas and encourages questions
- *Consults:* The leader consults with subordinates before taking decisions
- *Joins:* The leader specifies the problem and invites discussion with subordinates. The leader manages the process and draws together the potential solutions in a joint decision-making fashion
- *Delegates:* The leader defines the limits and asks the group to make the decision
- *Abdicates:* The leader leaves the group to operate within defined limits of responsibility and authority, to identify issues and make decisions independent of the leader.

In this theory, as the categories represent a continuum, there will be situations or contexts when one of the styles is more appropriate than the others. It implies flexibility in leadership and sensitivity to context.

The action-centred leadership model was proposed by Adair in 1973. In this model, leadership represents getting things done through the work team and relationships with fellow managers and staff. According to Adair, an action-centred leader must:

- direct the job to be done (task)
- support and review the individual people doing it (individual)
- coordinate and foster the work team as a whole (team).

These three elements, task, individual, team, are found in his well-known three interlocking circles diagram, representing the intersections and overlaps in human interaction.

GURU GUIDE

John Adair was born in Luton in 1934. After working as a senior lecturer at the Royal Military Academy, Sandhurst, he later worked for the Industrial Society before becoming the first professor of leadership studies at the University of Surrey in 1979. He also worked with ICI to develop an in-house leadership development strategy programme that helped to change the loss-making, bureaucratic giant into the first British company to make a billion pounds profit. He became a fellow of the Royal Historical Society and also an emeritus fellow at the Windsor Leadership Trust. More recently, the People's Republic of China awarded him the title of Honorary Professor of Leadership at the China Executive Leadership Academy.

John Adair is one of the foremost authorities on leadership and leadership development. He has written over 40 books on leadership and change management which have been translated into several languages, he is an experienced teacher, and has acted as a consultant. Over a million managers worldwide have taken part in the action-centred leadership programmes he has pioneered.

5

Transactional theory

The **transactional theory** of leadership is based on reward and punishment.

The transactional theory of leadership is based on reward and punishment. The transactional leader works by creating clear structures, whereby it is clear what is required of their subordinates, and the rewards they will gain for following orders. Punishments are not always mentioned, but they are well understood and formal systems of discipline are usually in place. The approach emphasizes the importance of the relationship between leader and followers in the pursuit of mutual benefits.

Transformational theory

The transformational theory of leadership contends that people will follow a leader who inspires them. This requires the leader to have vision, empathy and passion about a shared cause or vision. They will draw on elements of trait and behaviour theory through exhibiting charisma, enthusiasm, energy and personalization. In effect, they care about the people they lead and want shared success.

The **transformational theory** of leadership contends that people will follow a leader who inspires them.

The stages in transformational leadership tend to follow a pattern of:

- Develop a vision
- Sell the vision
- Map the way forward
- Lead the 'charge'.

Burns (1978, p. 103) draws on the humanistic psychology movement in his writing by proposing that the 'transforming leader shapes, alters, and elevates the motives, values and goals of followers achieving significant change in the process'. This requires clarity of values and principles and, to a high degree, respect.

Bass (1990) developed Burns' concept of transforming leadership by suggesting that the leader transforms followers, and so 'transformational leaders' may:

- expand a follower's portfolio of needs
- transform a follower's self-interest
- increase the confidence of followers
- elevate followers' expectations
- heighten the value of the leader's intended outcomes for the follower
- encourage behavioural change
- motivate others to higher levels of personal achievement.

Other authors in the area include Tichy and Devanna (1986), Bass and Avolio (1994), Hooper and Potter (1997), and Covey (1992), who offers a distinction between transactional leadership and transformational leadership (Table 17.4).

Table 17.4 Transactional leadership and transformational leadership compared

Transactional leadership	Transformational leadership
Builds on man's need to get a job done and make a living	Builds on a man's need for meaning
Is preoccupied with power and position, politics and perks	Is preoccupied with purposes and values, morals and ethics
Is mired in daily affairs	Transcends daily affairs
Is oriented to hard data and short-term goals	Is oriented towards long-term goals without compromising human values and principles
Focuses on tactical issues	Focuses more on missions and strategies
Relies on human relations to lubricate human interactions	Releases human potential – identifying and developing new talent
Follows and fulfils role expectations by striving to work effectively within current systems	Designs and redesigns jobs to make them meaningful and challenging
Supports structures and systems that reinforce the bottom line, maximize efficiency, and guarantee short-term profits	Aligns internal structures and systems to reinforce overarching values and goals

Source: Adapted from Covey, 1992

In the 1970s, the Swiss wristwatch industry was facing ruin. Swiss watches had always been known for their style, appearance and distinctiveness. Marques such as Tissot and Omega were held in great regard, and customers were prepared to pay very high prices. The centre of the Swiss watch industry was La Chaux-de-Fonds, a small town near the border with France, and the watches were handmade by craftspeople and experts working in small companies in the towns and villages around this region. The rural and prosperous location, the crafting by hand, and the sense of community all added to the overall perceived quality of the industry itself. In particular, the Swiss industry had never felt the need for a mass-market, cheap or good value offering – it survived on its exclusivity and perceived product and brand quality.

Then the digital watch was invented. The digital watch was far more accurate than the handmade version, although it was perceived to diminish the quality of the work, and the expert input necessary. When the digital products were presented to the Swiss industry, they were rejected on the spot. So the idea and technology were sold to Casio and Seiko, the Japanese calculator and digital equipment manufacturing companies. These companies embraced the new approach and began to develop their own ranges of watches. As large companies with mass and batch production capacity, Casio, Seiko and others were also able to produce the watches far more quickly and cheaply than the Swiss companies, which preferred to rely on the traditional methods. The Japanese companies were also able to produce their own distinctive designs, so that their offerings quickly came to be as recognizable as the Swiss products, and with the additional benefits of accuracy. Seiko and Casio also produced ranges of very cheap and good quality watches, and these products now found ready outlets in European and North American markets. They were able to attract large numbers of new customers who had long since sought good quality watches but had never before been able to afford them.

Consequently, the bottom dropped out of the Swiss market, and the small companies found themselves facing ruin. The Swiss industry as a whole had met the challenge from Japan with a combination of disdain, disbelief and arrogance, and only when many of the companies started to go out of business was the problem addressed. The Swiss government was called in, and asked to support what was after all a traditional and well-known domestic industry. First, the government prevaricated and then declined. For a time it seemed as if the whole industry would be sold off to Japanese interests. Then UBS, one of the Swiss industry's main backers, decided to consult Nicolas Hayek.

Hayek was known as a manufacturing and industrial expert. He had made his name advising the Swiss army on its sourcing and choice of weaponry and military hardware, and he was known to deliver high-quality and cost-effective results. He was also known to be straightforward to the point of rudeness; if the watch industry could not be saved, he would not prevaricate, but would say so.

Hayek stated that the industry could be saved, but that it would have to be done his way. The requirement was to create an industry in Switzerland that would be profitable and durable, and able to compete on cost and price with the Japanese competitors. Having gained the agreement and support of the banks and the government, he restructured and reorganized the whole industry. He created a holding company, SMH. He reorganized the entire industry into three separate companies, which would operate under the governance and direction of SMH. One company would manufacture the top and mid-range brands, one would produce a cheap/good value product/brand with which to compete directly against the mass-market products of Seiko and Casio, and the third would manufacture the components for the other two.

Hayek became chief executive of SMH, and he set about assembling a team of the world's best watch designers and engineers. He employed manufacturing experts. He built an expert marketing and sales team, whose remit was to get the Swiss industry back on its feet and into profit.

The designs of the workings of all the ranges of watches were streamlined and simplified, and the numbers of components used were reduced in all the brands. This meant that the top and mid-range brands were now as reliable and accurate as the branded goods.

The component manufacturing facility was capitalized and made accurate to the point at which the components themselves, manufactured in Switzerland, using Swiss labour and staff paid at Swiss labour rates, were cheaper and more cost-effective – and more accurate and a higher quality – than the Japanese alternatives.

SMH then introduced its cheap/good value brand, which it called 'Swatch'. Swatch had two different connotations – it appeared as a contraction of 'Swiss watch', and it also gave a marketing and sales platform for a 'second watch', one to be worn on a daily basis rather than something to be kept for smart and dress occasions. As stated above, this was unheard of in the Swiss watch industry. However, SMH built and reinforced the Swatch brand with regular new designs,

5

including use of new materials, especially wood and plastic, and different colours, logos and images on the watches themselves. There was immediate recognition of the brand, and this was (and remains) reinforced by regular Swatch conventions, sales drives, design competitions and the use of limited editions.

Hayek became actively involved in every aspect of SMH's growth and development, and this led to accusations of meddling and interference. Many of the experts that he hired found themselves able to work for him for short periods of time only. His response was (and remains) always:

> I never want executives who are only good. I want people who are expert and fully involved in every

aspect of what we need to be doing. If they will not do this, and if they will not accept this from me, I do not want them here.

Case study questions

1   What were the barriers to change that had to be overcome?
2   What are the strengths and weaknesses of restructuring a company or industry in crisis?
3   What are the leadership qualities brought by Hayek to this situation? What else would you need to be aware of when appointing a leader to such a situation?

For test questions, extra case studies, audio case studies, weblinks, videolinks and more to help you understand the topics covered in this chapter, visit our companion website at www.macmillanihe.com/companion/business/campbell.

VOCAB CHECKLIST FOR ESL STUDENTS

Autocratic	Personification	Scapegoating
Comfort zone	Power asymmetry (see 'power'	'Shaking up' phase (see
Democratic	and 'asymmetry')	'shake-up')
Impetus	Prevaricate	Tinker
Ingenuity	'Rank and file'	
Laissez-faire	Reconfiguration	

Definitions for these terms can be found in the 'Vocab Zone' of the companion website, which provides free access to the Macmillan English Dictionary online at www.macmillanihe.com/companion/business/campbell.

REVIEW QUESTIONS

1   Explain how the nature of change can influence the strategy implementation process.
2   What are the issues associated with the change management process?
3   Explain the role of leadership in managing change.
4   Explain the different leadership theories that are common in business strategy and how each differs.

DISCUSSION TOPIC

Leaders are born not made. Discuss.

HOT TOPICS – Research project areas to investigate

If you have a project to do, why not investigate …

- … which leadership styles are adopted in organizations during periods of crisis.
- … whether national culture/gender influences leadership style.
- … how rapid growth organizations cope with change.

Recommended reading

Adair, J.E. (2002) *Effective Strategic Leadership*, Basingstoke: Palgrave – now Palgrave Macmillan.

Cartwright, R. (2002) *Mastering Team Leadership*, Basingstoke: Palgrave – now Palgrave Macmillan.

Clawson, J.G. (2003) *Level Three Leadership: Getting below the Surface* (2nd edn), Englewood Cliffs, NJ: Prentice Hall.

Coch, L. and French, J.R. (1948) 'Overcoming resistance to change', *Human Relations*, 1: 512–32.

Covey, S.R. (1999) *Principle Centred Leadership*, London: Simon & Schuster.

Cranwell-Ward, J., Bacon, A. and Mackie, R. (2002) *Inspiring Leadership: Staying Afloat in Turbulent Times*, London: Thomson Learning.

Evans, M.G. (1970) 'The effect of supervisory behavior on the path-goal relationship', *Organizational Behavior and Human Performance*, 5: 277–98.

French, J.R., Israel, J. and As, D. (1960) 'An experiment on participation in a Norwegian factory', *Human Relations*, **13**(1): 3–19.

Gillen, T. (2002) *Leadership Skills for Boosting Performance*, London: CIPD.

Godard, A. and Lenhardt, J. (2000) *Transformational Leadership: Shared Dreams to Succeed*, Basingstoke: Palgrave – now Palgrave Macmillan.

Goleman, D., Boyatzis, R. and McKee, A. (2002) *The New Leaders: Transforming the Art of Leadership into the Science of Results*, London: Little, Brown.

Hesselbein, F. and Johnstone, R. (2002) *On Mission and Leadership: A Leader to Leader Guide*, San Fransisco, CA: Jossey-Bass.

Hughes, R., Ginnett, R. and Curphy, G. (2002) *Leadership: Enhancing the Lessons of Experience*, London: McGraw-Hill.

Johnson, G. (1987) *Strategic Change and the Management Process*, Oxford: Blackwell.

Landsberg, M. (2001) *The Tools of Leadership*, London: HarperCollins.

Lewin, K. (1951) *Field Theory in Social Science*, New York: Harper & Brothers.

Mintzberg, H. (1990) 'The design school: reconsidering the basic premises of strategic management', *Strategic Management Journal*, 11: 171–95.

Moss Kanter, R. (1989) *The Change Masters: Innovation and Entrepreneurship in the American Corporation*, New York: Simon & Schuster.

Nahavandi, A. (2000) *The Art & Science of Leadership* (2nd edn), Englewood Cliffs, NJ: Prentice Hall.

Olmstead, J. (2000) *Executive Leadership: Building World Class Organizations*, Houston, TX: Cashman Dudley.

Parker, B. and Stone, C. (2003) *Developing Management Skills for Leadership*, Englewood Cliffs, NJ: Prentice Hall.

Pettigrew, A.M. (1988) *The Management of Strategic Change*, Oxford: Blackwell.

Quinn, J.B. (1980) *Strategies for Change*, Homewood, IL: Irwin.

Quinn, J.B. (1980) 'Managing strategic change', *Sloan Management Review*, **21**(4): 3–20.

Schein, E.H. (1985) *Organizational Culture and Leadership*, San Francisco, CA: Jossey-Bass.

Shriberg, A., Shriberg, D. and Lloyd, C. (2002) *Practicing Leadership: Principles and Applications*, New York: Wiley.

Stacey, R.D. (1993) *Strategic Management and Organisational Dynamics*, London: Pitman.

Stringer, R. (2002) *Leadership and Organizational Climate*, Englewood Cliffs, NJ: Prentice Hall.

Tannenbaum, A.S. and Alport, F.H. (1956) 'Personality structure and group structure: an interpretive structure of their relationship through an event structure hypothesis', *Journal of Abnormal and Social Psychology*, 53: 272–80.

Topping, P. (2002) *Managerial Leadership*, New York: McGraw-Hill.

Williamson, O. (1975) *Markets and Hierarchies*, New York: Free Press.

Chapter references

5

Adair, J.E. (1973) *Action-Centred Leadership,* London: McGraw-Hill.

Adair, J.E. (2002) *100 Ideas for Effective Leadership & Management*, Oxford: Capstone.

Andrews, K. (1987) *The Concept of Corporate Strategy*, Homewood, IL: Irwin.

Ansoff, H.I. (1965) *Corporate Strategy: An Analytical Approach to Business Policy for Growth and Expansion*, New York: McGraw-Hill.

Bass, B.M. (1985) *Leadership and Performance Beyond Expectation*, New York: Free Press.

Bass, B.M. (1990) 'From transactional to transformational leadership: learning to share the vision', *Organizational Dynamics*, **18**(3): 19–31.

Bass, B.M. and Avolio, B. (1994) *Improving Organizational Effectiveness Through Transformational Leadership.* Thousands Oaks, CA: Sage.

Bass, B.M. and Steidlmeier, P. (1998) *Ethics, Character and Authentic Transformational Leadership,* http://cls.binghampton.edu/BassSteid.html.

Bennis, W. and Biederman, P. (1998) *Organizing Genius: The Secrets of Creative Collaboration*, Cambridge, MA: Perseus Books.

Blake, R.R. and Mouton, J.S. (1961) *Group Dynamics: Key to Decision Making*, Houston, TX: Gulf Publishing.

Blake, R.R. and Mouton, J.S. (1964) *The Managerial Grid: The Key to Leadership Excellence*, Houston, TX: Gulf Publishing.

Burns, J.M. (1978) *Leadership,* New York: Harper & Row.

Covey, S. (1992) *Principle-centred Leadership*, New York: Simon & Schuster.

Dansereau, F. Jr, Graen, G. and Haga, W.J. (1975) 'A vertical dyad linkage approach to leadership within formal organizations: a longitudinal investigation of the role making process', *Organizational Behavior and Human Performance*, 13: 46–78.

Fiedler, F.E. (1967) *A Theory of Leadership Effectiveness*, New York: McGraw-Hill.

Fiedler, F.E. and Garcia, J.E. (1987) *New Approaches to Leadership: Cognitive Resources and Organizational Performance*, New York: Wiley.

Graen, G. and Cashman, J.F. (1975) 'A role making model of leadership in formal organizaitons: a developmental approach', in J.G. Hunt and L.L. Larson (eds) *Leadership Frontiers*, Kent, OH: Kent State University Press.

Hersey, P. and Blanchard, K.H. (1969) *Management of Organizational Behavior: Utilizing Human Resources*, Englewood Cliffs, NJ: Prentice Hall.

Hickson, D.J., Hinigs, C.R., Lee, C.A. et al. (1971) 'A strategic contingencies theory of intra-organizational power', *Administrative Science Quarterly*, 16: 216–29.

Hooper, R.A. and Potter, J.R. (1997) *The Business of Leadership*, Aldershot: Ashgate.

House, R.J. and Mitchell, T.R. (1974) 'Path-goal theory of leadership', *Contemporary Business*, 3: 81–98.

Kouzes, J.M. and Posner, B.Z. (2003) *The Leadership Challenge* (3rd edn), San Francisco, CA: Jossey-Bass.

Lewin, K. (1947) 'Feedback problems of social diagnosis and action: Part II-B of frontiers in group dynamics, *Human Relations*, 1: 147–53.

Lewin, K., Llippit, R. and White, R.K. (1939) 'Patterns of aggressive behavior in experimentally created social climates', *Journal of Social Psychology*, 10: 271–301.

Likert, R. (1967) *The Human Organization: Its Management and Value*, New York: McGraw-Hill.

McCall, M.W. Jr and Lombardo, M.M. (1983) *Off the Track: Why and How Successful Executives Get Derailed*, Greenboro, NC: Centre for Creative Leadership.

McGregor, D. (1960) *The Human Side of Enterprise*, New York: McGraw-Hill.

Maier, N.R. (1963) *Problem-solving Discussions and Conferences: Leadership Methods and Skills*, New York: McGraw-Hill.

Merton, R.K. (1957) *Social Theory and Social Structure*, New York: Free Press.

Pfeffer, J. and Salancik, G.R. (1975) 'Determinants of supervisory behavior: a role set analysis', *Human Relations*, 28: 139–53.

Quinn, J.B. and Voyer, J. (1998) Logical incrementalism: managing strategy formation, in H. Mintzberg, J.B. Quinn and S. Ghoshal (eds) *The Strategy Process,* Englewood Cliffs, NJ: Prentice Hall.

Stogdill, R.M. (1974) *Handbook of Leadership: A Survey of the Literature*, New York: Free Press.

Tannenbaum, A.S. and Schmitt, W.H. (1958) 'How to choose a leadership pattern', *Harvard Business Review*, 36: 95–101.

Tichy, N.M. and Devanna, M.A. (1986) *The Transformational Leader*, New York: John Wiley.

Vroom, V.H. and Yetton, P.W. (1973) *Leadership and Decision-making*, Pittsburg: University of Pittsburg Press.

Yukl, G.A. (1989) *Leadership in Organizations*, Englewood Cliffs, NJ: Prentice Hall.

PART 6

CONTEMPORARY ISSUES IN BUSINESS STRATEGY

We have now explored all the elements involved in the business strategy process. Part 6 highlights some key issues that are either impacting on strategy right now, or will do so in the future. We explore four different areas.

Chapter 18 examines the nature of emerging technologies and how these will impact on organizations and the way business is done. It focuses on the web and how new technology is changing the shape of organizations and their business models.

Chapter 19 explores the concepts of quality and quality management. While this is firmly rooted in the domain of operations management, we feel that quality is at the heart of nearly all organizations and is often a threshold expectation of consumers. With this in mind, we look at the various approaches to quality management and introduce the concepts of benchmarking and Six Sigma.

Chapter 20 deals with the issue of sustainability. We explore this from the business perspective through the concepts of social responsibility and business ethics.

Chapter 21 examines emerging markets and the industrial superpowers. In this final chapter, we do not seek to offer any solutions but to raise awareness of what the future may hold for business strategy in the 21st century.

Chapter 18

The web, new technology and new organizational forms

Margaret McCann[1]

Introduction and chapter overview

This chapter explores a key area for the future development of organizations and therefore business strategy, existing and emerging web technologies. The chapter starts by setting the context of web growth and the basic terminology needed to understand the technology. The impact of the web is then explored, in particular the influence it has had on business and industry, relationships and value-adding properties. The chapter then explores new and emerging technologies, including Web 2.0 and the mobile web, and ends by exploring issues associated with the digital economy, management issues and strategies relating to the use of the web.

Learning objectives

By the end of this chapter, you should be able to:

- explain the impact that the web has had on business
- describe related emerging web technologies including Web 2.0 and the mobile web and their business applications
- discuss various issues related to the digital age, including the digital divide, information overload and privacy of data
- understand management issues related to business use of the web and relevant management strategies that may be applied

18.1 The web

The **internet** is a global network comprising millions of computers.

The **web** is a way of accessing information via the internet.

Although the terms are commonly used interchangeably, the internet and the World Wide Web (known as the 'web') are two different technologies. The internet is a global network comprising millions of computers, while the web is a way of accessing information via the internet, typically using browsers, such as Internet Explorer or Firefox, to access information on web pages. Other ways to access or transmit information on the internet include email, newsgroups and instant messaging.

1 Caledonian Business School, Glasgow Caledonian University.

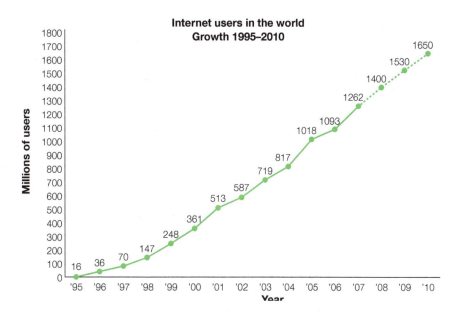

Figure 18.1 **Worldwide growth of internet users, 1995–2010**

Source: www.internetworldstats.com, copyright © Miniwatts Marketing Group

There are currently 1.9 billion internet users worldwide, which accounts for 28.7% of the world's population. The number of users has grown 444.8% from 2000 to 2010 (www.internetworldstats.com/stats.htm). Figure 18.1 demonstrates the rapid rise in internet users from 1995 to 2010.

The web first saw commercial use in the early 1990s. At that time, the web presence of a business mainly comprised a website in order to communicate and transmit information about its products and services. The web did not change the fundamental business model, as it did not provide new products and services but supported and extended processes, allowing access to a wider audience. Recently, the web has changed from the mainly read only medium, where businesses posted information on products and services, to one where users are encouraged to interact and contribute to web content. This is changing the way that businesses use the web, allowing them to interact openly and freely with customers, receive feedback on products and services, and collaborate with customers and suppliers.

Nowadays, the web is so fundamental to everyday life that no business can ignore the potential that it offers, and the way businesses adopt and exploit web technologies can determine their success or failure. Some businesses use the web to expand their business operations or change the way they operate and hence find new opportunities, while for others, it is fundamental to their very operation, for example Amazon, eBay, Google, Yahoo!. Without the web, these businesses could not and would not exist.

There are many different terminologies used when conducting business over the web. One of the most common is e-commerce, which can be defined as the buying or selling of goods or services via the internet. However, since the way business is conducted on the web is not restricted to the online transactions of buying and selling but also involves the important exchange of information between various parties, such as enquiries and feedback, a more accurate term to

E-commerce is the buying or selling of goods or services via the internet.

6

E-business is the use of technology throughout the supply chain of the business and the carrying out of business on the internet. It refers not only to buying and selling but also servicing customers and collaborating with business partners.

use is e-business. So we can define e-business as the use of technology throughout the supply chain of the business and the carrying out of business on the internet. It refers not only to buying and selling but also servicing customers and collaborating with business partners. This chapter discusses the web in the wider context of e-business.

Such e-business between businesses and consumers or customers can be conducted in the following ways:

- *Business-to-business (B2B):* involves businesses transactions from one business to another in the supply chain (producer to wholesaler or wholesaler to retailer). Alibaba.com is a popular example of B2B in action. This site is a virtual marketplace linking exporters and importers, where buyers and sellers post leads on the products/services of interest. The site mainly caters to small and medium-sized businesses and has now morphed into a virtual monopoly for sourcing products from mainland China.

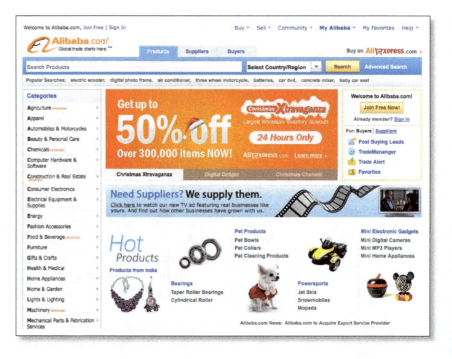

- *Business-to-customer/consumer (B2C):* the activities involved in the supply of products or services from a business to the end user. The most common and familiar facet of e-business is B2C. The electronics giant Apple not only sells its stylish, cutting-edge products through its B2C website, but also advises its customers to buy and download music from its popular iTunes music store.
- *Customer-to-customer/consumer-to-consumer (C2C):* the exchange of goods or services directly from consumer to consumer. This can typically involve auction sites such as eBay. Starting as a B2C site, Amazon's business model now allows the option to earn revenue through its C2C initiatives. Amazon's UK website allows individuals to sell/buy products from other individuals. Amazon benefits by charging a small referral fee for hosting and conducting the transaction.

18.2　The impact of the web on business

There are numerous ways that the web has impacted on business activities, ranging from small-scale efficiency gains to the transformation of an entire industry. In general, the web has been used to improve efficiency as it speeds up transactions and lowers the costs associated with business activities, such as the processing of enquiries and orders, and the creation, storage and distribution of information. It has increased flexibility and widened choice as customers can shop day or night, search for a range of suppliers regardless of location, shop in different ways (online store, auction site) and use comparison websites to compare prices, products and services.

We now cover some of the more important ways the web has impacted on business.

Transformation of industries

The web has changed the very way that business is conducted in some industries, such as the music and travel industries. The downloading of music from sites such as iTunes has changed the structure of the industry, forcing record companies and distributors to seek new business models. Artists can now publicize their own material through video-sharing sites such as YouTube (www.youtube.com) or social networking sites such as Facebook (www.facebook.com). Similarly, in the travel industry, high-street travel agents traditionally acted as intermediaries when customers were booking holidays. However, the web now allows customers to search for and book the various components associated with holidays directly, as well as read reviews and ratings from other travellers through sites such as Expedia (www.expedia.com) and TripAdvisor (www.tripadvisor.com), enabling them to make more informed decisions about their booking. This has forced some travel companies to change their business model to form strategic alliances with their competitors to offer a more cost-effective, extensive service (Deloitte, 2003). Others have remained competitive through improved customer relationship management or increased non-ticket revenue such as charging for baggage/check-in and so on (IBM, 2008).

Eliminate distance boundaries

Web technology can eliminate time and distance boundaries and offer flexibility in the location of work as there is no necessity for employees to be in the same location to work together. Employees may be able to access work systems remotely and so have the flexibility to work from home or any convenient location. Web or video-conferencing allows meetings to be conducted at any time of day or night without the need to travel. An international business can set up working practices so that different teams around the world share the workload. For example, one team can work during the day, while another team on the other side of world can take over at night. This allows the working day to be extended and does not involve pay for overtime or unsociable working hours.

Web technology also allows organizations to set up practices where better workforce skills are available or where the cost of work is cheaper. Outsourcing is the movement of a business process to another company with a more appropriate skills base, whereas offshoring is the movement of a business process from one location to another, usually another country, where the skills are

Outsourcing is the movement of a business process to another company with a more appropriate skills base.

Offshoring is the movement of a business process from one location to another, usually another country, where the skills are cheaper.

6

cheaper. Outsourcing or offshoring can be set up for a range of manufacturing or support services. A good example of outsourcing is the call centre operations of UK insurance companies, the majority of which outsource their call centre operations to India with a view to reducing costs and a renewed focus on core competence. Typical conditions such as low-cost labour, time difference, and English-speaking professionals have contributed to this 'look east' policy of UK insurance majors.

Collaboration

Web technology can be used to encourage internal and external collaboration. Internally, employees can be encouraged to use technology to work together and share information and ideas with their colleagues. Businesses throughout the supply chain can use the web as a platform to work together by automating order processing between businesses, and the shipment and supply of goods or services.

Building alliances may lead to virtual/strategic alliances being formed between businesses. These alliances may exist as a virtual business, with no or limited physical premises and be composed of different geographically dispersed businesses such as developers, producers and suppliers working together.

Web 2.0 technology (see below) can also be used to find and build associations with other businesses. For example, social business networking sites such as LinkedIn (www.linkedin.com) and Ecademy (www.ecademy.com) can be used to find and build professional contacts, and there are a host of online forums and communities, which can be used to share knowledge and support.

Example   **Virtual teaching at the Open University**

Another interesting example of collaboration is the Open University's attempt to create virtual worlds for educational purposes. The OU owns six islands at Second Life, a multi-user virtual environment, home to more than 17 million users. 'Open Life', the name of one of the islands, is a virtual teaching environment where staff and students meet and participate in pedagogical activities. OU staff frequently use the environment to hold meetings, deliver lecturers and carry out the normal student-centred activities one would traditionally associate with the 'bricks and mortar' university learning environments.

For more information, go to http://www.open.ac.uk/cetl-workspace/cetlcontent/documents/496357225a459.pdf.

Customer relationships

The web allows businesses to build relationships with their customers as enquiries can be received directly and dealt with personally and more efficiently. Customers can be encouraged to offer feedback, either directly via email or comment forms or indirectly through electronic communities, providing a business with vital information on how customers perceive their goods or services. Argos, the catalogue retailer, allows its customers to write reviews on products sold at its website. Customers are free to write about their shopping experience, including product reviews and customer service, through online forms. This not only helps Argos to keep tabs on the performance of its products but also to improve customer relationships.

Improve marketing

Using a variety of means, such as previous sales data, registration information, or monitoring programs such as cookies stored on a customer's computer (see below), information can be gathered about a customer's profile and preferences. This then allows a business to segment customers and target marketing products according to information gathered on preferences. This may involve sending customers personalized adverts on special offers, promotions and other information relative to that customer. In the near future, the media company Sky hopes to be able to advertise directly to customers based on their preferences via their TV, using viewing information gained from their Sky+ boxes.

Personalization

Web technology can be used to offer personalized products/services. For example, the PC retailer Dell allows customers to place their order online, specifying details of the exact requirements of their system. The customer's computer is then built to order and shipped to them in a few days. Direct ordering reduces warehouse costs as the exact quantities are known. In addition, customers can track their order online. Another business offering customized products is the sports retailer Nike. Its website (www.nikeid.nike.com) allows customers to personalize their own training shoes by choosing the colour, pattern, material and other design features.

The long tail

The **long tail** describes the strategy of selling a large number of niche products to a relatively small number of customers.

The 'long tail' is a term used to describe the way businesses have used the web to impact on the market. The long tail describes the strategy of selling a large number of niche products to a relatively small number of customers (Anderson, 2004). This is in contrast to 'traditional' retailers who tend to focus on selling a smaller range of popular items to the mass market. The total of the small volume of niche product sales can be larger than the high volume of sales of popular brands.

The online book retailer Amazon has been successful in selling a large range of books not available in traditional 'bricks and mortar' bookstores. In fact, many of the books that Amazon sell would be out of print if sold only through traditional methods. The web has allowed Amazon and other similar businesses to stock a wider choice of products, as they have used technology to ensure that their costs are low and to build alliances with other businesses. The use of technology to sell niche products can enable small businesses to compete against, and work with, larger enterprises.

18.3 The changing face of the web

The term **Web 2.0** is commonly associated with web applications that facilitate interactive information sharing, interoperability, social networking, user-centred design and collaborative working.

The web was originally used in a rather passive way, as businesses created 'shopfront' websites to provide customers with up-to-date information on their products and services. Now the power of the web has shifted, as content is created and shared by many and customers are encouraged to use technology to interact and collaborate. This interactive web is termed Web 2.0 – a term that is difficult to define precisely but is generally used for the content-sharing nature of today's web. It relates to the concept of social connections, participation and

6

interaction, where businesses, customers, employees and partners connect with each other and generate content by sharing data, collaborating, socializing and contributing their own thoughts, ideas, experiences and knowledge. It allows businesses to communicate directly with their customers and understand their preferences and needs in detail and so target their specific requirements. Web 2.0 applications are easy to use and inexpensive, so offer tremendous potential for businesses of all sizes, even small businesses that may be unable to take advantage of more 'traditional' web technologies.

As a marketing tool, Web 2.0 applications can enable businesses to engage with existing customers and to be proactive about finding new ones. Web 2.0 can change the type of marketing from general communications about products and services published on a website to community interaction through lots of conversations. Marketing professionals can use the wealth of information on these networks to better understand customers' needs or inform (push content to) existing customers.

The following are some Web 2.0 applications, with suggestions for their possible business application.

Blogs

Blogs are websites that host frequently updated journals, which are used for writing short and typically informal communications.

Originating from the term 'web-log', blogs are websites that host frequently updated journals, which are used for writing short and typically informal communications. Corporate blogs are often used for internal and external communication as well as for marketing and promotion by providing information on the business and its market to local and global, existing and potential customers. Blogs can be used for knowledge transfer, to showcase and share expertise, to respond to frequently asked questions (FAQs), to present advice and solutions and, in so doing, retain customer loyalty. Customers can be invited to post comments to blog entries, so blogs can be used to interact and gain feedback or ideas from customers and help maintain close links. Blog posts may contain links to other related web pages, encouraging collaboration and joint ventures between businesses.

Blogs can also be used internally within a company for information dissemination on recent business developments or even for staff feedback. Owner/manager blogging gives news straight from the decision maker. Infosys, the Indian software major, has another use for blogging; it uses blogs written by its employees to monitor views and opinions on job satisfaction, training needs, remuneration and so on. It encourages employees to write blogs on its intranet site to gather first-hand information on potential problems with a view to solving them at the earliest opportunity.

A recent blogging phenomenon is microblogging, which is blogging limited to shorter message length. Although microblogging has, to date, proved limited as a business tool (BBC, 2009), it may be useful for status updates for collaboration or for marketing of goods (Jin, 2009). The most popular microblogging tool is Twitter.

Wikis

A **wiki** is a web page that easily allows anyone to create, view and modify web content.

The word 'wiki' is the Hawaiian word for quick, thus WikiWikiWeb was the first wiki software. A wiki is a web page that easily allows anyone to create, view and modify web content. The most well-known wiki is Wikipedia – the online

encyclopedia written and policed by its users, who try to maintain quality of content. Wikis can be public (such as Wikipedia) or private, as security restrictions can be implemented which allow access only to certain users.

Wikis enable users to communicate and work together on documents, empowering all to contribute and so promote knowledge transfer and collective intelligence. When a wiki is edited, version control means that all previous versions are saved and can be referred to or resurrected if required.

Wikis encourage internal or inter-company collaboration, as teams, especially if located in several locations, can work on documents and are good for project work, from the initial stages of brainstorming to organizing meetings and documentation. They are also ideal for centralizing company documents in one accessible location.

Social networking

The web can indeed be a powerful tool for interacting and expanding social relationships. This is especially evident in social networking sites, which allow users to build a personal web presence and connect with contacts (business or social) to communicate and share content. The membership of popular social networking sites such as MySpace and Facebook has expanded over the past few years and each now has millions of users. There are specific business social networking sites such as LinkedIn, which are commonly used to meet and communicate with business contacts and even hire staff. Although initially social networking sites attracted a younger audience, popularity among over 35s is growing (Cachia et al., 2007) and businesses are starting to exploit social networking to build business connections.

Within each site, users initially set up a profile of personal (or company) details, which will generally be visible to other users. B2B or B2C networks are built by searching profiles for communities of interest and requesting them to be 'friends'. In this way, potential customers can be targeted and views and content exchanged. Such networking can be viral as users pass content and information around. It has been found that marketers who can engage customers by interacting through social networking can form a closer bond (Vasquez, 2006).

Virtual worlds

The increasing power and sophistication of technology allows users to create an avatar, or virtual character, in a virtual world, such as Second Life. Avatars can communicate and interact in real-time emulating real-life business activities such as conducting meetings with new or existing customers, networking with other business users or buying and selling real or virtual products. Second Life even uses its own currency for trading, the Linden dollar.

Different business models exist within virtual worlds such as Second Life. Traditional businesses can set up a store for virtual trading or use the environment to experiment with new products and gain customer feedback, as Nike and IBM have done. On the other hand, many virtual businesses exist within Second Life, ranging from fashion retail to virtual wedding or party planning for avatars.

RSS (rich site summary or really simple syndication) is a technology that allows information to be sent to the user whenever a web page is updated.

RSS

RSS (rich site summary or really simple syndication) is a technology that allows information to be sent to the user whenever a web page is updated. So rather

6

than searching continuously for updates on an item of interest, the web page is sent as soon as new content is added. RSS can be used by businesses for keeping interested parties up to date with company news or for marketing to existing or potential customers or suppliers. The BBC provides RSS services for users to keep abreast with the latest and developing news stories. Users can subscribe to the BBC's service and can benefit from updated coverage on news items and reporting from their favourite correspondents.

Podcasting and media sharing

Podcasting is the distribution of audio or video files that can be downloaded onto PCs or mobile devices such as MP3 players. Businesses can create and broadcast their own podcasts or subscribe to those produced by others. Podcasts can be used as a communication tool for marketing and showcasing of products or even for knowledge transfer in areas such as staff training. Regularly produced podcasts can be subscribed to using RSS, which informs the user when new podcasts are available and downloads them.

Podcasting is the distribution of audio or video files that can be downloaded onto PCs or mobile devices such as MP3 players.

Highly popular video-sharing sites such as YouTube or Google Video allow users to upload their own videos or view those produced by others. When content is added to these sites, tags are also incorporated, which are used to label, organize and identify content, allowing it to be found when searched by others. Video-sharing sites offer small businesses unique opportunities. For example, where TV advertising is prohibitive for small businesses, video-sharing sites can offer an ideal opportunity to showcase products.

Software as a service

The popularity of the web is changing the way that software can be purchased and used. Instead of businesses buying software as a package (product), software as a service is hosted by a service provider and made available to customers over the web. There is no need for customers to install the software on their own machine; instead, they can use the software via the web, from any location. There are many advantages to software as a service such as lower acquisition costs for businesses. Also, since the software is automatically updated, the latest version is always available and all users will use the same version. Some software as a service such as Google Docs (http://docs.google.com) is free to use and designed for easy collaboration, as documents can be shared with different users, saved locally or to a Google file server, or published online for all users to access. Thus it is easy to access documents from any location with web access.

The mobile web

The web is increasingly becoming more than a PC-based phenomenon as the trend towards smaller technology enables access by a range of mobile devices such as smartphones, netbooks, personal digital assistants (PDAs), MP3 players and even games consoles. The mobile web refers to browser-based access to the internet from a mobile device, such as a smartphone or PDA, connected to a wireless network. The mobile web is quickly becoming a part of our day-to-day lives. These devices increase the overall audience and use of the web, allowing anytime, anywhere access, which has huge implications for business in terms of market size, mobility and flexibility. It is important that businesses realize the opportunities the mobile web can offer and adapt their web presence to optimize mobile business advantages.

The **mobile web** refers to browser-based access to the internet from a mobile device, such as a smartphone or PDA, connected to a wireless network.

Although mobile devices are extremely convenient, most have a small screen and limited keyboard for input. Accessing web pages can also be very slow, with limited scrolling and navigation. Therefore using web pages designed for PC viewing can be impractical and so businesses must specifically design a mobile version of their web presence, which takes into account the reduced screen size and limited typing ability of these devices. Typically, mobile websites will be simplified with less content but contextualized for the mobile business needs.

Mobile technology

To access the web wirelessly, users will typically use their mobile phone and/or Wi-Fi (wireless fidelity), using devices such as PCs, laptops, netbooks, PDAs or MP3 players. The convergence of technology means that mobile devices are becoming increasingly powerful, with smartphones now incorporating features previously found on PDAs.

The new generation of smartphones includes features such as large touch screens, while others incorporate pull-out keyboards. These devices allow users access to the web to send and receive emails, to social networking sites and satellite navigation. Many have one-button access to encourage users onto certain applications such as social networking sites, maps and mobile browsers, such as Google Mobile (www.google.com/mobile).

Wi-Fi-enabled equipment can connect to the web when it is within range of a wireless network. Any Wi-Fi-enabled device can be used to connect – including some mobile phones. Access to such networks can be free of charge or users can subscribe to private networks. For example, Wi-Fi is available in public hotspots, businesses, university campuses, trains, coaches, as well as in millions of homes. Hotels, bars, restaurants and airports often provide free access to wireless networks and many cities have announced plans to allow wireless access on a city-wide basis. Thanks to Wi-Fi, there is now a cybercafé at the base of Mount Everest.

18.4 Business opportunities

There are currently 3 billion subscriptions to mobile phones worldwide compared to 1 billion PCs (Ahonen, 2009). The global popularity of mobile phones, together with advances in mobile technology, offers new business and revenue opportunities to a wider market.

Businesses can use mobile technology to boost their productivity rate. The mobility and flexibility provided by mobile devices makes communication easier as employees can send and receive emails, create or edit documents or access company data from any location. Employees on the move can reach customers directly, at any time, regardless of geography, reducing response time, offering a more individualized and accurate service, and so improving customer relations. In addition, mobile devices can be more convenient as they are quicker to boot up than a PC or laptop. Speed of information access can be crucial for a business's competitive advantage.

This mobile web access can be combined with mobile marketing to great effect. Advertising can take the form of multimedia banners on the screen, email

6

CASE STUDY   Facebook

Facebook, founded in 2004, is a social networking website that allows interaction among people and helps them to connect with friends, relatives and co-workers. It offers a virtual space where members can chat, share photos, form groups, buy/sell products and play games. Mark Zuckerberg, one of the founders and a Harvard sophomore at that time, wrote codes for a website that allowed the posting of profiles of Harvard students, which was extended to include students from other universities and later went on to develop as Facebook.com.

Initial investments for the company came from venture capitalists and as the site developed, further finance was sourced externally. In its present form, the company regularly attracts investors and has its international offices in London, Dublin, Paris, Milan, Stockholm, Toronto and Sydney. Anyone over the age of 13 with an active email account can become a Facebook user. The website primarily targets adults and has a global reach in terms of its coverage. Recent estimates note that Facebook is typically active in western markets; it is the most popular social networking site with users in Europe, Canada and Australia and has a near monopoly in these markets. In the US market, it is fast catching up with MySpace and according to recent reports, it will overtake MySpace to become the most influential US social utility website by 2010.

The tag of the most dominant social networking website is backed up by some impressive figures:

- it has over 500 million active users – as of July 2010
- it adds approximately 200,000 users every week
- it accounts for 5.0% of all page views on the internet
- more than 30% of global internet users visit Facebook every day
- it is ranked second only to Google in overall website traffic statistics
- more than 700,000 websites link with Facebook
- approximately 4.1 billion photos have been uploaded since its inception
- it accounted for nearly 390 million unique users for the first three months of 2010
- site statistics indicate that, on average, a user spends about 30 minutes interacting with the website
- in English-speaking countries, Facebook is the market leader; its nearest rivals are MySpace, Bebo, LinkedIn, Hi5, Friendster and Open Social.

Facebook faces competition from regionally dominated social utility sites. Facebook lags behind companies in non-English speaking countries, which can offer social networking in native languages. For example, the Chinese language site qq.com is popular not only in China but also in Taiwan and other Southeast Asian countries. Similarly, the Arabic site Maktoob.com dominates the Middle Eastern market.

The domination of Facebook can be explored by examining the products and services it offers the market. Facebook's products can be broadly divided into two categories:

1   core site functions relating to products like inbox, profiles, networks, friends
2   applications like photos, notes, posted items and any other third party application a user decides to add to their profile account.

These work in tandem to offer a unique user experience that not only allows them to mimic real-world social interactions but also create newer ones that are exclusive to the online medium. For example, a user account has a fundamental profile page, which contains inbox, chat window, networks and pages. These features allow communication and information sharing between users and form the basis of the social networking platform. The applications are there to enhance user experience. Photo applications allow users to upload their pictures and another application allows them to be rotated, cut, edited and tagged. The group application allows users to create groups and invite other users who share similar ideas and viewpoints to join them. Yet another application allows users to sell/buy products through the online marketplace, while mobile applications allow interaction through mobile phones. This combination of core products and applications plays a major part in creating environments of extreme personalization and experiences that are distinctive and inimitable.

At the root of Facebook's success is technology, its own proprietary technology as well third party content developers. Facebook not only develops its own technology but also encourages third party participation in the development of applications through open source platforms and software. Overall, Facebook has agreements with more than

80,000 developers to come up with applications that are innovative, useful and can offer distinct user experiences. Facebook has its own custom-built search engine and an efficient remote procedure call framework. These technologies allow rapid information retrieval and a seamless integration of various subsystems written in a myriad of programming languages. Apart from its own technology, Facebook's strength lies in its ability to embrace open source software. Facebook was developed from open source software and the company actively encourages engineers and independent programmers to work with open source software and platforms. It provides opportunities for external companies and developers to produce applications that can be integrated and run from Facebook's platforms. This adoption of open source software has helped Facebook to come out with applications that not only provide a varied and a unique consumer experience but also a core competence against its rivals and competitors.

Facebook has 1,200+ employees and is privately owned – its founders still have control over the company and it is not listed in any of the world's stock markets. This means that very little information regarding its revenue and balance sheet information is available. Primarily, Facebook earns its revenues through onsite advertising and the sale of virtual goods; reports from popular research firms (TBI

Research, Inside Facebook) indicate that the company earned about $640m (2009) in revenues from online advertising and a further $10m from the sale of virtual goods. According to Zuckerberg, in 2009, the company registered a cash flow positive for the first time and there is an expectation that it will reach the magical figure of $1bn in revenues by 2010. The private nature of the company and the inaccuracies with revenue information make it difficult to estimate the value of Facebook, but it is said to be worth around $10–15bn and there are talks of the company going public. Notwithstanding the huge valuation, it is expected to achieve operating profits in 2010 and with its significant user base, it may very well do so.

Case study questions

1 Do you think Facebook's sources of revenue are sustainable? Can online firms make a profit? What other opportunities are available for Facebook to increase its revenues?

2 As a technology-intensive organization, what are the pros and cons of Facebook's open source platform strategy?

3 It is said that Facebook benefits from network externalities and is highly dependent on huge user numbers. Do you agree with this?

---

messages or advertising within mobile games or videos. Using global positioning systems (GPS), marketers can send targeted, location-sensitive adverts directly to mobile devices such as adverts for local restaurants or shops.

There is currently much research being conducted to enable mobile phones to be used as an electronic wallet, as an alternative to debit/credits cards. This is already popular in Japan, where mobile technology tends to be more advanced, and enables customers to make payments or purchases in stores using their phones (Sutter, 2009). Banks are also carrying out research to enable customers to use their mobile handsets to carry out banking services such as accessing account information, bill payments and money transfers (McGlasson, 2008). This means that mobile phones can be used not only to retrieve information quickly and efficiently, but also to compare prices and make payments from the one small device.

Other business examples of the mobile web include:

- estate agents have used mobile technology to display houses to potential buyers as they are travelling around viewing properties (Roberts, 2007)
- iPhone customers can upload airline tickets to their phone and scan the barcode directly rather than printing the ticket (Sutter, 2009)
- many restaurants now use mobile technology such as PDAs for wireless ordering so that a customer's order can immediately be sent and displayed on an electronic board in the kitchen. Such systems can also be connected to stock and ingredient ordering systems
- in storerooms, wireless inventory checking allows for speedy customer feedback and faster decision-making

6

- eBay mobile allows users of the auction site to keep in touch with their sales or bids and to be notified if they are outbid
- the sports website ESPN has, on occasion, had more fans check its mobile website for up-to-date scores than its PC site (Cuneo, 2007)
- tracking deliveries, such as pizza deliveries from Domino's or Papa John's.

18.5   Issues in the digital age

There are several important issues around the digital age, such as the digital divide and how to overcome it, information overload and the privacy of data, and these are discussed in some detail.

The digital divide

The web has the potential to improve lives through access to a greater amount of information than ever before, which, in turn, can lead to greater equity among society. However, it is recognized that not everyone has the same access to the technology required to retrieve the vast amount of information available, share global knowledge or compete through global markets. The digital divide refers to the gap between those who own, or have access to, technology and the web and those who do not. The divide not only refers to access to the physical equipment but also those who have limited skills to use the technology to access the associated information. Table 18.1 outlines some of the factors associated with the digital divide.

> The **digital divide** refers to the gap between those who own, or have access to, technology and the web and those who do not.

Table 18.1 **Factors associated with the digital divide**

Socioeconomic	Lack of computer ownership or access to web, which may be linked to income
Education	Lack of education and training leading to poor online skills
Employment	Those in professional occupations tend to have the skills and access to technology as part of their job, while manual workers or the unemployed do not
Generational	Older people who did not grow up with the technology may not be as at ease using it as younger people
Attitudinal	Willingness to use and learn new technology, which may be related to computer anxiety
Disabilities	Although the web may provide some people with disabilities access to facilities otherwise unavailable, it must be provided in a format that is accessible for different disabilities
Language	More than 50% of websites are written in English, therefore users require proficiency in the English language
Geographical	People who reside in rural areas or citizens of underdeveloped, poorer countries may not have broadband access
Security	Users may have various fears about the security of personal information or concerns by parents of children accessing unsuitable content

The digital divide can exist both within and between countries but what may be the greatest divide is the gap between developed and underdeveloped countries (Cullen, 2001).

Bridging the global divide

In the developed world, individual governments generally have policies in place to bridge the divide in their respective country, which can range from funding for community access to technology to telecommunications infrastructure to educational initiatives (Cullen, 2001) but these are not suitable for all countries. Although access to the web may be rare in some of the poorest parts of the world, there are currently some projects designed to help overcome this problem. The One Laptop per Child project (http://laptop.org/en/) aims to distribute inexpensive and robust laptops to schoolchildren in developing countries throughout the world. This project is described not as a technology project but as an educational project to provide skills and access to IT to empower children out of poverty and help the future economies of the countries involved.

Mobile phone technology is likely to improve web access in some rural communities and is already helping to bridge the divide in some areas. In Africa, the number of mobile phones subscriptions has risen from 16 million in 2000 to more than 280 million in 2009 (Rudebeck, 2009). This technology can help reduce isolation in some areas; for example, in Kenya, farmers can access prices from fruit and vegetable markets, and in Brazil, the unemployed are sent information on job opportunities by text. However, this, in itself, can lead to a further divide between those who own a mobile phone and those who do not (Rudebeck, 2009).

Information overload

The different technologies that can be used to access and communicate information, for example emails, mobile phones, blogs, social networks, together with the ease of publishing information on the internet, have led to a rapid increase in the amount of information available. When using a search engine to find information online, it is common to obtain results listing many thousands of websites. In addition, since these sites can be written and published by anyone, they may not provide information of any quality or accuracy. Users of the web must be aware of the issues involved in finding accurate and relevant information and be able to evaluate websites to differentiate between good and bad. There are no strict guidelines to evaluate the quality of websites but factors such as ensuring the website is up to date, author credentials, authority or publishing body and links to other quality sites can help to give an indication of quality.

Search engine features can be used to filter and so obtain fewer, more relevant results. Using the advanced search features to enter accurate search terms (and excluding other terms) can help to improve results. Search engines are becoming more sophisticated and increasingly more personalized and can now track a user's interests and previous searches to produce more relevant personalized results. Google takes into account a user's location through their computer's IP address to enable localized research results (Google, 2009). The latest metasearch engines, such as Yippy (http://search.yippy.com/), cluster results into subsets, and the search engine Mooter (www.mooter.com) can present these clusters visually (Mostafa, 2005).

Businesses can use search engine optimization strategies to help improve their ranking within search result listings. Although individual search engines will not disclose exactly how they calculate the ranking of individual websites,

6

they include consideration of the number of occurrences of keywords within the page, number of previous hits and links to the site from other quality sites. It is also common to pay for sponsorship to enable a page to receive an enhanced place within the results list.

Privacy of data

The vast amount of data derived from global business activities, together with the increase in Web 2.0 applications designed to encourage sharing of information, has inevitably led to issues regarding the privacy and security of personal data.

The online activities of web users can be tracked through the use of cookies. Cookies are computer programs designed to collect information on a user's browsing activities, which provides important information on that person's interests, preferences and so on. Although users can block the use of cookies on their machine, the ethics of the use of such programs is debatable.

> **Cookies** are computer programs designed to collect information on a user's browsing activities, which provides important information on that person's interests, preferences and so on.

Within the working environment, technology exists that can be used to monitor the online activity of a workforce such as keystroke tracking, web browsing or email monitoring. Although various countries' legal systems offer different guidelines on how such surveillance methods can or cannot be used – and an employer may argue that they are being utilized to provide a safe working environment or safeguard intellectual property – there are still ethical arguments over employees' rights to privacy.

When dealing with the privacy and security of personal data, it is important to distinguish between the data obtained through business transactions as opposed to the voluntary sharing of personal information on social networking sites. Members of such sites are often happy to disclose their activities, likes and dislikes, which can provide a wealth of useful information for marketers. On the other hand, businesses must protect any personal data obtained during business transactions to avoid adverse disclosure or threats from security misdemeanours, such as hacking or identity theft.

Despite attempts to standardize international guidelines on privacy, to date no uniform global regulation exists, with different countries offering different guidelines or legislation on data protection and privacy (Wafa, 2009). Therefore complex privacy issues exist for data that is sent from country to country and businesses cannot assume that the legislation of the country in which they primarily operate will satisfy the requirements in other countries that they may deal with.

In a high-profile case in 2000 involving Yahoo! Inc and LICRA, the main object of contention was whether the French judicial system had the power to address content on Yahoo!'s international American website. The French legal system wanted to block content relating to the sale of Nazi memorabilia to French visitors of the website, but Yahoo! argued that while it could block the content on the French version (Yahoo.fr) of the website, it could not do the same on its international site (Yahoo.com), which is governed by American law and jurisdiction. Since both the French and the American version were freely available to French consumers, the question was how to selectively block the objectionable content to the target audience. In the end, Yahoo! was forced to accept the French court's rulings.

18.6   Management issues and strategies for web activity

It is becoming increasingly difficult for businesses to gain competitive advantage through activities such as cost cutting or mergers and acquisitions (Robinson, 2008), therefore managers must consider more innovative ways to improve business performance. The web is now an integral part of everyday life and is increasingly central to business activities. This chapter has highlighted how the web can offer many innovative business opportunities, including how it can:

- Change the business model
- Provide a wealth of information – formal and informal
- Increase market for products and services
- Improve efficiency
- Improve flexibility
- Increase mobility of the workforce
- Improve customer relations
- Increase internal and external collaboration
- Provide information for direct marketing
- Personalization of products or services.

It is crucial that managers understand the potential and role that the web may play as well as the value, impact and competitive advantage that can be gained from its effective use. The strategy for web activity must fit with the overall business strategy, otherwise any investment in time and money may be more than the potential value gained, or even be detrimental to achieving overall business goals. Therefore anyone involved in designing or setting up web activities should be aware of the overall business objectives and priorities to ensure that all activities work towards achieving the same business goals.

When designing a strategy for web activity, management must first consider the extent of the web presence required. Questions to address must include:

- What does the web presence hope to achieve?
- What extent of business operations will be conducted via the web?
- Will the web be used to widen the market – to go global?
- Who are our customers?
- How are they likely to access the web (PC or mobile)?
- Will the web presence be a 'shop-front' website for product or service information? Or will it also be used to:
    - build alliances with other businesses?
    - accept customer queries, orders or payments?
    - incorporate Web 2.0 features such as blogs, wikis and social networking?

The following sections expand on the questions that management must address when designing the strategy for web activity.

Website design and content strategy

Any business website must work towards the overall business goals and ensure that the correct business image is portrayed. Therefore a content strategy should be in place to ensure that the website reflects businesses objectives, priorities and activities. Managers must define roles and responsibilities so that content is edited and presented in a uniform manner as well as ensuring that information on the website is well written, relevant, accurate, up to date, easy to navigate and

6

optimizes the relationship with customers. There should also be mechanisms in place that consider:

- *Search engine optimization:* can customers find appropriate information about the business when using a search engine? If the business name is entered in a search engine, it should appear towards the top of the results listing. If not, keyword advertising and sponsorship may be considered.
- *Tracking statistics:* how many people, and who, is accessing the website?
- *Cross-linking:* what other websites does the site link to and vice versa?
- *Advertising:* should there be advertising on the business website? If so, it must be consistent with the purpose and image of the website.

Interaction with other businesses

The web can be used to build alliances with other businesses, making it easier to communicate, and buy and sell to others in the supply chain. The strategy for web activity must take into consideration if the web will be used to link with other businesses and, if so, which businesses; what links will be set up for (communicating, ordering, transfer of payment and so on); and who will be responsible for setting up the alliance and ensuring security.

Interaction with customers

There are many ways that the web can be used to interact with customers, therefore the strategy for web activity must also consider if the web will be used to interact with customers and how. This may be through the ordering of products or services, payment for products or services, and communication with customers. If setting up ordering and payment systems, security is paramount and customers must be confident that their details are protected.

Communication with customers can involve simple feedback through email or feedback forms, or wider communication using Web 2.0 applications. Web 2.0 applications such as blogs, wikis or social networking can be used to generate lots of valuable information but the strategy implemented must ensure that the information is used productively and that there is a return on investment. As part of the strategy, the following must be considered:

- What type of communication is being promoted?
- What is the most appropriate application for the purpose?
- What type of content should be included?
- Who will write content and keep it up to date?
- What writing style should be adopted?
- Who will manage comments and feedback?

Management must also understand that Web 2.0 can change the type of communication and how people express themselves to one that is more sociable, open and public and is only suitable for certain types of information. Communicating openly and promoting participation with customers can be used to gain valuable feedback as well as increase customer loyalty. However, it can also lead to negative feedback from them, so any strategy for the use of Web 2.0 must consider reputation monitoring. There must be procedures in place to regularly check the web for anything that might be negative to the business and to react quickly and effectively to such negativity. This may involve responding directly to negative feedback, making visible, positive statements to counteract customer complaints, and ensuring that positive (or even neutral) information is highly visible.

Businesses must also determine the most likely technologies that customers will use to access the web. Mobile web access is increasingly common, so part of the strategy for web activity may include a mobile strategy. The business may need a different web presence for mobile access, allowing customers with mobile devices to view the content more easily. Since mobile users may be accessing the website for only specific information or features, the content of the mobile web presence must be designed accordingly. Other factors to consider may include payment via mobile devices and using GPS to offer location-specific information.

Any web strategy should take into consideration issues associated with the digital age, as highlighted above. Understanding their customers in terms of social status, education, employment, age and so on will help a business to address issues associated with the digital divide. For example, there is little point in a business developing a complex web presence if their typical customers do not have access to web technology or have the skills or desire to use it. Understanding the geography of the customer base will determine if a global web presence is required and/or the language(s) required.

Global aspects

If the web is used as a tool to conduct business on a global scale, the strategy for the web presence must address international issues. Conducting business on a global scale requires cultural awareness – not only language translation but the business practice may have to be adopted to reflect the different cultures and take account of cultural differences. Pricing policies and shipping arrangements as well as contact information may also be required locally. In addition, the web presence must satisfy the legal and data protection requirements in all countries in which the business operates. This may involve designing a different web presence for all different countries and recruiting international lawyers to ensure they adhere to legal requirements of every country.

Privacy of data

The strategy must also include procedures that consider the privacy and security associated with the storage of customer data as well as any business transactions carried out over the web. Customers must be confident that the business has security procedures in place to protect customer data and ensure that the risk of security breaches is minimized. A visible privacy policy on a website is a way of communicating the importance of security and privacy of data to customers. This may include information such as what information the business collects, how it is collected, what it is used for, how customers can view and check their own information and how they can change it, if desired.

For test questions, extra case studies, audio case studies, weblinks, videolinks and more to help you understand the topics covered in this chapter, visit our companion website at www.macmillanihe.com/companion/business/campbell.

REVIEW QUESTIONS

1 Explain the impact the web has had on business.
2 Explain what we mean by the digital divide and how it can be resolved.
3 Evaluate the different web technologies and explain what Web 2.0 is.

DISCUSSION TOPIC

There is a popular belief that online networking sites like Facebook are detrimental to society – 'it further alienates people'. Discuss.

HOT TOPICS – Research project areas to investigate

For your research project, why not investigate ...

- ... how organizations use Web 2.0 technology to improve customer service.
- ... the extent to which the digital divide disadvantages users of government services.
- ... how mobile technologies could be used to improve efficiency of the supply chain of a ... organization.

Recommended reading

Fuller, A.W. and Thursby, M.C (2008) 'Technology commercialization: cooperative versus competitive strategies', *Advances in the Study of Entrepreneurship, Innovation & Economic Growth*, 18: 227–50.

O'Reilly, T. (2007) 'What is Web 2.0: design patterns and business models for the next generation of software', *Communications and Strategies*, **65**(1): 17–38.

Shuen, A. (2008) *Web 2.0: A Strategy Guide: Business Thinking and Strategies behind Successful Web 2.0 Implementations*, Cambridge: O'Reilly Books.

Weitz, B.A. (2001) Electronic retailing: market dynamics and entrepreneurial opportunities, in G.D. Libecap (ed.) *Entrepreneurship and Economic Growth in the American Economy*, vol. 12, Elsevier Science.

Chapter references

Ahonen, T. (2009) *Tomi Ahonen Almanac 2009: Mobile Telecoms Industry Review*, eBook, http://www.tomiahonen.com/.

Anderson, C. (2004) 'The long tail', http://www.wired.com/wired/archive/12.10/tail.html.

BBC (2009) 'Twitter tweets are 40% babble', http://news.bbc.co.uk/1/hi/technology/8204842.stm.

Cachia, R., Compano, R. and Da Costa, O. (2007) 'Grasping the potential of online social networks for foresight',

Technological Forecasting and Social Change, **74**(8): 1179–203.

Cullen, R. (2001) 'Addressing the digital divide', *Online Information Review*, **25**(5): 311–20.

Cuneo, A. (2008) 'More football fans hit ESPN's mobile site than its PC pages', *Advertising Age*, January, https://adage.com/.

Deloitte (2003) 'Online travel agents cast their web wide', http://www.htrends.com/researcharticle7447.html.

Google (2009) 'Google becomes more local', http://googleblog.blogspot.com/2009/04/google-becomes-more-local.html.

IBM (2008) 'The enterprise of the future ... in the travel industry', http://www-935.ibm.com/services/us/gbs/bus/pdf/gbe03111-usen-ceo-travel.pdf.

Jin, L. (2009) 'Businesses using Twitter, Facebook to market goods', http://www.post-gazette.com/pg/09172/978727-96.stm.

McGlasson, L. (2008) 'Emerging technologies: mobile banking, remote capture are key to attracting gen Y', http://www.bankinfosecurity.com/articles.php?art_id=897.

Mostafa, J. (2005) 'Seeking better web searches', *Scientific American*, **292**(2): 51–7.

Roberts, G. (2007) 'Trends in mobile technology, part 2: mobile matters in real estate', http://www.taggline.com/Mobile_Matters_Part2.pdf.

Robinson, R. (2008) 'Enterprise Web 2.0, Part 1: Web 2.0 – catching a wave of business innovation', http://www.ibm.com/developerworks/webservices/library/ws-enterprise1/.

Rudebeck, C. (2009) 'Closing the digital divide: how the spread of ICT is improving quality of life for millions in the third world', http://www.independent.co.uk/news/business/sustainit/closing-the-digital-divide-1640433.html.

Sutter, J.D. (2009) 'Wallet of the future? Your mobile phone', http://www.cnn.com/2009/TECH/08/13/cell.phone.wallet/index.html?eref=rss_tech.

Vasquez, D. (2006) 'Growing ad appeal of social networks: advertisers are beginning to overcome their fears', http://www.medialifemagazine.com/cgi-bin/artman/exec/view.cgi?archive=398&num=8514.

Wafa, T. (2009) 'Cyberspace law and internet regulation – global internet privacy rights: a pragmatic approach', *University of San Francisco Intellectual Property Law Bulletin*, **13**(2): 131–58.

6

Chapter 19
Quality

Introduction and chapter overview

The strategic development of many companies has been marked by recognition that good quality in operations can contribute significantly to competitive advantage, so we have seen the emergence and prominence of concepts such as service quality, Six Sigma, lean sigma and quality frameworks. In particular, total quality management (TQM) is seen by many companies as an important part of this operational emphasis, especially for those that aim to be world-class organizations. In order to recognize the importance of quality, each of the world's major industrialized nations has its own quality award. These awards act as an important strategic tool and can assist in an organization's product and market positioning.

In this chapter, we explain how this emphasis on quality management has come about and explore the main features demonstrated by those organizations that have successfully adopted a TQM philosophy. Key features of the quality award frameworks are discussed and, finally, the chapter explains the various types of operational benchmarking in common use.

Learning objectives

After studying this chapter, you should be able to:

- define quality and total quality management
- explain how TQM evolved
- explain the main principles of TQM
- describe and distinguish between the enablers and results elements of the EFQM excellence model
- describe how self-assessment frameworks are used and say what benefits they can bring to businesses
- distinguish between the different types of benchmarking and explain the benefits of each

19.1 Quality as a strategic imperative

The most important set of factors that impact on any organization's operations strategy are those set by the customers. The purpose of any operation's function is to manage the value-adding activities inside the business in such a way that customer requirements are met in full.

What 'matters' to the customer will, of course, vary from market to market. For each element of product that is of concern to a customer, organizations will have an internal response that facilitates the satisfaction of that concern. The most successful businesses are those that can most effectively configure their operations to meet customer requirements.

The various areas of focus for an organization when developing a competitive strategy are listed in Table 19.1 below. It is notable from this list just how important quality and customer focus become in the overall strategy. The quality of products (goods and services) can be seen to extend from the original design, to on-time delivery, reliability in service, through to after-sales service. This is what we mean by 'customer-driven quality'.

Quality begins with the quality of product design. Do the specifications achieve what the customer wants? Does the company fully understand customers' needs and requirements? Quality extends into the manufacturing or service processes. Can the company deliver the products at the right price? The efficiency of work processes and the competences of employees need to be such that products can be made cost-effectively and consistently to design specifications. Have all wasteful processes, those which do not add value, been eliminated? In the case of service operations, the customer is often in face-to-face contact with the employee providing the service. The customer should feel confident that the service is speedy, professional, efficient and provides value for money.

Product reliability is another important issue. From the customers' perspective, product reliability is measured by the product's functional performance and so the product must perform as expected. Continuous good functional performance over time is also important. The product must continue performing throughout what the customer considers to be a reasonable life expectancy. Reliable, fast delivery of products or off-the-shelf availability of consumer products is also a major consideration. Can the company meet the delivery lead time requirements? Does it do so reliably and consistently? In the case of service industries, the service provided is less tangible than physical products and therefore it is often the customers' perception of the reliability and timeliness of the service provided that is important.

For many businesses, 'what really matters to customers' can be seen to extend beyond the above issues. Customer-driven quality often requires innovation and the use of cutting-edge technologies. This innovation can be applied to materials

Table 19.1 Factors affecting customer-driven quality and the operating performance characteristics of an organization

What matters to customers in selecting a product purchase	How a business responds to customer demands
Low price (value for money)	Producing efficiently at low or reasonable unit cost
High-quality products and services	Building quality into processes and products
Fast delivery	Having short manufacturing lead times, finished goods stock or fast distribution
Product and service reliability	Building reliability into products and delivering dependable service
Innovation, using cutting-edge technologies	Keeping abreast of latest developments and emphasizing R&D
Wide product choice	Responding to change and providing a wide product mix
Responsive to changes in customer requirements	Being flexible and responding quickly to volume and delivery changes

6

and product design, or even to manufacturing processes or the way services and facilities are provided.

The list in Table 19.1 is useful as a starting point to identifying the wide range of issues that must be addressed by manufacturing and service sector organizations in the quest to become leaders in their own markets. Many 'winning' organizations – those with a competitive advantage in their industry – have arrived at the conclusion that one area of concern in operations is more important than any other – quality.

19.2   Quality and quality management

A number of academics and practitioners have attempted to provide a coherent definition of quality. The fact that there are so many definitions is testimony to the fact that it is a complicated matter on which to agree.

For a common product such as a car, we might think of quality as referring to reliability, build or safety features. For a service such as plastering a wall, we would probably arrive at a different set of things to describe a 'quality' job, such as the finish of the surface, the flushness of the edges and the extent to which it is even. It is the fact that the quality criteria vary from product to product that makes it difficult to agree on a definition.

Some of the most noted thinkers in the field have described quality with respect to 'excellence' or, more accurately, 'perceived excellence'. Although quality means many things to different people, in general, we can consider quality as meeting customer needs or expectations. Table 19.2 summarizes some of the most widely used definitions, while the major thinkers in this area are described in Table 19.3.

Table 19.2 **Some definitions of quality**

Quality guru	Definition of quality
Deming	Quality should be aimed at meeting the needs of the consumer, present and future
Juran	Quality is fitness for the purpose for which the product is intended
Crosby	Quality is conformance to requirements, either customer requirements or the specification predetermined for it
Oakland	Quality is meeting customer requirements

KEY CONCEPT

A **quality guru** is someone who has been recognized for their contribution to the management of quality within business and whose messages have led to major changes in the way organizations operate. There are a number people who are highly regarded as major contributors in the field of quality management, including Juran, Deming and Peters.

Table 19.3 **The quality gurus**

Quality guru	Main messages
W. Edwards Deming	Sometimes referred to as 'the father of TQM', Deming believed that bad management is responsible for more than 90% of quality problems. He argued that quality improvement is achieved by continuous reduction in process variation using statistical process control and employee involvement. Later, Deming developed his 'system of profound knowledge', in which he stressed the need for the organization to operate as a coherent system with everybody working together towards the overall aims. Good quality relies in large part on an understanding of the nature of variation (statistical theory), careful planning and prediction based on experience. Finally, he stressed the importance of psychology, recognizing the relationships of extrinsic and extrinsic motivation factors in the workplace
Joseph M. Juran	Juran proposed a general management approach with human elements. He believed that less than 20% of quality problems were due to the workers themselves. He defined quality as 'fitness for use'. Juran recommended a project approach to improvements by setting targets, planning to achieve targets set, assigning responsibility, and rewarding results achieved
Armand V. Feigenbaum	Feigenbaum proposed a systematic approach of total quality control involving every employee and all functions. He emphasized the need for 'quality-mindedness' through employee participation. He made the point that expenditure on prevention costs would lead to an overall reduction in product failure costs
Kaoru Ishikawa	Ishikawa stressed the importance of statistical methods, using his 'seven tools of quality' for problem solving. Also recognized for his contributions to the company-wide quality control movement, involving all staff at all levels through 'quality circles'
Genichi Taguchi	Taguchi developed the 'quality loss function' concerned with the optimization of products and processes prior to manufacture. His methods can be applied in the design phase of products or systems, or in production to optimize process variables
Shigeo Shingo	Shingo introduced a practical approach to achieve zero defects. With careful design of products and tooling systems, he eliminated the need for sample inspection, through his system of mistake proofing known as 'poka-yoke'. He is also acknowledged for his work on fast tooling changeovers. Commonly known as SMED (single minute exchange of dies), this is one of the most important contributions to JIT (just-in-time) operating systems
Philip B. Crosby	Crosby's 14-step approach to quality improvement sets out to achieve conformance to requirements through prevention not inspection. Believing that 'quality is free' and 'zero defects' should be the target, Crosby rejected statistically acceptable levels of quality. He believed in a 'top-down' approach to quality management and proposed his four absolutes of quality: quality is defined as conformance to requirements; the system of quality is prevention; the performance standard is zero defects; the measurement of quality is the financial cost of nonconformance
Tom Peters	Peters' early work stressed the importance of visible leadership and he encouraged MBWA (management by walking about), giving managers the opportunity to listen and solve problems through face-to-face contact with workers. His later work focused on customer orientation and he stressed that managers need to be 'obsessed' with quality, never accepting shoddy goods. He recognized that everyone needs to be trained in quality tools, and supported the use of cross-functional teams. He believed that organizations should overcome complacency by creating 'endless Hawthorne effects' (after the work of Elton Mayo) through the generation of new goals and environments. He also stressed the importance of the role of suppliers and customers in the quest for improvement

6

Historical perspective of quality

Quality has been an issue for as long as business has been carried out. For traditional crafts such as masons, blacksmiths, tailors, thatchers and carpenters, it was the craftsmen themselves who were responsible for the price, delivery and degree of quality of their wares and services. Reputations were established on the quality of workmanship, which in turn led to more demand for their skills and higher levels of profitability and prosperity for the individual. The more successful 'masters' recruited apprentices and employed other tradesmen, and quality was assured informally and depended on the pride that each individual had in their own work. In Europe, craft guilds were established, which aimed to ensure that adequate training was given and that apprentices 'qualified' only when they were demonstrably capable of producing adequate standards of workmanship. Much of this pride in workmanship was lost during the Industrial Revolution in the late 18th century with the introduction of machinery and high-volume manufacturing. However, large-scale production methods brought about a need to ensure consistent reproduction of parts, manufactured to exacting specifications and so the concept of 'quality control' was born.

In the early 1900s, Frederick W. Taylor introduced his ideas on scientific management. His methodology was to separate the planning (thinking) function from the physical work elements in production. By breaking down each job into smaller elements of work, he was able to train workers to perform simple mechanical tasks, which comprised only a part of the total production process. High-volume repeatability allowed gains in speed and efficiency, and this in turn led to cheaper products. Quality control techniques enabled specially trained inspectors to test finished components against a predetermined specification. This enabled defective parts to be identified and then removed or reworked before they reached the customer.

Frederick **Winslow Taylor** was born in Philadelphia in 1856. His early education was at Philips Exeter Academy in New Hampshire and in 1873 he joined the Midvale Steel Works as an apprentice pattern maker. Later on he became the chief engineer in the firm. Taylor obtained a degree in mechanical engineering from Stevens Institute of Technology. From 1890 to 1893 he was employed as a consulting engineer to management at the Manufacturing Investment Company of Philadelphia.

He joined the faculty of Tuck School of Business at Dartmouth College and was one of the first figures to offer management consultancy services to firms. He was awarded an honorary doctorate from the University of Pennsylvania. Professor Taylor won a gold medal at the Paris Exposition in 1900 for developing high-speed steel and was a recipient of the Elliott Cresson Medal awarded by the Franklin Institute, Philadelphia. He died in 1915.

He is regarded as the founding father of scientific management and is one of the most influential figures in the study of social sciences.

The modern quality movement

The modern quality movement began in the 1950s. The demand for goods and merchandise saw western industrial nations producing higher volumes of product, with a resulting decline in quality. In Japan, during the rebuilding of its industrial base after the Second World War, help was given by a number of management consultants. In particular, the work of Deming and Juran led the Japanese to completely review the accepted views on quality management.

GURU GUIDE

William Edwards Deming was born in 1900 in Iowa. He worked as a mathematical physicist with the US Department of Agriculture for nearly 12 years before becoming a statistical adviser to the US Census Bureau. He has also been a professor of statistics at New York University's Graduate School of Business Administration.

Professor Deming is a quality guru and was instrumental in developing concepts related to the statistical control of processes and overall quality management. He is widely credited for improving production in the USA and is known for his work in revitalizing Japanese industries after the Second World War, contributing to Japan's later reputation for high-quality, innovative products. From 1950 onward in Japan, he taught top management how to improve design (and thus service), product quality, testing and sales. He was a consultant for a number of private firms and was involved in the compilation of American War Standards. He is credited for introducing the concept of total quality management and for the application of statistical methods to improve the design and manufacture of products. He died in 1993.

Statistical quality control techniques were introduced to reduce variation in the production processes. Much emphasis was placed on the way that quality was managed, rather than simply concentrating on the technical issues. The focus shifted from one of quality inspection to one of preventing quality problems. Management began educating and involving all employees to look for ways to improve product quality and work methods. The Japanese developed a new culture of continuous improvement, where everyone was encouraged to believe that they had two jobs – doing the work and improving the work. They called this approach 'kaizen'.

The kaizen process begins with an examination of the work processes and operating practices, continuously looking for improvement opportunities. It is important that every employee strives for improvement and so an acceptance of kaizen by the organizational culture is an important element. Employees are empowered to experiment and make incremental changes and are sometimes provided with their own limited budgets for doing so. It is important that kaizen activities are actively supported by management, who will usually provide additional resources if required, perhaps when ideas for change are complex, requiring technical expertise, extra finance or help in other ways.

This new manufacturing philosophy gradually evolved and led to the Japanese domination in manufacturing industries by the late 1970s. During the 1980s, the rest of the world awoke to this transformation and the TQM movement was born.

Joseph Moses Juran was born in 1904 in Braila, Romania. With his family, he immigrated to the USA in 1912 and graduated with a bachelor's degree in electrical engineering from the University of Minnesota in 1924. As a hedge against the uncertainties of the Great Depression, Juran qualified as a lawyer, although he never practised. He joined the faculty of New York University as an adjunct professor in the industrial engineering department, and after the Second World War became a freelance consultant. His many clients included Gilette, Bausch & Lomb, General Foods and Borg-Warner.

Juran, well known for his work in quality management, was a prolific figure in introducing statistical testing and control chart techniques in manufacturing process. He wrote several books on quality management and his work with Bell Labs in promoting quality control made him one of the most influential figures in TQM. He died in 2008.

KEY CONCEPTS

Kaizen is a culturally embedded concept of continual improvement pioneered in Japanese companies. It concentrates on small gradual changes involving all employees in every area of business. According to Imai (1986), it is 'the single most important concept in Japanese management – the key to Japanese competitive success'. Kaizen is process-oriented change, involving operators continuously searching for better ways to do their job.

Kaizen teams take responsibility for identifying opportunities for improvement. Typically, ideas for change will be investigated, tested and measured by the team. Any savings in job cycle time, even a few seconds, will be introduced as the new standard method of production. Staff are encouraged to participate in kaizen teams and are given full training in problem-solving tools and techniques.

19.3 Total quality management

Total quality management (TQM) is a holistic approach, which provides awareness of the customer–supplier relationship and continuous improvement effort in all departments and functions.

Today, total quality management (TQM) is a holistic approach, which provides awareness of the customer–supplier relationship and continuous improvement effort in all departments and functions. Much has been written on the subject of TQM, and the philosophy means many things to different people.

Some have used an external customer focus, aiming to ensure employee awareness of customer needs and an elimination of faulty goods or services. Others have focused on the use of quality tools, such as brainstorming, statistical tools or control charts, to encourage problem solving and a right-first-time attitude. Many have used teamwork and 'empowerment' in an effort to develop a 'quality' culture, to improve staff motivation and an ongoing cycle of quality improvement.

There are as many approaches to TQM as there are consultants selling their own formula for success, but whatever the approach, the following features of TQM are usually present:

- it is strongly led by senior management
- it is customer oriented
- it recognizes internal customers in the value chain and external customers

- it represents a fundamental change away from *controlling* bad quality to *preventing* bad quality from happening – it *causes* good quality
- it encourages a right-first-time approach to all activities
- everybody is made responsible for quality
- there is an emphasis on kaizen
- training and quality tools are introduced in support of the quality regime
- employees are encouraged to look for ways for improving quality in their own areas, for example by process 'tightening'
- the introduction of measurement systems to eliminate and control waste.

Waste describes any activity in an operations process that is not value adding. It costs money but does not create value commensurate with its cost. Examples include:

- process inefficiency, say, as a result of bad design
- any process that does not add value, such as unnecessary inspection activities or materials handling activities, say, from station to station in the process
- any stock that is not actually being processed and to which value is therefore not being added. This includes all raw materials, all FG and any WIP that is queuing between production stages
- stocks that have failed a quality test, either in-process or at final quality control
- machine 'downtime', that is, production time lost through machines not being operable for any reason such as breakdown or through tooling up or tooling down between batches
- the time and stock involved in producing unsold or unsaleable stocks.

> **Waste** describes any activity in an operations process that is not value adding. It costs money but does not create value commensurate with its cost.

Oakland's model for total quality management

A number of frameworks for TQM have been developed. The earliest were proposed by academics trying to explain and rationalize the TQM concepts, to facilitate implementation by managers in industry. Many business consultants followed with their own ideas and a proliferation of TQM models ensued.

John Oakland developed a relatively simple framework, which usefully described the main features of TQM (Figure 19.1). According to Oakland (1993, p. 30), TQM is 'an approach to improving the competitiveness, effectiveness and flexibility of a whole organization'. TQM is thus a way of managing people and business process to ensure complete customer satisfaction at every stage, resulting in organizations doing things right first time.

Performance

At the heart of Oakland's model is performance, representing the processes, people and planning of customer–supplier chains in order to recognize the importance of meeting customer requirements. The model recognizes that all organizations have chains of internal customers and suppliers, therefore performance must be achieved across all levels of activity and combines planning, people and the processes. In essence, TQM is about

Figure 19.1 Oakland's model of TQM
Source: Oakland, 2003, 2004

6

managing people, business processes and planning to ensure the customer is satisfied at every stage of the process.

For example, in a manufacturing plant, raw materials are received into stores from suppliers, and are then fed into the first production process. Here the materials are worked on in some way and then passed on to the next department (the next internal customer) where they are worked again. At each stage value is added until the final product is sold to the external customer. Each operator in the chain is therefore both a customer and a supplier, with each having the responsibility of meeting their respective customer's requirements. Failing to do so at any stage results in inferior quality and a need to correct or rework the WIP stock or the FG. At every stage, the work process and the skills of the operator must be capable of doing the job correctly to the designed specification.

Process: quality systems

To achieve consistency in work processes, a company must be organized so that the required standards are known and understood by all employees. This requires management systems to plan, monitor and control all activities. For many organizations, this is achieved by setting out objectives through a quality 'policy' and the use of a fully documented quality system such as ISO 9000. Using such a system ensures a consistent level of quality, which, in turn, promotes customer confidence. In addition, these systems help the organization to manage internal and external operations in a cost-effective and efficient way.

Planning: tools and techniques of quality

The quality system provides a framework for recording and dealing with quality problems. However, simply asking staff to take responsibility for solving their own quality problems is usually not enough. Employees often must be trained and educated so that they can identify problems and deal with them effectively. Many organizations now train staff in basic problem-solving tools and other quality techniques, encouraging them to become proactive in quality improvement activities.

People: teams and the organization

Clear lines of authority and responsibility are important in most organizational structures. Just as important, however, is the need to ensure that departments and functions do not become so compartmentalized that barriers develop. In most modern manufacturing and service companies, work processes are complex in nature and are often beyond the control of any one individual. A team approach, therefore, offers a number of advantages.

The use of teams allows more complex problems to be solved because it brings together different skills and expertise. Interdepartmental teams can resolve issues that cross over functional boundaries and will also help reduce problems of internal politics. Teamworking can also help develop skills and knowledge and it is often more satisfying for the individuals involved – improving morale, participation and decision-making.

Commitment, culture and communication

Achieving right-first-time quality requires a dedicated, well-motivated and loyal workforce who have been educated and trained to do the job properly. This requires leadership, policy setting, careful planning and the provision of appropriate resources at every level of the company. Senior managers must demonstrate their own commitment and the 'quality message' must be communicated and understood by everyone in the organization. The development of a TQM culture usually takes many years and must be demonstrated from senior management level down through the whole organization.

Example   Walmart: setting standards

The US supermarket Walmart implemented TQM practices to improve various elements of its business operations, including continuously sourcing quality products from supply networks to deliver the best products at the lowest available prices to the consumer. By continuously working with its suppliers, Walmart ensures that its products are of a standard that meets consumer expectations and are therefore deemed of an acceptable quality. The quality requirements also ensure that Walmart's standards remain competitive and comparable with industry best practices.

Quality award and assessment frameworks

The realization that quality is a key determinant of the competitive position of a business has brought about a number of methods of recognition. Accordingly, every developed economy has its own government-sponsored award to recognize those organizations that have achieved high quality and to stimulate others to follow the same path. These frameworks are all based on the philosophy of TQM and have much in common. The high profile and publicity gained by the winners of these internationally recognized awards give organizations significant marketing opportunities. Three of the major frameworks in use today are the Deming Prize (Japan), the Malcolm Baldrige Award (USA) and the EFQM European Quality Award.

These frameworks have continued to evolve and are now becoming adopted by countries worldwide in similar forms. The primary use of the frameworks is as a self-assessment tool by which companies can critically review their own activities against a comprehensive set of criteria. Typically, an organization prepares a detailed written submission of strengths and weaknesses for all aspects of its operations and business performance. For the best companies – those which demonstrate the highest levels of achievement – the submission can be used to judge them for the award. More importantly, and for most organizations, any weaknesses they have identified can be prioritized and developed into an action plan for business improvement.

The Deming Prize, established in 1950 in honour of W. Edwards Deming, has several categories including prizes for individuals, small companies and factories. Hundreds of companies apply for the Deming Prize each year. Each applicant must submit a detailed account of quality practices and methods and from these submissions, a shortlist of companies is selected for site visits and assessment. The Malcolm Baldrige National Quality Award, named after a former US secretary of commerce, was designed to operate in a similar manner to the Deming Prize.

Table 19.4 **Companies that have received the Baldrige Award**

Year	Recipients
2009	Honeywell Federal Manufacturing & Technologies, MidwayUSA, AtlantiCare, Heartland Health and VA Cooperative Studies Program Clinical Research Pharmacy Coordinating Center
2008	Cargill Corn Milling North America, Poudre Valley Health System and Iredell-Statesville Schools
2007	PRO-TEC Coating Co., Mercy Health System, Sharp HealthCare, City of Coral Springs and U.S. Army Research, Development and Engineering (ARDEC)
2006	Premier, Inc. MESA Products Inc. and North Mississippi Medical Center
2005	Sunny Fresh Foods Inc., DynMcDermott Petroleum Operations, Park Place Lexus, Jenks Public Schools, Richland College and Bronson Methodist Hospital
2004	The Bama Companies, Texas Nameplate Company Inc., Kenneth W. Monfort College of Business and Robert Wood Johnson University Hospital Hamilton
2003	Medrad Inc., Boeing Aerospace Support, Caterpillar Financial Services Corp., Stoner Inc., Community Consolidated School District 15, Baptist Hospital Inc. and Saint Luke's Hospital of Kansas City
2002	Motorola Inc. Commercial, Government and Industrial Solutions Sector, Branch Smith Printing Division and SSM Health Care
2001	Clarke American Checks Inc., Pal's Sudden Service, Chugach School District, Pearl River School District and University of Wisconsin-Stout
2000	Dana Corp.-Spicer Driveshaft Division, KARLEE Company Inc., Operations Management International Inc. and Los Alamos National Bank
1999	STMicroelectronics Inc.-Region Americas, BI Performance Services, The Ritz-Carlton Hotel Co. and Sunny Fresh Foods
1998	Boeing Airlift and Tanker Programs, Solar Turbines Inc. and Texas Nameplate Co. Inc.
1997	3M Dental Products Division, Solectron Corp., Merrill Lynch Credit Corp. and Xerox Business Services
1996	ADAC Laboratories, Dana Commercial Credit Corp., Custom Research Inc. and Trident Precision Manufacturing Inc.
1995	Armstrong World Industries Building Products Operation and Corning Telecommunications Products Division
1994	AT&T Consumer Communications Services, GTE Directories Corp. and Wainwright Industries Inc.
1993	Eastman Chemical Co. and Ames Rubber Corp.
1992	AT&T Network Systems Group/Transmission Systems Business Unit, Texas Instruments Inc. Defence Systems & Electronics Group, AT&T Universal Card Services, The Ritz-Carlton Hotel Co. and Granite Rock Co.
1991	Solectron Corp., Zytec Corp. and Marlow Industries
1990	Cadillac Motor Car Division, IBM Rochester, Federal Express Corp. and Wallace Co. Inc.
1989	Milliken & Co. and Xerox Corp. Business Products and Systems
1988	Motorola Inc., Commercial Nuclear Fuel Division of Westinghouse Electric Corp. and Globe Metallurgical Inc.

Source: Baldrige National Quality Programme, National Institute of Standard and Technology, 2009

Baldrige awards are given in manufacturing, service, small business, education and healthcare. They have the specific aim of improving the competitiveness and performance of organizations by promoting performance excellence, recognizing achievements and publicizing their successful strategies. Promotion of successful strategies in this way guides other organizations to observe and learn from them through benchmarking (see Table 19.4).

It is the third of the awards mentioned above that we will consider in more detail – the EFQM model.

19.4　The EFQM excellence model

Following the success of the Deming Prize and the Malcolm Baldrige Award, 14 leading European organizations, supported by the European Commission, formed the Brussels-based European Foundation for Quality Management (EFQM) in 1988. By 2001, across Europe, membership of the EFQM had grown to over 850 member organizations in most sectors of commercial and not-for-profit activity. EFQM's mission is: 'To energise leaders who want to learn, share and innovate using the EFQM Excellence Model as a common framework' (www.efqm.org/en). The EFQM excellence model is shown in Figure 19.2.

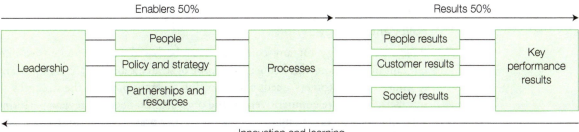

Figure 19.2 **The EFQM excellence model**
Source: www.efqm.org/en/

The EFQM excellence model is based on the following premise: 'Excellent results with respect to Performance, Customers, People and Society are achieved through Leadership driving Policy and Strategy, that is delivered through People, Partnerships and Resources, and Processes' (www.saeto.com/efqm.htm). Excellence is defined by the EFQM as outstanding practice in managing the organization and achieving results and is based on eight fundamental concepts (EFQM, 2010a, 2010b).

The excellence model contains nine criteria, five 'enablers', which cover what an organization does, and four 'results', which cover what an organization achieves. Results are caused by enablers and enablers are improved using feedback from results. The model can be used by all types and sizes of organization. Published guidelines are specifically written by the EFQM (www.efqm.org/en/PdfResources/EFQMcatalogue.pdf). The model offers a rigorous and structured self-assessment approach to business improvements based on hard facts. Careful assessment against each criterion allows an organization to calculate an overall score from a total possible 1,000 points. This score can then be viewed as a benchmark for comparisons with other organizations. Award-winning organizations achieve scores of around 700 points.

One of the most powerful attractions of the model is its use as a self-assessment diagnostic tool. This forms the basis for a company-wide plan of improvement activities, which can be prioritized to yield best results. Improvements can be measured and revisited year after year to observe progress. Benchmarking both internally and externally provides a powerful method of setting realistic improvement targets, and is referred to constantly within the model. Because of its importance, benchmarking will be discussed in more detail later in this chapter.

6

The enabler criteria

The first five criteria of the EFQM excellence model examine how an organization sets itself out to manufacture goods or provide services to customers.

Leadership

This first element looks for a visible demonstration of commitment to excellence by all managers within the organization. Managers must develop the mission, vision and be 'role model' leaders of a culture of excellence. They should define priorities, provide the resources and ensure the management system is developed, implemented and continuously improved. They should also be involved with customers and suppliers, promoting partnerships and joint improvement 'win–win' activities.

Policy and strategy

Policy and strategy for any company must be based on comprehensive and relevant information (this being the purpose of strategic analysis). It is important to understand customers' needs and to exploit, as far as possible, the strengths of suppliers. To ensure competitiveness, the organization needs to review performance and use benchmarking to compare with best practice, the competition and other best-in-class organizations.

People

The knowledge, competences and capabilities of employees must be identified, managed and developed. The organization should encourage individual and team participation in improvement activities and empower staff to take action.

Partnerships and resources

Partnerships and resources refer to all the resources employed by the company, other than the human resources covered above. These include external partnerships, financial resources, information resources, suppliers and materials, buildings, plant and equipment, technology and intellectual property. The company must demonstrate how it manages and exploits its resources to gain competitive advantage.

Processes

Each key process must be systematically designed, measured and managed to established standards (ISO 9000). Constantly striving to be more competitive requires regular reviews of processes and actual performance levels. Excellent companies talk to their customers and suppliers, and proactively involve them in the design of products and services. The use of best practice benchmarking helps to identify innovation and new technologies and leads to improvements.

The results criteria

The remaining four criteria of the EFQM excellence model examine what the organization is actually achieving, with regard to 'customer results', 'people results', 'society results' and 'key performance results'. To achieve a high score, a company must have strong positive trends for at least five years in business results and profitability. Measures must also be in place showing strong satisfaction trends from all stakeholders – customers, suppliers, employees and the wider community.

In 2010, there were five prize winners and eight finalists for the EFQM Excellence Award:

- Alpenresort Schwarz – Finalist
- Bradstow School – Prize Winner in Leading with Vision, Inspiration & Integrity and a Prize Winner in Succeeding through People
- Domino-World – Finalist
- Dr. Germain Becker & Associés – Finalist
- Eskisehir Maternity and Child Illness Hospital – Prize Winner in Leading with Vision, Inspiration and Integrity
- Liverpool John Moores University – Finalist
- Olabide Ikastola – Prize Winner in Adding Value for Customers and a Prize Winner in Succeeding through People
- Osakidetza - Comarca Gipuzkoa Ekialde – Finalist
- Robert Bosch Fahrzeugelektrik Eisenach – Finalist
- Siemens Congelton – Finalist
- Stavropol State Agrarian University – Prize Winner in Nurturing Creativity & Innovation and a Prize Winner in Leading with Vision, Inspiration & Integrity
- Vamed-KMB – Prize Winner in Succeeding through People
- Worthington Cylinders – Finalist.

The EFQM award

19.5 Six Sigma and lean sigma

Six Sigma is a relatively new concept compared to TQM as a whole. It began in 1986 when Bill Smith, a Motorola Inc. employee, introduced a statistically based method to reduce variation in electronic manufacturing processes in the company in the USA. Initially, Six Sigma was developed as an alternative to TQM; however, Six Sigma and TQM have many similarities and are compatible in varied business environments, making both equally valid. TQM has helped companies (both service and manufacturing) to improve quality, while Six Sigma has the potential to deliver statistically tested, quantitative results.

We have seen that TQM is often associated with the development, deployment and maintenance of organizational systems that are required for various business processes. It is based on a strategic approach that focuses on maintaining existing quality standards as well as making incremental quality improvements. Six Sigma, on the other hand, is more than just a process improvement programme, as it is based on concepts that focus on continuous quality improvements for achieving near perfection by restricting the number of possible defects to less than 3.4 defects per million. Thus the basic difference between Six Sigma and TQM is the approach. Six Sigma is based on DMAIC – define-measure-analyse-improve-control. Other abbreviations include DMAICT, which is DMAIC, plus transfer of best practice, and DMADV – define-measure-analyse-design-verify. Six Sigma is designed to help in making precise measurements, identifying exact problems and providing solutions that can be measured. It is driven by data, and provides quantifiable and measurable results. So, while TQM views quality as conformance to internal requirements, Six Sigma focuses on improving quality by reducing the number of defects. The end result may be the same in both concepts. Table 19.5 shows the DMAIC steps and the various tools

Six Sigma is based on concepts that focus on continuous quality improvements for achieving near perfection by restricting the number of possible defects to less than 3.4 defects per million.

6

and techniques that can be used. Table 19.5 is sourced from iSixSigma.com, the largest community of professionals with an interest in Six Sigma. The website is worth viewing for more detail on current thinking in the field of Six Sigma.

Table 19.5 The DMAIC steps and tools used for Six Sigma

DMAIC Phase Steps	Tools Used
D – Define Phase: Define the project goals and customer (internal and external) deliverables.	
• Define Customers and Requirements (CTQs) • Develop Problem Statement, Goals and Benefits • Identify Champion, Process Owner and Team • Define Resources • Evaluate Key Organizational Support • Develop Project Plan and Milestones • Develop High Level Process Map	• Project Charter • Process Flowchart • SIPOC Diagram • Stakeholder Analysis • DMAIC Work Breakdown Structure • CTQ Definitions • Voice of the Customer Gathering
Define Tollgate Review	
M – Measure Phase: Measure the process to determine current performance; quantify the problem.	
• Define Defect, Opportunity, Unit and Metrics • Detailed Process Map of Appropriate Areas • Develop Data Collection Plan • Validate the Measurement System • Collect the Data • Begin Developing $Y=f(x)$ Relationship • Determine Process Capability and Sigma Baseline	• Process Flowchart • Data Collection Plan/Example • Benchmarking • Measurement System Analysis/Gage R&R • Voice of the Customer Gathering • Process Sigma Calculation
Measure Tollgate Review	
A – Analyze Phase: Analyze and determine the root cause(s) of the defects.	
• Define Performance Objectives • Identify Value/Non-Value Added Process Steps • Identify Sources of Variation • Determine Root Cause(s) • Determine Vital Few x's, $Y=f(x)$ Relationship	• Histogram • Pareto Chart • Time Series/Run Chart • Scatter Plot • Regression Analysis • Cause and Effect/Fishbone Diagram • 5 Whys • Process Map Review and Analysis • Statistical Analysis • Hypothesis Testing (Continuous and Discrete) • Non-Normal Data Analysis
Analyze Tollgate Review	
I – Improve Phase: Improve the process by eliminating defects.	
• Perform Design of Experiments • Develop Potential Solutions • Define Operating Tolerances of Potential System • Assess Failure Modes of Potential Solutions • Validate Potential Improvement by Pilot Studies • Correct/Re-Evaluate Potential Solution	• Brainstorming • Mistake Proofing • Design of Experiments • Pugh Matrix • House of Quality • Failure Modes and Effects Analysis (FMEA) • Simulation Software
Improve Tollgate Review	
C – Control Phase: Control future process performance.	
• Define and Validate Monitoring and Control System • Develop Standards and Procedures • Implement Statistical Process Control • Determine Process Capability • Develop Transfer Plan, Handoff to Process Owner • Verify Benefits, Cost Savings/Avoidance, Profit Growth • Close Project, Finalize Documentation • Communicate to Business, Celebrate	• Process Sigma Calculation • Control Charts (Variable and Attribute) • Cost Savings Calculations • Control Plan
Control Tollgate Review	

Source: http://www.isixsigma.com/index.php?option=com_k2&view=item&layout=item&id=1477&Itemid=343

Lean Six Sigma is an evolution of Six Sigma, where lean manufacturing/production approaches and principles are merged with those of Six Sigma. Lean is an approach that seeks to improve flow in the value stream and eliminate waste. Six Sigma uses the DMAIC framework and statistical tools to uncover root causes to understand and reduce variation. A combination of both provides a structured improvement approach and effective tools to solve problems. This creates rapid transformational improvement at lower cost.

Lean is an approach that seeks to improve flow in the value stream and eliminate waste.

Example **Six Sigma in action**

Apart from being an active continuous improvement methodology in the manufacturing industry, Six Sigma has also found acceptance in the service sector. The banking industry provides an active platform for the application of Six Sigma as a continuous improvement philosophy and tool. Major financial institutions in the USA, Europe and South Asia (Llyods TSB, NatWest, GE, JPMorgan Chase, Bank of America, ICICI Bank) have adopted Six Sigma methodologies in order to improve their service quality, increase customer satisfaction, reduce expenses, increase earnings and reduce risk. For example, using Six Sigma tools, JPMorgan Chase identified several expense reduction areas and saved $500,000 per annum in the use of unnecessary SWIFT messages (Doganoksoy et al., 2000). Similarly, GE improved its call centre performance by reviewing its processes using Six Sigma methodology. The net result was that the rate of a caller reaching a live person in GE improved from 76% to 99% (Pande et al., 2000).

19.6 Quality and strategic analysis

Garvin (1987) proposes eight dimensions of quality that can provide a guiding framework for strategic analysis. These dimensions are performance, features, reliability, conformance, durability, serviceability, aesthetics and perceived quality (Table 19.6). Delivering these eight dimensions will lead to a degree of competitive advantage and enhance the strategic position of organizations.

Table 19.6 Garvin's eight dimensions of quality

Dimension	Description
Performance	The primary operating characteristics of a product or service must be seen to perform to users' expectations
Features	A secondary aspect to performance, as they are supplementary to the basic functioning of the product or service
Reliability	A measure of the probability of the product or service failing to work. The more durable a good is, the greater the requirement for reliability
Conformance	The degree to which characteristics meet established standards
Durability	The measure of a product's life, often a balance against value for money
Serviceability	The speed, competence and ease of repair
Aesthetics	A highly subjective measure, reflecting looks, sensory pleasure and individual preference
Perceived quality	The degree of incomplete information held by the consumer and the value attached to the good, based on what is expected or inferred rather than reality itself

6

19.7   Benchmarking

One of the key features within the above frameworks is the importance of benchmarking. Superior performers in most industries regularly review themselves against the competition and other best-in-class companies to remain at the top. *Fit for the Future*, a report published by the Confederation of British Industry (CBI) in 1997 examined the strengths of UK companies. The report concluded: 'The most powerful process any company can adopt and which delivers immediate, measurable and sustainable productivity improvements is the transfer of Best Practice.'

This is the key to successful benchmarking – for an organization to analyse its own performance and then compare performance in several areas against competitors. If, for example, one competitor in an industry enjoys a lower rate of waste or higher quality than others, questions can be asked as to what this company has done to bring about the superior performance. By using benchmarking in this way, best practice procedures can be emulated and performance improved in the lower performers.

Successful benchmarking usually rests on the premise that competitors in an industry are willing, to some extent, to share, collaborate or make information available on their performance and processes. The happy result of successful benchmarking is that all participants in an industry have improved quality performance, so improving customer satisfaction with the industry's products.

In recent years, the interest in benchmarking has grown. What started out as a relatively simple concept has become increasingly complicated. Benchmarking has proved to be a profitable source of income for management consultants who have developed and published many different approaches and methodologies. For any organization just beginning to benchmark, reading the literature will confirm that there are many types of benchmarking in existence. Where do they start? Which form of benchmarking is best? We will consider the different types under three broad headings, metric, diagnostic and process benchmarking. A simple way is to view them along a continuum, as shown in Figure 19.3.

From Figure 19.3, we can see that there is an increase in effort, resources and costs as we move from metric benchmarking through to full process benchmarking. At the lower end, metric benchmarking can provide an indication of relative performance and perhaps identify leading competitors, but it is unlikely to yield any real ideas on how to change. At best, it will only help to define performance gaps.

Moving up, diagnostic benchmarking requires a little more effort but in return will identify areas of strength and more detail on areas of weakness for the organization. Done correctly, it will also help to prioritize which processes should be targeted for improvement activities.

Process benchmarking requires considerably more resource, effort and time, but organizations successfully completing the process will be rewarded with many benefits of transferred best practice.

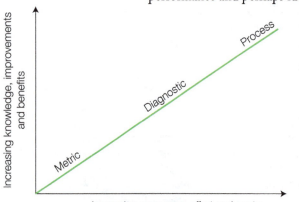

Figure 19.3 Types of benchmarking

Metric benchmarking

Many organizations, in both manufacturing and service-based sectors, use metric benchmarking as a means of direct comparison both internally and externally with other organizations. Metrics are performance indicators used as comparative measures. There are many published forms of metric data from which simple comparisons can be drawn, for example league tables published by government agencies or public sector organizations such as (in the UK) the NHS. Another example is the university league tables published by the *Financial Times*. In the manufacturing sector, we have the Best Factory Awards from *Works Management*/Cranfield University.

> **Metrics** are performance indicators used as comparative measures.

Metric benchmarking is often used by companies to make inter-site comparisons using key performance indicators, such as product costs, staffing levels, resources per unit produced, waste or rework levels, stock turnover rates and so on. These can be useful, provided that each site is measured in the same way using like-for-like comparisons. Perhaps the biggest disadvantage of metric benchmarking is that even when it shows a performance gap between two companies, it does not explain how better performance can be achieved.

Example   Xerox and benchmarking

In the early 1980s, Xerox initiated the Leadership through Quality programme, aimed at reducing costs and improving quality within Xerox. When Xerox had benchmarked itself against its Japanese rivals, it found that its products were of lower quality and the lead time between product design and market was considerably higher in comparison with Japanese competitors. Accepting its lack of focus, Xerox introduced the Leadership Through Quality programme, and defined benchmarking as 'the process of measuring its products, services, and practices against its toughest competitors, identifying the gaps and establishing goals. Our goal is always to achieve superiority in quality, product reliability and cost.' Gradually, Xerox developed and successfully implemented its own benchmarking model. Xerox is now considered a world-class player in quality initiatives and its practices have redefined benchmarking standards.

Source: http://www.improvementandinnovation.com/features/project/benchmarking-how-xerox-regained-its-competitive-edge.

Diagnostic benchmarking

PROBE (PROmoting Business Excellence) is a suite of diagnostic and best practice benchmarking tools, developed by the CBI in conjunction with industry leaders and leading academics in the early 1990s. PROBE helps businesses to understand how their performance and practices compare with world-class companies, by measuring and comparing businesses on world-class performance scales. *Made in Europe* (Hanson et al., 1994) was a large-scale study that compared hundreds of manufacturing organizations across Europe, examining the relationship between practice and performance. The research found that good practice correlated strongly with performance. PROBE has been followed by a number of similar instruments, some of which have been designed for particular industry sectors. Examples include Learning PROBE, developed for use by the further education sector, and Service PROBE, which looks at the components of world-class excellence in the services industry.

CASE STUDY   Foreshore Engineering Ltd

Foreshore Engineering Ltd makes, delivers and installs high value, energy-efficient water, heating and lighting systems for the building industry. Starting from a small base in a small town in north Yorkshire, Foreshore has grown to the point at which it has contracts all over the UK. Last year, the total turnover was £42m, with retained profit of £9.5m.

The vast majority of work comes from fitting these systems in new buildings, especially offices, shops and factories. In recent years, Foreshore has extended its operations into fitting these systems into existing premises, which can be difficult and complex, because Foreshore staff have to operate while work is going on in these premises. Foreshore therefore charges much more for installations in existing working premises than it does for working on new facilities. This area of its work, although a small part of the company's operations at present, is one it wishes to explore and develop further if at all possible.

Foreshore is at the cutting edge of what is still a young industry. By being an early mover, it has secured a strong position in this part of the building and construction industry. However, it is an attractive, growing field, and new companies are coming in all the time.

The company makes the systems to individual order for each customer. Foreshore guarantees its work for five years. The quality of the engineering is very good, and the Foreshore installation builders and engineers have a reputation for cheerfulness as well as expertise. Projects are nearly always delivered on time and to the cost and quality required. Complaints only come in once every two or three months, and when this does happen, each is assessed and put right to the satisfaction of the individual customer. All remedial work takes place by agreement, and, to date, Foreshore has lost no business as the result of customer complaints.

Foreshore is due to be inspected by the Health and Safety Executive (HSE) and the trade federation of which it is a member. It is also due to receive a major visit from a consortium of clients, which, if successful, will lead to major new contracts being awarded.

The HSE and trade federation visits duly came and went, and Foreshore received a clean bill of health from both. They found that the factory and the quality of the work was fine, all the premises were clean, working practices were excellent and staff training was fully in place and rigorously carried out. The only criticism that either had to make was on the comprehensiveness of the documentation, and the factory general manager was given the task of putting this right.

It quickly became clear that this was a crucial task that needed completing before the client consortium asked to see full evidence of the approach to quality management in the production and installation of systems, in the nature of the service delivery, including after-sales and post-installation relationships, and in the management and rectifying of complaints. The factory general manager was not sure how to proceed with this, and so turned to the trade federation for advice.

The trade federation sent in a small team of consultants. The consultants found that everything was being done, but nothing was being recorded. The documentation would not pass a quality audit, and it would not gain any British, European or ISO 9000 accreditation. If Foreshore wanted the new client consortium contracts, it would have to have a full audit and comprehensive documentation. Because of the imminent visit of the consortium, the work would have to be carried out immediately. This would be expensive, in the order of £400,000. However, all things being equal, the standards would be then awarded, which would lead to the new batch of contracts, and would be good for the long-term future of the business.

The Foreshore board of directors met to discuss the matter and, after a brief debate, engaged the consultants to do the quality audit. The consultants found that everything was indeed in order as promised, and the standards were duly awarded. The new client consortium awarded the contracts to Foreshore, and everything returned to normal.

However, events took another turn. First, the consultants wanted Foreshore to benchmark its practices and operations against others in similar lines of work; and they recommended comparison with a specialist motorcycle manufacturer with nearby premises. The consultants also introduced the concept of zero defects, with all that this entailed – no defects in the manufacturing or engineering processes. Most crucially, they stressed the need for 'quality' in customer service and the establishment of standards to which everyone could subscribe.

Having read their report, the factory manager spent the next three days quietly observing things. She found that, in practice, much of the quality side of the work was being managed on an ad hoc basis. The manufacturing and installation leaned heavily on people checking each other's work – there were no procedures. The customer service side had no rules at all – everything was done on a purely reactive basis, which she knew was fine until a crisis happened. However, she also knew that the natural environment that existed within Foreshore meant that there was every likelihood that any attempt to introduce formal procedures would be met with resistance.

Case study questions

1 What positive benefits has the consultancy exercise delivered for Foreshore?

2 What are the strengths and shortcomings of benchmarking in the establishment and assessment of quality standards? Can Foreshore possibly learn from the local manufacturer with whom it was recommended to benchmark?

3 How might the question of quality management in delivering customer and client service be best established?

Researchers from the Newcastle Business School at Northumbria University developed a scaled-down version of PROBE, called PILOT. It was a questionnaire-based survey instrument, which asked around 50 questions on practice and performance measures, suitable for both manufacturing and service sector organizations. On completion of the questionnaire, the participating organizations received feedback showing them how they compared against other organizations in the area. Like the PROBE analysis, the PILOT study found that good practice correlated strongly with business performance.

Process benchmarking

By far the most involved form of benchmarking, process benchmarking is where the most substantial benefits can be found. The focus is on any key business process that has been identified as an area for improvement.

Fundamental to the success of process benchmarking is the recognition that many organizations have functions that use generically similar business processes, regardless of sector or industry type. Thus one main advantage of process benchmarking is that businesses need not restrict themselves to observing practices in companies that are considered direct competition. Most business organizations issue invoices, collect payables (debts), appoint new people and so on and these types of 'generic' activities can be benchmarked regardless of industry.

Benchmarking activities can be widened to include partners from different sectors and this can enable completely new ways of working to be identified. This can lead to significant improvements in operating efficiency across industrial sectors.

Process benchmarking can be divided into four stages:

1 Understanding the nature and complexity of the business processes that are to be benchmarked. This requires careful process mapping and measurement of process metrics.

2 Identifying potential and willing benchmarking partners – not always a straightforward task as some corporate cultures resist 'opening up' to outside organizations.

3 Data collection and measurement. It is important to ensure that processes are compared on a like-for-like basis.

4 Implementation of change and transfer of best practice for a given process. This is not always easy because cultural, demographic or technological barriers may present unforeseen problems.

VOCAB CHECKLIST FOR ESL STUDENTS

Baseline
Blacksmiths
Brainstorming
Commensurate
Compartmentalized
Conformance
Consortium
Diagnostic

Extrinsic
Flowchart
Flushness (refers to straightness
    of edges. See 'plumb' in
    'plumb line')
Histogram
Interdepartmental
Metrics

Proliferation
Remedial
Role model
Scatter plot (see 'scatter
    diagram')
Tangible
Testimony
Transformational

Definitions for these terms can be found in the 'Vocab Zone' of the companion website, which provides free access to the Macmillan English Dictionary online at www.macmillanihe.com/companion/business/campbell.

REVIEW QUESTIONS

1   Explain what is meant by the term 'quality' and 'total quality management'.
2   Describe the EFQM model and explain the difference between enablers and results.
3   Explain how benchmarking may help an organization improve its quality regime.

DISCUSSION TOPIC

Statistical techniques for improving quality, like Six Sigma, are a fad. What is important is people. Discuss.

HOT TOPICS – Research project areas to investigate

For your research project, why not investigate ...

- ... whether lean sigma can be applied to a voluntary organization.
- ... what consumers in the luxury car market believe constitutes good quality.
- ... how organizations measure the quality of their processes.

Recommended reading

Badri, M.A., Davis, D. and Davis, D. (1995) 'A study of measuring the critical factors of quality management', *International Journal of Quality & Reliability Management*, **12**(2): 36–53.

Black, S.A. and Porter, L.J. (1996) 'Identification of the CSFs of TQM', *Decision Sciences*, **27**(1): 1–21.

Breyfogle, F.W. III, Cupello, J.M. and Meadows, B. (2001) *Managing Six Sigma*, New York: John Wiley.

Davis, A. (2003) 'Six Sigma for small companies', *Troy*, **42**(11): 20.

Ghobadian, A. and Gallear, D. (1997) 'TQM and organisation size', *International Journal of Operations & Production Management*, **17**(2): 121–63.

Harry, M. and Schroeder, R. (2000) *Six Sigma: The Breakthrough Management Strategy Revolutionizing the World's Top Corporations*, New York: Random House.

Hoerl, R. (1998) 'Six Sigma and the future of the quality profession', *Quality Progress*, **35**(1): 35–42.

Klefsjo, B., Wiklund, H. and Edgeman, R.L. (2001) 'Six Sigma seen as a methodology for TQM', *Measuring Business Excellence*, **5**(1): 31–5.

Lee, G.L. and Oakes, I. (1995) 'The pros and cons of TQM for smaller forms in manufacturing: some experiences down the supply chain', *Total Quality Management*, **6**(4): 413–26.

McAdam, R. (2000) 'Quality models in an SME context: a critical perspective using a grounded approach', *International Journal of Quality & Reliability Management*, **17**(3): 305–23.

Yusof, S.M. and Aspinwall, E. (2000) 'TQM implementation: issues, review and case study', *International Journal of Operations & Production Management*, **20**(6): 634–55.

Chapter references

CBI (Confederation of British Industry) (1997) *Fit for the Future, How Competitive is British Manufacturing?*, London: CBI, http://webarchive.nationalarchives.gov.uk/+/http://www.dti.gov.uk/comp/competitive/wh_int1.htm.

EFQM (European Foundation for Quality Management) (2010a) *The EFQM Excellence Model*, Brussels: EFQM.

EFQM (European Foundation for Quality Management) (2010b) *The Fundamental Concepts of Excellence*, Brussels: EFQM.

Garvin, D.A. (1987) 'Competing on the eight dimensions of quality', *Harvard Business Review*, November–December: 108–9.

Hanson, P., Voss, C., Blackmon, K. and Oak, B. (1994) *Made in Europe: A Four Nations Best Practice Study*, London: IBM UK/London Business School.

Imai, M. (1986) *Kaizen: The Key to Japan's Competitive Success*, New York: McGraw-Hill.

Oakland, J.S. (1993) *Total Quality Management: The Route to Improving Performance* (2nd edn), Oxford: Butterworth-Heinemann.

Oakland, J.S. (2003) *TQM: Text with Cases* (3rd edn), Oxford: Butterworth-Heinemann.

Oakland, J.S. (2004) *Oakland on Quality Management*, Oxford: Butterworth-Heinemann.

Pande, P.S., Neuman, R.P. and Cavanagh, R.R. (2000) *The Six Sigma Way*, New York: McGraw-Hill.

6

Chapter 20

Social responsibility and business ethics

Introduction and chapter overview

Business ethics is one of the most hotly debated areas of business research. Almost every possible opinion position is reflected in the literature. This chapter aims to set out an impartial discussion of the subject, beginning with an introduction to the issues surrounding the debate about the relationships between business and society. The stockholder and stakeholder positions are discussed. The stakeholder position is presented as a kind of social contract and the ways in which stakeholders are classified are discussed. The debate is explored further using Donaldson and Preston's (1995) framework for understanding the stakeholder debate. The nature of stakeholder concerns are presented and the strategic postures that businesses can adopt with respect to social concerns are outlined. The ways in which businesses attempt to discharge social responsibility are discussed and, finally, the important areas of sustainability and the eco-agenda are introduced.

Learning objectives

After studying this chapter, you should be able to:

- understand the business–society relationship
- explain the different positions on social responsibility
- describe several ways of classifying stakeholders
- explain the nature of stakeholder concerns
- explain the strategic posture on social responsibility
- describe the concept of sustainability and the main themes of the eco-agenda

20.1 Business and its relationship to society

Any regular reader of the news will be aware of a trend over recent years towards an increasing awareness of the behaviour of business in respect of what have become known as 'ethical' or 'social' issues. Alleged 'bad' behaviour such as irresponsible environmental behaviour, the way employees are sometimes treated, suspect product safety and responses to accidents like oil spills are often reported and discussed in some depth in the press and on television.

The traditional **economic theory of the firm** posits the notion that businesses exist primarily to make profits for their owners.

Events such as these raise an important strategic question: what is the precise nature of a business's relationship to society? The traditional economic theory of the firm posits the notion that businesses exist primarily to make profits for their owners. Some writers in this field have taken the view that the only moral behaviour of business is that which is dedicated to maximizing profits for its shareholders (see for example Friedman, 1970). Others have adopted the diametrically opposite position – that businesses have a moral obligation to those constituencies from which they directly or indirectly benefit (see for example Evan and Freeman, 1993; Freeman, 1994; Clarkson, 1995). This area of argument has been called the 'stakeholder–stockholder debate'. It can be broadly understood in terms of a continuum, with two notional extremes but 'real life' existing at various points along the continuum (Figure 20.1).

Pure stockholder theory		Pure stakeholder theory
Single fiduciary duty		Multi-fiduciary duty
Accountable to principals alone		Accountable to all
(shareholders in business companies)		(some) stakeholders

Figure 20.1 **The stakeholder–stockholder continuum**

KEY CONCEPT

A **fiduciary duty** is a duty of care and trust that one party has towards another. While some fiduciary duties are non-contestable, others are. In the case of business ethics, the question is: To whom does the board of a company owe a fiduciary duty? It is usually accepted that it owes such a duty to the company's shareholders, as that agency relationship underpins the structure of capitalism. The question, then, is who else is owed such a duty and how is it weighted against the duty towards shareholders? In a dispute between employees and shareholders, for example, to which party does the board of directors owe the main fiduciary duty?

The stockholder position

The **stockholder position** on businesses' responsibility to society argues that businesses exist primarily for their owners (usually shareholders).

At one end of the continuum is the 'pure' stockholder position. The stockholder position on businesses' responsibility to society argues that businesses exist primarily for their owners (usually shareholders). This means that only a fiduciary duty to shareholders is recognized. Accordingly, any business behaviour that renders profit performance suboptimal is not only theft from shareholders but will also, eventually, lead to a level of business performance that will harm all the stakeholders (including employees and suppliers).

In a now well-known article in the *New York Times Magazine*, Nobel Laureate Professor Milton Friedman (1970) contended that 'the moral obligation of business is to increase its profits'. Friedman argued that the one and only obligation of company directors – the legal agents of shareholders' financial interests – is to act in such a way as to maximize the financial rate of return on the owners' shares. The capitalist system on which western economies are based rests in large part on the assumption that investments made in shares, for example in pension funds, unit trusts and so on, will perform well, that is, there will be an increase in the share's value and in the rate of dividend per share – objectives that can only be served by financial profits.

6

Milton Friedman was born in New York in 1912. He graduated from Rutgers University with a BA in mathematics and gained an MA from the University of Chicago. He held a fellowship at the University of Columbia and worked for a year as a research assistant for the renowned economist Professor Harold Hotelling. He graduated with a PhD in 1946 and later joined the faculty of the University of Chicago. He was instrumental in developing the Chicago School of economics and was a Fulbright visiting fellow at Cambridge University. He was also an economic adviser to President Regan and Republican presidential candidate Barry Goldwater.

Professor Friedman was a renowned economist and a recipient of the Nobel Prize in Economics. He is best known for his theoretical and empirical work in microeconomics, macroeconomics, economic history and public policy. He died in 2006.

Proponents of stockholder theory argue that because the only moral duty of directors is to maximize shareholder wealth, the activities of business beyond making profits are no concern of other stakeholders. The intellectual pedigree of this view of social responsibility can be traced back over 200 years.

The classical economic philosophy of Adam Smith (from his book *The Wealth of Nations*, published in 1776) concerns the maximization of benefit to society through the economic mechanism, whereby all individuals and businesses act freely in their own economic best interests. Smith's 'invisible hand' principle shows how, when each individual and business is free of external influence to make economic decisions, ultimately, everybody in society will benefit. Profitable businesses stimulate economic growth in the macroeconomy and increase employment. In turn, increased rates of employment stimulate spending power in the economy and businesses further increase their profits. If this virtuous cycle can be maintained, society becomes prosperous and the net effect is positive.

The stakeholder position

The **stakeholder position** posits that organizations, like individual people, are citizens of society, and as such, we have certain rights, obligations and responsibilities.

The stakeholder position posits that organizations, like individual people, are citizens of society. Citizenship carries with it certain rights from which we benefit, as well as certain obligations and responsibilities. Evidently, we enjoy the benefits of society, such as civil peace, freedom under the rule of law, the right to own and enjoy our property and so on. In return, we accept our obligations – both legal and social. Legally, we collectively agree to obey the law, to pay our taxes and to respect civil authority. Socially, most of us accept that society works best when we accord each other certain basic civilities. We apologize when we bump into somebody in a corridor, we sympathize with and comfort those going through hard times and we celebrate with each other when one of us gets good news.

Turning to business, it is obvious that businesses enjoy certain benefits from society. They gain finance capital and employees from society and they rely on the continuing support of customers, local communities, suppliers and others. The stakeholder view of the business–society relationship argues that because businesses benefit from the goodwill of society, they owe certain duties in return.

The implications of this proposition are far-reaching. In essence, stakeholder theory argues that shareholders are neither the sole owners of a business nor the sole beneficiaries of its activities. While shareholders are undeniably one stakeholder group, they are far from being the only group who expect to benefit from business activity and, accordingly, are just one of those groups who have a legitimate right to influence a company's strategic objectives.

Seven positions on social responsibility

Gray et al. (1996) identified seven distinctive positions along the stakeholder/stockholder continuum (Figure 20.1). From left to right, they are:

- Pristine capitalists
- Expedients
- Social contractarians
- Social ecologists
- Socialists
- Radical feminists
- Deep greens.

1 *Pristine capitalist position:* This is the first position at the stockholder extreme. We use the adjective 'pristine' because this position is untainted with any other concern other than those of shareholders. It does not recognize the rights of any other stakeholders (other than shareholders). Anything – any action or policy taken by a company's management – that is not in the economic best interests of shareholders is direct theft of shareholder value and therefore unethical. It thus follows that all social responsibility efforts, because they cost money and consume management time, are unethical and unacceptable.

2 *Expedient position:* Expedient means 'appropriate' and so this position recognizes that although the underlying values are those of maximizing profits, it is sometimes necessary to take social and environment actions in order to maximize economic returns. In other words, this position takes a purely strategic and instrumental view of business responsibility: some responsibility towards other stakeholders is necessary in order to maximize shareholder value.

3 *Social contractarian position:* This the first of the seven positions to depart from the purely capitalist assumption of the pristine capitalists and the expedients. In order to understand the social contractarian position, it is necessary to understand what the social contract is (see Key concept box below).

Under a social contract, social institutions (such as governments or businesses) can only continue to enjoy social legitimacy if they continually modify their policies and activities to accord with societal opinion. We can readily appreciate that this must be the case for a democratically elected government, as political parties seeking office offer policies that they feel

6

will accord with the electorate's aspirations. If, during a government's term of office, policy objectives diverge from those of the electorate, the probability that it will be removed from office at the next election is increased.

The point here is that what businesses want to do is align themselves with the norms and beliefs of society so that they will be seen to be in agreement with society. So if, for example, society shows more concern about the environment or the conditions of workers in developing countries, the business will also demonstrate concern for these things. The underlying belief is that the business will prosper best when it is fully aligned with the norms and aspirations of society, even if, in the short term, that involves investment in 'social responsibility' measures. The business doesn't necessarily intrinsically care about greater ethical responsibility, but rather, it believes that demonstrating society's norms back to society will result in greater benefit to the business.

KEY CONCEPT

Social contract theory posits the notion that any social institution exists alongside its constituencies via a social contract. The concept is an old one but successive thinkers since the 17th century have modified our understanding of it. The English philosophers Thomas Hobbes (1588–1679) and John Locke (1632–1704) developed the theory to explain the relationship between a government and the people over which it governs. In the 20th century, the theory was modified to help to explain the relationship between powerful business organizations and the stakeholders they can influence (see for example, Rawls, 1971; Donaldson, 1982).

The essence of the theory is one of reciprocal responsibility. The constituency agrees to accept the authority of the powerful institution, while the institution agrees to act in the best interests of its constituencies. If either party breaks the terms of the contract, then, it is argued, the nature of the contract is destroyed.

In respect to the business–stakeholder relationship, a social contract is said to exist between an organization and those groups in society that rely on it. The stakeholders (in effect) agree to support the activities of the organization, as employees, customers and so on, as long as the organization acts in a manner that is acceptable to the stakeholders.

4 *Social ecologist position:* This is the first position to recognize the belief that organizations, and businesses in particular, are partly responsible for the inequalities in society and environmental degradation. If businesses are part of the problem, they should be part of the solution. It thus follows that businesses should – from an ethical perspective – include social and environmental measures as part of their strategies. Given that most economic activity takes place at a net cost to the environment, it follows that this impact should be minimized.

KEY CONCEPT

Socialism is an economic theory or system in which the means of production, distribution and exchange are owned by the community collectively, usually through the state.

5 *Socialist position:* Although derived from political theory, socialism is more a set of beliefs than a political ideology. Essentially a worldview that sees economic relationships in terms of socioeconomic class, socialism views

capitalism as one class (the capitalist) controlling and subjugating lower classes. In the same way that early Marxist socialists interpreted society as a hegemony (domination) of the rich and powerful, in the context of business, socialists see businesses as potential or actual oppressors. They might believe, for example, that businesses concentrate wealth in society rather then redistributing it, or they might point to the exploitation of workers in a business's supply chain (perhaps in developing countries) as evidence of subjugation.

What has this to do with business ethics? Socialists, in this context, believe there is something wrong with society and that businesses are a manifestation of that malaise. Society should be reconfigured to make businesses much more publicly accountable and much more socially contributive. Businesses must exist for the net benefit of society and not just for capitalist shareholders. This isn't, therefore, about being more ethical in doing business. Rather, it is about changing the role of business in society and is thus a much more radical prescription than merely changing business practice.

6　*Radical feminist position:* Often misunderstood, this position also argues for a realignment of society (as with the socialists) but sees economic and social relationships through a feminist lens. One of the features of feminism as an intellectual 'school' is to view the world in terms of masculine and feminine characteristics. The radical feminist view is that society, and hence society's structures (including businesses), would be better if composed of more feminist characteristics rather than the masculine characteristics that, they argue, society is based around. Masculine characteristics include those associated with aggression, hierarchy, power, competitiveness and the will to dominate. When we assume, for example, that competitive strategy is about gaining competitive advantage, what we are effectively saying is that the world is a place that rewards aggression and power. Radical feminists argue that these characteristics are typical of those displayed by individuals and organizations in a modern capitalist society. They argue that society would be better served by the more feminist characteristics of interconnectedness, equality, mercy, cooperation and compassion. Clearly, this would have a dramatic effect on business and how capitalism is structured.

7　*Deep green or deep ecologist position:* As the most radical of the seven positions, the deep green position rejects the claimed advantages of capitalism and business and argues instead that the entire system must be replaced. Humans have quite wrongly claimed for themselves primacy over the world's environment and have, in the process, created an environmental crisis capable of threatening the future of human life on earth. Business activity is responsible for the environmental degradation of the earth and cannot be trusted to clean it up. A radical restructuring of society involving the dismantling of capitalism is the only realistic solution.

The notion of corporate social responsibility (CSR) only really fits with the first four of these seven positions (up to and including social ecologist). The socialist, radical feminist and deep green positions would see CSR efforts as crude manipulation intended to maintain and increase the power of capital in society. This seven-point scale therefore demonstrates just how uninformed those are who advocate CSR as a solution to environmental and social problems. The assumption that business is capable of finding a solution to social and environmental problems (called 'ecological modernism') is thus highly contestable.

20.2   Ways of classifying stakeholders

Stakeholders are at the heart of the ethical debate in business, and the extent to which the claims of different stakeholders are recognized is a key ethical issue. If a stakeholder model is appropriate for business, the question still has to be asked about which stakeholders should be recognized. It is not possible to say that 'we will consult stakeholders' or 'we will take stakeholder needs into account', as different stakeholders have different claims on an organization and often want completely different things. This section is about the ways that have been examined to consider stakeholders and how the plethora of stakeholders in a business's environment can be distinguished from each other.

We encountered the idea of stakeholders in Chapter 3, where we learned that stakeholders are the people who can influence or are influenced by the organization. Freeman (1994, p. 46) defines stakeholders as: 'Any group or individual who can affect or [be] affected by the achievement of an organisation's objectives.'

However, given the broad range of parties that are included in most definitions of 'stakeholder', there are bound to be difficulties in formulating strategy if all stakeholder opinions are to be treated with equal weight. Who could honestly argue, for example, that a barperson at a local bar should or does have the same influence over strategy as the owner? It seems, therefore, that not all stakeholders are equal. A number of ways of classifying stakeholders have been advanced and these are examined.

GURU GUIDE

R. Edward Freeman taught at the University of Minnesota and the Wharton School, University of Pennsylvania. He is currently the Elis and Signe Olsson Professor of Business Administration at the Darden School of Business at the University of Virginia and the academic director of the Business Roundtable Institute for Corporate Ethics.

He has received a number of awards for teaching excellence from Wharton School, University of Pennsylvania and Carlson School of Management at the University of Minnesota. He is also the recipient of the Lifetime Achievement Award from the World Resources Institute and the Aspen Institute. At its 2010 annual meeting, the Society for Business Ethics gave its Outstanding Contributions to Scholarship Award to Freeman, noting that there were more than 12,000 citations to his work on stakeholder theory.

He is well known for developing the stakeholder approach for managing businesses and has written several influential books and texts in the area of stakeholder management. His best known work is the award-winning *Strategic Management: A Stakeholder Approach*, in which he suggests that businesses build their strategy around their relationships with key stakeholders.

Criteria for distinguishing between stakeholders

Many writers have attempted to classify stakeholders according to how they relate to the organization's activities. Some of these distinctions are now outlined.

Internal and external stakeholders

Perhaps the easiest and most straightforward distinction is between stakeholders inside the organization and those outside. Internal stakeholders will typically include staff and management, whereas external stakeholders will include customers, competitors or suppliers. Some stakeholders will be more difficult to categorize, such as trade unions, which may have elements of both internal and external membership.

Narrow and wide stakeholders

Evan and Freeman (1993) view stakeholders as either being or not being influenced by an organization. Narrow stakeholders are most affected by the organization's policies and will usually include shareholders, management, employees, suppliers and customers who are dependent on the organization's output. Wider stakeholders are less affected and typically may include government, less dependent customers, the wider community, as opposed to local communities, and other peripheral groups. The Evan and Freeman model may lead some to conclude that an organization has a higher degree of responsibility and accountability to its narrower stakeholders.

Primary and secondary stakeholders

According to Clarkson (1995, p. 106), 'A primary stakeholder group is one without whose continuing participation the corporation cannot survive as a going concern.' Clarkson sees the important distinction as being between those who influence an organization and those who do not. For most organizations, primary stakeholders – those most vital to an organization – will include government, through its tax and legislative influence, customers and suppliers. Secondary stakeholders – those without whose 'continuing participation' the company can probably still exist – will therefore include communities and, in some cases, the management of the organization itself.

Active and passive stakeholders

Mahoney (1994) divided stakeholders between those who are active and those who are passive. Active stakeholders seek to participate in the organization's activities. These stakeholders may or may not be a part of the organization's formal structure. Management and employees obviously fall into this active category but some parties outside an organization may also fall into this category, such as regulators, in the case of, say, UK privatized utilities, and environmental pressure groups. Passive stakeholders do not normally seek to participate in an organization's policy making. This is not to say that passive stakeholders are any less interested nor any less powerful, but that they do not seek to take an active part in the organization's strategy. Passive stakeholders will normally include most shareholders, government and local communities.

Voluntary and involuntary stakeholders

This distinction describes stakeholders who engage with the organization voluntarily and those who become stakeholders involuntarily. Voluntary stakeholders will include, for example, employees with transferable skills, that is, they could work elsewhere, most customers, suppliers and shareholders. Some stakeholders, however, do not choose to be stakeholders but nevertheless are. Involuntary

6

stakeholders include those affected by the activities of large organizations, local communities and 'neighbours', the natural environment, future generations and most competitors.

Legitimate and illegitimate stakeholders

This is one of the more difficult categorizations to make as a stakeholder's legitimacy depends on your viewpoint – one person's terrorist is another's freedom fighter. While those with an active economic relationship with an organization will almost always be considered legitimate, others who make claims without such a link or who have no mandate to make a claim will be considered illegitimate by some, meaning that there is no possible case for taking their views into account when making decisions. While terrorists will usually be considered illegitimate, there is more debate on the legitimacy of the claims of lobby groups, campaigning organizations and non-governmental/charitable organizations.

Recognized and unrecognized (by the organization) stakeholders

The categorization by recognition follows on from the debate over legitimacy. If an organization considers a stakeholder's claim to be illegitimate, it is likely that their claim will not be recognized. This means that the stakeholder's claim will not be taken into account when making decisions.

Known about and unknown stakeholders

Finally, some stakeholders are known about by the organization in question and others are not. This means, of course, that whether their claims are considered legitimate or not, it is difficult to recognize the claims of unknown stakeholders, for example nameless sea creatures, undiscovered species, communities around overseas supplier businesses and so on. Some say that it is an organization's moral duty to seek out all possible stakeholders invoved in a decision before it is taken, and this can sometimes mean, for example, adopting minimum impact policies. The exact identity of a nameless sea creature need not be known about but it might be the case that low emissions can normally be assumed to be better for these creatures than pollution and high emissions.

20.3 Descriptions of the organization–stakeholder relationship

Whichever stakeholder model one finds most appealing, we turn now to the question as to why organizations do or do not take account of stakeholder concerns in their strategy formulation and implementation. A parallel can be drawn between the ways in which organizations view their stakeholders and the ways in which individual people consider, or do not consider, the views of other people. Some people are concerned about others' opinions of them, while other people seem to have little or no regard for others' concerns. Furthermore, the reasons why individuals care about others' concerns will also vary.

In attempting to address this issue, Donaldson and Preston (1995) drew a distinction between two motivations describing why organizations accede to stakeholder concerns. They describe these two contrasting motivations as the instrumental and the normative.

The instrumental view of stakeholders

The instrumental view of stakeholder theory posits that organizations take stakeholder opinions into account only insofar as they are consistent with other, more important economic objectives, for example profit maximization. Accordingly, it may be that a business modifies its objectives in the light of environmental concerns but only because acquiescence to stakeholder opinion is the best way of optimizing profit or achieving other business success. If the loyalty or commitment of an important primary or active stakeholder group is threatened, it is likely that the organization will modify its objectives because not to do so would threaten to reduce its economic performance, for example profitability. It follows from the instrumental stakeholder approach that an organization's values are guided by its stakeholders' opinions – it may not have any inherent moral values of its own except for the overriding profit motive.

The normative view of stakeholders

The normative view of stakeholder theory differs from the instrumental view because it describes not what is, but what should be, that is, what should be the 'norm' in an ideal situation. The most commonly cited moral framework used in describing that which should be is derived from the philosophy of German ethical thinker Immanual Kant (1724–1804). Kant's moral philosophy centred around the notion of civil duties, which, Kant argued, are important in maintaining and increasing the net good in society. Kantian ethics are, in part, based on the notion that we each have a moral obligation to each other in respect of taking account of each others' concerns and opinions. Not to do so will result in the atrophy of social cohesion and will ultimately lead to everybody being morally, and possibly economically, worse off.

Extending this argument to stakeholder theory, the normative view argues that organizations should accommodate stakeholder concerns not because of what the organization can 'get out of it' for its own profit, but because it should observe its moral duty to each stakeholder. The normative view sees stakeholders as ends in themselves and not as merely instrumental to the achievement of other ends.

20.4 Stakeholder concerns

If it can be coherently argued that organizations do (for whatever reason) have some degree of responsibility to their constituencies, then we now turn to the issues that are most frequently raised as being areas of concern. The most frequently mentioned stakeholder concerns can be divided into two broad and interconnected categories:

1 Concerns over an organization's attitude towards the *natural environment*
2 Concerns over the *ethical behaviour* of organizations.

Table 20.1 describes how these broad categories are linked and subdivided.

The environmental and ethical concerns outlined in Table 20.1 are matters for which organizations are accountable, according to stakeholder theory proponents. Given that different stakeholders have raised these matters as being of concern, all of them are part of the portfolio of issues for which organizations are, in part, responsible to society.

Table 20.1 **A taxonomy of stakeholder concerns**

Key area	Subsidiary concerns	Examples
Environmental concerns	The state of natural resources	• Energy resources and conservation • Mineral resources and conservation • Extinction and overfishing
	The way in which business activities affect environmental pollution	• Global warming ('greenhouse' effect) • Ozone layer depletion • Health concerns (skin cancer, asthma) • Industrial emissions (into rivers) • Rubbish and waste (landfill, nuclear) • 'Acid' rain (emissions from coal-fired power stations)
Ethical concerns	The asymmetric nature of markets	• Developing countries' debt and its repayment terms to developed countries' banks • 'Fair trade' between companies in rich, developed countries and producers in poorer, developing countries • Multinational companies alleged 'exploitation' of weaker developing economies
	The business's alleged responsibility to society	• Community involvement • Marketing practices (corporate sponsorships and advertising) • Animal 'cruelty' issues • Product health and safety • Compensation and reparations (drugs, oil spills)
	The internal and industry activities of the business	• Employment practices (employment rate of minorities, disabled people, women) • Health and safety in the workplace (over and above the legal minimum) • Treatment of suppliers, customers and other stakeholders (days taken to pay smaller creditors)

20.5   Strategic postures in social responsibility

Social responsibility means that organizations are not free to act as though the concerns outlined above did not exist. However, it is evident that not all organizations espouse the same attitudes in respect to social and environmental concerns. Four general degrees of responsiveness have been identified (Campbell and Craig, 2005) and these are outlined below.

Socially obstructive organizations

Some businesses are actively socially obstructive. This description can be applied to organizations that actively resist any pressure or attempts to modify pure business objectives in the light of social concerns. Such organizations may resist attempts to make them abide by even the minimum legal standards of behaviour – behaviour which may be followed by denial and an attempt to keep 'interfering' bodies out of their business. Some have argued that tobacco manufacturers fall into this category, because in order to protect their cigarette sales, they may effectively deny that tobacco causes as much harm as some health professionals have suggested may be the case. These companies would presumably argue that it would not be in their strategic interests to respond to stakeholder concerns.

Koch Industries, for example, a $100bn a year conglomerate in the oil and chemical industry, has donated nearly $48m to climate opposition groups. It has been reported that, between 2005 and 2008, Koch Industries donated substantial amounts to groups not only opposed to clean energy but also to

CASE STUDY   Sunrise Farms Ltd

At home in the countryside near Mombassa, Kenya, Paul Potter sat back contentedly on his verandah. He had just secured a deal for his company, an international wholesale farming conglomerate called Sunrise Farms Ltd, to supply the largest UK, French and German supermarket chains with a wide range of organic fruit and vegetable produce. The deal was worth £630m over five years, and represented a major victory for Sunrise.

Sunrise was founded in London in 1961. Originally it was purely a trading company, buying wholesale on behalf of independent fruit and vegetable sellers in Covent Garden. The company then took advantage of opportunities to buy out the independents and establish itself as one of the largest, most reliable and, above all, fairest of wholesalers. It also began to buy up its own farms, so that it could guarantee as much domestic produce as possible, as far as possible. It was one of the first companies in the UK to move into indoor, industrial and all-year-round farming. It used artificial lighting and growing environment management to produce year-round strawberry and raspberry crops that would otherwise only be available in season.

The company subsequently sold its farming operations in order to concentrate on wholesale buying and selling. Starting in the UK, it quickly expanded into the other EU countries, and opened up in Africa in 1990. Sunrise gained a reputation for fair trading across the whole continent, always giving fair prices to independent farmers and farming combines and cooperatives. The produce would then be sold on wholesale to the large UK, French and German supermarket chains.

Potter had worked for Sunrise for 20 years. Starting as a marketing assistant at the company head office in London, he had worked his way up the company, and moved to purchasing and supply seven years ago. There he had quickly made a mark for securing long-term supplies at good prices. From time to time this had antagonized more senior managers, who did not see why he could not get the prices down still further. Whenever the question arose, Potter always replied: 'Do we want the supplies, or do we want cheapness? We cannot have both.'

Potter had become purchasing director for the whole of Sunrise's business in Africa three years ago and since then had doubled the volume of business. In spite of his insistence on paying fair prices, Sunrise's African turnover had gone up fivefold, from £23m to £130m. Paul himself was well known and highly respected in the wholesale markets across the continent.

However, the recent round had been a tough competition. In particular, Potter had been worried about being undercut by South African farming conglomerates, all of which had promised to deliver the same volumes and quality as Sunrise, but at far lower prices. In particular, one of the South African companies had come in at 66% lower, and Potter had resigned himself to defeat. Before doing so, however, he had telephoned head office in London, and asked what he should do. 'Stick to your guns', was the reply, 'the South African bid will be turned down.' When Paul had asked how they could possibly be certain of this, he was told that the French and UK supermarkets had inspected the South African farms, and had found them to be substandard in terms of cleanliness, working conditions and wage rates.

Paul had known then to keep quiet and indeed 'stick to his guns'. Sunrise had been one of the first companies to adopt the fair trade logo, and this had gone a long way towards building the reputation and securing Sunrise's position in Africa as the European trader of choice. Paul always inspected the farms himself, and he did his best to make sure that everything was is order in terms of wages, working conditions, management practices and farming methods. This last had now become important because of the huge expansion in the 'organic market', which in 2007 was worth £19bn in the UK alone, and which would nearly double over the coming two years.

Consequently, Sunrise was now able to attach the fair trade logo to all its produce that came out of Africa as a matter of policy, which had helped to secure long-term, valuable contracts with Morrisons, Sainsbury's and Waitrose in the UK, and E.Leclerc and Carrefour in France. He also knew that if the business did come through, on average two plane loads per hour and one ship load per day would be heading from Africa to Europe, carrying produce for Sunrise's clients in the European supermarket and grocery sector.

6

senators and influential lobbyists to support the use of fossil fuels. It has been accused of spreading false and misleading information regarding climate change and, on several occasions, it has used its financial power to target policy groups representing renewable energies or global warming. Its action is mainly understood to protect its interests centred around oil, gas and chemical industries (Vidal, 2010).

Social obligation only organizations

Some businesses observe no more than their minimum social obligations. This description can be applied to organizations that are prepared to abide by whatever restrictions are placed on them by governments, that is, the legal minimum. They are unwilling to give credence to any pressure or lobby groups which, in the opinion of the organization, do not have any statutory influence over them.

Companies operating in the oil and gas industry fall into this category. The case of Shell Nigeria (the colloquial name for Royal Dutch Shell's Nigerian operations) is a well-known example. Shell was legally extracting oil and natural gas from the Niger Delta, but its attitude towards the welfare of the indigenious Ogoni people and the environment created a storm in the 1980 and 90s. Oil companies operating in the Niger Delta, including Shell, were responsible for both environmental degradation and social unrest in the region. They came under severe criticism and pressure from human rights and environmental groups to improve conditions but still resisted any moves towards concrete action. Shell's CSR approach pre-1997 can be termed as obligatory and its corporate objective at that time reflects its approach and attitude – typically, it was 'to find, produce and deliver hydrocarbons safely, responsibly and economically for the benefit of our stakeholders'.

Socially responsive organizations

Socially responsive organizations submit to minimum legal standards for corporate behaviour towards society and the environment, but will do more to address people's concerns if pressurized to do so by stakeholders such as pressure groups.

Many high-street brands can be called socially responsive. For example, Starbucks mission and objective statements reflect its attitude towards society and environment (see below). Through its CAFE (Coffee and Farmer Equity Practices) initiative (an incentive-based system under which Starbucks' growers receive economic incentives for following a comprehensive set of sourcing guidelines), it has been aware of the needs of small coffee farmers, and its business, as far as possible, is conducted in an environmentally aware manner. Recycling, reducing waste and investing in communities are some of its operating mantras, and within the CSR community, it is well known for its environmental leadership and sustainability initiatives.

Social contribution organizations

Social contribution organizations willingly do all they reasonably can to extend their social and environmental involvement. These organizations seek to make a positive contribution to the communities they serve, to help protect the natural environment and to avoid any unethical business practices. Some of these organizations may exist primarily for the purpose of promoting social responsibility and ethical business practice.

Voluntary and non-governmental organizations fall into this category. A well-known example is Greenpeace, which has been at the forefront of environmental activism for over three decades. One of its main objectives is to protect earth's diversity and it organizes campaigns to raise awareness on issues ranging from climate change to genetically modified organisms. A different kind of social contribution organization is TreeHugger (treehugger.com), the leading eco-lifestyle website dedicated to driving sustainability mainstream. Its main mission is to deliver cutting-edge scoops on green architecture, design, gadgets, technology, fashion, health, politics and science to more than 2.5 million visitors each month.

20.6   Responding to the ethical agenda

Given the extent to which organizations vary in their postures towards social responsibility, it is not surprising that a range of mechanisms have been adopted to express such responsibility. Essentially, this section is concerned with answering the question: How do organizations express their concerns over social issues?

A key distinction to be drawn here is between having a corporate social responsibility (CSR) strategy and adopting a strategic approach to CSR. To have a CSR strategy means 'the firm is orderly in the methods and procedures it uses [in its CSR]' (Saiia et al., 2003, p. 185), whereas 'strategic CSR' means 'the corporate resources that are given have meaning and impact on the firm as well as the community that receives those resources' (Saiia et al., 2003, p. 185). So CSR strategy means that the company has considered how it will respond to certain stakeholders and a range of ethical issues, and strategic CSR means that the company sees CSR as a part of its overall business strategy. To be strategic about CSR means that CSR measures, such as charitable giving, social involvement, environmental impact reduction and so on, will only be undertaken if the benefits can be seen and measured for the company's shareholders.

When it comes to CSR measures themselves, most companies consider a range of items for inclusion in the CSR strategy. Some frame these into a formal code of ethics and the measures typically include:

- relations with customers
- relations with shareholders and other investors
- relations with employees
- relations with suppliers
- relations with the government and the local community
- the environment
- taxation
- relations with competitors
- issues relating to international business
- behaviour in relation to mergers and takeovers

6

- ethical issues concerning directors and managers
- compliance and verification.

Starbucks mission statement highlights some the important concepts addressed above, and includes Starbucks commitment to its stakeholders, customers, community and environment.

> *Our mission: to inspire and nurture the human spirit – one person, one cup and one neighborhood at a time.*

Here are the principles of how we live that every day:

Our Coffee

It has always been, and will always be, about quality. We're passionate about ethically sourcing the finest coffee beans, roasting them with great care, and improving the lives of people who grow them. We care deeply about all of this; our work is never done.

Our Partners

We're called partners, because it's not just a job, it's our passion. Together, we embrace diversity to create a place where each of us can be ourselves. We always treat each other with respect and dignity. And we hold each other to that standard.

Our Customers

When we are fully engaged, we connect with, laugh with, and uplift the lives of our customers – even if just for a few moments. Sure, it starts with the promise of a perfectly made beverage, but our work goes far beyond that. It's really about human connection.

Our Stores

When our customers feel this sense of belonging, our stores become a haven, a break from the worries outside, a place where you can meet with friends. It's about enjoyment at the speed of life – sometimes slow and savoured, sometimes faster. Always full of humanity.

Our Neighborhood

Every store is part of a community, and we take our responsibility to be good neighbors seriously. We want to be invited in wherever we do business. We can be a force for positive action – bringing together our partners, customers, and the community to contribute every day. Now we see that our responsibility – and our potential for good – is even larger. The world is looking to Starbucks to set the new standard, yet again. We will lead.

Our Shareholders

We know that as we deliver in each of these areas, we enjoy the kind of success that rewards our shareholders. We are fully accountable to get each of these elements right so that Starbucks – and everyone it touches – can endure and thrive.

Environmental Mission Statement

> *Starbucks is committed to a role of environmental leadership in all facets of our business.*

We fulfil this mission by a commitment to:

- Understanding of environmental issues and sharing information with our partners.
- Developing innovative and flexible solutions to bring about change.
- Striving to buy, sell and use environmentally friendly products.
- Recognizing that fiscal responsibility is essential to our environmental future.
- Instilling environmental responsibility as a corporate value.
- Measuring and monitoring our progress for each project.
- Encouraging all partners to share in our mission.

Source: http://www.starbucks.com/about-us/company-information/mission-statement.

One of the most important changes in recent years has been the growth in social and environmental reporting and accounting. This is when a company voluntarily informs its stakeholders of its behaviour in respect of environmental, ethical and social concerns. Organizations have no legal obligations to make such disclosures but some do so nevertheless. The disclosures may be of a social or environmental nature and, it has been argued, are designed to legitimize the organization's behaviour in the eyes of potentially critical stakeholders (see for example Guthrie and Parker, 1989; Gray et al., 1995).

Social reporting disclosures can be carried in a number of company-produced documents. The practice is more established among larger companies who have more complex stakeholder relationships than smaller ones. While the annual report remains the primary vehicle for social disclosure for most companies, some companies produce separate environmental or social reports (see next section). These are non-mandatory documents that set out in more detail how the company has behaved in respect of environmental or social concerns over the past year. The concerns over the environmental impacts of businesses lead us to the final section, that of the environmental sustainability of businesses.

20.7   Businesses and sustainability

The concept of sustainability was defined in 1987 in an influential UN report by the former Norwegian prime minister Mrs Gro Harlem Brundtland. She said that sustainable development, say, of businesses, is 'development that meets the needs of the present without compromising the ability of future generations to meet their own needs'. This guideline has become increasingly influential over time. At its root is the observation that most economic activity impacts on the environment in two ways – it takes from the environment and it emits into the environment. The point is that nothing is infinitely sustainable because there is only so much capacity in the natural environment to provide inputs and absorb outputs.

Sustainable development is 'development that meets the needs of the present without compromising the ability of future generations to meet their own needs'.

A typical business will take from the environment in its energy use, water, inventories (stocks) and emit into the environment its emissions, products (what happens when they are disposed of) and any accidental spillages or leaks. The point is that once the environment has exceeded its capacity for these, it will deteriorate. Because we and our progeny must live in the environment, the state of the environment is extremely important.

To be sustainable, then, a business must not use inputs to produce outputs that cannot be offset or replaced at the same rate at which they are consumed or produced. This is why many government and business measures are aimed at reducing resource consumption or offsetting, such as by the use of recycling. A key problem, however, is that some industries are, by their very nature, unsustainable. Petrochemicals, for example, extract a non-renewable energy source from the ground (oil), which is burned to produce energy (in power stations and cars, for example), which then produces greenhouse gases.

To some extent, then, the sustainability of business is an aspiration rather than a realistic policy agenda. The eco-agenda that is linked to the aim of sustainability has pervaded many aspects of business activity and is becoming increasingly important.

6

Given that almost all business activity takes place at net cost to the environment (it destroys more than it remediates) and that environmental concerns have risen as a public issue in recent years, businesses have been increasingly turning to environmental issues in their strategies. It is common to criticize businesses for **greenwashing** (a wordplay on 'whitewashing') – the deceptive use of green PR or green marketing in order to promote a misleading perception that a company's policies or products (such as goods or services) are environmentally friendly.

The point is that competitive pressures mean that a single business can rarely 'break ranks' with its industry and introduce genuinely meaningful environmental measures. It is thus generally seen as (at best) an incremental and slow change towards more environmental responsibility.

Greenwashing is a term describing the deceptive use of green PR or green marketing in order to promote a misleading perception that a company's policies or products (such as goods or services) are environmentally friendly.

Example   Scottish whisky industry

A different take on the concepts discussed above is when a industry truly starts focusing on developing and implementing sustainable strategies. The Scottish whisky industry is a prime example, being a forerunner in the employment of sustainable initiatives, with clear policies to promote long-term economic, environmental and social sustainability.

Some of its commitments and targets include:

- *reducing reliance on fossil fuels:* By 2020, the industry aims to derive 20% of its primary energy requirements from non-fossil sources
- *forest management:* All casks will henceforth be sourced from sustainable forests
- *supply chain management:* The industry hopes to work with its supply chain stakeholders, even those who are not under its direct control, in developing sustainable strategies
- *packaging materials:* By 2020, the industry expects all its packaging materials will either be fully reusable or recyclable, and not find their way to waste landfill.

Source: http://www.scotch-whisky.org.uk/swa/files/EnvironmentalStrategy09.pdf.

For test questions, extra case studies, audio case studies, weblinks, videolinks and more to help you understand the topics covered in this chapter, visit our companion website at www.macmillanihe.com/companion/business/campbell.

REVIEW QUESTIONS

1 Explain the different positions on social responsibility.
2 Describe the concept of sustainability and the main themes of the eco-agenda.
3 Explain the nature of stakeholder concerns.
4 Explain what is meant by the strategic posture in social responsibility.

DISCUSSION TOPIC

Organizations should 'live for today' and only focus on repaying the wealth invested in them by shareholders. Discuss.

HOT TOPICS – Research project areas to investigate

For your research project, why not investigate ...

- ... how sustainability issues are communicated internally within an organization.
- ... approaches by organizations to offset their carbon footprint.
- ... what issues are likely to drive the next phase of CSR in Europe.

6

Recommended reading

Bansal, P. and Roth, R. (2000) 'Why companies go green: a model of ecological responsiveness, *Academy of Management Journal*, **43**(4): 717–36.

Campbell, D.J. (1997) *Organisations and the Business Environment*, Oxford: Butterworth Heinemann.

Fields, S. (2002) 'Sustainable business makes dollars and cents, *Environmental Health Perspectives*, **110**(3): A142–5.

Fry, L.W., Keim, G.D. and Meiners, E. (1982) 'Corporate contributions: altruistic or for profit?', *Academy of Management Journal*, **25**(1): 94–106.

Hemingway, C.A. (2005) 'Personal values as a catalyst for corporate social entrepreneurship', *Journal of Business Ethics,* **60**(3): 233–49.

Maignan, I.O. Ferrell, G. and Tomas, G. (1999) 'Corporate

citizenship: cultural antecedents and business benefits, *Journal of the Academy of Marketing Science*, **27**(4): 455–69.

Roux, M. (2007) 'Climate conducive to corporate action', *The Australian*, p. 14.

Sacconi, L. (2004) 'A social contract account for CSR as extended model of corporate governance (Part II): compliance, reputation and reciprocity', *Journal of Business Ethics*, 11: 77–96.

Sun, W. (2010) *How to Govern Corporations so They Serve the Public Good: A Theory of Corporate Governance Emergence*, New York: Edwin Mellen.

Chapter references

Campbell, D.J. and Craig, T. (2005) *Organisations and the Business Environment* (2nd edn), Oxford: Elsevier.

Clarkson, M.B. (1995) 'A stakeholder framework for analysing and evaluating corporate social performance', *Academy of Management Review*, **20**(1): 92–117.

Donaldson, T. (1982) *Corporate Morality*, Englewood Cliffs, NJ: Prentice Hall.

Donaldson, T. and Preston, L.E. (1995) 'The stakeholder theory of the corporation: concepts, evidence and implications', *Academy of Management Review*, **20**(1): 65–91.

Evan, W.M. and Freeman, R.E. (1993) 'A stakeholder theory of the modern corporation: Kantian capitalism', in T.L. Beauchamp and N.E. Bowie (eds) *Ethical Theory and Business*, Englewood Cliffs, NJ: Prentice Hall.

Freeman, R.E. (1994) 'The politics of stakeholder theory: some future directions', *Business Ethics Quarterly*, **4**(4): 409–21.

Friedman, M. (1970) 'The social responsibility of business is to increase its profits', *New York Times Magazine*, 13 September, 7–13.

Gray, R., Kouhy, R. and Lavers, S. (1995) 'Corporate social and environmental reporting: a review of the literature and a longitudinal study of UK disclosures', *Accounting, Auditing and Accountability Journal*, **8**(2): 47–77.

Guthrie, J.E. and Parker, L.D. (1989) 'Corporate social reporting: a rebuttal of legitimacy theory', *Accounting and Business Research*, **9**(76): 343–52.

Mahoney, J. (1994) 'Stakeholder responsibilities: turning the ethical tables', *Business Ethics – A European Review*, **3**(4): 212–18.

Rawls, J. (1971) *A Theory of Justice*, Cambridge, MA: Harvard University Press.

Saiia, D.H, Carroll, A.B. and Buchholtz, A.K. (2003) 'Philanthropy as strategy, when corporate charity begins at home', *Business and Society*, **42**(2): 169–201.

Smith, A. (1776) *An Inquiry into the Nature & Causes of The Wealth of Nations*, Glasgow edn, 2 vols, 1982, Glasgow: Liberty Fund.

Vidal, J. (2010) 'US oil company donated millions to climate sceptic groups, says Greenpeace', *The Gurdian*, 30 March, www.guardian.co.uk/environment/2010/mar/30/us-oil-donated-millions-climate-sceptics.

Chapter 21

Emerging markets and industry superpowers

Introduction and chapter overview

This is the final chapter of our book, and here we want you to start to think about what business developments are on the horizon. We want you to use the knowledge you now have about the environment and environmental scanning to think about how the changing nature of business, consumers and global markets may influence societies and the organizations operating within them.

The chapter explores the nature of generation Y and profiles geographic regions which may be termed superpowers or emerging markets – India, China, Brazil, the Middle East, elements of Central Europe and Russia. We have not included countries in Africa but in terms of natural resources, agriculture and emerging tourism, African nations will be ones to watch in the future.

We conclude by briefly examining strategic management implications. We do not offer any answers in this chapter, rather, its purpose is to pose some questions and make you think about the world in the 21st century.

Learning objectives

After studying this chapter, you will be able to:

- understand what is meant by emerging markets and emerging industries
- explain what is meant by generation Y and outline the characteristics displayed by this generation
- profile the characteristics of different superpower or emerging economies
- suggest which industries are growing and developing across different regions of the globe
- identify areas where new products are emerging and begin to consider the impact of such changes on society

21.1 Emerging markets: industry and products

In understanding the changing nature of the world markets, it is useful for us to look at four key things. First, we shall consider which markets seem to be emerging, and second, which industries are growing as a result of such market emergence, although this is tricky as each market changes depending on geographic location. Then, given that markets are often driven by a combination of demand and new technology, we explore the concept of generation Y and how this emerging generation of consumers could impact on industry and markets. Finally, we take a look at the current industry superpowers and emerging countries.

Emerging markets

The term emerging
markets refers to countries
or markets that are just
beginning to industrialize
and, in the process, are
displaying strong economic
growth.

The term emerging markets refers to countries or markets that are just beginning to industrialize and, in the process, are displaying strong economic growth. This strong growth usually results in the GDP (gross domestic product) and disposable income of the population increasing. The result of this increase is consumers' ability to buy goods and services they would not normally have been able to afford. So developing countries represent a potential emerging market for existing products and for companies already established in the 'developed' world. In this respect, companies like Coca-Cola and Vodafone have found new outlets for their products. In contrast, advertising firms like Omnicom Group and Interpublic Group have flourished on the back of the domestic growth in countries like Russia, India and China by providing advertising and media consultancy services as competition in emerging markets has increased and the need for advertising has arisen.

KEY CONCEPTS

Gross domestic product (GDP) is a measure of a country's overall official economic output. It is the market value of all final goods and services officially made within the borders of a country in a year. It is often positively correlated with the standard of living.

Gross national income (GNI) per capita is the dollar value of a country's final income in a year, divided by its population. It reflects the average income of a country's citizens.

In addition to emerging markets built on existing products and services offered to developing countries, markets also emerge as a result of the introduction of new technology. It is widely recognized that to achieve long-term economic growth, investment is required in new technology and the development and transfer of technical know-how. This knowledge transfer leads to efficiency and/or effectiveness but is often sporadic in nature, resulting in a mixture of incremental technology introduction and more sporadic or radical developments. Often, it is the radical developments that provide for the structural changes that lead to higher returns, including things like the development of the mobile phone, or Windows operating systems. In some cases, it is not so much the technology that allows for the creation of the market but the drive to become the industry standard. This was clearly seen in the development of the video recorder and the battle between Betamax and VHS in the late 1970s and 80s. Despite the former being a better technological product, the latter became the industry standard, because of mass production, consumerism and better meeting consumer expectations, wants and needs. A similar battle is currently underway between the producers of 3D television.

Emerging industry

On the whole, most industry is driven by consumer behaviour and demand patterns, and so the emerging industry reflects the emerging markets.

To understand and perhaps forecast emerging industries, it is useful to understand that, across the globe, different countries have different industrial priorities and that a government's economic policies are often a good measure of where such priorities, or perceived growth industries, lie. Take Malaysia for example. The economic policy of Malaysia has one key objective, the achievement of long-term stable and sustainable growth. This is intended to improve the standard of living of the population and secure the economic future of the country. To achieve this, in a way similar to many of the Middle East, oil-rich countries, the government recognized the need for economic diversification and thus the need to supplement traditional industries with new or emerging industries. In Malaysia, this can be seen in a number of key areas:

- More effective use of palm oil biomass (the waste products of palm oil, one of Malaysia's main agricultural industries)
- Development of the biotechnology sector to focus on herbal-based pharmaceuticals and treatment of tropical diseases
- Growth in the manufacturing sector around high-tech and knowledge-based industries, including defence, marine, fabricated metals and food manufacturing
- Growth in the service sector, for example education, health tourism, Islamic finance and professional or consultancy services.

Overall, these sectors have been and are being promoted, resourced and supported by government policy, the education sector, research and a host of other initiatives in a coordinated effort to grow the sectors.

The same pattern is seen across the globe, be it funded/orchestrated by government, monarchy or dictatorship.

To see how economies are changing, we look at two economies that traditionally were at the forefront of economic development, namely the USA and Japan.

The USA

In the USA, according to the Bureau of Labor Statistics (2009), service industries represent the largest growth sector and are predicted to add an estimated 14.6 million jobs between 2008 and 2018, a 96% increase in employment. In this sector, the two largest employment growth areas are expected to be professional and business services (4.2 million) and healthcare and social assistance (4 million). On the other hand, manufacturing and production are forecast to remain stagnant.

In the USA, the top 10 growth industries (by employment) are:

1 Management, scientific and technical consulting services
2 Offices of physicians
3 Computer systems design and related services
4 Other general merchandise stores
5 Employment services
6 Local government, excluding education and hospitals
7 Home healthcare services
8 Services for the elderly and persons with disabilities
9 Nursing care facilities
10 Full-service restaurants (Bureau of Labor Statistics, 2009).

6

The 10 most in decline are:

1 Department stores
2 Semiconductor and other electronic component manufacturing
3 Motor vehicle parts manufacturing
4 Postal service
5 Printing and related support activities
6 Cut and sew apparel manufacturing
7 Newspaper publishers
8 Support activities for mining
9 Gasoline stations
10 Wired telecommunications carriers (Bureau of Labor Statistics, 2009).

These trends in employment show how the economy in the USA is being shaped and changed by the new technologies and perhaps what the future may hold for economies across the world that are currently at the manufacturing-based stage of economic growth.

Adopting a different measure, the Fortune 500 survey highlighted the following as the largest growth sectors by profit growth (*Fortune*, 2009):

1 Pipelines
2 Engineering and construction
3 Petroleum refining
4 Mining, crude oil production
5 Oil and gas equipment, services
6 Energy
7 Construction and farm machinery
8 Metals
9 Food production
10 Industrial machinery.

From the USA, we can see an emerging trend in industry related to health and wellbeing, services and the creative industries. The green and alternative energy industry is developing and gathering pace. Overall, change is quicker and organizational life cycles shorter, making organization renewal, strategic networks, and open source innovation central to many organizations.

Japan

In Japan, there have been two key periods of economic development, 1868–1940, and 1945 to the mid-1990s. During both periods, the Japanese government encouraged economic change by fostering a national revolution from above and advising in every aspect of society. The national goal was to make Japan so powerful and wealthy that its independence would never be threatened. The success of Japan's economy is well known; however, there were also resulting downsides. The preoccupation with growth led to a focus on production and manufacturing and a resultant neglect of the environment, for example increasing industrial pollution, and consumer services. Many social services, such as housing, roads, sewerage, social security and public health, suffered, as focus was placed on private sector manufacturing and productivity. As we will see next, these are side effects that future economies will need to avoid if they are to meet the needs of generation Y.

Generation Y

Before exploring some country profiles, it is useful for us to take a look at generation Y. We have seen that markets and industries are, in effect, shaped and developed by a mixture of technology and consumers' wants, needs and desires. Here we focus on the nature of future consumers, those termed 'generation Y' (or millennial generation, generation next or net generation). Generation Y describes the demographic cohort following generation X, roughly speaking, those born in the 1980s and 90s. Understanding a little about generation Y allows us to think about how we may need to adapt organizations and strategy to serve these markets and how to manage these new employees.

Generation Y describes the demographic cohort following generation X, roughly speaking, those born in the 1980s and 90s.

The members of generation Y have been termed 'digital natives' – they have been reared with the internet and 24-hour access to information and so are shaped by this in terms of their outlook and demands. They are vastly different from generation X (their parents' generation). They are characterized as being passionate, strong-willed and optimistic, they have great expectations and expect to get what they want. They expect information to be quickly and readily available, 24/7. Members of generation Y will change jobs, on average, 29 times in their lifetime and will want maximum flexibility and freedom – only around 6% will join any form of union or political party – and they will be motivated by 'organizations that offer more than money' (Braid, 2007). Indeed, these tendencies raise questions as to whether there will be any generation Y members available to lead companies in the future – an issue which may require organizations to rethink their governance structures.

These are some of the characteristics of members of generation Y:

- In the USA, the population is 80 million, with a spend power of $200bn
- Reared with the internet, social media, 24-hour information, email, instant messaging and texting, their lives are characterized by being continuously connected and by multitasking
- They have been selected and protected, in that they were born during the rise of contraceptives and legal abortion, and have been protected by elements such as mandatory seatbelts, cycle helmets, food standards, medical advancements and a more protective parenting approach
- They are more civic-minded, motivated by what friends think and do, confident, untrusting of authority and strive for self-fulfilment.

In terms of employment characteristics, Anni Macbeth, forecaster and futurist, highlighted that generation Y members will have five key characteristics that employers will need to be aware of (http://blog.litmos.com/2008_08_01_archive.html):

- they will only give one chance to gain their trust; if deceived, they will disconnect
- they are multi-channellers and can focus fully on many variables at once
- they care and are committed to saving the planet
- they avoid authority and the establishment
- they have a sense of immediacy and have high expectations of service and relationships.

It is clear that generation Y members will have a massive impact on business and organizations of the future, so we need to think how they will change and shape the future.

6

CASE STUDY   Swann Wind Farms Ltd

By common consent, the wind farm and alternative energy industries are as safe as any in the world. As well as contributing to the overall prosperity, development and wellbeing of the world, there is great scope for enterprise and organizational and managerial acumen in business and market development. So the prospects for anyone wanting a career in this sector look well assured, with scope for being at the cutting edge of business, technology, social, economic and political development, and making a real and lasting contribution to the future of international society.

After he qualified as a mechanical engineer, Simon Rose determined that he would work in an industry that would give him a good career, lots of interest and, above all, would make a real impact on the future of the world. So when he was given the opportunity to join Swann Wind Farms Ltd (SWF), he jumped at the chance. His prospects were excellent, the interest high, and the scope for work virtually unlimited.

This was three years ago. Since then the company has had work all over the world and Simon himself has worked in France, Germany, Latvia and Lithuania. He has just come back from a six-month trip assessing the feasibility of installing 5,000 windmills in the Yangtze valley in China over the coming three years.

Located near Portsmouth on the south coast of England, SWF manufacture, produce and deliver the windmills. They also project manage the installation of the windmills themselves, and their integration with the national and local electricity grids of the countries and locations in which they work. SWF is happy to work for either nationalized, privatized or fully commercial electricity providers. SWF charges premium rates for a top-quality service, delivered on time and to budget, with fully guaranteed products, and, over the past decade, has made a worldwide name for its work. The company's finances are strong and sound, with no deficit financing and an extensive reinvestment programme based purely on retained profit (see table).

SWF: main financial and other data

	Last year	This year
Income/turnover	£130m	£170m
Retained profit	£30m	£32m
Company valuation*	£590m	£630m

* Share value, plus valuation of recent completions, work in progress and order book, plus goodwill/technology/expertise.

However, since his return, Simon has become aware of a number of problems. First, for reasons never explained, SWF was not awarded any of the contracts for wind farm and wind turbine development around the coast of the UK, in spite of the fact that it had (and has) a proven track record in the field and was the only fully UK-owned bidder for the work. Also, while SWF would indeed have been more expensive than some, it would not have been as expensive as the largest successful bidder, and would have delivered a higher quality project six months in advance. One of the public authorities has since gone on record asking why SWF has not been awarded any of the work.

It has also become clear that the company will not get the full share of the work in China, on which Simon has spent so much time and effort. It is clear that while SWF will get the project management part of the contract, the equipment and technology are to be supplied by other preferred bidders from France, Germany and the USA. The result of this is going to be a serious short- to medium-term cash flow problem, and depending on other orders, this may in turn hinder the ability of SWF to invest in its own capability in the next generations of wind generation technology and other alternative energy sources.

Under direction from the company's top and senior management, Simon now tried to get to the bottom of why SWF was having so much trouble moving itself forwards. He began by asking the clients that SWF had served so well, and the answers seemed to fall into three categories:

■ *protectionism* – the large national utilities of the UK, France, Spain, Germany, the USA and Japan were doing their very best to carve up the market for the present and next generation of wind turbines

■ *envy* – brought on by the reputation of SWF for

delivering quality products, on time and within budget, which, in turn, made the large companies in the industry look cumbersome, sloppy, complacent and inefficient

■ *financial structure and size* – which Simon knew remained a constant problem for otherwise strong and effective providers across the sector, and was a more or less universal problem for many otherwise excellent businesses in all spheres of activity.

Simon also knew that the last point remained a constant headache to SWF top and senior management. SWF had a notional value of £630m (see table above), which did not remotely compare with EDF (£32bn) in France or British Energy (£17bn) in the UK, which became part of EDF Energy in 2009.

Case study questions

1 What are the main lessons for managers in companies in emerging industries?
2 What are the problems facing industries such as alternative energy technology and how might those in charge begin to tackle them?
3 What alternatives are open to Swann Wind Farms in addressing the cash flow and capital/financial situation?
4 How might Swann Wind Farms deal with the industrial/structural problem of envy, and the universal counter-publicity that this invariably generates?

21.2 Industry superpowers: China and India

In this section we focus on what can now be classed as two world industrial superpowers, namely China and India. Our intention is to profile each country to provide an understanding of the scale, speed of growth and nature of each.

China

China has emerged as an economic superpower after years of expansion, with around 9% per annum GDP growth as the norm. In 2005, GDP was around $2,000bn rising to $5,000bn in 2010, representing 7.92% of the world economy (http://www.tradingeconomics.com/Economics/GDP.aspx?Symbol=CNY).

Clearly, China is one of the world's most developing and potentially rich countries. It is a top exporter and attracts record amounts of foreign investment. The government is also investing billions in infrastructure and supporting business. As China is now a member of the World Trade Organization (an organization whose purpose is to supervise and liberalize international trade), it can access foreign markets and foreign markets can access it. As such, the opportunities for organizations are immense if the cultural barriers can be overcome.

China is the most populous nation in the world, with 1.3 billion inhabitants or one in three of the world's population.

Nation facts: China

The People's Republic of China had a population of 1.34 billion in 2009. The capital city is Beijing and the largest city is Shanghai.

Social factors	*Economic factors*
■ Major language: Mandarin Chinese	■ Monetary unit: 1 renminbi (yuan) = 10 jiao = 100 fen
■ Major religions: Buddhism, Christianity, Islam, Taoism	■ Main exports: manufactured goods, including textiles, garments, electronics, arms
■ Life expectancy: 71 years (men), 75 years (women)	■ GNI per capita: US$2,930 (World Bank, 2008, http://devdata.worldbank.org/AAG/chn_aag.pdf)

6

China has the world's largest internet-using population, but the government regularly and routinely blocks access to certain websites. Indeed, Google's withdrawal from China was a result of such policy and action. The existing infrastructure and willingness of the population to engage with technology allows for a major potential for e-business, e-commerce and new business models.

An examination of the top 20 biggest companies in China (taken from Fortune, 2010, http://money.cnn.com/magazines/fortune/global500/2010/countries/China.html) will highlight the prominence of certain industries in the country. It will also show where these companies within these key industries rank in the world, since their number in the 'Global 500' ranking is included.

For example, the dominance of the utilities industry can be seen from the appearance of companies in the list, such as China Mobile Communications which ranks 4th in the country and 77th in the Global 500, making $71,749 in revenue in 2010; China Telecommunications which ranks 16th in the country and 204th in the Global 500, making $35,557 in revenue in 2010; and the China Southern Power Grid which ranks 12th in the country and 156th in the Global 500, making $45,735 in revenue in 2010. The revenue from these companies constitutes a large portion of the total revenue made by each company in the list.

Also among the top 20 biggest companies in China are China Railway Construction which ranks 8th in the country and 133rd in the Global 500, making $52,044 in revenue in 2010; China Communications Construction which ranks 18th in the country and 224th in the Global 500, making $33,465 in revenue in 2010; and finally China State Construction Engineering which ranks 14th in the country and 187th in the Global 500, making $38,117 in revenue in 2010. This shows just how important the construction industry is in China.

Finally, the prominence of more 'traditional industries', such as banking and oil, is demonstrated by the appearance of Sinopec which is the top company in the country and 7th in the Global 500, making $187,518 in revenue in 2010; China National Petroleum which ranks 3rd in the country and 10th in the Global 500, making $165,496 in revenue in 2010; and the Industrial and Commercial Bank of China which ranks 5th in the country and 87th in the Global 500, making $69,296 in revenue in 2010.

This industry profile has major implications for the ecosystem and the sustainability agenda as well as the competitive environment for such industries. The growth and development of the economy, combined with more freedom of information and wealth (for some), have raised market profiles, purchasing power and buyer bargaining power.

China is undoubtedly an attractive prospect for developing organizations and provides great potential market opportunities. However, the political and cultural environments are not easy to navigate and pose massive challenges for companies to overcome.

India

India is the second most populous nation in the world, with 1.2 billion inhabitants, and has the highest fertility rate, indicating that, by 2030, India will have overtaken China in terms of population and will be the most inhabited nation. The country has many languages, cultures and religions and so is highly diverse.

Nation facts: India
The Republic of India had a population of 1.2 billion in 2009. The capital city is New Delhi and the most populated city is Mumbai (Bombay).

Social factors	*Economic factors*
■ Major languages: Hindi, English and at least 16 other official languages ■ Major religions: Hinduism, Islam, Christianity, Sikhism, Buddhism, Jainism ■ Life expectancy: 62 years (men), 65 years (women)	■ Monetary unit: 1 Indian rupee = 100 paise ■ Main exports: agricultural products, textile goods, gems and jewellery, software services and technology, engineering goods, chemicals, leather products ■ GNI per capita: US$1,180 (World Bank, 2010, http://data.worldbank.org/country/india)

As with China, economic, social and environmental problems are a concern. There are vast wealth gaps and the social and digital divides are increasing. India has seen dramatic growth in GDP of 7% over the past few years and is forecast to grow GDP by a further 9% from the current $1.4 trillion in 2009 (World Bank, http://data.worldbank.org/country/india). Indeed, PricewaterhouseCoopers predicts that India will grow to third largest (by GDP) country in 2012 and then second by 2020 (http://www.pwc.com/pt_BR/br/sala-de-imprensa/assets/release-pib-2030-uk.pdf). This makes India (with its population resource) a formidable industrial superpower.

The top eight largest companies in India (from Fortune, 2010, http://money.cnn.com/magazines/fortune/global500/2010/countries/India.html) are: Indian Oil which ranks 1st in the country and 125th in the Global 500, it is based in New Delhi and made $54,288 in revenue in 2010; Reliance Industries which ranks 2nd in the country and 175th in the Global 500, it is based in Mumbai and made $41,085 in revenue in 2010; the State Bank of India which ranks 3rd in the country and 282nd in the Global 500, it is based in Mumbai and made $28,213 in revenue in 2010; Bharat Petroleum which ranks 4th in the country and 307th in the Global 500, it also based in Mumbai and made $26,596 in revenue in 2010; Hindustan Petroleum which ranks 5th in the country and 354th in the Global 500, it made $23,881 in revenue in 2010; Tata Steel which ranks 6th in the country and 410th in the Global 500 and made $21,582 in revenue in 2010; Oil and Natural Gas which ranks 7th in the country and 413th in the Global 500, it is based in Dehradun and made $21,448 in revenue in 2010; and finally, Tata Motors which ranks 8th in the country and 413th in the Global 500, it is based in Mumbai and made $19,501 in revenue in 2010.

These top eight companies are dominated by extraction and manufacturing industries. However, there are a number of other industries growing in India. It is estimated that the Indian semiconductor and embedded design industry has grown from $3.25bn in 2005 to $14.42bn in 2010 and will grow to $43.07bn in 2015 (http://www.ciol.com/semicon/special-report/feature/india-ascends-in-embedded-value-chain/2570798551/0/).

6

As the core and developing industries grow, so too will those supporting these industries, for example glass production, silicon, plastics, logistics, exports and education (Vaswani, 2006). The opportunities for trade with and into India are truly immense and its future prospect as 'the' superpower looks entirely possible.

Having examined our two superpowers, we can now profile some of the key emerging economies.

21.3   Emerging industry superpowers

While the USA, Western Europe and Japan have traditionally been seen as the global leaders of international trade, we have seen that India and China are now beginning to dominate. However, there are also a host of emerging nations (in a global trade sense) that will shape the future of the international economy. We profile a few interesting and key ones in this section.

Brazil

Brazil is probably the most prominent and economically stable Latin American economy. Most wealth is created around natural resources, particularly iron ore, oil and wood. The latter, combined with cattle ranching, has led to issues associated with deforestation and exploitation of the Amazon rainforest.

Nation facts: Brazil	
The Federative Republic of Brazil had a population of 193.7 million in 2009. The capital city is Brasilia and the largest city is São Paulo.	
Social factors	*Economic factors*
■ Major language: Portuguese ■ Major religion: Christianity ■ Life expectancy: 69 years (men), 76 years (women)	■ Monetary unit: 1 real = 100 centavos ■ Main exports: manufactured goods, iron ore, coffee, oranges, other agricultural produce ■ GNI per capita: US$8,040 in 2009 (World Bank, 2010, http://data.worldbank.org/country/brazil)

Much arable land is controlled by a few wealthy families, although efforts are being made to redistribute such wealth. In addition to agriculture and mining, there is a sizeable manufacturing and service sector. The top seven biggest companies in Brazil (from Fortune, 2010, http://money.cnn.com/magazines/fortune/global500/2010/countries/Brazil.html) are: Petrobas which ranks 1st in the company and 54th in the Global 500, based in Rio de Janeiro it made $91,869 in revenue in 2010; Itaúsa-Investimentos Itaú which ranks 2nd in the country and 117th in the Global 500, it is based in São Paulo and made $57,859 in revenue in 2010; Banco Bradesco which ranks 3rd in country and 135th in the Global 500, it is based in Osasco and made $51,608 in revenue in 2010; Banco do Brasil which ranks 4th in the country and 148th in the Global 500, it is based in Brasília and made $48,122 in revenue in 2010; Vale which ranks 5th in the country and 363rd in the Global 500, it is based in Rio de Janeiro and made $23,311 in revenue in 2010; Ultrapar Holdings which ranks 6th in the country and 471st in the Global 500, it is based in São Paulo and made $18,064 in revenue in 2010; and finally JBS which ranks 7th in the country and 496th in the Global 500, it is based in São Paulo and made $17,161 in revenue in 2010.

Brazil had significant growth in 2007 and 2008 before the 2008 financial crisis and, like other nations, suffered through 2008 and into 2009. However, Brazil was one of the first economies to emerge from the crisis and growth has continued again. Growth for 2010 is forecast at 5%, highlighting the opportunities this country poses for foreign investment. The implications of this are that Brazil has built the infrastructure to act as a springboard for Latin American business to develop and network with other superpowers.

Middle East: United Arab Emirates and Iran

The United Arab Emirates (UAE) is a federation of seven states formed in 1971 by the Trucial States after it had gained independence from Britain.

Before the 1950s, the economy was dependent on fishing and pearling. When oil was discovered and began to be exported in 1962, the society and economy were transformed.

In strategic terms, the economy has shown distinct foresight by directing oil revenues into healthcare, education and national infrastructure. It was recognized that oil reserves would be limited and therefore active diversification was undertaken into business, tourism and construction, particularly in Dubai. Now oil and gas output is only 25% of UAE's GDP and in less than 30 years, the UAE has transformed itself into a key destination for events, sports, tourism and business, and a centre for construction, distribution and biotechnology.

Nation facts: United Arab Emirates
The United Arab Emirates had a population of 4.6 million in 2009. The capital city is Abu Dhabi and the largest city is Dubai.

Social factors	Economic factors
■ Major language: Arabic ■ Major religion: Islam ■ Life expectancy: 77 years (men), 79 years (women)	■ Monetary unit: 1 dirham = 100 fils ■ Main exports: oil, gas ■ GNI per capita: US$22,491 (World Bank, 2006, http://www.pdwb.de/archiv/weltbank/gni06.pdf)

The UAE strategic plan for the next few years focuses on further diversification (into biotechnology and pharmaceuticals) and creating more opportunities for nationals through improved education and increased private sector employment. However, the recent financial crisis and debt position of Dubai, in particular, may stall further developments for a while.

Iran provides for an interesting contrast to UAE. Known as Persia until 1935, Iran was one of the greatest empires of the ancient world. The country has long maintained a distinct cultural identity within the Islamic world by retaining its own language and adhering to the Shia interpretation of Islam. This makes the country somewhat difficult to penetrate or understand.

6

The country has an abundance of energy resources in the form of oil and natural gas reserves, which are second only to Russia. Most economic activity is controlled by the state, with private sector activity limited to small and medium-sized enterprises in farming, workshops and services.

Nation facts: Iran	
The Islamic Republic of Iran had a population of 74.2 million in 2009. The capital city is Tehran.	
Social factors	*Economic factors*
■ Major language: Persian ■ Major religion: Islam ■ Life expectancy: 70 years (men), 73 years (women)	■ Monetary unit: 10 Iranian rials = 1 toman ■ Main exports: petroleum, carpets, agricultural products ■ GNI per capita: US$4,530 (World Bank, 2010, http://data.worldbank.org/country/iran-islamic-republic)

Iran is something of a 'sleeping state' in commercial terms. The potential for emerging development is clear and the implications in terms of eco-impacts (including nuclear) are significant. However, if political reform occurs, the commercial potential of the country would be significant.

Central Europe: Czech Republic and Poland

Czechoslovakia emerged from 41 years of communist rule after the Velvet Revolution of 1989. The 'velvet divorce' in January 1993 saw Czechoslovakia peacefully dissolve into its constituent states of the Czech Republic and Slovakia, and in 2004 the Czech Republic became part of the European Union (EU).

Nation facts: Czech Republic	
The Czech Republic had a population of 10.4 million in 2009. The capital city is Prague.	
Social factors	*Economic factors*
■ Major language: Czech ■ Major religion: Christianity ■ Life expectancy: 73 years (men), 80 years (women)	■ Monetary unit: 1 koruna = 100 halers ■ Main exports: manufactured goods, machinery, cars and transport equipment, beer ■ GNI per capita: US$17,310 (World Bank, 2010, http://data.worldbank.org/country/czech-republic)

The Czech Republic has a robust democratic tradition, highly developed economy and a rich cultural heritage. It is one of the most stable and prosperous of the post-communist states and has an open investment economy. The Czech Republic is attractive to foreign investors as it is centrally located in Europe, has a low-cost structure, well-qualified workforce, and is a member of the EU. Key developments include the tourism sector, banking and logistics.

Poland has a rich cultural heritage of over 1,000 years, positioned at the heart of Europe. In recent years, the country has had some success in creating a market economy and attracting foreign investment. There has been a massive move-ment of workers to Western Europe, with Poland still operating a large farming community. However, skilled workers are now returning and the economy is beginning to flourish.

Nation facts: Poland

The Republic of Poland had a population of 38.1 million in 2009. The capital city is Warsaw.

Social factors	*Economic factors*
■ Major language: Polish	■ Monetary unit: 1 zloty = 100 groszy
■ Major religion: Christianity	■ Main exports: machinery and transport equipment, foodstuffs, chemicals
■ Life expectancy: 71 years (men), 80 years (women)	■ GNI per capita: US$12,260 (World Bank, 2010, http://data.worldbank.org/country/poland)

Poland has pursued a policy of economic liberalization since 1990 and stands out as a success story among transition economies. Poland's economic performance could improve over the longer term if the country is able to address the deficiencies in road and rail infrastructure and its business environment.

Russia

Russia has undergone significant change since the collapse of the Soviet Union in 1991, moving from a globally isolated, centrally planned economy to a more market-based, globally integrated economy.

Nation facts: Russia

The Russian Federation had a population of 140.9 million in 2009. The capital city is Moscow.

Social factors	*Economic factors*	
■ Major language: Russian	■ Monetary unit: 1 rouble = 100 kopecks	
■ Major religions: Christianity, Islam	■ Main exports: oil and oil products, natural gas, wood and wood products, metals, chemicals, weapons and military equipment	
■ Life expectancy: 60 years (men), 73 years (women)	■ GNI per capita: US$9,370 (World Bank, 2010, http://data.worldbank.org/country/russian-federation)	

The economic reforms of the 1990s privatized most industries, with the exception of the energy and defence sectors. The result has been industry split into commodity producers, which are highly competitive and represent increasing degrees of economic domination. This includes the natural gas sector, where Russia is the largest provider in the world. Russia is the second largest provider of oil, and the third largest provider of steel and aluminium. Russia's top six biggest companies include (from Fortune, 2010, http://money.cnn.com/magazines/fortune/global500/2010/countries/Russia.

6

html): Gazprom which ranks 1st in the country and 50th in the Global 500, it is based in Moscow and made $94,472 in revenue in 2010; Lukoil which ranks 2nd in the country and 93rd in the Global 500, it is based in Moscow and made $68,025 in revenue in 2010; Rosneft Oil which ranks 3rd in the country and 211th in the Global 500, it made $34,695 in revenue in 2010; Sberbank which ranks 4th in the country and 256th in the Global 500, it made $30,394 in revenue in 2011; TNK-BP Holding which ranks 5th in the country and 318th in the Global 500, it made $25,696 in revenue in 2010; and finally, Sistema ranks 6th in the country and 460th in the Global 500, it made $18,750 in revenue in 2010.

Russia is currently trying to build up its high-tech sector but it still has some way to go to compete with the key players in the world. Agriculture remains a significant provision, although much of the industry suffered as a result of the financial crisis. This said, Russia's position of being in the top three suppliers of gas, oil and steel will provide a significant base from which to build the economy and support the emerging industries.

21.4   General implications for business strategy

In Part 3, we saw the importance of analysing the external environment in terms of macroenvironments and microenvironments. As such, the changing nature of the world stage will obviously impact on any future business strategy developed.

While the impacts can be massive and often unpredictable, we do know the following:

1   Countries that are currently growing and developing the manufacturing base of their economy are doing so more quickly than previously. Their next stage of development will be into services and support.

2   Generation Y will have a major impact on both what is offered by organizations and how it is offered. Products and markets will evolve and develop but organizational structures, working patterns, ethics and resources will also need to evolve.

3   We need to rethink the 'way' we do business in order to ensure business is effective between the various emerging nations (see Morrison et al., 1994).

We have tried to highlight some significant elements of the changing world economy but to do so more fully is a book in its own right. There are many developments also happening in Latin America, Africa, Scandinavian countries, the Balkan states and Australasia. We hope we have opened your eyes enough for you to now explore these areas in more detail and with more focus around the organizations, industries and product areas that interest you most.

This is a helpful chapter to refer to when completing 1.1.3 Industry Life Cycle within the External Analysis section in Phase 2 of the **Strategic Planning Software** (www.planning-strategy.com), particularly the section on emerging industries. Chapter 13 is also useful here.

For test questions, extra case studies, audio case studies, weblinks, videolinks and more to help you understand the topics covered in this chapter, visit our companion website at www.macmillanihe.com/companion/business/campbell.

VOCAB CHECKLIST FOR ESL STUDENTS

Acumen	Ecosystem	Populous
Agriculture	Futurist	Protectionism
Apparel	Goodwill	Prudent
Arable	Monarchy	Semiconductor
Biomass	Natural resources	Superpowers
Dictatorship	Orchestrated	Wind turbine
Disposable income	Petrochemicals	

Definitions for these terms can be found in the 'Vocab Zone' of the companion website, which provides free access to the Macmillan English Dictionary online at www.macmillanihe.com/companion/business/campbell.

REVIEW QUESTIONS

1 Explain how the 'environmental' profile of a country can influence business strategy across the globe.
2 Explain which industries and markets are likely to be the most significant in business terms over the next 10 years.
3 Explain what we mean by generation Y.

DISCUSSION TOPIC

The developed economies will always rule supreme in terms of international trade as they are more technically advanced. Discuss.

HOT TOPICS – Research project areas to investigate

For your research project, why not investigate ...

- ... how organizations monitor changes in the business environment.
- ... how companies react to changing consumer trends.
- ... which sectors of the economy are growing fastest and why.

Recommended reading

Business Week (1999) Generation Y, *Business Week Online*, 15 February, http://www.businessweek.com/1999/99_07/b3616001.htm.

Chow, I., Holbert, N., Kelley, L. and Yu, J. (1997) *Business Strategy, An Asia-Pacific Focus*, Singapore: Prentice Hall.

Clarkson, M.B. (1995) 'A stakeholder framework for analysing and evaluating corporate social performance', *Academy of Management Review*, **20**(1): 92–117.

Walde, K. (2002) 'The economic determinants of technology shocks in a real business cycle model', *Journal of Economic Dynamics and Control*, **27**(1): 1–28.

6

Chapter references

Braid, M. (2007) 'How to connect with generation Y', *Sunday Times*, 20 May.

Bureau of Labor Statistics (2009) *Employment Prediction 2008–2018: Summary*, 10 December.

Clarkson, M.B. (1995) 'A stakeholder framework for analysing and evaluating corporate social performance', *Academy of Management Review*, **20**(1): 92–117.

Fortune (2009) Fortune 500 'Top industries: fast growers', *Fortune*, 4 May.

Morrison, T., Conaway, W. and Borden, G. (1994) *Kiss, Bow, or Shake Hands*, Holbrook, MA: Adams Media.

Vaswani, K. (2006) 'Indian factories prepare for growth', BBC, 24 May.

GLOSSARY

A

An **acquisition** is a joining of unequal partners, with one organization buying and subsuming the other party.

Adaptive learning centres on changing in response to developments in the business environment.

The audited **annual report and accounts** has five compulsory components, as set out in the UK in the Companies Act 1985 (as amended): chairman's statement, auditor's report, profit and loss (P&L) statement, balance sheet and cash flow statement. All limited companies are required to file these. The accounting rules by which they are to be constructed are prescribed in International Financial Reporting Standards to ensure that all companies mean the same thing when they make an entry in one of the financial statements. When they are completed, following the company's financial year end, they become publicly available. Each shareholder has the right to receive a copy, and a copy is lodged at UK Companies House in Cardiff or London (or Edinburgh if it is a Scottish company).

B

Backward vertical development or backward integration represents a move backwards in the supply chain, towards the supplier or raw materials.

The **balanced scorecard** is a management tool for managers to 'balance' the various indicators of success (or 'perspectives') for a given business.

The **bargaining power of buyers** is the extent to which the buyers of a product exert power over an industry.

The **bargaining power of suppliers** will not be determined solely by their relationship with one industry but by their relationships with all the industries they serve.

The **behavioural theory** of leadership believes that leaders can be made rather than born, so leadership can be learned if the behaviours can be isolated and taught.

Benchmarking is a process where an organization compares elements of its business, processes or performance against the industry norms, best practice or 'best in class'. The metrics can include quality, time or cost. Benchmarking involves management identifying the best firms in their industry, or any other industry where similar processes exist, and mapping how well they perform against them.

Blogs are websites that host frequently updated journals, which are used for writing short and typically informal communications.

C

Capital is money that is used to invest in the business – to buy new equipment, new capacity, extra factory space and so on. The investment of capital enables the business to expand and, through that expansion, increase its revenue and profits in future years. Capital can be raised from shareholders, through retained profits, rights issues, loan capital or the disposal of assets.

The **combined market value** of a merger or acquisition is the two company's values added together. It is an indication of what the company will be valued at after the integration goes ahead.

A **competence** is an attribute or collection of attributes possessed by all or most of the companies in an industry.

Competence building takes place when the business builds new core competences, based on its resources and competences. It is often necessary to build new competences alongside existing ones when entering new markets, as it is unlikely that existing competences will fully meet new customer needs.

Competence leveraging refers to the ability of a business to exploit its core competences in new markets, thus meeting new customer needs. It can also refer to the ability of the business to modify and improve existing core competences.

Competitive advantage is often seen as the overall purpose of business strategy. Some texts use the phrase 'superior performance' to mean the same thing. Essentially, a business can be said to possess competitive advantage if it is able to return higher profits than its competitors. The higher profits mean that it will be able to commit more retained profit to reinvest in its strategy, thus maintaining its lead over its competitors in an industry. When this superiority is maintained successfully over time, we refer to it as a 'sustainable' competitive advantage. Competitive advantage can be lost when management fail to reinvest the superior profits in such a way that the advantage is not maintained.

A **consortium** is a group of companies that combine to exploit each others' resources and competences to the benefit of the group and to provide a critical mass beyond their own means directed towards a particular task.

The **contingency theory** of leadership states that a leader's ability to lead is contingent on a variety of situational and behavioural factors.

Convenience goods are products where purchase is relatively frequent, at low prices, and the customer sees little interest or risk in the purchase.

Cookies are computer programs designed to collect information on a user's browsing activities, which provides important information on that person's interests, preferences and so on.

A **core competence** is an attribute, or collection of attributes, specific to a particular organization that enables it to produce above-average performance.

The **cost of capital** can be viewed as the annual amount payable (as a percentage) against the principal amount of money.

A **cost leadership strategy** is based on a business organizing and managing its value-adding activities so as to be the lowest cost producer of a product (a good or service) within an industry.

Critical success factors (CSFs) are those human factors that would help achieve the desired level of an organization's goal.

The **cultural web** is a schematic representation of the elements of an organization's culture so that we can see how each element influences the paradigm.

Culture is 'the collective programming of the mind which distinguishes the members of one organization from another'.

D

Data is facts, numbers in their recorded but unprocessed state.

Decision support systems (DSS) support middle and senior managers, and focus on facilitating decision-making.

Deliberate strategy, sometimes called planned or prescriptive strategy, is meant to happen. It is preconceived, premeditated and usually monitored and controlled from start to finish. It has a specific objective.

Demographic variables are used to define market segments in consumer markets. It is self-evident that people can be divided from each other in many ways and the more variables that are applied to a total market, the smaller and more homogeneous the segment becomes. The most commonly used demographic variables are those that are readily identifiable. Differences such as sex, age, occupation, type of residence and stage of family life cycle are all easy to identify. Less easy – and therefore less usable – are differences such as religious affiliation, sexual orientation, political persuasion and musical preferences. It is unfortunate, then, that some of this latter category of variables are powerful in respect of their ability to predict patterns of demand for some product types.

Demography is the social science concerned with the charting of the size and structure of a population of people.

A **differentiation strategy** is based on persuading customers that a product is superior to that offered by competitors.

The **digital divide** refers to the gap between those who own, or have access to, technology and the web and those who do not.

Direct exporting is the transfer of goods (or services) across national borders from the home production facility.

Disposals (demergers and divestments) involve taking a part of a company and selling it off as a 'self-contained' unit, with its own management, structure and employees in place.

Distinctive capability can develop from reputation, architecture (internal and external relationships), innovation and strategic assets.

Diversification is business growth through new products and new markets. It is an appropriate option when current markets are saturated or when products are reaching the end of their life cycle.

Dividend yield is calculated by dividing the dividend per share at the last year end by the current price.

Dynamic capabilities represent the ability of organizations to innovate, adapt and adopt in terms of their tangible and intangible resources.

E

Earnings per share (EPS) is calculated by dividing profit after interest and tax (called earnings) by the number of shares.

E-business is the use of technology throughout the supply chain of the business and the carrying out of business on the internet. It refers not only to buying and selling but also servicing customers and collaborating with business partners.

E-commerce is the buying or selling of goods or services via the internet.

The traditional **economic theory of the firm** posits the notion that businesses exist primarily to make profits for their owners.

Economies of scale describe the benefits that are gained when increasing volume results in lower unit costs. Although economies of scale can arise in all parts of the value chain, it is probably best understood by illustrating it using purchasing as an example. An individual purchasing one single item will pay more *per item* than a large company buying many of the same item. It is said that the purchaser who is able to purchase in bulk (because of the size and structure of the buyer) enjoys scale economies over smaller organizations who buy in at lower volumes.

Economy of scope describes the benefits that can arise in one product or market area as a result of activity in another. For example, research into material properties for the benefit of the NASA space programme (one area of scope) has resulted in advances in other areas such as fabrics, non-stick pans and coatings for aircraft. Organizations that invest heavily in R&D (such as pharmaceutical companies) are among those who are always seeking economies of scope – seeking to use breakthroughs in one area to benefit another.

Effectiveness is the ability to deliver the expected result or value for the user or consumer.

Efficiency is the ability to accomplish a task with minimum, time, effort or use of resources.

Efficiency ratios show how efficiently a company has used its assets to generate sales.

Emergent strategy has no specific objective. It does not have a preconceived route to success but it may be just as effective as a deliberate strategy. By following a consistent pattern of behaviour, an organization may arrive at the same position as if it had planned everything in detail.

The term **emerging markets** refers to countries or markets that are just beginning to industrialize and, in the process, are displaying strong economic growth.

In an **equity carve-out**, the selling company retains a shareholding in the disposal, with the balance of shares being offered to the stock market.

Explicit knowledge is knowledge whose meaning is clearly stated, details of which can be recorded and stored, such as important formulations, procedures or ways of acting.

F

A **fiduciary duty** is a duty of care and trust that one party has towards another. While some fiduciary duties are non-contestable, others are. In the case of business ethics, the question is: To whom does the board of a company owe a fiduciary duty? It is usually accepted that it owes such a duty to the company's shareholders, as that agency relationship underpins the structure of capitalism. The question, then, is who else is owed such a duty and how is it weighted against the duty towards shareholders? In a dispute between employees and shareholders, for example, to which party does the board of directors owe the main fiduciary duty?

Financial resources comprise money for capital investment and working capital. Sources include shareholders, banks, bondholders.

Finished goods (FG) stocks are those which have passed through the process and are ready for distribution to the customers.

Fiscal policy is the regulation of the national economy through the management of government revenues and expenditures. Each fiscal year, a government raises so much in revenues (through taxation) and it spends another amount through its various departments (health, education and defence). The government is able to influence the economic climate in a country by varying either or both of these sides of the fiscal equation. In the UK, the chancellor of the exchequer is in charge of fiscal policy.

A **focus strategy** is aimed at a segment of the market for a product rather than at the whole market or many markets.

Forward vertical development is growth towards the next stage in the supply chain by gaining an interest in a buyer of the company's outputs.

A **franchise** is an arrangement under which a franchisor supplies a franchisee with a tried-and-tested brand name, products and expertise in return for the payment of a proportion of profits or sales.

G

Gearing is an indication of how the company has arranged its capital structure.

Generation Y describes the demographic cohort following generation X, roughly speaking, those born in the 1980s and 90s.

Generative learning is about building new competences or identifying or creating opportunities for leveraging existing competences in new competitive arenas.

Geographic information systems (GIS) are IS that have a 'map' as a key component.

Global industries are those in which competition is global.

A **good** is tangible and is something that can be owned.

The **great man theory** of leadership is based on the premise that leaders are born and not made.

Greenwashing is a term describing the deceptive use of green PR or green marketing in order to promote a misleading perception that a company's policies or products (such as goods or services) are environmentally friendly.

Gross domestic product (GDP) is a measure of a country's overall official economic output. It is the market value of all final goods and services officially made within the borders of a country in a year. It is often positively correlated with the standard of living.

Gross national income (GNI) per capita is the dollar value of a country's final income in a year, divided by its population. It reflects the average income of a country's citizens.

Group decision support systems (GDSS) support the decision-making activities of groups.

H

Horizontal development is a move resulting in higher market share within the same industry.

A **hostile takeover** describes an offer for the shares of a target public limited company which the target's directors reject.

Human resources comprise appropriately skilled employees to add value in operations and to support those who add value, which may include supporting employees in marketing, accounting or personnel functions. Sources include the labour markets for the appropriate skill levels required by the organization.

I

Implicit or tacit knowledge is often unstated, based on individual experience and difficult to record and store.

Incremental change offers the advantage of a step-by-step approach to change, and enables management to gain acceptance before and during the change process.

Industries produce goods and services – the supply side of the economic system.

Industry analysis aims to establish the nature of the competition in an industry and the competitive position of a business with respect to its microenvironment.

Industry attractiveness represents the potential to make a profit or gain strategic rent from a specific industry configuration.

Inertia refers to the force that needs to be exerted on a body to overcome its state in relation to its motion.

Information is data that has been processed to make it meaningful to the person who receives it.

Information systems are the systems that deliver information and communication services, and the organizational function that plans, develops and manages the information systems.

Information technology (IT) refers to hardware, software and telecommunications networks technology.

Innovation is the commercialization or exploitation of creativity and is often represented by a degree of novelty – novelty being relative to the organization, the situation or the process.

The **instrumental view of stakeholder theory** posits that organizations take stakeholder opinions into account only insofar as they are consistent with other, more important economic objectives, for example profit maximization.

Intangible assets include skills, knowledge, brand names, goodwill and patent rights.

Intellectual (intangible) resources comprise inputs that cannot be seen or felt but which are essential for continuing business success. Included here are elements of tacit knowledge such as technical know-how, legally defensible patents and licences, brand names, registered designs, logos, 'secret' formulations and recipes, business contact networks or databases.

Internal (organic) growth is expansion by means of the reinvestment of the previous year's profits and loan capital in the same business that generated the profits. This results in increased capacity, increased employment and, ultimately, increased turnover. Its advantages are: lower risk, is within existing area of expertise, and avoids high exposure to costs of alternative growth mechanisms, for example by debt servicing. Its disadvantages are: slower than external growth, little scope for diversification, and relies on existing management skills in the business.

The **internet** is a global network comprising millions of computers.

Inventory used to be called stock.

J

Joint ventures represent contractually legal binding agreements between two or more companies with shared benefit and risk (as per the contract).

K

Kaizen is a culturally embedded concept of continual improvement pioneered in Japanese companies. It concentrates on small gradual changes involving all employees in every area of business. According to Imai (1986), it is 'the single most important concept in Japanese management – the key to Japanese competitive success'. Kaizen is process-oriented change, involving operators continuously searching for better ways to do their job.

Kaizen teams take responsibility for identifying opportunities for improvement. Typically, ideas for change will be investigated, tested and measured by the team. Any savings in job cycle time, even a few seconds, will be introduced as the new standard method of production. Staff are encouraged to participate in kaizen teams and are given full training in problem-solving tools and techniques.

The **knowledge-based view** of competitive advantage is based on the assumption that knowledge is the most important resource in complex, dynamic and uncertain environments, where knowledge is viewed as being at the centre of wealth-creating/value-adding activity.

Knowledge management is primarily concerned with the creation of new knowledge, the storage and sharing of knowledge and the control of knowledge.

L

Lean is an approach that seeks to improve flow in the value stream and eliminate waste.

Lean production (or lean manufacturing) is often known simply as lean. The approach works from the perspective of value creation and the consumer, or user of the system. Value is any process or activity that the consumer will pay for and, as such, all other elements are deemed wasteful, and thus targeted for elimination.

The **learning curve** describes the rate at which an individual or an organization learns to perform a particular task.

Licensing involves a producer transferring certain rights to a licensee for the sole use in a host country of its established brand, recipe, registered design or similar piece of intellectual property.

Liquidity ratios test the company's ability to meet its short-term debts.

The **long tail** describes the strategy of selling a large number of niche products to a relatively small number of customers.

M

The **macroenvironment** is the broad environment outside an organization's industry and markets.

A **management buyout** (MBO) is when a company that a parent company wishes to dispose of is sold to its current management.

Management information systems (MIS) are integrated information systems that connect different levels of management for the sharing of information.

Market development is based on entry into new markets or new segments of existing markets while employing existing products.

Market/industry fit is the matching of an organization's resources to the industry and market structure within which it operates.

Market penetration aims to increase market share using existing products within existing markets.

Market risk is incurred whenever a business attempts to develop markets or differentiate using customer groups it has hitherto not served.

Markets consume goods and services that have been produced by industries – the demand side of the economic system.

Market segmentation is the division of larger markets into submarkets that represent and reflect distinct market characteristics. Such characteristics could be based on price, wants, needs, product features, demand profiles or geographic locations.

Market share is a measure of an organization's performance with regard to its ability to win and retain customers.

The **market value** of public limited companies equals the number of shares on the stock market (the share volume) multiplied by the share price. It is taken to be a good indicator of the value of a company because it accounts for the company's asset value plus the 'goodwill' that the market attaches to the share.

In a **merger**, the organization's shareholders come together, normally willingly, to share the resources of the enlarged (merged) organization.

Metrics are performance indicators used as comparative measures.

The **microenvironment** is that which immediately surrounds a business, the parts of which the business interacts with frequently and over which it may have some influence. For most purposes, we can identify competitors, suppliers and customers as comprising the main constituents of this strata of the environment.

The **mission statement** provides direction for the organization by defining what the organization is and its reason for existing. As such, the mission statement often encapsulates the vision and values.

The **mobile web** refers to browser-based access to the internet from a mobile device, such as a smartphone or PDA, connected to a wireless network.

Monetary policy is the regulation of the national economy by varying the supply and price of money. Money supply concerns the volume of money (in its various forms) in the economy and the 'price' of money is the base rate, which determines the interest rate that banks and other lenders charge for borrowings. Since May 1997, monetary policy has been overseen by the Monetary Policy Committee of the Bank of England.

Multi-domestic industries are those where competition in each nation is essentially independent.

A **multinational company** is an international company whose foreign interests are not coordinated from a strategic centre.

Multinational global customers seek the best suppliers in the world but then use the product or service obtained in many countries.

N

National global customers seek the best suppliers in the world and then use the product or service in one country.

A **need** is a good or service that is deemed essential or is currently lacking.

Non-current assets used to be known as fixed assets (plant, machinery, real estate) – distinguishes them from current assets, which are assets used to manage the business in the short term in the form of working capital.

Non-price competition will take the form of branding, advertising, promotion, additional services to customers and product innovation.

The **normative view of stakeholder theory** differs from the instrumental view because it describes not what is, but what should be, that is, what should be the 'norm' in an ideal situation.

O

Offshoring is the movement of a business process from one location to another, usually another country, where the skills are cheaper.

Operational decisions are those that are concerned with how the internal parts of the organization should be configured and managed so that they best achieve the strategic objectives.

Organizational structure refers to the 'shape' of the business, in terms of its 'height', 'width' and complexity.

The **organization's industry** consists of the business and a group of companies producing similar products, employing similar capabilities and technology.

Outsourcing is the movement of a business process to another company with a more appropriate skills base.

P

A **paradigm** is a worldview – a way of looking at the world. It is expressed in the assumptions people make and their deep-rooted beliefs. The paradigm of an organization or a national culture is important because it determines how it will behave in a given circumstance. Given a certain moral dilemma or similar choice, we might expect the paradigms of, for example, an orthodox Jew and an atheist to lead them to arrive at different conclusions. The things that cause one culture to adopt one paradigm and another culture to espouse a different one are set out in the cultural web.

Payables used to be known as creditors – reminds us that creditors are those a company owes money to.

Performance ratios test to see how well a company has turned its inputs into profits.

Person cultures can be found in learned professional societies, trade unions, cooperatives, some charities and some religious organizations.

Physical (tangible) resources comprise land, buildings (offices, warehouses and so on), plant, equipment, stock for production, IT and so on. Sources include estate agents, builders and trade suppliers.

Pioneer companies are those that are first to market with a particular product.

A **placing** involves the selling of shares directly to a small number of investors, usually large financial institutions.

Podcasting is the distribution of audio or video files that can be downloaded onto PCs or mobile devices such as MP3 players.

The **political environment** is that part of the macroenvironment that is either under the direct control or influence of the government and/or the state.

Power cultures are common in small entrepreneurial (owner-managed) companies and in some notable larger organizations with a charismatic leader.

Power distance is 'how removed subordinates feel from superiors in a social meaning of the word "distance". In a high power distance culture, inequality is accepted … in a low power distance culture, inequalities and overt status symbols are minimized and subordinates expect to be consulted and to share decisions with approachable managers' (Hickson and Pugh, 1995, p. 21).

Price competition involves businesses trying to undercut each other's prices, which will, in turn, be dependent on their ability to reduce their costs of production.

The **price/earnings ratio** (P/E) is calculated by dividing the current market price of the company's ordinary shares by its EPS.

The term **price elasticity of demand** describes the extent to which the volume of demand for a product is dependent upon its price.

Process innovation reflects an attempt to re-engineer or design the flow of activity in the organization.

A **product** is anything that is offered for sale.

Product development centres on the development of new products for existing markets.

Product innovation represents the development of new technologies and products as well as new uses for existing products.

The **product life cycle** is the complete 'life' of a product or service from its inception and growth, through shake-out and maturity, to its eventual decline and death.

Product markets are those where businesses deploy their competences and sell their products.

The **product portfolio** is the range of products offered.

Product positioning is the way in which a product or a brand is perceived in relation to the preferences of market segments, and in relation to competitive products.

Product risk is incurred whenever a business introduces a new product.

Q

A **quality guru** is someone who has been recognized for their contribution to the management of quality within business and whose messages have led to major changes in the way organizations operate. There are a number people who are highly regarded as major contributors in the field of quality management, including Juran, Deming and Peters.

R

Raw materials or purchased parts are stocks in their 'raw' state. Raw materials are those goods that are purchased, before they undergo any processing within the manufacturing process.

Receivables used to be known as debtors – reminds us that debtors are those who owe money (usually customers on account).

A **resource audit** is the purposeful checking or testing of resources for sufficiency, adequacy and availability.

Resource inputs (sometimes called factors of production) are essential inputs that are central to the normal functioning of the organizational process.

Resource markets are those where organizations obtain finance, human resources, materials, equipment, services and so on.

Retained profit, that element of operating profit not paid to shareholders in the form of a dividend, is the most common method of funding strategic developments.

Revenue is money that is earned through normal business transactions – sales, rents or whatever the company does in its normal activities.

A **rights issue** is when a company issues new shares to the stock market.

Role cultures are common in traditional bureaucracies, such as the civil service, banks, insurance companies and in some newer business types such as call centres.

RSS (rich site summary or really simple syndication) is a technology that allows information to be sent to the user whenever a web page is updated.

S

A **segmentation base** is a way of distinguishing one customer type from another.

A **service** is something that is done on the buyer's behalf and is intangible in nature.

Share capital has, historically, comprised the majority of capital for a limited company's start-up and subsequent development.

Shareholders are the financial owners of the company.

Share value is the price of a company's shares at a given point in time. Like any other commodity, their value is determined by the forces of supply and demand. In normal circumstances, the supply is fixed over the short to medium term, so price is determined by how many people want to buy shares. If the market has confidence in a company's prospects, demand for shares will rise and so, accordingly, will their price. If a company's prospects are considered poor, investors will sell their shares, fewer will want to buy them and the price will fall.

Share volume is the number of shares issued by a company in total. This is usually determined at the foundation or flotation of a company, although rights issues and similar events can increase the share volume. It is generally true that larger companies have higher share volumes than smaller concerns.

Shopping goods are those that are typically more expensive, of more interest to the purchaser, and some risk is seen in the purchase.

Shorter structures involve few management layers and are suitable for smaller organizations that are engaged in few products or market structures. They are cheaper to operate and facilitate a greater degree of senior management control.

The **situational and participative theories** of leadership view leadership as relating to context and the involvement of others.

Six Sigma is based on concepts that focus on continuous quality improvements for achieving near perfection by restricting the number of possible defects to less than 3.4 defects per million.

A **social benefit** will result in an improvement in the condition of society, for example increasing employment, cleaner industry, better working conditions and so on.

Social contract theory posits the notion that any social institution exists alongside its constituencies via a social contract. The concept is an old one but successive thinkers since the 17th century have modified our understanding of it. The English philosophers Thomas Hobbes (1588–1679) and John Locke (1632–1704) developed the theory to explain the relationship between a government and the people over which it governs. In the 20th century, the theory was modified to help to explain the relationship between powerful business organizations and the stakeholders they can influence (see for example, Rawls, 1971; Donaldson, 1982). The essence of the theory is one of reciprocal responsibility. The constituency agrees to accept the authority of the powerful institution, while the institution agrees to act in the best interests of its constituencies. If either party breaks the terms of the contract,

then, it is argued, the nature of the contract is destroyed. In respect to the business–stakeholder relationship, a social contract is said to exist between an organization and those groups in society that rely on it. The stakeholders (in effect) agree to support the activities of the organization, as employees, customers and so on, as long as the organization acts in a manner that is acceptable to the stakeholders.

A **social cost** is a deterioration in the condition of society, for example an increase in unemployment, higher levels of emissions and pollution, declining salaries and so on.

Socialism is an economic theory or system in which the means of production, distribution and exchange are owned by the community collectively, usually through the state.

Social responsibility can be described as the obligation of an organization's management towards the welfare and interests of the society which provides it the environment and resources to survive and flourish, and which is affected by the organization's actions and policies.

Specialty goods are seen as products that are so differentiated from others, often carrying considerable prestige, that customers may insist on only one brand.

The **stakeholder position** posits that organizations, like individual people, are citizens of society, and as such, we have certain rights, obligations and responsibilities.

Stakeholders are the people who can influence or are influenced by the organization. They can be primary (active) stakeholders, such as customers, suppliers, labour, financial institutions, or secondary (passive) such as government, local community, lobby groups.

Step change offers the advantage of 'getting it over with', and enables the organization to respond quickly to changes in its environment.

The **stockholder position** on businesses' responsibility to society argues that businesses exist primarily for their owners (usually shareholders).

Stocks are the physical goods that are bought in, converted and then sold to the customers in a manufacturing or assembly business. There are three types of stock, depending on where they are along the production process – raw materials, work-in-progress and finished goods.

The **strategic aim** is a statement of organizational intent specified in terms of where the organization wishes to 'go' and when it wishes to get there.

A **strategic alliance** describes a range of collaborative arrangements between two or more organizations that agree to act in a particular way for the achievement of a common goal or aim.

Strategic decisions are those that are concerned with how the whole organization will be positioned in respect of its product and resource markets, its competitors and its macro-influences.

Strategic groups are collections of firms operating in the same strategic space trying to compete for premium share of profit.

Strategic objectives often form the strategy road map for an organization. They are 'stepping stones' to achieving the strategic aim and should be SMART in nature, that is, specific, measurable, achievable, relevant and time bound.

Strategic thinking is about combining strategic knowledge, context and organizational awareness to shape, reshape and redefine the business boundaries, direction and resources in order to gain a competitive advantage, be it short, medium or longer term.

A **substitute** can be regarded as something that meets the same needs as the product of the industry.

Sustainable development is 'development that meets the needs of the present without compromising the ability of future generations to meet their own needs'.

Switching costs refer to substitute products, one of the barriers to mobility in a market. Switching costs are the cost (actual or perceived) of changing from one product or service provider to another. Such costs can be tangible or intangible in nature. Switching costs may be financial, but may also be expressed in terms of lower quality, reduced confidence in the competitor's product or poorer product performance.

Synergy refers to the benefits that can be gained when organizations join forces rather than work apart. An integration can be said to be synergistic when the whole is greater than the sum of the parts.

T

A **takeover** is technically the same as an acquisition.

Tall structures, involving more layers of specialist managers, enable the organization to coordinate a wider range of activities across different product and market sectors. They are more difficult for senior management to control and obviously more expensive in terms of management overheads.

Tangible assets include stocks, materials, machinery, buildings, human resources, finance and so on.

Task cultures are found in organizations engaged in activities of a non-repetitive nature, often high value, one-off tasks.

The **threat of new entrants** to the industry depends on the 'height' of entry barriers.

Total quality management (TQM) is a holistic approach, which provides awareness of the customer–supplier relationship and continuous improvement effort in all departments and functions.

Trait theory is based on the premise that leaders are born rather than made and focuses on identifying the traits.

The **transactional theory** of leadership is based on reward and punishment.

Transaction processing systems (TPS) are the building blocks for a company's information management policy.

Transferable marketing describes the extent to which elements of the marketing mix, like brand names and promotions, can be used globally without local adaptations.

The **transformational theory** of leadership contends that people will follow a leader who inspires them.

A **transnational company** has a high degree of coordination in its international interests. It usually has a strategic centre that manages the global operation such that all parts act in accordance with a centrally managed strategic purpose.

U

The concept of **utility** infers that whenever a consumer makes a purchase, they make a cost–benefit calculation, wherein they judge that the benefit they receive from the product is worth more than the price paid.

V

The **value added** to a good or service is the difference in the financial value of the finished product compared to the financial value of the inputs. As a sheet of metal passes through the various stages in car production, value is added so that a tonne of metal worth a few hundred pounds becomes a car worth several thousand pounds. The rate at which value is added depends on how well the operations process is managed. If the car manufacturer suffers a cost disadvantage by, say, holding a high level of stock or working with out of date machinery, then the value added over the process will be lower.

Value chain analysis seeks to provide an understanding of how much value an organization's activities add to its products (goods and services) for its consumers compared to the costs of the resources used in their production (the value margin).

Values are the underlying principles, perspectives and beliefs that guide action and behaviour in the organization.

Vertical development allows for growth based on moving backwards (backward integration) or forwards (forward integration) along the supply chain of which it is a part.

A **virtual organization** is a network of linked businesses that coordinate and integrate their activities so effectively that they give the appearance of a single business organization.

The **vision** is an attempt to articulate what the organization should be like in the future. It is what the organization is seeking to become.

W

A **want** is a good or service that is desired but is not necessarily essential.

Waste describes any activity in an operations process that is not value adding. It costs money but does not create value commensurate with its cost.

The **web** is a way of accessing information via the internet.

The term **Web 2.0** is commonly associated with web applications that facilitate interactive information sharing, interoperability, social networking, user-centred design and collaborative working.

A **wiki** is a web page that easily allows anyone to create, view and modify web content.

Working capital is the amount of money a company has tied up in the normal operation of its business. Working capital comprises money tied up in inventories, receivables (money owed to the business), payables (money the company owes), and cash or current bank deposits. A company's objective is usually to minimize this figure.

Work-in-progress (WIP) is the name given to stocks that are actually being worked on in the manufacturing process.

INDEX

Campbell, Edgar & Stonehouse
Business Strategy: An Introduction, **Third edition**

This is your purchase code for free access to the Strategic Planning Software (SPS):

Students: To access SPS visit **www.planning-strategy.com.** Select your user type as 'Student', click 'Create', enter your purchase code and press 'Submit' to log on. Fill in your contact and course information, and create a username and password to enable you to log in directly from the homepage.

Lecturers: To get started e-mail technical support at **spstechnicalassistance@gmail. com**, requesting your institution to be set up on the system. Once your institution has been verified you can set up an account at **www.planning-strategy.com** by selecting the 'Instructor' option under 'Select User Type' and clicking 'Create'. You will then be prompted to enter in details about yourself and to set a username and password. Once the registration is complete, you can log in as an instructor, add a new course and then a section to the course. When adding a section, a start and end date HAVE to be entered – students and other users CANNOT access the software after the course expires.

Please see p. xxiii of this book, and also our companion website, **www.macmillanihe.com/ companion/Campbell-Business-Strategy/** for more information about SPS, including a 'how to' guide, a video demo and further registration instructions.

CPSIA information can be obtained
at www.ICGtesting.com
Printed in the USA
LVHW050608120123
736923LV00002B/32

9 780230 218581